## *More Advance Praise for* Blown to Bits

"Most writing about the digital world comes from techies writing about technical matter for other techies or from pundits whose turn of phrase greatly exceeds their technical knowledge. In *Blown to Bits*, experts in computer science address authoritatively the practical issues in which we all have keen interest."

—Howard Gardner, Hobbs Professor of Cognition and Education,
Harvard Graduate School of Education,
author of *Multiple Intelligences* and *Changing Minds*

"Regardless of your experience with computers, *Blown to Bits* provides a uniquely entertaining and informative perspective from the computing industry's greatest minds.

A fascinating, insightful and entertaining book that helps you understand computers and their impact on the world in a whole new way.

This is a rare book that explains the impact of the digital explosion in a way that everyone can understand and, at the same time, challenges experts to think in new ways."

—Anne Margulies, Assistant Secretary for Information Technology and
Chief Information Officer of the Commonwealth of Massachusetts

"*Blown to Bits* is fun and fundamental. What a pleasure to see real teachers offering such excellent framework for students in a digital age to explore and understand their digital environment, code and law, starting with the insight of Claude Shannon. I look forward to you teaching in an open online school."

—Professor Charles Nesson, Harvard Law School,
Founder, Berkman Center for Internet and Society

"To many of us, computers and the Internet are magic. We make stuff, send stuff, receive stuff, and buy stuff. It's all pointing, clicking, copying, and pasting. But it's all mysterious. This book explains in clear and comprehensive terms how all this gear on my desk works and why we should pay close attention to these revolutionary changes in our lives. It's a brilliant and necessary work for consumers, citizens, and students of all ages."

—Siva Vaidhyanathan, cultural historian and media scholar
at the University of Virginia and author of *Copyrights and Copywrongs:
The Rise of Intellectual Property and How it Threatens Creativity*

"The world has turned into the proverbial elephant and we the blind men. The old and the young among us risk being controlled by, rather than in control of, events and technologies. *Blown to Bits* is a remarkable and essential Rosetta Stone for beginning to figure out how all of the pieces of the new world we have just begun to enter—law, technology, culture, information—are going to fit together. Will life explode with new possibilities, or contract under pressure of new horrors? The precipice is both exhilarating and frightening. Hal Abelson, Ken Ledeen, and Harry Lewis, together, have ably managed to describe the elephant. Readers of this compact book describing the beginning stages of a vast human adventure will be one jump ahead, for they will have a framework on which to hang new pieces that will continue to appear with remarkable speed. To say that this is a 'must read' sounds trite, but, this time, it's absolutely true."

—**Harvey Silverglate**, criminal defense and civil liberties lawyer and writer

# Blown to Bits

*Your Life, Liberty,
and Happiness After
the Digital Explosion*

Hal Abelson
Ken Ledeen
Harry Lewis

✦ Addison-Wesley

Upper Saddle River, NJ • Boston • Indianapolis • San Francisco
New York • Toronto • Montreal • London • Munich • Paris • Madrid
Cape Town • Sydney • Tokyo • Singapore • Mexico City

The publisher offers excellent discounts on this book when ordered in quantity for bulk purchases or special sales, which may include electronic versions and/or custom covers and content particular to your business, training goals, marketing focus, and branding interests. For more information, please contact:

U.S. Corporate and Government Sales
(800) 382-3419
corpsales@pearsontechgroup.com

For sales outside the United States, please contact:

International Sales
international@pearson.com

Visit us on the Web: www.informit.com/aw

*Library of Congress Cataloging-in-Publication Data:*

Abelson, Harold.
  Blown to bits : your life, liberty, and happiness after the digital explosion / Hal Abelson, Ken Ledeen, Harry Lewis.
      p. cm.
  ISBN 0-13-713559-9 (hardback : alk. paper) 1. Computers and civilization. 2. Information technology—Technological innovations. 3. Digital media. I. Ledeen, Ken, 1946- II. Lewis, Harry R. III. Title.
  QA76.9.C66A245 2008
  303.48'33—dc22

                                                                                    2008005910

  For information regarding permissions, write to:

    Pearson Education, Inc.
    Rights and Contracts Department
    501 Boylston Street, Suite 900
    Boston, MA 02116
    Fax (617) 671 3447

ISBN-13: 978-0-13-713559-2
ISBN-10: 0-13-713559-9
Text printed in the United States on recycled paper at RR Donnelley in Crawfordsville, Indiana.
Tenth printing November 2014

**This Book Is Safari Enabled**

The Safari® Enabled icon on the cover of your favorite technology book means the book is available through Safari Bookshelf. When you buy this book, you get free access to the online edition for 45 days.

Safari Bookshelf is an electronic reference library that lets you easily search thousands of technical books, find code samples, download chapters, and access technical information whenever and wherever you need it.

To gain 45-day Safari Enabled access to this book:

- Go to http://www.informit.com/onlineedition
- Complete the brief registration form
- Enter the coupon code 9SD6-IQLD-ZDNI-AGEC-AG6L

If you have difficulty registering on Safari Bookshelf or accessing the online edition, please e-mail customer-service@safaribooksonline.com.

**Editor in Chief**
Mark Taub

**Acquisitions Editor**
Greg Doench

**Development Editor**
Michael Thurston

**Managing Editor**
Gina Kanouse

**Senior Project Editor**
Kristy Hart

**Copy Editor**
Water Crest Publishing, Inc.

**Indexer**
Erika Millen

**Proofreader**
Williams Woods Publishing Services

**Publishing Coordinator**
Michelle Housley

**Interior Designer and Composition**
Nonie Ratcliff

**Cover Designer**
Chuti Prasertsith

*To our children, Amanda, Jennifer, Joshua, Elaheh, Annie,
and Elizabeth, who will see the world changed
yet again in ways we cannot imagine.*

# Contents

# Preface

For thousands of years, people have been saying that the world is changing and will never again be the same. Yet the profound changes happening today are different, because they result from a specific technological development.

It is now possible, in principle, to remember everything that anyone says, writes, sings, draws, or photographs. *Everything.* If digitized, the world has enough disks and memory chips to save it all, for as long as civilization can keep producing computers and disk drives. Global computer networks can make it available to everywhere in the world, almost instantly. And computers are powerful enough to extract meaning from all that information, to find patterns and make connections in the blink of an eye.

In centuries gone by, others may have dreamed these things could happen, in utopian fantasies or in nightmares. But now they are happening. We are living in the middle of the changes, and we can see the changes happening.

But we don't know how things will turn out.

Right now, governments and the other institutions of human societies are deciding how to use the new possibilities. Each of us is participating as we make decisions for ourselves, for our families, and for people we work with. Everyone needs to know how their world and the world around them is changing as a result of this explosion of digital information. Everyone should know how the decisions will affect their lives, and the lives of their children and grandchildren and everyone who comes after.

That is why we wrote this book.

Each of us has been in the computing field for more than 40 years. The book is the product of a lifetime of observing and participating in the changes it has brought. Each of us has been both a teacher and a learner in the field. This book emerged from a general education course we have taught at Harvard, but it is not a textbook. We wrote this book to share what wisdom we have with as many people as we can reach. We try to paint a big picture, with dozens of illuminating anecdotes as the brushstrokes. We aim to entertain you at the same time as we provoke your thinking.

You can read the chapters in any order. The Appendix is a self-contained explanation of how the Internet works. You don't need a computer to read this book. But we would suggest that you use one, connected to the Internet, to explore any topic that strikes your curiosity or excites your interest. Don't be afraid to type some of the things we mention into your favorite search engine and see what comes up. We mention many web sites, and give their complete descriptors, such as bitsbook.com, which happens to be the site for this book itself. But most of the time, you should be able to find things more quickly by searching for them. There are many valuable public information sources and public interest groups where you can learn more, and can participate in the ongoing global conversation about the issues we discuss.

We offer some strong opinions in this book. If you would like to react to what we say, please visit the book's web site for an ongoing discussion.

Our picture of the changes brought by the digital explosion is drawn largely with reference to the United States and its laws and culture, but the issues we raise are critical for citizens of all free societies, and for all people who hope their societies will become freer.

Cambridge, Massachusetts
January 2008

# Acknowledgments

While we take full responsibility for any errors in the book, we owe thanks to a great many others for any enlightenment it may provide. Specifically, we are grateful to the following individuals, who commented on parts of the book while it was in draft or provided other valuable assistance: Lynn Abelson, Meg Ausman, Scott Bradner, Art Brodsky, Mike Carroll, Marcus Cohn, Frank Cornelius, Alex Curtis, Natasha Devroye, David Fahrenthold, Robert Faris, Johann-Christoph Freytag, Wendy Gordon, Tom Hemnes, Brian LaMacchia, Marshall Lerner, Anne Lewis, Elizabeth Lewis, Jessica Litman, Lory Lybeck, Fred vonLohmann, Marlyn McGrath, Michael Marcus, Michael Mitzenmacher, Steve Papa, Jonathan Pearce, Bradley Pell, Les Perelman, Pamela Samuelson, Jeff Schiller, Katie Sluder, Gigi Sohn, Debora Spar, René Stein, Alex Tibbetts, Susannah Tobin, Salil Vadhan, David Warsh, Danny Weitzner, and Matt Welsh.

# About the Authors

**Hal Abelson** is Class of 1922 Professor of Computer Science and Engineering at MIT, and an IEEE Fellow. He has helped drive innovative educational technology initiatives such MIT OpenCourseWare, cofounded Creative Commons and Public Knowledge, and was founding director of the Free Software Foundation. **Ken Ledeen**, Chairman/CEO of Nevo Technologies, has served on the boards of numerous technology companies. **Harry Lewis**, former Dean of Harvard College, is Gordon McKay Professor of Computer Science at Harvard and Fellow of the Berkman Center for Internet and Society. He is author of *Excellence Without a Soul: Does Liberal Education Have a Future?* Together, the authors teach Quantitative Reasoning 48, an innovative Harvard course on information for non-technical, non-mathematically oriented students.

# CHAPTER 1

# Digital Explosion

## Why Is It Happening, and What Is at Stake?

On September 19, 2007, while driving alone near Seattle on her way to work, Tanya Rider went off the road and crashed into a ravine.* For eight days, she was trapped upside down in the wreckage of her car. Severely dehydrated and suffering from injuries to her leg and shoulder, she nearly died of kidney failure. Fortunately, rescuers ultimately found her. She spent months recuperating in a medical facility. Happily, she was able to go home for Christmas.

Tanya's story is not just about a woman, an accident, and a rescue. It is a story about bits—the zeroes and ones that make up all our cell phone conversations, bank records, and everything else that gets communicated or stored using modern electronics.

Tanya was found because cell phone companies keep records of cell phone locations. When you carry your cell phone, it regularly sends out a digital "ping," a few bits conveying a "Here I am!" message. Your phone keeps "pinging" as long as it remains turned on. Nearby cell phone towers pick up the pings and send them on to your cellular service provider. Your cell phone company uses the pings to direct your incoming calls to the right cell phone towers. Tanya's cell phone company, Verizon, still had a record of the last location of her cell phone, even after the phone had gone dead. That is how the police found her.

So why did it take more than a week?

If a woman disappears, her husband can't just make the police find her by tracing her cell phone records. She has a privacy right, and maybe she has good reason to leave town without telling her husband where she is going. In

---

* Citations of facts and sources appear at the end of the book. A page number and a phrase identify the passage.

Tanya's case, her bank account showed some activity (more bits!) after her disappearance, and the police could not classify her as a "missing person." In fact, that activity was by her husband. Through some misunderstanding, the police thought he did not have access to the account. Only when the police suspected Tanya's husband of involvement in her disappearance did they have legal access to the cell phone records. Had they continued to act on the true presumption that he was blameless, Tanya might never have been found.

New technologies interacted in an odd way with evolving standards of privacy, telecommunications, and criminal law. The explosive combination almost cost Tanya Rider her life. Her story is dramatic, but every day we encounter unexpected consequences of data flows that could not have happened a few years ago.

When you have finished reading this book, you should see the world in a different way. You should hear a story from a friend or on a newscast and say to yourself, "that's really a bits story," even if no one mentions anything digital. The movements of physical objects and the actions of flesh and blood human beings are only the surface. To understand what is really going on, you have to see the virtual world, the eerie flow of bits steering the events of life.

This book is your guide to this new world.

## The Explosion of Bits, and Everything Else

The world changed very suddenly. Almost everything is stored in a computer somewhere. Court records, grocery purchases, precious family photos, pointless radio programs.... Computers contain a lot of stuff that isn't useful today but somebody thinks might someday come in handy. It is all being reduced to zeroes and ones—"bits." The bits are stashed on disks of home computers and in the data centers of big corporations and government agencies. The disks can hold so many bits that there is no need to pick and choose what gets remembered.

So much digital information, misinformation, data, and garbage is being squirreled away that most of it will be seen only by computers, never by human eyes. And computers are getting better and better at extracting meaning from all those bits—finding patterns that sometimes solve crimes and make useful suggestions, and sometimes reveal things about us we did not expect others to know.

The March 2008 resignation of Eliot Spitzer as Governor of New York is a bits story as well as a prostitution story. Under anti-money laundering (AML) rules, banks must report transactions of more than $10,000 to federal regulators. None of Spitzer's alleged payments reached that threshold, but his bank's computer found that transfers of smaller sums formed a suspicious pattern. The AML rules exist to fight terrorism and organized crime. But while the computer was monitoring small banking transactions in search of big-time crimes, it exposed a simple payment for services rendered that brought down the Governor.

Once something is on a computer, it can replicate and move around the world in a heartbeat. Making a million perfect copies takes but an instant—copies of things we want everyone in the world to see, and also copies of things that weren't meant to be copied at all.

The digital explosion is changing the world as much as printing once did—and some of the changes are catching us unaware, blowing to bits our assumptions about the way the world works.

When we observe the digital explosion at all, it can seem benign, amusing, or even utopian. Instead of sending prints through the mail to Grandma, we put pictures of our children on a photo album web site such as Flickr. Then not only can Grandma see them—so can Grandma's friends and anyone else. So what? They are cute and harmless. But suppose a tourist takes a vacation snapshot and you just happen to appear in the background, at a restaurant where no one knew you were dining. If the tourist uploads his photo, the whole world could know where you were, and when you were there.

Data leaks. Credit card records are supposed to stay locked up in a data warehouse, but escape into the hands of identity thieves. And we sometimes give information away just because we get something back for doing so. A company will give you free phone calls to anywhere in the world—if you don't mind watching ads for the products its computers hear you talking about.

And those are merely things that are happening today. The explosion, and the social disruption it will create, have barely begun.

We already live in a world in which there is enough memory *just in digital cameras* to store every word of every book in the Library of Congress a hundred times over. So much email is being sent that it could transmit the full text of the Library of Congress in ten minutes. Digitized pictures and sounds take more space than words, so emailing all the images, movies, and sounds might take a year—but that is just today. The explosive growth is still happening. Every year we can store more information, move it more quickly, and do far more ingenious things with it than we could the year before.

So much disk storage is being produced every year that it could be used to record a page of information, every minute or two, about you *and every other human being on earth*. A remark made long ago can come back to haunt a political candidate, and a letter jotted quickly can be a key discovery for a biographer. Imagine what it would mean to record every word every human being speaks or writes in a lifetime. The technological barrier to that has already been removed: There is enough storage to remember it all. Should any social barrier stand in the way?

Sometimes things seem to work both better and worse than they used to. A "public record" is now *very* public—before you get hired in Nashville, Tennessee, your employer can figure out if you were caught ten years ago taking an illegal left turn in Lubbock, Texas. The old notion of a "sealed court record" is mostly a fantasy in a world where any tidbit of information is duplicated, cataloged, and moved around endlessly. With hundreds of TV and radio stations and millions of web sites, Americans love the variety of news sources, but are still adjusting uncomfortably to the displacement of more authoritative sources. In China, the situation is reversed: The technology creates greater government control of the information its citizens receive, and better tools for monitoring their behavior.

This book is about how the digital explosion is changing everything. It explains the technology itself—why it creates so many surprises and why things often don't work the way we expect them to. It is also about things the information explosion is destroying: old assumptions about our privacy, about our identity, and about who is in control of our lives. It's about how we got this way, what we are losing, and what remains that society still has a chance to put right. The digital explosion is creating both opportunities and risks. Many of both will be gone in a decade, settled one way or another. Governments, corporations, and other authorities are taking advantage of the chaos, and most of us don't even see it happening. Yet we all have a stake in the outcome. Beyond the science, the history, the law, and the politics, this book is a wake-up call. The forces shaping your future are digital, and you need to understand them.

## The Koans of Bits

Bits behave strangely. They travel almost instantaneously, and they take almost no space to store. We have to use physical metaphors to make them understandable. We liken them to dynamite exploding or water flowing. We even use social metaphors for bits. We talk about two computers agreeing on some bits, and about people using burglary tools to steal bits. Getting the right metaphor is important, but so is knowing the limitations of our metaphors. An imperfect metaphor can mislead as much as an apt metaphor can illuminate.

**CLAUDE SHANNON**

Claude Shannon (1916–2001) is the undisputed founding figure of information and communication theory. While working at Bell Telephone Laboratories after the Second World War, he wrote the seminal paper, "A mathematical theory of communication," which foreshadowed much of the subsequent development of digital technologies. Published in 1948, this paper gave birth to the now-universal realization that the bit is the natural unit of information, and to the use of the term.

Alcatel-Lucent, http:www.bell-labs.com/news/2001/february/26/shannon2_lg.jpeg.

We offer seven truths about bits. We call them "koans" because they are paradoxes, like the Zen verbal puzzles that provoke meditation and enlightenment. These koans are oversimplifications and over-generalizations. They describe a world that is developing but hasn't yet fully emerged. But even today they are truer than we often realize. These themes will echo through our tales of the digital explosion.

## Koan 1: It's All Just Bits

Your computer successfully creates the illusion that it contains photographs, letters, songs, and movies. All it really contains is bits, lots of them, patterned in ways you can't see. Your computer was designed to store just bits—all the files and folders and different kinds of data are illusions created by computer programmers. When you send an email containing a photograph, the computers that handle your message as it flows through the Internet have no idea that what they are handling is part text and part graphic. Telephone calls are also just bits, and that has helped create competition—traditional phone companies, cell phone companies, cable TV companies, and Voice over IP (VoIP) service providers can just shuffle bits around to each other to complete calls. The Internet was designed to handle just bits, not emails or attachments, which are inventions of software engineers. We couldn't live without those more intuitive concepts, but they are artifices. Underneath, it's all just bits.

This koan is more consequential than you might think. Consider the story of Naral Pro-Choice America and Verizon Wireless. Naral wanted to form a text messaging group to send alerts to its members. Verizon decided not to allow it, citing the "controversial or unsavory" things the messages might contain. Text message alert groups for political candidates it would allow, but not for political causes it deemed controversial. Had Naral simply wanted telephone service or an 800 number, Verizon would have had no choice. Telephone companies were long ago declared "common carriers." Like railroads, phone companies are legally prohibited from picking and choosing customers from among those who want their services. In the bits world, there is no difference between a text message and a wireless phone call. It's all just bits, traveling through the air by radio waves. But the law hasn't caught up to the technology. It doesn't treat all bits the same, and the common carriage rules for voice bits don't apply to text message bits.

> ### EXCLUSIVE AND RIVALROUS
>
> Economists would say that bits, unless controlled somehow, tend to be *non-exclusive* (once a few people have them, it is hard to keep them from others) and *non-rivalrous* (when someone gets them from me, I don't have any less). In a letter he wrote about the nature of ideas, Thomas Jefferson eloquently stated both properties. *If nature has made any one thing less susceptible than all others of exclusive property, it is the action of the thinking power called an idea, which an individual may exclusively possess as long as he keeps it to himself; but the moment it is divulged, it forces itself into the possession of every one, and the receiver cannot dispossess himself of it. Its peculiar character, too, is that no one possesses the less, because every other possesses the whole of it.*

Verizon backed down in the case of Naral, but not on the principle. A phone company can do whatever it thinks will maximize its profits in deciding whose messages to distribute. Yet no sensible engineering distinction can be drawn between text messages, phone calls, and any other bits traveling through the digital airwaves.

## Koan 2: Perfection Is Normal

To err is human. When books were laboriously transcribed by hand, in ancient scriptoria and medieval monasteries, errors crept in with every copy. Computers and networks work differently. Every copy is perfect. If you email a photograph to a friend, the friend won't receive a fuzzier version than the original. The copy will be identical, down to the level of details too small for the eye to see.

Computers do fail, of course. Networks break down too. If the power goes out, nothing works at all. So the statement that copies are normally perfect is only relatively true. Digital copies are perfect only to the extent that they can be communicated at all. And yes, it is possible in theory that a single bit of a big message will arrive incorrectly. But networks don't just pass bits from one place to another. They check to see if the bits seem to have been damaged in transit, and correct them or retransmit them if they seem incorrect. As a result of these error detection and correction mechanisms, the odds of an actual error—a character being wrong in an email, for example—are so low that we would be wiser to worry instead about a meteor hitting our computer, improbable though precision meteor strikes may be.

The phenomenon of perfect copies has drastically changed the law, a story told in Chapter 6, "Balance Toppled." In the days when music was distributed on audio tape, teenagers were not prosecuted for making copies of songs, because the copies weren't as good as the originals, and copies of copies would be even worse. The reason that thousands of people are today receiving threats from the music and movie industries is that their copies are perfect—not just as good as the original, but identical to the original, so that even the notion of "original" is meaningless. The dislocations caused by file sharing are not over yet. The buzzword of the day is "intellectual property." But bits are an odd kind of property. Once I release them, everybody has them. And if I give you my bits, I don't have any fewer.

## Koan 3: There Is Want in the Midst of Plenty

Vast as world-wide data storage is today, five years from now it will be ten times as large. Yet the information explosion means, paradoxically, the loss of information that is not online. One of us recently saw a new doctor at a clinic he had been using for decades. She showed him dense charts of his blood chemistry, data transferred from his home medical device to the clinic's computer—more data than any specialist could have had at her disposal five years ago. The doctor then asked whether he had ever had a stress test and what the test had shown. Those records should be all there, the patient explained, in the medical file. But it was in the *paper* file, to which the doctor did not have access. It wasn't in the *computer's* memory, and the patient's memory was being used as a poor substitute. The old data might as well not have existed at all, since it wasn't digital.

Even information that exists in digital form is useless if there are no devices to read it. The rapid progress of storage engineering has meant that data stored on obsolete devices effectively ceases to exist. In Chapter 3, "Ghosts in the Machine," we shall see how a twentieth-century update of the eleventh-century British Domesday Book was useless by the time it was only a sixtieth the age of the original.

Or consider search, the subject of Chapter 4, "Needles in the Haystack." At first, search engines such as Google and Yahoo! were interesting conveniences, which a few people used for special purposes. The growth of the World Wide Web has put so much information online that search engines are for many people the first place to look for something, before they look in books or ask friends. In the process, appearing prominently in search results has become a matter of life or death for businesses. We may move on to purchase from a competitor if we can't find the site we wanted in the first page or two of results. We may assume something didn't happen if we can't find it quickly in an online news source. If it can't be found—and found quickly—it's just as though it doesn't exist at all.

## Koan 4: Processing Is Power

### MOORE'S LAW

Gordon Moore, founder of Intel Corporation, observed that the density of integrated circuits seemed to double every couple of years. This observation is referred to as "Moore's Law." Of course, it is not a natural law, like the law of gravity. Instead, it is an empirical observation of the progress of engineering and a challenge to engineers to continue their innovation. In 1965, Moore predicted that this exponential growth would continue for quite some time. That it has continued for more than 40 years is one of the great marvels of engineering. No other effort in history has sustained anything like this growth rate.

The speed of a computer is usually measured by the number of basic operations, such as additions, that can be performed in one second. The fastest computers available in the early 1940s could perform about five operations per second. The fastest today can perform about a trillion. Buyers of personal computers know that a machine that seems fast today will seem slow in a year or two.

For at least three decades, the increase in processor speeds was exponential. Computers became twice as fast every couple of years. These increases were one consequence of "Moore's Law" (see sidebar).

Since 2001, processor speed has not followed Moore's Law; in fact, processors have hardly grown faster at all. But that doesn't mean that computers won't continue to get faster. New chip designs include multiple processors on the same chip so the work can be split up and performed in parallel. Such design innovations promise to achieve the same effect as continued increases in raw processor speed. And the same technology improvements that make computers faster also make them cheaper.

The rapid increase in processing power means that inventions move out of labs and into consumer goods very quickly. Robot vacuum cleaners and self-parking vehicles were possible in theory a decade ago, but now they have become economically feasible. Tasks that today seem to require uniquely human skills are the subject of research projects in corporate or academic laboratories. Face recognition and voice recognition are poised to bring us new inventions, such as telephones that know who is calling and surveillance cameras that don't need humans to watch them. The power comes not just from the bits, but from being able to do things with the bits.

## Koan 5: More of the Same Can Be a Whole New Thing

Explosive growth is exponential growth—doubling at a steady rate. Imagine earning 100% annual interest on your savings account—in 10 years, your money would have increased more than a thousandfold, and in 20 years, more than a millionfold. A more reasonable interest rate of 5% will hit the same growth points, just 14 times more slowly. Epidemics initially spread exponentially, as each infected individual infects several others.

When something grows exponentially, for a long time it may seem not to be changing at all. If we don't watch it steadily, it will seem as though something discontinuous and radical occurred while we weren't looking.

That is why epidemics at first go unnoticed, no matter how catastrophic they may be when full-blown. Imagine one sick person infecting two healthy people, and the next day each of those two infects two others, and the next day after that each of those four infects two others, and so on. The number of newly infected each day grows from two to four to eight. In a week, 128 people come down with the disease in a single day, and twice that number are now sick, but in a population of ten million, no one notices. Even after two weeks, barely three people in a thousand are sick. But after another week, 40% of the population is sick, and society collapses

Exponential growth is actually smooth and steady; it just takes very little time to pass from unnoticeable change to highly visible. Exponential growth of anything can suddenly make the world look utterly different than it had been. When that threshold is passed, changes that are "just" quantitative can look qualitative.

Another way of looking at the apparent abruptness of exponential growth—its explosive force—is to think about how little lead time we have to respond to it. Our hypothetical epidemic took three weeks to overwhelm the population. At what point was it only a half as devastating? The answer is *not* "a week and a half." The answer is *on the next to last day.* Suppose it took a week to develop and administer a vaccine. Then noticing the epidemic after a week and a half would have left ample time to prevent the disaster. But that would have required understanding that there *was* an epidemic when only 2,000 people out of ten million were infected.

The information story is full of examples of unperceived changes followed by dislocating explosions. Those with the foresight to notice the explosion just a little earlier than everyone else can reap huge benefits. Those who move a little too slowly may be overwhelmed by the time they try to respond. Take the case of digital photography.

In 1983, Christmas shoppers could buy digital cameras to hook up to their IBM PC and Apple II home computers. The potential was there for anyone to see; it was not hidden in secret corporate laboratories. But digital photography did not take off. Economically and practically, it couldn't. Cameras were too bulky to put in your pocket, and digital memories were too small to hold many images. Even 14 years later, film photography was still a robust industry. In early 1997, Kodak stock hit a record price, with a 22% increase in quarterly profit, "fueled by healthy film and paper sales...[and] its motion picture film business," according to a news report. The company raised its dividend for the first time in eight years. But by 2007, digital memories had become huge, digital processors had become fast and compact, and both were cheap. As a result, cameras had become little computers. The company that was once synonymous with photography was a shadow of its former self. Kodak announced that its employee force would be cut to 30,000, barely a fifth the size it was during the good times of the late 1980s. The move would cost the company more than $3 billion. Moore's Law moved faster than Kodak did.

In the rapidly changing world of bits, it pays to notice even small changes, and to do something about them.

## Koan 6: Nothing Goes Away

2,000,000,000,000,000,000,000.

That is the number of bits that were created and stored away in 2007, according to one industry estimate. The capacity of disks has followed its own version of Moore's Law, doubling every two or three years. For the time being at least, that makes it possible to save everything though recent projections suggest that by 2011, we may be producing more bits than we can store.

In financial industries, federal laws now *require* massive data retention, to assist in audits and investigations of corruption. In many other businesses, economic competitiveness drives companies to save everything they collect and to seek out new data to retain. Wal-Mart stores have tens of millions of transactions every day, and every one of them is saved—date, time, item, store, price, who made the purchase, and how—credit, debit, cash, or gift card. Such data is so valuable to planning the supply chain that stores will pay money to get more of it from their customers. That is really what supermarket loyalty cards provide—shoppers are supposed to think that the store is granting them a discount in appreciation for their steady business, but actually the store is paying them for information about their buying patterns. We might better think of a privacy tax—we pay the regular price *unless* we want to keep information about our food, alcohol, and pharmaceutical purchases from the market; to keep our habits to ourselves, we pay extra.

The massive databases challenge our expectations about what will happen to the data about us. Take something as simple as a stay in a hotel. When you check in, you are given a keycard, not a mechanical key. Because the keycards can be deactivated instantly, there is no longer any great risk associated with losing your key, as long as you report it missing quickly. On the other hand, the hotel now has a record, accurate to the second, of every time you entered your room, used the gym or the business center, or went in the back door after-hours. The same database could identify every cocktail and steak you charged to the room, which other rooms you phoned and when, and the brands of tampons and laxatives you charged at the hotel's gift shop. This data might be merged with billions like it, analyzed, and transferred to the parent company, which owns restaurants and fitness centers as well as hotels. It might also be lost, or stolen, or subpoenaed in a court case.

The ease of storing information has meant asking for more of it. Birth certificates used to include just the information about the child's and parents' names, birthplaces, and birthdates, plus the parents' occupations. Now the electronic birth record includes how much the mother drank and smoked during her pregnancy, whether she had genital herpes or a variety of other medical conditions, and both parents' social security numbers. Opportunities for research are plentiful, and so are opportunities for mischief and catastrophic accidental data loss.

And the data will all be kept forever, unless there are policies to get rid of it. For the time being at least, the data sticks around. And because databases are intentionally duplicated—backed up for security,

*The data will all be kept forever, unless there are policies to get rid of it.*

or shared while pursuing useful analyses—it is far from certain that data can ever be permanently expunged, even if we wish that to happen. The Internet consists of millions of interconnected computers; once data gets out, there is no getting it back. Victims of identity theft experience daily the distress of having to remove misinformation from the record. It seems never to go away.

## Koan 7: Bits Move Faster Than Thought

The Internet existed before there were personal computers. It predates the fiber optic communication cables that now hold it together. When it started around 1970, the ARPANET, as it was called, was designed to connect a handful of university and military computers. No one imagined a network connecting tens of millions of computers and shipping information around the world in the blink of an eye. Along with processing power and storage capacity, networking has experienced its own exponential growth, in number of computers interconnected and the rate at which data can be shipped over long distances, from space to earth and from service providers into private homes.

The Internet has caused drastic shifts in business practice. Customer service calls are outsourced to India today not just because labor costs are low there. Labor costs have *always* been low in India, but international telephone calls used to be expensive. Calls about airline reservations and lingerie returns are answered in India today because it now takes almost no time and costs almost no money to send to India the bits representing your voice. The same principle holds for professional services. When you are X-rayed at your local hospital in Iowa, the radiologist who reads the X-ray may be half a world away. The digital X-ray moves back and forth across the world faster than a physical X-ray could be moved between floors of the hospital. When you place an order at a drive-through station at a fast food restaurant, the person taking the order may be in another state. She keys the order so it appears on a computer screen in the kitchen, a few feet from your car, and you are none the wiser. Such developments are causing massive changes to the global economy, as industries figure out how to keep their workers in one place and ship their business as bits.

In the bits world, in which messages flow instantaneously, it sometimes seems that distance doesn't matter at all. The consequences can be startling. One of us, while dean of an American college, witnessed the shock of a father receiving condolences on his daughter's death. The story was sad but familiar, except that this version had a startling twist. Father and daughter were both in Massachusetts, but the condolences arrived from half-way around the world before the father had learned that his daughter had died. News, even the most intimate news, travels fast in the bits world, once it gets out. In the fall of 2007, when the government of Myanmar suppressed protests by Buddhist monks, television stations around the world showed video clips taken by cell phone, probably changing the posture of the U.S. government. The Myanmar rebellion also shows the power of information control when information is just bits. The story dropped off the front page of the news-papers once the government took total control of the Internet and cell phone towers.

The instantaneous communication of massive amounts of information has created the misimpression that there is a place called "Cyberspace," a land without frontiers where all the world's people can be interconnected as though they were residents of the same small town. That concept has been decisively refuted by the actions of the world's courts. National and state bor-ders still count, and count a lot. If a book is bought online in England, the publisher and author are subject to British libel laws rather than those of the homeland of the author or publisher. Under British law, defendants have to prove their innocence; in the U.S., plaintiffs have to prove the guilt of the defendants. An ugly downside to the explosion of digital information and its movement around the world is that information may become less available even where it would be legally protected (we return to this subject in Chapter 7, "You Can't Say That on the Internet"). Publishers fear "libel tourism"–lawsuits in countries with weak protection of free speech, designed to intim-idate authors in more open societies. It may prove simpler to publish only a single version of a work for sale everywhere, an edition omitting information that might somewhere excite a lawsuit.

## Good and Ill, Promise and Peril

The digital explosion has thrown a lot of things up for grabs and we all have a stake in who does the grabbing. The way the technology is offered to us, the way we use it, and the consequences of the vast dissemination of digital infor-mation are matters not in the hands of technology experts alone. Governments and corporations and universities and other social institutions have a say. And ordinary citizens, to whom these institutions are accountable, can influence their decisions. Important choices are made every year, in government offices and legislatures, in town meetings and police stations, in the corporate offices of banks and insurance companies, in the purchasing departments of chain stores and pharmacies. We all can help raise the level of discourse and understanding. We can all help ensure that technical decisions are taken in a context of ethical standards.

We offer two basic morals. The first is that information technology is inherently neither good nor bad—it can be used for good or ill, to free us or to shackle us. Second, new technology brings social change, and change comes with both risks and opportunities. All of us, and all of our public agencies and private institutions, have a say in whether technology will be used for good or ill and whether we will fall prey to its risks or prosper from the opportunities it creates.

## *Technology Is Neither Good nor Bad*

Any technology can be used for good or ill. Nuclear reactions create electric power and weapons of mass destruction. The same encryption technology that makes it possible for you to email your friends with confidence that no eavesdropper will be able to decipher your message also makes it possible for terrorists to plan their attacks undiscovered. The same Internet technology that facilitates the widespread distribution of educational works to impoverished students in remote locations also enables massive copyright infringement. The photomanipulation tools that enhance your snapshots are used by child pornographers to escape prosecution.

The key to managing the ethical and moral consequences of technology while nourishing economic growth is to *regulate the use* of technology without *banning or restricting its creation.*

It is a marvel that anyone with a smart cell phone can use a search engine to get answers to obscure questions almost anywhere. Society is rapidly being freed from the old limitations of geography and status in accessing information.

The same technologies can be used to monitor individuals, to track their behaviors, and to control what information they receive. Search engines need not return unbiased results. Many users of web browsers do not realize that the sites they visit may archive their actions. Technologically, there could be a record of exactly what you have been accessing and when, as you browse a library or bookstore catalog, a site selling pharmaceuticals, or a service offering advice on contraception or drug overdose. There are vast opportunities to use this information for invasive but relatively benign purposes, such as marketing, and also for more questionable purposes, such as blacklisting and blackmail. Few regulations mandate disclosure that the information is being collected, or restrict the use to which the data can be put. Recent federal laws, such as the USA PATRIOT Act, give government agencies sweeping authority to sift through mostly innocent data looking for signs of "suspicious activity" by potential terrorists—and to notice lesser transgressions, such as Governor Spitzer's, in the process. Although the World Wide Web now reaches into millions of households, the rules and regulations governing it are not much better than those of a lawless frontier town of the old West.

> ### BLACKLISTS AND WHITELISTS
> In the bits world, providers of services can create blacklists or whitelists. No one on a blacklist can use the service, but everyone else can. For example, an auctioneer might put people on a blacklist if they did not pay for their purchases. But service providers who have access to other information about visitors to their web sites might use undisclosed and far more sweeping criteria for blacklisting. A whitelist is a list of parties to whom services are available, with everyone else excluded. For example, a newspaper may whitelist its home delivery subscribers for access to its online content, allowing others onto the whitelist only after they have paid.

## New Technologies Bring Both Risks and Opportunities

The same large disk drives that enable anyone with a home computer to analyze millions of baseball statistics also allow anyone with access to confidential information to jeopardize its security. Access to aerial maps via the Internet makes it possible for criminals to plan burglaries of upscale houses, but technologically sophisticated police know that records of such queries can also be used to solve crimes.

Even the most un-electronic livelihoods are changing because of instant worldwide information flows. There are no more pool hustlers today—journeymen wizards of the cue, who could turn up in pool halls posing as out-of-town bumpkins just looking to bet on a friendly game, and walk away with big winnings. Now when any newcomer comes to town and cleans up, his name and face are on AZBilliards.com instantly for pool players everywhere to see.

Social networking sites such as facebook.com, myspace.com, and match.com have made their founders quite wealthy. They have also given birth to many thousands of new friendships, marriages, and other ventures. But those pretending to be your online friends may not be as they seem. Social networking has made it easier for predators to take advantage of the naïve, the lonely, the elderly, and the young.

In 2006, a 13-year-old girl, Megan Meier of Dardenne Prairie, Missouri, made friends online with a 16-year-old boy named "Josh." When "Josh" turned against her, writing "You are a bad person and everybody hates you.... The world would be a better place without you," Megan committed suicide. Yet Josh did not exist. Josh was a MySpace creation—but of whom? An early police report stated that the mother of another girl in the neighborhood acknowledged "instigating" and monitoring the account. That woman's lawyer later blamed someone who worked for his client. Whoever may have sent the final message to Megan, prosecutors are having a hard time identifying any law that might have been broken. "I can start MySpace on every single one of you and spread rumors about every single one of you," said Megan's mother, "and what's going to happen to me? Nothing."

Along with its dazzling riches and vast horizons, the Internet has created new manifestations of human evil—some of which, including the cyber-harassment Megan Meier suffered, may not be criminal under existing law. In a nation deeply committed to free expression as a legal right, which Internet evils should be crimes, and which are just wrong?

Vast data networks have made it possible to move work to where the people are, not people to the work. The results are enormous business oppor-tunities for entrepreneurs who take advantage of these technologies and new enterprises around the globe, and also the other side of the coin: jobs lost to outsourcing.

The difference every one of us can make, to our workplace or to another institution, can be to ask a question at the right time about the risks of some new technological innovation—or to point out the possibility of doing something in the near future that a few years ago would have been utterly impossible.

---

✳

---

We begin our tour of the digital landscape with a look at our privacy, a social structure the explosion has left in shambles. While we enjoy the benefits of ubiquitous information, we also sense the loss of the shelter that privacy once gave us. And we don't know what we want to build in its place. The good and ill of technology, and its promise and peril, are all thrown together when information about us is spread everywhere. In the post-privacy world, we stand exposed to the glare of noonday sunlight—and sometimes it feels strangely pleasant.

# CHAPTER 2

# Naked in the Sunlight

*Privacy Lost, Privacy Abandoned*

## 1984 Is Here, and We Like It

On July 7, 2005, London was shaken as suicide bombers detonated four explosions, three on subways and one on a double-decker bus. The attack on the transit system was carefully timed to occur at rush hour, maximizing its destructive impact. 52 people died and 700 more were injured.

Security in London had already been tight. The city was hosting the G8 Summit, and the trial of fundamentalist cleric Abu Hamza al-Masri had just begun. Hundreds of thousands of surveillance cameras hadn't deterred the terrorist act, but the perpetrators were caught on camera. Their pictures were sent around the world instantly. Working from 80,000 seized tapes, police were able to reconstruct a reconnaissance trip the bombers had made two weeks earlier.

George Orwell's *1984* was published in 1948. Over the subsequent years, the book became synonymous with a world of permanent surveillance, a society devoid of both privacy and freedom:

> ...there seemed to be no color in anything except the posters that were plastered everywhere. The black-mustachio'd face gazed down from every commanding corner. There was one on the house front immediately opposite. BIG BROTHER IS WATCHING YOU ...

The real 1984 came and went nearly a quarter century ago. Today, Big Brother's two-way telescreens would be amateurish toys. Orwell's imagined

London had cameras everywhere. His actual city now has at least half a million. Across the UK, there is one surveillance camera for every dozen people. The average Londoner is photographed hundreds of times a day by electronic eyes on the sides of buildings and on utility poles.

Yet there is much about the digital world that Orwell did not imagine. He did not anticipate that cameras are far from the most pervasive of today's tracking technologies. There are dozens of other kinds of data sources, and the data they produce is retained and analyzed. Cell phone companies know not only what numbers you call, but where you have carried your phone. Credit card companies know not only where you spent your money, but what you spent it on. Your friendly bank keeps electronic records of your transactions not only to keep your balance right, but because it has to tell the government if you make huge withdrawals. The digital explosion has scattered the bits of our lives everywhere: records of the clothes we wear, the soaps we wash with, the streets we walk, and the cars we drive and where we drive them. And although Orwell's Big Brother had his cameras, he didn't have search engines to piece the bits together, to find the needles in the haystacks. Wherever we go, we leave digital footprints, while computers of staggering capacity reconstruct our movements from the tracks. Computers re-assemble the clues to form a comprehensive image of who we are, what we do, where we are doing it, and whom we are discussing it with.

Perhaps none of this would have surprised Orwell. Had he known about electronic miniaturization, he might have guessed that we would develop an astonishing array of tracking technologies. Yet there is something more fundamental that distinguishes the world of *1984* from the actual world of today. We have fallen in love with this always-on world. We accept our loss of privacy in exchange for efficiency, convenience, and small price discounts. According to a 2007 Pew/Internet Project report, "60% of Internet users say they are not worried about how much information is available about them online." Many of us publish and broadcast the most intimate moments of our lives for all the world to see, even when no one requires or even asks us to do so. 55% of teenagers and 20% of adults have created profiles on social networking web sites. A third of the teens with profiles, and half the adults, place no restrictions on who can see them.

In Orwell's imagined London, only O'Brien and other members of the Inner Party could escape the gaze of the telescreen. For the rest, the constant gaze was a source of angst and anxiety. Today, we willingly accept the gaze. We either don't think about it, don't know about it, or feel helpless to avoid it except by becoming hermits. We may even judge its benefits to outweigh its risks. In Orwell's imagined London, like Stalin's actual Moscow, citizens spied on their fellow citizens. Today, we can all be Little Brothers, using our search engines to check up on our children, our spouses, our neighbors, our colleagues, our enemies, and our friends. More than half of all adult Internet users have done exactly that.

The explosive growth in digital technologies has radically altered our expectations about what will be private and shifted our thinking about what *should* be private. Ironically, the notion of privacy has become fuzzier at the same time as the secrecy-enhancing technology of encryption has become widespread. Indeed, it is remarkable that we no

> **PUBLIC ORGANIZATIONS INVOLVED IN DEFENDING PRIVACY**
>
> Existing organizations have focused on privacy issues in recent years, and new ones have sprung up. In the U.S., important forces are the American Civil Liberties Union (ACLU, www.aclu.org), the Electronic Privacy Information Center (EPIC, epic.org), the Center for Democracy and Technology (CDT, www.cdt.org), and the Electronic Frontier Foundation (www.eff.org).

longer blink at intrusions that a decade ago would have seemed shocking. Unlike the story of secrecy, there was no single technological event that caused the change, no privacy-shattering breakthrough—only a steady advance on several technological fronts that ultimately passed a tipping point.

Many devices got cheaper, better, and smaller. Once they became useful consumer goods, we stopped worrying about their uses as surveillance devices. For example, if the police were the only ones who had cameras in their cell phones, we would be alarmed. But as long as we have them too, so we can send our friends funny pictures from parties, we don't mind so much that others are taking pictures of us. The social evolution that was supported by consumer technologies in turn made us more accepting of new enabling technologies; the social and technological evolutions have proceeded hand in hand. Meanwhile, international terrorism has made the public in most democracies more sympathetic to intrusive measures intended to protect our security. With corporations trying to make money from us and the government trying to protect us, civil libertarians are a weak third voice when they warn that we may not want others to know so much about us.

So we tell the story of privacy in stages. First, we detail the enabling technologies, the devices and computational processes that have made it easy and convenient for us to lose our privacy—some of them familiar technologies, and some a bit more mysterious. We then turn to an analysis of how we have lost our privacy, or simply abandoned it. Many privacy-shattering things have happened to us, some with our cooperation and some not. As a result, the sense of personal privacy is very different today than it was two decades ago. Next, we discuss the social changes that have occurred—cultural shifts that were facilitated by the technological diffusion, which in turn made new technologies easier to deploy. And finally we turn to the big question: What does privacy even mean in the digitally exploded world? Is there any hope of keeping anything private when everything is bits, and the bits are stored, copied, and moved around the world in an instant? And if we can't—or won't—keep our personal information to ourselves anymore, how can we make ourselves less vulnerable to the downsides of living in such an exposed world? Standing naked in the sunlight, is it still possible to protect ourselves against ills and evils from which our privacy used to protect us?

# Footprints and Fingerprints

As we do our daily business and lead our private lives, we leave footprints and fingerprints. We can see our footprints in mud on the floor and in the sand and snow outdoors. We would not be surprised that anyone who went to the trouble to match our shoes to our footprints could determine, or guess, where we had been. Fingerprints are different. It doesn't even occur to us that we are leaving them as we open doors and drink out of tumblers. Those who have guilty consciences may think about fingerprints and worry about where they are leaving them, but the rest of us don't.

> ### THE UNWANTED GAZE
>
> *The Unwanted Gaze* by Jeffrey Rosen (Vintage, 2001) details many ways in which the legal system has contributed to our loss of privacy.

In the digital world, we all leave both electronic footprints and electronic fingerprints—data trails we leave intentionally, and data trails of which we are unaware or unconscious. The identifying data may be useful for forensic purposes. Because most of us don't consider ourselves criminals, however, we tend not to worry about that. What we don't think about is that the various small smudges we leave on the digital landscape may be useful to someone else—someone who wants to use the data we left behind to make money or to get something from us. It is therefore important to understand how and where we leave these digital footprints and fingerprints.

## Smile While We Snap!

Big Brother had his legions of cameras, and the City of London has theirs today. But for sheer photographic pervasiveness, nothing beats the cameras in the cell phones in the hands of the world's teenagers. Consider the alleged misjudgment of Jeffrey Berman. In early December 2007, a man about

60 years old committed a series of assaults on the Boston public transit system, groping girls and exposing himself. After one of the assaults, a victim took out her cell phone. Click! Within hours, a good head shot was up on the Web and was shown on all the Boston area television stations. Within a day, Berman was under arrest and charged with several crimes. "Obviously we, from time to time, have plainclothes officers on the trolley, but that's a very difficult job to do," said the chief of the Transit Police. "The fact that this girl had the wherewithal to snap a picture to identify him was invaluable."

That is, it would seem, a story with a happy ending, for the victim at least. But the massive dissemination of cheap cameras coupled with universal access to the Web also enables a kind of vigilante justice—a ubiquitous Little-Brotherism, in which we can all be detectives, judges, and corrections officers. Mr. Berman claims he is innocent; perhaps the speed at which the teenager's snapshot was disseminated unfairly created a presumption of his guilt. Bloggers can bring global disgrace to ordinary citizens.

In June 2005, a woman allowed her dog to relieve himself on a Korean subway, and subsequently refused to clean up his mess, despite offers from others to help. The incident was captured by a fellow passenger and posted online. She soon became known as "gae-ttong-nyue" (Korean for "puppy poo girl"). She was identified along with her family, was shamed, and quit school. There is now a Wikipedia entry about the incident. Before the digital explosion—before bits made it possible to convey information instantaneously, everywhere—her actions would have been embarrassing and would have been known to those who were there at the time. It is unlikely that the story would have made it around the world, and that it would have achieved such notoriety and permanence.

> There are many free webcam sites, at which you can watch what's happening right now at places all over the world. Here are a few:
>
> www.camvista.com
> www.earthcam.com
> www.webcamworld.com
> www.webworldcam.com

Still, in these cases, at least someone thought someone did something wrong. The camera just happened to be in the right hands at just the right moment. But looking at images on the Web is now a leisure activity that anyone can do at any time, anywhere in the world. Using Google Street View, you can sit in a café in Tajikistan and identify a car that was parked in my driveway when Google's camera came by (perhaps months ago). From Seoul, you can see what's happening right now, updated every few seconds, in Picadilly Circus or on the strip in Las Vegas. These views were always available to the public, but cameras plus the Web changed the meaning of "public."

And an electronic camera is not just a camera. *Harry Potter and the Deathly Hallows* is, as far as anyone knows, the last book in the Harry Potter series. Its arrival was eagerly awaited, with lines of anxious Harry fans stretching around the block at bookstores everywhere. One fan got a pre-release copy, painstakingly photographed every page, and posted the entire book online before the official release. A labor of love, no doubt, but a blatant copyright violation as well. He doubtless figured he was just posting the pixels, which could not be traced back to him. If that was his presumption, he was wrong. His digital fingerprints were all over the images.

Digital cameras encode metadata along with the image. This data, known as the Exchangeable Image File Format (EXIF), includes camera settings (shutter speed, aperture, compression, make, model, orientation), date and time, and, in the case of our Harry Potter fan, the make, model, and serial number of his camera (a Canon Rebel 350D, serial number 560151117). If he registered his camera, bought it with a credit card, or sent it in for service, his identity could be known as well.

## Knowing Where You Are

Global Position Systems (GPSs) have improved the marital lives of count-less males too stubborn to ask directions. Put a Garmin or a Tom Tom in a car, and it will listen to precisely timed signals from satellites reporting their positions in space. The GPS calculates its own location from the satellites' locations and the times their signals are received. The 24 satellites spinning 12,500 miles above the earth enable your car to locate itself within 25 feet, at a price that makes these systems popular birthday presents.

If you carry a GPS-enabled cell phone, your friends can find you, if that its what you want. If your GPS-enabled rental car has a radio transmitter, you can be found whether you want it or not. In 2004, Ron Lee rented a car from Payless in San Francisco. He headed east to Las Vegas, then back to Los Angeles, and finally home. He was expecting to pay $150 for his little vacation, but Payless made him pay more—$1,400, to be precise. Mr. Lee forgot to read the fine print in his rental contract. He had not gone too far; his contract was for unlimited mileage. He had missed the fine print that said, "Don't leave California." When he went out of state, the unlimited mileage clause was invalidated. The fine print said that Payless would charge him $1 per Nevada mile, and that is exactly what the company did. They knew where he was, every minute he was on the road.

A GPS will locate you anywhere on earth; that is why mountain climbers carry them. They will locate you not just on the map but in three dimensions, telling you how high up the mountain you are. But even an ordinary cell phone will serve as a rudimentary positioning system. If you are traveling in settled territory—any place where you can get cell phone coverage—the signals from the cell phone towers can be used to locate you. That is how Tanya Rider was found (see Chapter 1 for details). The location is not as precise as that supplied by a GPS—only within ten city blocks or so—but the fact that it is possible at all means that photos can be stamped with identifying information about where they were shot, as well as when and with what camera.

## Knowing Even Where Your Shoes Are

A Radio Frequency Identification tag—RFID, for short—can be read from a distance of a few feet. Radio Frequency Identification is like a more elaborate version of the familiar bar codes that identify products. Bar codes typically identify what kind of thing an item is—the make and model, as it were. Because RFID tags have the capacity for much larger numbers, they can provide a unique serial number for each item: not just "Coke, 12 oz. can" but "Coke can #12345123514002." And because RFID data is transferred by radio waves rather than visible light, the tags need not be visible to be read, and the sensor need not be visible to do the reading.

RFIDs are silicon chips, typically embedded in plastic. They can be used to tag almost anything (see Figure 2.1). "Prox cards," which you wave near a sensor to open a door, are RFID tags; a few bits of information identifying you are transmitted from the card to the sensor. Mobil's "Speedpass" is a little RFID on a keychain; wave it near a gas pump and the pump knows whom to charge for the gasoline. For a decade, cattle have had RFIDs implanted in their flesh, so individual animals can be tracked. Modern dairy farms log the milk production of individual cows, automatically relating the cow's identity to its daily milk output. Pets are commonly RFID-tagged so they can be reunited with their owners if the animals go missing for some reason. The possibility of tagging humans is obvious, and has been proposed for certain high-security applications, such as controlling access to nuclear plants.

But the interesting part of the RFID story is more mundane—putting tags in shoes, for example. RFID can be the basis for powerful inventory tracking systems.

RFID tags are simple devices. They store a few dozen bits of information, usually unique to a particular tag. Most are passive devices, with no batteries, and are quite small. The RFID includes a tiny electronic chip and a small coil, which acts as a two-way antenna. A weak

### SPYCHIPS

This aptly named book by Katherine Albrecht and Liz McIntyre (Plume, 2006) includes many stories of actual and proposed RFID uses by consumer goods manufacturers and retailers.

current flows through the coil when the RFID passes through an electromagnetic field—for example, from a scanner in the frame of a store, under the carpet, or in someone's hand. This feeble current is just strong enough to power the chip and induce it to transmit the identifying information. Because RFIDs are tiny and require no connected power source, they are easily hidden. We see them often as labels affixed to products; the one in Figure 2.1 was between the pages of a book bought from a bookstore. They can be almost undetectable.

 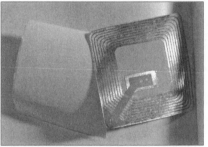

FIGURE 2.1   An RFID found between the pages of a book. A bookstore receiving a box of RFID-tagged books can check the incoming shipment against the order without opening the carton. If the books and shelves are scanned during stocking, the cash register can identify the section of the store from which each purchased copy was sold.

RFIDs are generally used to improve record-keeping, not for snooping. Manufacturers and merchants want to get more information, more reliably, so they naturally think of tagging merchandise. But only a little imagination is required to come up with some disturbing scenarios. Suppose, for example, that you buy a pair of red shoes at a chain store in New York City, and the shoes have an embedded RFID. If you pay with a credit card, the store knows your name, and a good deal more about you from your purchasing history. If you wear those shoes when you walk into a branch store in Los Angeles a month later, and that branch has an RFID reader under the rug at the entrance, the clerk could greet you by name. She might offer you a scarf to match the shoes—or to match anything else you bought recently from any other branch of the store. On the other hand, the store might know that you have a habit of returning almost everything you buy—in that case, you might find yourself having trouble finding anyone to wait on you!

The technology is there to do it. We know of no store that has gone quite this far, but in September 2007, the Galeria Kaufhof in Essen, Germany equipped the dressing rooms in the men's clothing department with RFID readers. When a customer tries on garments, a screen informs him of available sizes and colors. The system may be improved to offer suggestions about accessories. The store keeps track of what items are tried on together and what combinations turn into purchases. The store will remove the RFID tags from the clothes after they are purchased—if the customer asks; otherwise, they remain unobtrusively and could be scanned if the garment is returned to the store. Creative retailers everywhere dream of such ways to use devices to make money, to save money, and to give them small advantages over their competitors. Though Galeria Kaufhof is open about its high-tech men's department, the fear that customers won't like their clever ideas sometimes holds back retailers—and sometimes simply causes them to keep quiet about what they are doing.

## Black Boxes Are Not Just for Airplanes Anymore

On April 12, 2007, John Corzine, Governor of New Jersey, was heading back to the governor's mansion in Princeton to mediate a discussion between Don Imus, the controversial radio personality, and the Rutgers University women's basketball team.

His driver, 34-year-old state trooper Robert Rasinski, headed north on the Garden State Parkway. He swerved to avoid another car and flipped the Governor's Chevy Suburban. Governor Corzine had not fastened his seatbelt, and broke 12 ribs, a femur, his collarbone, and his sternum. The details of exactly what happened were unclear. When questioned, Trooper Rasinski said he was not sure how fast they were going—but we *do* know. He was going 91 in a 65 mile per hour zone. There were no police with radar guns around; no human being tracked his speed. We know his exact speed at the moment of impact because his car, like 30 million cars in America, had a black box—an "event data recorder" (EDR) that captured every detail about what was going on just before the crash. An EDR is an automotive "black box" like the ones recovered from airplane crashes.

EDRs started appearing in cars around 1995. By federal law, they will be mandatory in the United States beginning in 2011. If you are driving a new GM, Ford, Isuzu, Mazda, Mitsubishi, or Subaru, your car has one—whether anyone told you that or not. So do about half of new Toyotas. Your insurance company is probably entitled to its data if you have an accident. Yet most people do not realize that they exist.

EDRs capture information about speed, braking time, turn signal status, seat belts: things needed for accident reconstruction, to establish responsibility, or to prove innocence. CSX Railroad was exonerated of all liability in the death of the occupants of a car when its EDR showed that the car was stopped on the train tracks when it was hit. Police generally obtain search warrants before downloading EDR data, but not always; in some cases, they do not have to. When Robert Christmann struck and killed a pedestrian on October 18, 2003, Trooper Robert Frost of the New York State Police downloaded data from the car at the accident scene. The EDR revealed that Christmann had been going 38 MPH in an area where the speed limit was 30. When the data was introduced at trial, Christmann claimed that the state had violated his Fourth Amendment rights against unreasonable searches and seizures, because it had not asked his permission or obtained a search warrant before retrieving the data. That was not necessary, ruled a New York court. Taking bits from the car was not like taking something out of a house, and no search warrant was necessary.

Bits mediate our daily lives. It is almost as hard to avoid leaving digital footprints as it is to avoid touching the ground when we walk. Yet even if we live our lives without walking, we would unsuspectingly be leaving fingerprints anyway.

*It is almost as hard to avoid leaving digital footprints as it is to avoid touching the ground when we walk.*

Some of the intrusions into our privacy come because of the unexpected, unseen side effects of things we do quite voluntarily. We painted the hypothetical picture of the shopper with the RFID-tagged shoes, who is either welcomed or shunned on her subsequent visits to the store, depending on her shopping history. Similar surprises can lurk almost anywhere that bits are exchanged. That is, for practical purposes, pretty much everywhere in daily life.

## Tracing Paper

If I send an email or download a web page, it should come as no surprise that I've left some digital footprints. After all, the bits have to get to me, so some part of the system knows where I am. In the old days, if I wanted to be anonymous, I could write a note, but my handwriting might be recognizable, and I might leave fingerprints (the oily kind) on the paper. I might have typed, but Perry Mason regularly solved crimes by matching a typewritten note with the unique signature of the suspect's typewriter. More fingerprints.

So, today I would laserprint the letter and wear gloves. But even that may not suffice to disguise me. Researchers at Purdue have developed techniques for matching laser-printed output to a particular printer. They analyze printed sheets and detect unique characteristics of each manufacturer and each individual printer—fingerprints that can be used, like the smudges of old typewriter hammers, to match output with source. It may be unnecessary to put the microscope on individual letters to identify what printer produced a page.

The Electronic Frontier Foundation has demonstrated that many color printers secretly encode the printer serial number, date, and time on every page that they print (see Figure 2.2). Therefore, when you print a report, you should not assume that no one can tell who printed it.

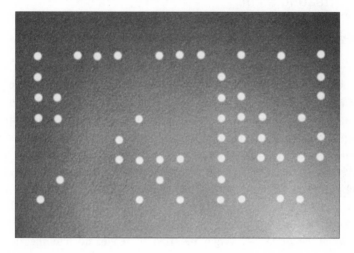

Source: Laser fingerprint. Electronic Frontier Foundation. http://w.2.eff.org/Privacy/printers/docucolor/.

FIGURE 2.2   Fingerprint left by a Xerox DocuColor 12 color laser printer. The dots are very hard to see with the naked eye; the photograph was taken under blue light. The dot pattern encodes the date (2005-05-21), time (12:50), and the serial number of the printer (21052857).

There was a sensible rationale behind this technology. The government wanted to make sure that office printers could not be used to turn out sets of hundred dollar bills. The technology that was intended to frustrate counterfeiters makes it possible to trace every page printed on color laser printers back to the source. Useful technologies often have unintended consequences.

Many people, for perfectly legal and valid reasons, would like to protect their anonymity. They may be whistleblowers or dissidents. Perhaps they are merely railing against injustice in their workplace. Will technologies that undermine anonymity in political discourse also stifle free expression? A measure of anonymity is essential in a healthy democracy—and in the U.S., has been a weapon used to advance free speech since the time of the Revolution. We may regret a complete abandonment of anonymity in favor of communication technologies that leave fingerprints.

*The problem is not just the existence of fingerprints, but that no one told us that we are creating them.*

The problem is not just the existence of fingerprints, but that no one told us that we are creating them.

## The Parking Garage Knows More Than You Think

One day in the spring of 2006, Anthony and his wife drove to Logan Airport to pick up some friends. They took two cars, which they parked in the garage. Later in the evening, they paid at the kiosk inside the terminal, and left—or tried to. One car got out of the garage without a problem, but Anthony's was held up for more than an hour, in the middle of the night, and was not allowed to leave. Why? Because his ticket did not match his license plate.

It turns out that every car entering the airport garage has its license plate photographed at the same time as the ticket is being taken. Anthony had held both tickets while he and his wife were waiting for their friends, and then he gave her back one—the "wrong" one, as it turned out. It was the one he had taken when he drove in. When he tried to leave, he had the ticket that matched his wife's license plate number. A no-no.

Who knew that if two cars arrive and try to leave at the same time, they may not be able to exit if the tickets are swapped? In fact, who knew that every license plate is photographed as it enters the garage?

There is a perfectly sensible explanation. People with big parking bills sometimes try to duck them by picking up a second ticket at the end of their trip. When they drive out, they try to turn in the one for which they would have to pay only a small fee. Auto thieves sometimes try the same trick. So the system makes sense, but it raises many questions. Who else gets access to the license plate numbers? If the police are looking for a particular car, can they search the scanned license plate numbers of the cars in the garage? How long is the data retained? Does it say anywhere, even in the fine print, that your visit to the garage is not at all anonymous?

## All in Your Pocket

The number of new data sources—and the proliferation and interconnection of old data sources—is part of the story of how the digital explosion shattered privacy. But the other part of the technology story is about how all that data is put together.

On October 18, 2007, a junior staff member at the British national tax agency sent a small package to the government's auditing agency via TNT, a private delivery service. Three weeks later, it had not arrived at its destination and was reported missing. Because the sender had not used TNT's "registered mail" option, it couldn't be traced, and as of this writing has not been found. Perhaps it was discarded by mistake and never made it out of the mailroom; perhaps it is in the hands of criminals.

The mishap rocked the nation. As a result of the data loss, every bank and millions of individuals checked account activity for signs of fraud or identity theft. On November 20, the head of the tax agency resigned. Prime Minister Gordon Brown apologized to the nation, and the opposition party accused the Brown administration of having "failed in its first duty—to protect the public."

The package contained two computer disks. The data on the disks included names, addresses, birth dates, national insurance numbers (the British equivalent of U.S. Social Security Numbers), and bank account numbers of 25 million people—nearly 40% of the British population, and almost every child in the land. The tax office had all this data because every British child receives weekly government payments, and most families have the money deposited directly into bank accounts. Ten years ago, that much data would have required a truck to transport, not two small disks. Fifty years ago, it would have filled a building.

This was a preventable catastrophe. Many mistakes were made; quite ordinary mistakes. The package should have been registered. The disks should have been encrypted. It should not have taken three weeks for someone to speak up. But those are all age-old mistakes. Offices have been sending packages for centuries, and even Julius Caesar knew enough to encrypt information if he had to use intermediaries to deliver it. What happened in 2007 that could not have happened in 1984 was the assembly of such a massive database in a form that allowed it to be easily searched, processed, analyzed, connected to other databases, transported—and "lost."

Exponential growth—in storage size, processing speed, and communication speed—have changed the same old thing into something new. Blundering, stupidity, curiosity, malice, and thievery are not new. The fact that sensitive data about everyone in a nation could fit on a laptop *is* new. The ability to search for a needle in the haystack of the Internet *is* new. Easily connecting "public" data sources that used to be stored in file drawers in Albuquerque and Atlanta, but are now both electronically accessible from Algeria—*that* is new too.

Training, laws, and software all can help. But the truth of the matter is that as a society, we don't really know how to deal with these consequences of the digital explosion. The technology revolution is outstripping society's capacity to adjust to the changes in what can be taken for granted. The Prime Minister had to apologize to the British nation because among the things that have been blown to bits is the presumption that no junior staffer could do that much damage by mailing a small parcel.

## Connecting the Dots

The way we leave fingerprints and footprints is only part of what is new. We have always left a trail of information behind us, in our tax records, hotel reservations, and long distance telephone bills. True, the footprints are far clearer and more complete today than ever before. But something else has changed—the harnessing of computing power to correlate data, to connect the dots, to put pieces together, and to create cohesive, detailed pictures from what would otherwise have been meaningless fragments. The digital explosion does not just blow things apart. Like the explosion at the core of an atomic bomb, it blows things together as well. Gather up the details, connect the dots, assemble the parts of the puzzle, and a clear picture will emerge.

Computers can sort through databases too massive and too boring to be examined with human eyes. They can assemble colorful pointillist paintings out of millions of tiny dots, when any few dots would reveal nothing. When a federal court released half a million Enron emails obtained during the corruption trial, computer scientists quickly identified the subcommunities, and perhaps conspiracies, among Enron employees, using no data other than the pattern of who was emailing whom (see Figure 2.3). The same kinds of clustering algorithms work on patterns of telephone calls. You can learn a lot by knowing who is calling or emailing whom, even if you don't know what they are saying to each other—especially if you know the time of the communications and can correlate them with the time of other events.

Sometimes even public information is revealing. In Massachusetts, the Group Insurance Commission (GIC) is responsible for purchasing health insurance for state employees. When the premiums it was paying jumped one year, the GIC asked for detailed information on every patient encounter. And for good reason: All kinds of health care costs had been growing at prodigious rates. In the public interest, the state had a responsibility to understand how it was spending taxpayer money. The GIC did not want to know patients' names; it did not want to track individuals, and it did not want people to *think* they were being tracked. Indeed, tracking the medical visits of individuals would have been illegal.

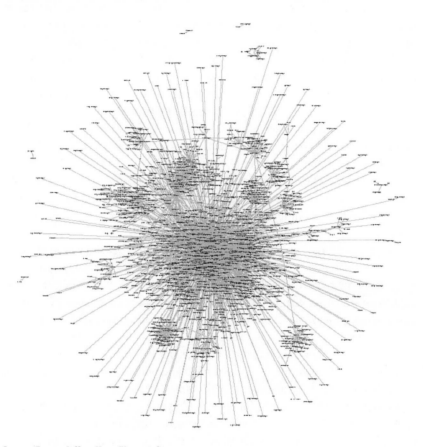

Source: Enron, Jeffrey Heer. Figure 3 from http://jheer.org/enron/v1/.

FIGURE 2.3    Diagram showing clusters of Enron emailers, indicating which employees carried on heavy correspondence with which others. The evident "blobs" may be the outlines of conspiratorial cliques.

So, the GIC data had no names, no addresses, no Social Security Numbers, no telephone numbers—nothing that would be a "unique identifier" enabling a mischievous junior staffer in the GIC office to see who exactly had a particular ailment or complaint. To use the official lingo, the data was "de-identified"; that is, stripped of identifying information. The data did include the gender, birth date, zip code, and similar facts about individuals making medical claims, along with some information about why they had sought medical attention. That information was gathered not to challenge any particular person, but to learn about patterns—if the truckers in Worcester are having lots of back injuries, for example, maybe workers in that region need better training on how to lift heavy items. Most states do pretty much the same kind of analysis of de-identified data about state workers.

Now this was a valuable data set not just for the Insurance Commission, but for others studying public health and the medical industry in Massachusetts. Academic researchers, for example, could use such a large inventory of medical data for epidemiological studies. Because it was all de-identified, there was no harm in letting others see it, the GIC figured. In fact, it was such good data that private industry—for example, businesses in the health management sector—might pay money for it. And so the GIC sold the data to businesses. The taxpayers might even benefit doubly from this decision: The data sale would provide a new revenue source to the state, and in the long run, a more informed health care industry might run more efficiently.

But how de-identified really was the material?

Latanya Sweeney was at the time a researcher at MIT (she went on to become a computer science professor at Carnegie Mellon University). She wondered how hard it would be for those who had received the de-identified data to "re-identify" the records and learn the medical problems of a particular state employee—for example, the governor of the Commonwealth.

Governor Weld lived, at that time, in Cambridge, Massachusetts. Cambridge, like many municipalities, makes its voter lists publicly available, for a charge of $15, and free for candidates and political organizations. If you know the precinct, they are available for only $.75. Sweeney spent a few dollars and got the voter lists for Cambridge. Anyone could have done the same.

According to the Cambridge voter registration list, there were only six people in Cambridge with Governor Weld's birth date, only three of those were men, and only one of those lived in Governor Weld's five-digit zip code. Sweeney could use that combination of factors, birth date, gender, and zip code to recover the Governor's medical records—and also those for members of his family, since the data was organized by employee. This type of re-identification is straightforward. In Cambridge, in fact, birth date alone was sufficient to identify more than 10% of the population. Nationally, gender, zip code, and date of birth are all it takes to identify 87% of the U.S. population uniquely.

The data set contained far more than gender, zip code, and birth date. In fact, any of the 58 individuals who received the data in 1997 could have identified any of the 135,000 people in the database. "There is no patient confidentiality," said Dr. Joseph Heyman, president of the Massachusetts Medical Society. "It's gone."

It is easy to read a story like this and scream, "Heads should roll!." But it is actually quite hard to figure out *who, if anyone, made a mistake.* Certainly collecting the information was the right thing to do, given that health costs are a major expense for all businesses and institutions. The GIC made an honest effort to de-identify the data before releasing it. Arguably the GIC might not have released the data to other state agencies, but that would be like saying that every department of government should acquire its heating oil independently. Data is a valuable resource, and once someone has collected it, the government is entirely correct in wanting it used for the public good. Some might object to selling the data to an outside business, but only in retrospect; had the data really been better de-identified, whoever made the decision to sell the data might well have been rewarded for helping to hold down the cost of government.

> *It is easy to read a story like this and scream, "Heads should roll!." But it is actually quite hard to figure out who, if anyone, made a mistake.*

Perhaps the mistake was the ease with which voter lists can be obtained. However, it is a tradition deeply engrained in our system of open elections that the public may know who is eligible to vote, and indeed who has voted. And voter lists are only one source of public data about the U.S. population. How many 21-year-old male Native Hawaiians live in Middlesex County, Massachusetts? In the year 2000, there were four. Anyone can browse the U.S. Census data, and sometimes it can help fill in pieces of a personal picture: Just go to factfinder.census.gov.

The mistake was thinking that the GIC data was truly de-identified, when it was not. But with so many data sources available, and so much computing power that could be put to work connecting the dots, it is very hard to know just how much information has to be discarded from a database to make it truly anonymous. Aggregating data into larger units certainly helps—releasing data by five-digit zip codes reveals less than releasing it by nine-digit zip codes. But the coarser the data, the less it reveals also of the valuable information for which it was made available.

How can we solve a problem that results from many developments, no one of which is really a problem in itself?

# Why We Lost Our Privacy, or Gave It Away

Information technology did not cause the end of privacy, any more than automotive technology caused teen sex. Technology creates opportunities and risks, and people, as individuals and as societies, decide how to live in the changed landscape of new possibilities. To understand why we have less privacy today than in the past, we must look not just at the gadgets. To be sure, we should be wary of spies and thieves, but we should also look at those who protect us and help us—and we should also take a good look in the mirror.

We are most conscious of our personal information winding up in the hands of strangers when we think about data loss or theft. Reports like the one about the British tax office have become fairly common. The theft of information about 45 million customers of TJX stores, described in Chapter 5, "Secret Bits," was even larger than the British catastrophe. In 2003, Scott Levine, owner of a mass email business named Snipermail, stole more than a billion personal information records from Acxiom. Millions of Americans are victimized by identity theft every year, at a total cost in the tens of billions of dollars annually. Many more of us harbor daily fears that just "a little bit" of our financial information has leaked out, and could be a personal time bomb if it falls into the wrong hands.

Why can't we just keep our personal information to ourselves? Why do so many other people have it in the first place, so that there is an opportunity for it to go astray, and an incentive for creative crooks to try to steal it?

We lose control of our personal information because of things we do to ourselves, and things others do to us. Of things we do to be ahead of the curve, and things we do because everyone else is doing them. Of things we do to save money, and things we do to save time. Of things we do to be safe from our enemies, and things we do because we feel invulnerable. Our loss of privacy is a problem, but there is no one answer to it, because there is no one reason why it is happening. It is a messy problem, and we first have to think about it one piece at a time.

We give away information about ourselves—voluntarily leave visible footprints of our daily lives—because we judge, perhaps without thinking about it very much, that the benefits outweigh the costs. To be sure, the benefits are many.

## Saving Time

For commuters who use toll roads or bridges, the risk-reward calculation is not even close. Time is money, and time spent waiting in a car is also anxiety and frustration. If there is an option to get a toll booth transponder, many commuters will get one, even if the device costs a few dollars up front. Cruising past the cars waiting to pay with dollar bills is not just a relief; it actually brings the driver a certain satisfied glow.

The transponder, which the driver attaches to the windshield from inside the car, is an RFID, powered with a battery so identifying information can be sent to the sensor several feet away as the driver whizzes past. The sensor can be mounted in a constricted travel lane, where a toll booth for a human tolltaker might have been. Or it can be mounted on a boom above traffic, so the driver doesn't even need to change lanes or slow down

And what is the possible harm? Of course, the state is recording the fact that the car has passed the sensor; that is how the proper account balance can be debited to pay the toll. When the balance gets too low, the driver's credit card may get billed automatically to replenish the balance. All that only makes the system better—no fumbling for change or doing anything else to pay for your travels.

The monthly bill—for the Massachusetts Fast Lane, for example—shows where and when you got on the highway—when, accurate to the second. It also shows where you got off and how far you went. Informing you of the mileage is another useful service, because Massachusetts drivers can get a refund on certain fuel taxes, if the fuel was used on the state toll road. Of course, you do not need a PhD to figure out that the state also knows when you got off the road, to the second, and that with one subtraction and one division, its computers could figure out if you were speeding. Technically, in fact, it would be trivial for the state to print the appropriate speeding fine at the bottom of the statement, and to bill your credit card for that amount at the same time as it was charging for tolls. That would be taking convenience a bit too far, and no state does it, yet.

What does happen right now, however, is that toll transponder records are introduced into divorce and child custody cases. You've never been within five miles of that lady's house? Really? Why have you gotten off the highway at the exit near it so many times? You say you can be the better custodial parent for your children, but the facts suggest otherwise. As one lawyer put it, "When a guy says, 'Oh, I'm home every day at five and I have dinner with my kids every single night,' you subpoena his E-ZPass and you find out he's crossing that bridge every night at 8:30. Oops!" These records can be subpoenaed, and have been, hundreds of times, in family law cases. They have also been used in employment cases, to prove that the car of a worker who said he was working was actually far from the workplace.

But most of us aren't planning to cheat on our spouses or our bosses, so the loss of privacy seems like no loss at all, at least compared to the time saved. Of course, if we actually *were* cheating, we *would* be in a big hurry, and might take some risks to save a few minutes!

## Saving Money

Sometimes it's money, not time, which motivates us to leave footprints. Such is the case with supermarket loyalty cards. If you do not want Safeway to keep track of the fact that you bought the 12-pack of Yodels despite your recent cholesterol results, you can make sure it doesn't know. You simply pay the "privacy tax"—the surcharge for customers not presenting a loyalty card. The purpose of loyalty cards is to enable merchants to track individual item purchases. (Item-level transactions are typically not tracked by credit card companies, which do not care if you bought Yodels instead of granola, so long as you pay the bill.) With loyalty cards, stores can capture details of cash transactions as well. They can process all the transaction data, and draw inferences about shoppers' habits. Then, if a lot of people who buy Yodels also buy Bison Brew Beer, the store's automated cash register can automatically spit out a discount coupon for Bison Brew as your Yodels are being bagged. A "discount" for you, and more sales for Safeway. Everybody wins. Don't they?

As grocery stores expand their web-based business, it is even easier for them to collect personal information about you. Reading the fine print when you sign up is a nuisance, but it is worth doing, so you understand what you are giving and what you are getting in return. Here are a few sentences of Safeway's privacy policy for customers who use its web site:

> Safeway may use personal information to provide you with news-
> letters, articles, product or service alerts, new product or service
> announcements, saving awards, event invitations, personally tailored
> coupons, program and promotional information and offers, and other
> information, which may be provided to Safeway by other companies.
> ... We may provide personal information to our partners and suppliers
> for customer support services and processing of personal information
> on behalf of Safeway. We may also share personal information with
> our affiliate companies, or in the course of an actual or potential sale,
> re-organization, consolidation, merger, or amalgamation of our busi-
> ness or businesses.

Dreary reading, but the language gives Safeway lots of leeway. Maybe you don't care about getting the junk mail. Not everyone thinks it is junk, and the company does let you "opt out" of receiving it (although in general, few people bother to exercise opt-out rights). But Safeway has lots of "affiliates," and who knows how many companies with which it *might* be involved in a merger or sale of part of its business. Despite privacy concerns voiced by groups like C.A.S.P.I.A.N. (Consumers Against Supermarket Privacy Invasion and Numbering, www.nocards.org), most shoppers readily agree to have the data collected. The financial incentives are too hard to resist, and most consumers just don't worry about marketers knowing their purchases. But whenever purchases can be linked to your name, there is a record, somewhere in a huge database, of whether you use regular or super tampons, lubricated or unlubricated condoms, and whether you like regular beer or lite. You have authorized the company to share it, and even if you hadn't, the company could lose it accidentally, have it stolen, or have it subpoenaed.

## Convenience of the Customer

The most obvious reason not to worry about giving information to a company is that you do business with them, and it is in your interest to see that they do their business with you better. You have no interest in whether they make more money from you, but you do have a strong interest in making it easier and faster for you to shop with them, and in cutting down the amount of stuff they may try to sell you that you would have no interest in buying. So your interests and theirs are, to a degree, aligned, not in opposition. Safeway's privacy policy states this explicitly: "Safeway Club Card information and other information may be used to help make Safeway's products, services, and programs more useful to its customers." Fair enough.

No company has been more progressive in trying to sell customers what they might want than the online store Amazon. Amazon suggests products to repeat customers, based on what they have bought before–or what they have simply looked at during previous visits to Amazon's web site. The algorithms are not perfect; Amazon's computers are drawing inferences from data, not being clairvoyant. But Amazon's guesses are pretty good, and recommending the wrong book every now and then is a very low-cost mistake. If Amazon does it too often, I might switch to Barnes and Noble, but there is no injury to me. So again: Why should anyone care that Amazon knows so much about me? On the surface, it seems benign. Of course, we don't want the credit card information to go astray, but who cares about knowing what books I have looked at online?

Our indifference is another marker of the fact that we are living in an exposed world, and that it feels very different to live here. In 1988, when a

## How Sites Know Who You Are

1. **You tell them.** Log in to Gmail, Amazon, or eBay, and you are letting them know exactly who you are.

2. **They've left cookies on one of your previous visits.** A *cookie* is a small text file stored on your local hard drive that contains information that a particular web site wants to have available during your current session (like your shopping cart), or from one session to the next. Cookies give sites persistent information for tracking and personalization. Your browser has a command for showing cookies—you may be surprised how many web sites have left them!

3. **They have your IP address.** The web server has to know where you are so that it can ship its web pages to you. Your IP address is a number like 66.82.9.88 that locates your computer in the Internet (see the Appendix for details). That address may change from one day to the next. But in a residential setting, your Internet Service Provider (your *ISP*—typically your phone or cable company) knows who was assigned each IP address at any time. Those records are often subpoenaed in court cases.

If you are curious about who is using a particular IP address, you can check the American Registry of Internet Numbers (www.arin.net). Services such as whatismyip.com, whatismyip.org, and ipchicken.com also allow you to check your own IP address. And www.whois.net allows you to check who owns a domain name such as harvard.com—which turns out to be the Harvard Bookstore, a privately owned bookstore right across the street from the university. Unfortunately, that information won't reveal who is sending you spam, since spammers routinely forge the source of email they send you.

videotape rental store clerk turned over Robert Bork's movie rental records to a Washington, DC newspaper during Bork's Supreme Court confirmation hearings, Congress was so outraged that it quickly passed a tough privacy protection bill, The Video Privacy Protection Act. Videotape stores, if any still exist, can be fined simply for keeping rental records too long. Twenty years later, few seem to care much what Amazon does with its millions upon millions of detailed, fine-grained views into the brains of all its customers.

## It's Just Fun to Be Exposed

Sometimes, there can be no explanation for our willing surrender of our privacy except that we take joy in the very act of exposing ourselves to public view. Exhibitionism is not a new phenomenon. Its practice today, as in the past, tends to be in the province of the young and the drunk, and those wishing to pretend they are one or the other. That correlation is by no means perfect, however. A university president had to apologize when an image of her threatening a Hispanic male with a stick leaked out from her MySpace page, with a caption indicating that she had to "beat off the Mexicans because they were constantly flirting with my daughter."

And there is a continuum of outrageousness. The less wild of the party photo postings blend seamlessly with the more personal of the blogs, where the bloggers are chatting mostly about their personal feelings. Here there is not exuberance, but some simpler urge for human connectedness. That passion, too, is not new. What *is* new is that a photo or video or diary entry, once posted, is visible to the entire world, and that there is no taking it back. Bits don't fade and they don't yellow. Bits are forever. And we don't know how to live with that.

*Bits don't fade and they don't yellow. Bits are forever. And we don't know how to live with that.*

For example, a blog selected with no great design begins:

> This is the personal web site of Sarah McAuley. ... I think sharing my life with strangers is odd and narcissistic, which of course is why I'm addicted to it and have been doing it for several years now. Need more? You can read the "About Me" section, drop me an email, or you know, just read the drivel that I pour out on an almost-daily basis.

No thank you, but be our guest. Or consider that there is a Facebook group just for women who want to upload pictures of themselves uncontrollably drunk. Or the Jennicam, through which Jennifer Kay Ringley opened her life to the world for seven years, setting a standard for exposure that many since have surpassed in explicitness, but few have approached in its endless ordinariness. We are still experimenting, both the voyeurs and viewed.

## Because You Can't Live Any Other Way

Finally, we give up data about ourselves because we don't have the time, patience, or single-mindedness about privacy that would be required to live our daily lives in another way. In the U.S., the number of credit, debit, and bank cards is in the billions. Every time one is used, an electronic handshake records a few bits of information about who is using it, when, where, and for what. It is now virtually unheard of for people to make large purchases of ordinary consumer goods with cash. Personal checks are going the way of cassette tape drives, rendered irrelevant by newer technologies. Even if you could pay cash for everything you buy, the tax authorities would have you in their databases anyway. There even have been proposals to put RFIDs in currency notes, so that the movement of cash could be tracked.

Only sects such as the Amish still live without electricity. It will soon be almost that unusual to live without Internet connectivity, with all the finger-prints it leaves of your daily searches and logins and downloads. Even the old dumb TV is rapidly disappearing in favor of digital communications. Digital TV will bring the advantages of video on demand—no more trips to rent movies or waits for them to arrive in the mail—at a price: Your television ser-vice provider will record what movies you have ordered. It will be so attrac-tive to be able to watch what we want when we want to watch it, that we won't miss either the inconvenience or the anonymity of the days when all the TV stations washed your house with their airwaves. You couldn't pick the broadcast times, but at least no one knew which waves you were grabbing out of the air.

# Little Brother Is Watching

So far, we have discussed losses of privacy due to things for which we could, in principle anyway, blame ourselves. None of us really needs a loyalty card, we should always read the fine print when we rent a car, and so on. We would all be better off saying "no" a little more often to these privacy-busters, but few of us would choose to live the life of constant vigilance that such res-olute denial would entail. And even if we were willing to make those sacri-fices, there are plenty of other privacy problems caused by things others do to us.

The snoopy neighbor is a classic American stock figure—the busybody who watches how many liquor bottles are in your trash, or tries to figure out whose Mercedes is regularly parked in your driveway, or always seems to know whose children were disorderly last Saturday night. But in Cyberspace, we are all neighbors. We can all check up on each other, without even open-ing the curtains a crack.

## Public Documents Become VERY Public

Some of the snooping is simply what anyone could have done in the past by paying a visit to the Town Hall. Details that were always public—but inacces-sible—are quite accessible now.

In 1975, Congress created the Federal Election Commission to administer the Federal Election Campaign Act. Since then, all political contributions have been public information. There is a difference, though, between "public" and "readily accessible." Making public data available on the Web shattered the veil of privacy that came from inaccessibility.

Want to know who gave money to Al Franken for Senate? Lorne Michaels from Saturday Night Live, Leonard Nimoy, Paul Newman, Craig Newmark (the "craig" of craigslist.com), and Ginnie W., who works with us and may not have wanted us to know her political leanings. Paul B., and Henry G., friends of ours, covered their bases by giving to both Obama and Clinton.

The point of the law was to make it easy to look up big donors. But since data is data, what about checking on your next-door neighbors? Ours definitely leaned toward Obama over Clinton, with no one in the Huckabee camp. Or your clients? One of ours gave heartily to Dennis Kucinich. Or your daughter's boyfriend? You can find out for yourself, at www.fec.gov or fundrace.huffingtonpost.com. We're not telling about our own.

Hosts of other facts are now available for armchair browsing—facts that in the past were nominally public but required a trip to the Registrar of Deeds. If you want to know what you neighbor paid for their house, or what it's worth today, many communities put all of their real estate tax rolls online. It was always public; now it's accessible. It was never wrong that people could get this information, but it feels very different now that people can browse through it from the privacy of their home.

If you are curious about someone, you can try to find him or her on Facebook, MySpace, or just using an ordinary search engine. A college would not peek at the stupid Facebook page of an applicant, would it? Absolutely not, says the Brown Dean of Admissions, "unless someone says there's something we should look at." *absolute w/ loup holes*

New participatory websites create even bigger opportunities for information-sharing. If you are about to go on a blind date, there are special sites just for that. Take a look at www.dontdatehimgirl.com, a social networking site with a self-explanatory focus. When we checked, this warning about one man had just been posted, along with his name and photograph: "Compulsive womanizer, liar, internet cheater; pathological liar who can't be trusted as a friend much less a boyfriend. Total creep! Twisted and sick—needs mental help. Keep your daughter away from this guy!" Of course, such information may be worth exactly what we paid for it. There is a similar site, www.platewire.com, for reports about bad drivers. If you are not dating or driving, perhaps you'd like to check out a neighborhood before you move in, or just register a public warning about the obnoxious revelers who live next door to you. If so, www.rottenneighbor.com is the site for you. When we

*check out*

typed in the zip code in which one of us lives, a nice Google map appeared with a house near ours marked in red. When we clicked on it, we got this report on our neighbor:

> you're a pretty blonde, slim and gorgeous. hey, i'd come on to you if i weren't gay. you probably have the world handed to you like most pretty women. is that why you think that you are too good to pick up after your dog? you know that you are breaking the law as well as being disrespectful of your neighbors. well, i hope that you step in your own dogs poop on your way to work, or on your way to dinner. i hope that the smell of your self importance follows you all day.

For a little money, you can get a lot more information. In January 2006, John Aravosis, creator of Americablog.com, purchased the detailed cell phone records of General Wesley Clark. For $89.95, he received a listing of all of Clark's calls for a three-day period. There are dozens of online sources for this kind of information. You might think you'd have to be in the police or the FBI to find out who people are calling on their cell phones, but there are handy services that promise to provide anyone with that kind of information for a modest fee. The *Chicago Sun Times* decided to put those claims to a test, so it paid $110 to locatecell.com and asked for a month's worth of cell phone records of one Frank Main, who happened to be one of its own reporters. The *Sun Times* did it all with a few keystrokes—provided the telephone number, the dates, and a credit card number. The request went in on Friday of a long weekend, and on Tuesday morning, a list came back in an email. The list included 78 telephone numbers the reporter had called—sources in law enforcement, people he was writing stories about, and editors in the newspaper. It was a great service for law enforcement—except that criminals can use it too, to find out whom the detectives are calling. These incidents stimulated passage of the Telephone Records and Privacy Act of 2006, but in early 2008, links on locatecell.com were still offering to help "find cell phone records in seconds," and more.

If cell phone records are not enough information, consider doing a proper background check. For $175, you can sign up as an "employer" with ChoicePoint and gain access to reporting services including criminal records, credit history, motor vehicle records, educational verification, employment verification, Interpol, sexual offender registries, and warrants searchers—they are all there to be ordered, with *a la carte* pricing. Before we moved from paper to bits, this information was publicly available, but largely inaccessible. Now, all it takes is an Internet connection and a credit card. This is one

> ### PERSONAL COMPUTER MONITORING SOFTWARE
>
> PC Pandora (www.pcpandora.com) enables you to "know everything they do on your PC," such as "using secret email accounts, chatting with unknown friends, accessing secret dating profiles or even your private records." Using it, you can "find out about secret email accounts, chat partners, dating site memberships, and more."
>
> Actual Spy (www.actualspy.com) is a "keylogger which allows you to find out what other users do on your computer in your absence. It is designed for the hidden computer monitoring and the monitoring of the computer activity. Keylogger Actual Spy is capable of catching all keystrokes, capturing the screen, logging the programs being run and closed, monitoring the clipboard contents."

of the most important privacy transformations. Information that was previously available only to professionals with specialized access or a legion of local workers is now available to everyone.

Then there is real spying. Beverly O'Brien suspected her husband was having an affair. If not a physical one, at a minimum she thought he was engaging in inappropriate behavior online. So, she installed some monitoring software. Not hard to do on the family computer, these packages are promoted as "parental control software"—a tool to monitor your child's activities, along with such other uses as employee monitoring, law enforcement, and to "catch a cheating spouse." Beverly installed the software, and discovered that her hapless hubby, Kevin, was chatting away while playing Yahoo! Dominoes. She was an instant spy, a domestic wire-tapper. The marketing materials for her software neglected to tell her that installing spyware that intercepts communications traffic was a direct violation of Florida's Security of Communications Act, and the trial court refused to admit any of the evidence in their divorce proceeding. The legal system worked, but that didn't change the fact that spying has become a relatively commonplace activity, the domain of spouses and employers, jilted lovers, and business competitors.

## Idle Curiosity

There is another form of Little Brother-ism, where amateurs can sit at a computer connected to the Internet and just look for something interesting—not about their neighbors or husbands, but about anyone at all. With so much data out there, anyone can discover interesting personal facts, with the investment of a little time and a little imagination. To take a different kind of example, imagine having your family's medical history re-identified from a paper in an online medical journal.

Figure 2.4 shows a map of the incidence of a disease, let's say syphilis, in a part of Boston. The "syphilis epidemic" in this illustration is actually a simulation. The data was just made up, but maps exactly like this have been common in journals for decades. Because the area depicted is more than 10 square kilometers, there is no way to figure out which house corresponds to a dot, only which neighborhood.

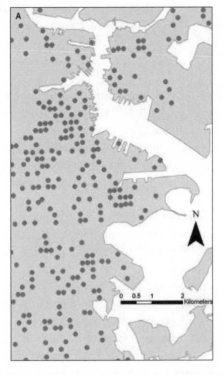

Source: John S. Brownstein, Christopher A. Cassa, Kenneth D. Mandl, No place to hide—reverse identification of patients from published maps, *New England Journal of Medicine*, 355:16, October 19, 2007, 1741-1742.

FIGURE 2.4   Map of part of Boston as from a publication in a medical journal, showing where a disease has occurred. (Simulated data.)

At least that was true in the days when journals were only print documents. Now journals are available online, and authors have to submit their figures as high-resolution JPEGs. Figure 2.5 shows what happens if you download the published journal article from the journal's web site, blow up a small part of the image, and superimpose it on an easily available map of the corresponding city blocks. For each of the seven disease locations, there is only a single house to which it could correspond. Anyone could figure out where the people with syphilis live.

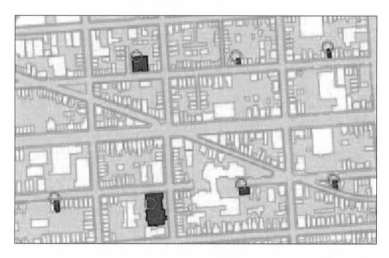

Source: John S. Brownstein, Christopher A. Cassa, Kenneth D. Mandl, No place to hide—reverse identification of patients from published maps, *New England Journal of Medicine*, 355:16, October 19, 2007, 1741-1742.

FIGURE 2.5    Enlargement of Figure 2.4 superimposed on a housing map of a few blocks of the city, showing that individual households can be identified to online readers, who have access to the high-resolution version of the epidemiology map.

This is a re-identification problem, like the one Latanya Sweeney noted when she showed how to get Governor Weld's medical records. There are things that can be done to solve this one. Perhaps the journal should not use such high-resolution images (although that could cause a loss of crispness, or even visibility—one of the nice things about online journals is that the visually impaired can magnify them, to produce crisp images at a very large scale). Perhaps the data should be "jittered" or "blurred" so what appears on the screen for illustrative purposes is intentionally incorrect in its fine details. There are always specific policy responses to specific re-identification scenarios.

Every scenario is a little different, however, and it is often hard to articulate sensible principles to describe what should be fixed.

In 2001, four MIT students attempted to re-identify Chicago homicide victims for a course project. They had extremely limited resources: no proprietary databases such as the companies that check credit ratings possess, no access to government data, and very limited computing power. Yet they were able to identify nearly 8,000 individuals from a target set of 11,000.

The source of the data was a free download from the Illinois Criminal Justice Authority. The primary reference data source was also free. The Social Security Administration provides a comprehensive death index including name, birth date, Social Security Number, zip code of last residence, date of death, and more. Rather than paying the nominal fee for the data (after all, they were students), these researchers used one of the popular genealogy web sites, RootsWeb.com, as a free source for the Social Security Death Index (SSDI) data. They might also have used municipal birth and death records, which are also publicly available.

The SSDI did not include gender, which was important to completing an accurate match. But more public records came to the rescue. They found a database published by the census bureau that enabled them to infer gender from first names—most people named "Robert" are male, and most named "Susan" are female. That, and some clever data manipulation, was all it took. It is far from clear that it was wrong for any particular part of these data sets to be publicly available, but the combination revealed more than was intended.

The more re-identification problems we see, and the more *ad hoc* solutions we develop, the more we develop a deep-set fear that our problems may never end. These problems arise because there is a great deal of public data, no one piece of which is problematic, but which creates privacy violations in combination. It is the opposite of what we know about salt—that the component elements, sodium and chlorine, are both toxic, but the compound itself is safe. Here we have toxic compounds arising from the clever combination of harmless components. What can possibly be done about *that?*

# Big Brother, Abroad and in the U.S.

Big Brother really is watching today, and his job has gotten much easier because of the digital explosion. In China, which has a long history of tracking individuals as a mechanism of social control, the millions of residents of Shenzhen are being issued identity cards, which record far more than the bearer's name and address. According to a report in the *New York Times*, the cards will document the individual's work history, educational background, religion, ethnicity, police record, medical insurance status, landlord's phone number, and reproductive history. Touted as a crime-fighting measure, the new technology—developed by an American company—will come in handy in case of street protests or any individual activity deemed suspicious by the authorities. The sort of record-keeping that used to be the responsibility of local authorities is becoming automated and nationalized as the country prospers and its citizens become increasingly mobile. The technology makes it easier to know where everyone is, and the government is taking advantage of that opportunity. Chinese tracking is far more detailed and pervasive than Britain's ubiquitous surveillance cameras.

## You Pay for the Mike, We'll Just Listen In

Planting tiny microphones where they might pick up conversations of underworld figures used to be risky work for federal authorities. There are much safer alternatives now that many people carry their own radio-equipped microphones with them all the time.

Many cell phones can be reprogrammed remotely so that the microphone is always on and the phone is transmitting, even if you think you have powered it off. The FBI used this technique in 2004 to listen to John Tomero's conversations with other members of his organized crime family. A federal court ruled that this "roving bug," installed after due authorization, constituted a legal from of wiretapping. Tomero could have prevented it by removing the battery, and now some nervous business executives routinely do exactly that.

The microphone in a General Motors car equipped with the OnStar system can also be activated remotely, a feature that can save lives when OnStar operators contact the driver after receiving a crash signal. OnStar warns, "OnStar will cooperate with official court orders regarding criminal investigations from law enforcement and other agencies," and indeed, the FBI has used this method to eavesdrop on conversations held inside cars. In one case, a federal court ruled against this way of collecting evidence—but not on privacy grounds. The roving bug disabled the normal operation of OnStar, and the court simply thought that the FBI had interfered with the vehicle owner's contractual right to chat with the OnStar operators!

## Identifying Citizens—Without ID Cards

In the age of global terrorism, democratic nations are resorting to digital surveillance to protect themselves, creating hotly contested conflicts with traditions of individual liberty. In the United States, the idea of a national identification card causes a furious libertarian reaction from parties not usually outspoken in defense of individual freedom. Under the REAL ID act of 2005, uniform federal standards are being implemented for state-issued drivers' licenses. Although it passed through Congress without debate, the law is opposed by at least 18 states. Resistance pushed back the implementation timetable first to 2009, and then, in early 2008, to 2011. Yet even fully implemented, REAL ID would fall far short of the true national ID preferred by those charged with fighting crime and preventing terrorism.

As the national ID card debate continues in the U.S., the FBI is making it irrelevant by exploiting emerging technologies. There would be no need for anyone to carry an ID card if the government had enough biometric data on Americans—that is, detailed records of their fingerprints, irises, voices, walking gaits, facial features, scars, and the shape of their earlobes. Gather a combination of measurements on individuals walking in public places, consult the databases, connect the dots, and—bingo!—their names pop up on the computer screen. No need for them to carry ID cards; the combination of biometric data would pin them down perfectly.

*As the national ID card debate continues in the U.S., the FBI is making it irrelevant by exploiting emerging technologies.*

Well, only imperfectly at this point, but the technology is improving. And the data is already being gathered and deposited in the data vault of the FBI's Criminal Justice Information Services database in Clarksburg, West Virginia. The database already holds some 55 million sets of fingerprints, and the FBI processes 100,000 requests for matches every day. Any of 900,000 federal, state, and local law enforcement officers can send a set of prints and ask the FBI to identify it. If a match comes up, the individual's criminal history is there in the database too.

But fingerprint data is hard to gather; mostly it is obtained when people are arrested. The goal of the project is to get identifying information on nearly everyone, and to get it without bothering people too much. For example, a simple notice at airport security could advise travelers that, as they pass through airport security, a detailed "snapshot" will be taken as they enter the secure area. The traveler would then know what is happening, and could have refused (and stayed home). As an electronic identification researcher puts it, "That's the key. You've chosen it. You have chosen to say, 'Yeah, I want this place to recognize me.'" No REAL ID controversies, goes the theory; all the data being gathered would, in some sense at least, be offered voluntarily.

## *Friendly Cooperation Between Big Siblings*

In fact, there are two Big Brothers, who often work together. And we are, by and large, glad they are watching, if we are aware of it at all. Only occasionally are we alarmed about their partnership.

The first Big Brother is Orwell's—the government. And the other Big Brother is the industry about which most of us know very little: the business of aggregating, consolidating, analyzing, and reporting on the billions of individual transactions, financial and otherwise, that take place electronically every day. Of course, the commercial data aggregation companies are not in the spying business; none of their data reaches them illicitly. But they do know a lot about us, and what they know can be extremely valuable, both to businesses and to the government.

The new threat to privacy is that computers can extract significant information from billions of apparently uninteresting pieces of data, in the way that mining technology has made it economically feasible to extract precious metals from low-grade ore. Computers can correlate databases on a massive level, linking governmental data sources together with private and commercial ones, creating comprehensive digital dossiers on millions of people. With their massive data storage and processing power, they can make connections in the data, like the clever connections the MIT students made with the Chicago homicide data, but using brute force rather than ingenuity. And the computers can discern even very faint traces in the data—traces that may help track payments to terrorists, set our insurance rates, or simply help us be sure that our new babysitter is not a sex offender.

And so we turn to the story of the government and the aggregators.

Acxiom is the country's biggest customer data company. Its business is to aggregate transaction data from all those swipes of cards in card readers all over the world—in 2004, this amounted to more than a billion transactions a day. The company uses its massive data about financial activity to support the credit card industry, banks, insurers, and other consumers of information about how people spend money. Unsurprisingly, after the War on Terror began, the Pentagon also got interested in Acxiom's data and the ways they gather and analyze it. Tracking how money gets to terrorists might help find the terrorists and prevent some of their attacks.

ChoicePoint is the other major U.S. data aggregator. ChoicePoint has more than 100,000 clients, which call on it for help in screening employment candidates, for example, or determining whether individuals are good insurance risks.

Acxiom and ChoicePoint are different from older data analysis operations, simply because of the scale of their operations. Quantitative differences have qualitative effects, as we said in Chapter 1; what has changed is not the technology, but rather the existence of rich data sources. Thirty years ago, credit cards had no magnetic stripes. Charging a purchase was a mechanical operation; the raised numerals on the card made an impression through carbon paper so you could have a receipt, while the top copy went to the company that issued the card. Today, if you charge something using your CapitalOne card, the bits go instantly not only to CapitalOne, but to Acxiom or other aggregators. The ability to search through huge commercial data sources—including not just credit card transaction data, but phone call records, travel tickets, and banking transactions, for example—is another illustration that more of the same can create something new.

Privacy laws do exist, of course. For a bank, or a data aggregator, to post your financial data on its web site would be illegal. Yet privacy is still developing as an area of the law, and it is connected to commercial and government interests in uncertain and surprising ways.

A critical development in privacy law was precipitated by the presidency of Richard Nixon. In what is generally agreed to be an egregious abuse of presidential power, Nixon used his authority as president to gather information on those who opposed him—in the words of his White House Counsel at the time, to "use the available federal machinery to screw our political enemies." Among the tactics Nixon used was to have the Internal Revenue Service audit the tax returns of individuals on an "enemies list," which included congressmen, journalists, and major contributors to Democratic causes. Outrageous as it was to use the IRS for this purpose, it was not illegal, so Congress moved to ban it in the future.

The Privacy Act of 1974 established broad guidelines for when and how the Federal Government can assemble dossiers on citizens it is not investigating for crimes. The government has to give public notice about what information it wants to collect and why, and it has to use it only for those reasons.

The Privacy Act limits what the government can do to gather information about individuals and what it can do with records it holds. Specifically, it states, "No agency shall disclose any record which is contained in a system of records by any means of communication to any person, or to another agency, except pursuant to a written request by, or with the prior written consent of, the individual to whom the record pertains, unless ...." If the government releases information inappropriately, even to another government agency, the affected citizen can sue for damages in civil court. The protections provided by the Privacy Act are sweeping, although not as sweeping as they may seem. Not every government office is in an "agency"; the courts are not, for example. The Act requires agencies to give public notice of the uses to which they will put the information, but the notice can be buried in the

Federal Register where the public probably won't see it unless news media happen to report it. Then there is the "unless" clause, which includes significant exclusions. For example, the law does not apply to disclosures for statistical, archival, or historical purposes, civil or criminal law enforcement activities, Congressional investigations, or valid Freedom of Information Act requests.

In spite of its exclusions, government practices changed significantly because of this law. Then, a quarter century later, came 9/11. *Law enforcement should have seen it all coming,* was the constant refrain as investigations revealed how many unconnected dots were in the hands of different government agencies. *It all could have been prevented if the investigative fiefdoms had been talking to each other. They should have been able to connect the dots.* But they could not—in part because the Privacy Act restricted inter-agency data transfers. A response was badly needed. The Department of Homeland Security was created to ease some of the interagency communication problems, but that government reorganization was only a start.

In January 2002, just a few months after the World Trade Center attack, the Defense Advanced Research Projects Agency (DARPA) established the Information Awareness Office (IAO) with a mission to:

> imagine, develop, apply, integrate, demonstrate, and transition information technologies, components and prototype, closed-loop, information systems that will counter asymmetric threats by achieving total information awareness useful for preemption; national security warning; and national security decision making. The most serious asymmetric threat facing the United States is terrorism, a threat characterized by collections of people loosely organized in shadowy networks that are difficult to identify and define. IAO plans to develop technology that will allow understanding of the intent of these networks, their plans, and potentially define opportunities for disrupting or eliminating the threats. To effectively and efficiently carry this out, we must promote sharing, collaborating, and reasoning to convert nebulous data to knowledge and actionable options.

Vice Admiral John Poindexter directed the effort that came to be known as "Total Information Awareness" (TIA). The growth of enormous private data repositories provided a convenient way to avoid many of the prohibitions of the Privacy Act. The Department of Defense can't get data from the Internal Revenue Service, because of the 1974 Privacy Act. *But they can both buy it from private data aggregators!* In a May 2002 email to Adm. Poindexter, Lt. Col Doug Dyer discussed negotiations with Acxiom.

Acxiom's Jennifer Barrett is a lawyer and chief privacy officer. She's testified before Congress and offered to provide help. One of the key suggestions she made is that people will object to Big Brother, wide-coverage databases, but they don't object to use of relevant data for specific purposes that we can all agree on. Rather than getting all the data for any purpose, we should start with the goal, tracking terrorists to avoid attacks, and then identify the data needed (although we can't define all of this, we can say that our templates and models of terrorists are good places to start). Already, this guidance has shaped my thinking.

Ultimately, the U.S. may need huge databases of commercial transactions that cover the world or certain areas outside the U.S. This information provides economic utility, and thus provides two reasons why foreign countries would be interested. Acxiom could build this mega-scale database.

The *New York Times* broke the story in October 2002. As Poindexter had explained in speeches, the government had to "break down the stovepipes" separating agencies, and get more sophisticated about how to create a big picture out of a million details, no one of which might be meaningful in itself. The *Times* story set off a sequence of reactions from the Electronic Privacy Information Center and civil libertarians. Congress defunded the office in 2003. Yet that was not the end of the idea.

The key to TIA was data mining, looking for connections across disparate data repositories, finding patterns, or "signatures," that might identify terrorists or other undesirables. The General Accountability Office report on Data Mining (GAO-04-548) reported on their survey of 128 federal departments. They described 199 separate data mining efforts, of which 122 used personal information.

Although IAO and TIA went away, Project ADVISE at the Department of Homeland Security continued with large-scale profiling system development. Eventually, Congress demanded that the privacy issues concerning this program be reviewed as well. In his June 2007 report (OIG-07-56), Richard Skinner, the DHS Inspector General, stated that "program managers did not address privacy impacts before implementing three pilot initiatives," and a few weeks later, the project was shut down. But ADVISE was only one of twelve data-mining projects going on in DHS at the time.

Similar privacy concerns led to the cancellation of the Pentagon's TALON database project. That project sought to compile a database of reports of suspected threats to defense facilities as part of a larger program of domestic counterintelligence.

The Transportation Security Administration (TSA) is responsible for airline passenger screening. One proposed system, CAPPS II, which was ultimately terminated over privacy concerns, sought to bring together disparate data sources to determine whether a particular individual might pose a transportation threat. Color-coded assessment tags would determine whether you could board quickly, be subject to further screening, or denied access to air travel.

The government creates projects, the media and civil liberties groups raise serious privacy concerns, the projects are cancelled, and new ones arise to take their place. The cycle seems to be endless. In spite of Americans' traditional suspicions about government surveillance of their private lives, the cycle seems to be almost an inevitable consequence of Americans' concerns about their security, and the responsibility that government officials feel to use the best available technologies to protect the nation. Corporate databases often contain the best information on the people about whom the government is curious.

# Technology Change and Lifestyle Change

New technologies enable new kinds of social interactions. There were no suburban shopping malls before private automobiles became cheap and widely used. Thirty years ago, many people getting off an airplane reached for cigarettes; today, they reach for cell phones. As Heraclitus is reported to have said 2,500 years ago, "all is flux"—everything keeps changing. The reach-for-your-cell phone gesture may not last much longer, since airlines are starting to provide onboard cell phone coverage.

The more people use a new technology, the more useful it becomes. (This is called a "network effect"; see Chapter 4, "Needles in the Haystack.") When one of us got the email address lewis@harvard as a second-year graduate student, it was a vainglorious joke; all the people he knew who had email addresses were students in the same office with him. Email culture could not develop until a lot of people had email, but there wasn't much point in having email if no one else did.

Technology changes and social changes reinforce each other. Another way of looking at the technological reasons for our privacy loss is to recognize that the social institutions enabled by the technology are now more important than the practical uses for which the technology was originally conceived. Once a lifestyle change catches on, we don't even think about what it depends on.

## Credit Card Culture

The usefulness of the data aggregated by Acxiom and its kindred data aggregation services rises as the number of people in their databases goes up, and as larger parts of their lives leave traces in those databases. When credit cards were mostly short-term loans taken out for large purchases, the credit card data was mostly useful for determining your creditworthiness. It is still useful for that, but now that many people buy virtually everything with credit cards, from new cars to fast-food hamburgers, the credit card transaction database can be mined for a detailed image of our lifestyles. The information is there, for example, to determine if you usually eat dinner out, how much traveling you do, and how much liquor you tend to consume. Credit card companies do in fact analyze this sort of information, and we are glad they do. If you don't seem to have been outside Montana in your entire life and you turn up buying a diamond bracelet in Rio de Janeiro, the credit card company's computer notices the deviation from the norm, and someone may call to be sure it is really you.

The credit card culture is an economic problem for many Americans, who accept more credit card offers than they need, and accumulate more debt than they should. But it is hard to imagine the end of the little plastic cards, unless even smaller RFID tags replace them. Many people carry almost no cash today, and with every easy swipe, a few more bits go into the databases.

## Email Culture

Email is culturally in between telephoning and writing a letter. It is quick, like telephoning (and instant messaging is even quicker). It is permanent, like a letter. And like a letter, it waits for the recipient to read it. Email has, to a great extent, replaced both of the other media for person-to-person communication, because it has advantages of both. But it has the problems that other communication methods have, and some new ones of its own.

Phone calls are not intended to last forever, or to be copied and redistributed to dozens of other people, or to turn up in court cases. When we use email as though it were a telephone, we tend to forget about what else might happen to it, other than the telephone-style use, that the recipient will read it and throw it away. Even Bill Gates probably wishes that he had written his corporate emails in a less telephonic voice. After testifying in an antitrust lawsuit that he had not contemplated cutting a deal to divide the web browser market with a competitor, the government produced a candid email he had sent, seeming to contradict his denial: "We could even pay them money as part of the deal, buying a piece of them or something."

*Email is as public as postcards, unless it is encrypted, which it usually is not.*

Email is bits, traveling within an ISP and through the Internet, using email software that may keep copies, filter it for spam, or submit it to any other form of inspection the ISP may choose. If your email service provider is Google, the point of the inspection is to attach some appropriate advertising. If you are working within a financial services corporation, your emails are probably logged—even the ones to your grandmother—because the company has to be able to go back and do a thorough audit if something inappropriate happens.

Email is as public as postcards, unless it is encrypted, which it usually is not. Employers typically reserve the right to read what is sent through company email. Check the policy of your own employer; it may be hard to find, and it may not say what you expect. Here is Harvard's policy, for example:

> Employees must have no expectation or right of privacy in anything they create, store, send, or receive on Harvard's computers, networks, or telecommunications systems. .... Electronic files, e-mail, data files, images, software, and voice mail may be accessed at any time by management or by other authorized personnel for any business purpose. Access may be requested and arranged through the system(s) user, however, this is not required.

Employers have good reason to retain such sweeping rights; they have to be able to investigate wrongdoing for which the employer would be liable. As a result, such policies are often less important than the good judgment and ethics of those who administer them. Happily, Harvard's are generally good. But as a general principle, the more people who have the authority to snoop, the more likely it is that someone will succumb to the temptation.

Commercial email sites can retain copies of messages even after they have been deleted. And yet, there is very broad acceptance of public, free, email services such as Google's Gmail, Yahoo! Mail, or Microsoft's Hotmail. The technology is readily available to make email private: whether you use encryption tools, or secure email services such as Hushmail, a free, web-based email service that incorporates PGP-based encryption (see Chapter 5). The usage of these services, though, is an insignificant fraction of their unencrypted counterparts. Google gives us free, reliable email service and we, in return, give up some space on our computer screen for ads. Convenience and cost trump privacy. By and large, users don't worry that Google, or its competitors, have all their mail. It's a bit like letting the post office keep a copy of every letter you send, but we are so used to it, we don't even think about it.

## Web Culture

When we send an email, we think at least a *little* bit about the impression we are making, because we are sending it to a human being. We may well say things we would not say face-to-face, and live to regret that. Because we can't see anyone's eyes or hear anyone's voice, we are more likely to over-react and be hurtful, angry, or just too smart for our own good. But because email is directed, we don't send email thinking that no one else will ever read what we say.

The Web is different. Its social sites inherit their communication culture not from the letter or telephone call, but from the wall in the public square, littered with broadsides and scribbled notes, some of them signed and some not. Type a comment on a blog, or post a photo on a photo album, and your action can be as anonymous as you wish it to be—you do not know to whom your message is going. YouTube has millions of personal videos. Photo-archiving sites are the shoeboxes and photo albums of the twenty-first century. Online backup now provides easy access to permanent storage for the contents of our personal computers. We entrust commercial entities with much of our most private information, without apparent concern. The generation that has grown up with the Web has embraced social networking in all its varied forms: MySpace, YouTube, LiveJournal, Facebook, Xanga, Classmates.com, Flickr, dozens more, and blogs of every shape and size. More than being taken, personal privacy has been given away quite freely, because everyone else is doing it—the surrender of privacy is more than a way to social connectedness, it is a social institution in its own right. There are 70 million bloggers sharing everything from mindless blather to intimate personal details. Sites like www.loopt.com let you find your friends, while twitter.com lets you tell the entire world where you are and what you are doing. The Web is a confused, disorganized, chaotic realm, rich in both gold and garbage.

The "old" web, "Web 1.0," as we now refer to it, was just an information resource. You asked to see something, and you got to see it. Part of the dis-inhibition that happens on the new "Web 2.0" social networking sites is due to the fact that they still allow the movie-screen illusion—that we are "just looking," or if we are contributing, we are not leaving footprints or finger-prints if we use pseudonyms. (See Chapter 4 for more on Web 1.0 and Web 2.0.)

But of course, that is not really the way the Web ever worked. It is important to remember that even Web 1.0 was never anonymous, and even "just looking" leaves fingerprints.

In July 2006, a *New York Times* reporter called Thelma Arnold of Lilburn, Georgia. Thelma wasn't expecting the call. She wasn't famous, nor was she involved in anything particularly noteworthy. She enjoyed her hobbies, helped her friends, and from time to time looked up things on the Web—stuff about her dogs, and her friends' ailments.

Then AOL, the search engine she used, decided to release some "anonymous" query data. Thelma, like most Internet users, may not have known that AOL had kept every single topic that she, and every other one of their users, had asked about. But it did. In a moment of unenlightened generosity, AOL released for research use a small sample: about 20 million queries from 658,000 different users. That is actually not a lot of data by today's standards. For example, in July 2007, there were about 5.6 billion search engine queries, of which roughly 340 million were AOL queries. So, 20 million queries comprise only a couple of days' worth of search queries. In an effort to protect their clients' privacy, AOL "de-identified" the queries. AOL never mentioned anyone by name; they used random numbers instead. Thelma was 4417149. AOL mistakenly presumed that removing a single piece of personal identification would make it hard to figure out who the users were. It turned out that for some of the users, it wasn't hard at all.

It didn't take much effort to match Thelma with her queries. She had searched for "landscapers in Lilburn, GA" and several people with the last name "Arnold," leading to the obvious question of whether there were any Arnolds in Lilburn. Many of Thelma's queries were not particularly useful for identifying her, but were revealing nonetheless: "dry mouth," "thyroid," "dogs that urinate on everything," and "swing sets."

Thelma was not the only person to be identified. User 22690686 (Terri) likes astrology, and the Edison National Bank, Primerica, and Budweiser. 5779844 (Lawanna) was interested in credit reports, and schools. From what he searched for, user 356693 seems to have been an aide to Chris Shays, Congressman from Connecticut.

One of the privacy challenges that we confront as we rummage through the rubble of the digital explosion is that information exists without context. Was Thelma Arnold suffering from a wide range of ailments? One might readily conclude that from her searches. The fact is that she often tried to help her friends by understanding their medical problems.

Or consider AOL user 17556639, whose search history was released along with Thelma Arnold's. He searched for the following:

how to kill your wife 23 Mar, 22:09
wife killer 23 Mar, 22:11
poop 23 Mar, 22:12
dead people 23 Mar, 22:13
pictures of dead people 23 Mar, 22:15
killed people 23 Mar, 22:16
dead pictures 23 Mar, 22:17
murder photo 23 Mar, 22:20
steak and cheese 23 Mar, 22:22
photo of death 23 Mar, 22:30
death 23 Mar, 22:33
dead people photos 23 Mar, 22:33
photo of dead people 23 Mar, 22:35
www.murderdpeople.com 23 Mar, 22:37
decapitated photos 23 Mar, 22:39
car crashes3 23 Mar, 22:40
car crash photo 23 Mar, 22:41

Is this AOL user a potential criminal? Should AOL have called the police? Is 17556639 about to kill his wife? Is he (or she) a researcher with a spelling problem and an interest in Philly cheese steak? Is reporting him to the police doing a public service, or is it an invasion of privacy?

There is no way to tell just from these queries if this user was contemplating some heinous act or doing research for a novel that involves some grisly scenes. When information is incomplete and decontextualized, it is hard to judge meaning and intent.

In this particular case, we happen to know the answer. The user, Jason from New Jersey, was just fooling around, trying to see if Big Brother was watching. He wasn't planning to kill his wife at all. Inference from incomplete data has the problem of false positives—thinking you have something that you don't, because there are other patterns that fit the same data.

Information without context often leads to erroneous conclusions. Because our digital trails are so often retrieved outside the context within which they were created, they sometimes suggest incorrect interpretations. Data interpretation comes with balanced social responsibilities, to protect society when there is evidence of criminal behavior or intent, and also to protect the individual when such evidence is too limited to be reliable. Of course, for every example of misleading and ambiguous data, someone will want to solve the problems it creates by collecting more data, rather than less.

# Beyond Privacy

There is nothing new under the sun, and the struggles to define and enforce privacy are no exception. Yet history shows that our concept of privacy has evolved, and the law has evolved with it. With the digital explosion, we have arrived at a moment where further evolution will have to take place rather quickly.

## *Leave Me Alone*

More than a century ago, two lawyers raised the alarm about the impact technology and the media were having on personal privacy:

> Instantaneous photographs and newspaper enterprise have invaded the sacred precincts of private and domestic life; and numerous mechanical devices threaten to make good the prediction that "what is whispered in the closet shall be proclaimed from the house-tops."

This statement is from the seminal law review article on privacy, published in 1890 by Boston attorney Samuel Warren and his law partner, Louis Brandeis, later to be a justice of the U.S. Supreme Court. Warren and Brandeis went on, "Gossip is no longer the resource of the idle and of the vicious, but has become a trade, which is pursued with industry as well as effrontery. To satisfy a prurient taste the details of sexual relations are spread broadcast in the columns of the daily papers. To occupy the indolent, column upon column is filled with idle gossip, which can only be procured by intrusion upon the domestic circle." New technologies made this garbage easy to produce, and then "the supply creates the demand."

And those candid photographs and gossip columns were not merely tasteless; they were bad. Sounding like modern critics of mindless reality TV, Warren and Brandeis raged that society was going to hell in a handbasket because of all that stuff that was being spread about.

> Even gossip apparently harmless, when widely and persistently circulated, is potent for evil. It both belittles and perverts. It belittles by inverting the relative importance of things, thus dwarfing the thoughts and aspirations of a people. When personal gossip attains the dignity of print, and crowds the space available for matters of

real interest to the community, what wonder that the ignorant and thoughtless mistake its relative importance. Easy of comprehension, appealing to that weak side of human nature which is never wholly cast down by the misfortunes and frailties of our neighbors, no one can be surprised that it usurps the place of interest in brains capable of other things. Triviality destroys at once robustness of thought and delicacy of feeling. No enthusiasm can flourish, no generous impulse can survive under its blighting influence.

The problem they perceived was that it was hard to say just why such invasions of privacy should be unlawful. In individual cases, you could say something sensible, but the individual legal decisions were not part of a general regime. The courts had certainly applied legal sanctions for defamation—publishing malicious gossip that was false—but then what about malicious gossip that was true? Other courts had imposed penalties for publishing an individual's private letters—but on the basis of property law, just as though the individual's horse had been stolen rather than the words in his letters. That did not seem to be the right analogy either. No, they concluded, such rationales didn't get to the nub. When something private is published about you, something has been taken from you, you are a victim of theft—but the thing stolen from you is part of your identity as a person. In fact, privacy was a right, they said, a "general right of the individual to be let alone." That right had long been in the background of court decisions, but the new technologies had brought this matter to a head. In articulating this new right, Warren and Brandeis were, they asserted, grounding it in the principle of "inviolate personhood," the sanctity of individual identity.

## Privacy and Freedom

The Warren-Brandeis articulation of privacy as a right to be left alone was influential, but it was never really satisfactory. Throughout the twentieth century, there were simply too many good reasons for *not* leaving people alone, and too many ways in which people *preferred* not to be left alone. And in the U.S., First Amendment rights stood in the way of privacy rights. As a general rule, the government simply cannot stop me from saying *anything*. In particular, it usually cannot stop me from saying what I want about your private affairs. Yet the Warren-Brandeis definition worked well enough for a long time, because, as Robert Fano put it, "The pace of technological progress was for a long time sufficiently slow as to enable society to learn pragmatically how to exploit new technology and prevent its abuse, with society maintaining its equilibrium most of the time." By the late 1950s, the emerging electronic technologies, both computers and communication, had destroyed that balance. Society could no longer adjust pragmatically, because surveillance technologies were developing too quickly.

The result was a landmark study of privacy by the Association of the Bar of the City of New York, which culminated in the publication, in 1967, of a book by Alan Westin, entitled *Privacy and Freedom*. (Fano was reviewing Westin's book when he painted the picture of social disequilibrium caused by rapid technological change.) Westin proposed a crucial shift of focus.

Brandeis and Warren had seen a loss of privacy as a form of personal injury, which might be so severe as to cause "mental pain and distress, far greater than could be inflicted by mere bodily injury." Individuals had to take responsibility for protecting themselves. "Each man is responsible for his own acts and omissions only." But the law had to provide the weapons with which to resist invasions of privacy.

Westin recognized that the Brandeis-Warren formulation was too absolute, in the face of the speech rights of other individuals and society's legitimate data-gathering practices. Protection might come not from protective shields, but from control over the uses to which personal information could be put. "Privacy," wrote Westin, "is the claim of individuals, groups, or institutions to determine for themselves when, how, and to what extent information about them is communicated to others."

> ... what is needed is a structured and rational weighing process, with definite criteria that public and private authorities can apply in comparing the claim for disclosure or surveillance through new devices with the claim to privacy. The following are suggested as the basic steps of such a process: measuring the seriousness of the need to conduct surveillance; deciding whether there are alternative methods to meet the need; deciding what degree of reliability will be required of the surveillance instrument; determining whether true consent to surveillance has been given; and measuring the capacity for limitation and control of the surveillance if it is allowed.

So even if there were a legitimate reason why the government, or some other party, might know something about you, your right to privacy might limit what the knowing party could do with that information.

This more nuanced understanding of privacy emerged from the important social roles that privacy plays. Privacy is not, as Warren and Brandeis had it, the right to be isolated from society—privacy is a right that makes society work. Fano mentioned three social roles of privacy. First, "the right to maintain the privacy of one's personality can be regarded as part of the right of self-preservation"—the right to keep your adolescent misjudgments and personal conflicts to yourself, as long as they are of no lasting significance to your ultimate position in society. Second, privacy is the way society allows deviations from prevailing social norms, given that no one set of social norms is universally and permanently satisfactory—and indeed, given that social progress requires social experimentation. And third, privacy is essential to the development of independent thought—it enables some decoupling of the individual from society, so that thoughts can be shared in limited circles and rehearsed before public exposure.

*Privacy is the way society allows deviations from prevailing social norms, given that social progress requires social experimentation.*

*Privacy and Freedom*, and the rooms full of disk drives that sprouted in government and corporate buildings in the 1960s, set off a round of soul-searching about the operational significance of privacy rights. What, in practice, should those holding a big data bank think about when collecting the data, handling it, and giving it to others?

## Fair Information Practice Principles

In 1973, the Department of Health, Education, and Welfare issued "Fair Information Practice Principles" (FIPP), as follows:

- **Openness.** There must be no personal data record-keeping systems whose very existence is secret.

- **Disclosure.** There must be a way for a person to find out what information about the person is in a record and how it is used.

- **Secondary use.** There must be a way for a person to prevent information about the person that was obtained for one purpose from being used or made available for other purposes without the person's consent.

- **Correction.** There must be a way for a person to correct or amend a record of identifiable information about the person.

- **Security.** Any organization creating, maintaining, using, or disseminating records of identifiable personal data must assure the reliability of the data for its intended use and must take precautions to prevent misuses of the data.

These principles were proposed for U.S. medical data, but were never adopted. Nevertheless, they have been the foundation for many corporate privacy policies. Variations on these principles have been codified in international trade agreements by the Organization of Economic Cooperation and Development (OECD) in 1980, and within the European Union (EU) in 1995. In the United States, echoes of these principles can be found in some state laws, but federal laws generally treat privacy on a case by case or "sectorial" basis. The 1974 Privacy Act applies to interagency data transfers within the federal government, but places no limitations on data handling in the private sector. The Fair Credit Reporting Act applies only to consumer credit data, but does not apply to medical data. The Video Privacy Act applies only to videotape rentals, but not to "On Demand" movie downloads, which did not exist when the Act was passed! Finally, few federal or state laws apply to the huge data banks in the file cabinets and computer systems of cities and towns. American government is decentralized, and authority over government data is decentralized as well.

The U.S. is not lacking in privacy laws. But privacy has been legislated inconsistently and confusingly, and in terms dependent on technological contingencies. There is no national consensus on what should be protected, and how protections should be enforced. Without a more deeply informed collective judgment on the benefits and costs of privacy, the current legislative hodgepodge may well get worse in the United States.

The discrepancy between American and European data privacy standards threatened U.S. involvement in international trade, because an EU directive would prohibit data transfers to nations, such as the U.S., that do not meet the European "adequacy" standard for privacy protection. Although the U.S. sectorial approach continues to fall short of European requirements, in 2000 the European Commission created a "safe harbor" for American businesses with multinational operations. This allowed individual corporations to establish their practices are adequate with respect to seven principles, covering notice, choice, onward transfer, access, security, data integrity, and enforcement.

> ### U.S. PRIVACY LAWS
>
> The Council of Better Business Bureaus has compiled a "Review of Federal and State Privacy Laws":
>
> www.bbbonline.org/
> UnderstandingPrivacy/library/
> fed_statePrivLaws.pdf
>
> The state of Texas has also compiled a succinct summary of major privacy laws:
>
> www.oag.state.tx.us/notice/
> privacy_table.htm.

It is, unfortunately, too easy to debate whether the European omnibus approach is more principled than the U.S. piecemeal approach, when the real question is whether either approach accomplishes what we want it to achieve. The Privacy Act of 1974 assured us that obscure statements would be buried deep in the Federal Register, providing the required official notice about massive governmental data collection plans—better than nothing, but providing "openness" only in a narrow and technical sense. Most large corporations doing business with the public have privacy notices, and virtually no one reads them. Only 0.3% of Yahoo! users read its privacy notice in 2002, for example. In the midst of massive negative publicity that year when Yahoo! changed its privacy policy to allow advertising messages, the number of users who accessed the privacy policy rose only to 1%. None of the many U.S. privacy laws prevented the warrantless wiretapping program instituted by the Bush administration, nor the cooperation with it by major U.S. telecommunications companies.

Indeed, cooperation between the federal government and private industry seems more essential than ever for gathering information about drug trafficking and international terrorism, because of yet another technological development. Twenty years ago, most long-distance telephone calls spent at least part of their time in the air, traveling by radio waves between microwave antenna towers or between the ground and a communication satellite. Government eavesdroppers could simply listen in (see the discussion of Echelon in Chapter 5). Now many phone calls travel through fiber optic cables instead, and the government is seeking the capacity to tap this privately owned infrastructure.

High privacy standards have a cost. They can limit the public usefulness of data. Public alarm about the release of personal medical information has led to major legislative remedies. The Health Information Portability and Accountability Act (HIPAA) was intended both to encourage the use of electronic data interchange for health information, and to impose severe penalties for the disclosure of "Protected Health Information," a very broad category including not just medical histories but, for example, medical payments. The bill mandates the removal of anything that could be used to re-connect medical records to their source. HIPAA is fraught with problems in an environment of ubiquitous data and powerful computing. Connecting the dots by assembling disparate data sources makes it extremely difficult to achieve the level of anonymity that HIPAA sought to guarantee. But help is available, for a price, from a whole new industry of HIPAA-compliance advisors. If you search for HIPAA online, you will likely see advertisements for services that will help you protect your data, and also keep you out of jail.

## EVER READ THOSE "I AGREE" DOCUMENTS?

Companies can do almost anything they want with your information, as long as you agree. It seems hard to argue with that principle, but the deck can be stacked against the consumer who is "agreeing" to the company's terms. Sears Holding Corporation (SHC), the parent of Sears, Roebuck and Kmart, gave consumers an opportunity to join "My Sears Holding Community," which the company describes as "something new, something different ... a dynamic and highly interactive online community ... where your voice is heard and your opinion matters." When you went online to sign up, the terms appeared in a window on the screen.

The scroll box held only 10 lines of text, and the agreement was 54 boxfuls long. Deep in the terms was a detail: You were allowing Sears to install software on your PC that "monitors all of the Internet behavior that occurs on the computer ..., including ... filling a shopping basket, completing an application form, or checking your ... personal financial or health information." So your computer might send your credit history and AIDS test results to SHC, and you said it was fine!

At the same time as HIPAA and other privacy laws have safeguarded our personal information, they are making medical research costly and sometimes impossible to conduct. It is likely that classic studies such as the Framingham Heart Study, on which much public policy about heart disease was founded, could not be repeated in today's environment of strengthened privacy rules. Dr. Roberta Ness, president of the American College of Epidemiology, reported that "there is a perception that HIPAA may even be having a negative effect on public health surveillance practices."

The European reliance on the Fair Information Practice Principles is often no more useful, in practice, than the American approach. Travel through London, and you will see many signs saying "Warning: CCTV in use" to meet the "Openness" requirement about the surveillance cameras. That kind of notice throughout the city hardly empowers the individual. After all, even Big Brother satisfied the FIPP Openness standard, with the ubiquitous notices that he was watching! And the "Secondary Use" requirement, that European citizens should be asked permission before data collected for one purpose is used for another, is regularly ignored in some countries, although compliance practices are a major administrative burden on European businesses and may cause European businesses at least to pause and think before "repurposing" data they have gathered. Sociologist Amitai Etzioni repeatedly asks European audiences if they have *ever* been asked for permission to re-use data collected about them, and has gotten only a single positive response—and that was from a gentleman who had been asked by a U.S. company.

The five FIPP principles, and the spirit of transparency and personal control that lay behind them, have doubtless led to better privacy practices. But they have been overwhelmed by the digital explosion, along with the insecurity of the world and all the social and cultural changes that have occurred in daily life. Fred H. Cate, a privacy scholar at the Indiana University, characterizes the FIPP principles as almost a complete bust:

> Modern privacy law is often expensive, bureaucratic, burdensome, and offers surprisingly little protection for privacy. It has substituted individual control of information, which it in fact rarely achieves, for privacy protection. In a world rapidly becoming more global through information technologies, multinational commerce, and rapid travel, data protection laws have grown more fractured and protectionist. Those laws have become unmoored from their principled basis, and the principles on which they are based have become so varied and procedural, that our continued intonation of the FIPPS mantra no longer obscures the fact that this emperor indeed has few if any clothes left.

## Privacy as a Right to Control Information

It is time to admit that we don't even really know what we want. The bits are everywhere; there is simply no locking them down, and no one really wants to do that anymore. The meaning of privacy has changed, and we do not have a good way of describing it. It is not the right to be left alone, because not even the most extreme measures will disconnect our digital selves from the rest of the world. It is not the right to keep our private information to ourselves, because the billions of atomic factoids don't any more lend themselves into binary classification, private or public.

*The bits are everywhere; there is simply no locking them down, and no one really wants to do that anymore.*

Reade Seligmann would probably value his privacy more than most Americans alive today. On Monday, April 17, 2006, Seligmann was indicted in connection with allegations that a 27-year-old performer had been raped at a party at a Duke fraternity house. He and several of his lacrosse teammates instantly became poster children for everything that is wrong with

American society—an example of national over-exposure that would leave even Warren and Brandeis breathless if they were around to observe it. Seligmann denied the charges, and at first it looked like a typical he-said, she-said scenario, which could be judged only on credibility and presumptions about social stereotypes.

But during the evening of that fraternity party, Seligmann had left a trail of digital detritus. His data trail indicated that he could not have been at the party long enough, or at the right time, to have committed the alleged rape. Time-stamped photos from the party showed that the alleged victim of his rape was dancing at 12:02 AM. At 12:24 AM, he used his ATM card at a bank, and the bank's computers kept records of the event. Seligmann used his cell phone at 12:25 AM, and the phone company tracked every call he made, just as your phone company keeps a record of every call you make and receive. Seligmann used his prox card to get into his dormitory room at 12:46 AM, and the university's computer kept track of his comings and goings, just as other computers keep track of every card swipe or RFID wave you and I make in our daily lives. Even during the ordinary movements of a college student going to a fraternity party, every step along the way was captured in digital detail. If Seligmann had gone to the extraordinary lengths necessary to avoid leaving digital fingerprints—not using a modern camera, a cell phone, or a bank, and living off campus to avoid electronic locks—his defense would have lacked important exculpatory evidence.

Which would we prefer—the new world with digital fingerprints everywhere and the constant awareness that we are being tracked, or the old world with few digital footprints and a stronger sense of security from prying eyes? And what is the point of even asking the question, when the world cannot be restored to its old information lock-down?

In a world that has moved beyond the old notion of privacy as a wall around the individual, we could instead regulate those who would inappropriately *use* information about us. If I post a YouTube video of myself dancing in the nude, I should expect to suffer some personal consequences. Ultimately, as Warren and Brandeis said, individuals have to take responsibility for their actions. But society has drawn lines in the past around which facts are relevant to certain decisions, and which are not. Perhaps, the border of privacy having become so porous, the border of relevancy could be stronger. As Daniel Weitzner explains:

> New privacy laws should emphasize usage restrictions to guard against unfair discrimination based on personal information, even if it's publicly available. For instance, a prospective employer might be able to find a video of a job applicant entering an AIDS clinic or a

mosque. Although the individual might have already made such facts public, new privacy protections would preclude the employer from making a hiring decision based on that information and attach real penalties for such abuse.

In the same vein, it is not intrinsically wrong that voting lists and political contributions are a matter of public record. Arguably, they are essential to the good functioning of the American democracy. Denying someone a promotion because of his or her political inclinations *would be* wrong, at least for most jobs. Perhaps a nuanced classification of the ways in which others are allowed to use information about us would relieve some of our legitimate fears about the effects of the digital explosion.

In *The Transparent Society*, David Brin wrote:

> Transparency is not about eliminating privacy. It's about giving us the power to hold accountable those who would *violate* it. Privacy implies serenity at home and the right to be let alone. It may be irksome how much other people know about me, but I have no right to police their minds. On the other hand I care very deeply about what others *do* to me and to those I love. We all have a right to some place where we can feel safe.

Despite the very best efforts, and the most sophisticated technologies, we cannot control the spread of our private information. And we often want information to be made public to serve our own, or society's purposes.

Yet there can still be principles of accountability for the *misuse* of information. Some ongoing research is outlining a possible new web technology, which would help ensure that information is used appropriately even if it is known. Perhaps automated classification and reasoning tools, developed to help connect the dots in networked information systems, can be retargeted to limit inappropriate use of networked information. A continuing border war is likely to be waged, however, along an existing free speech front: the line separating my right to tell the truth about you from your right not to have that information used against you. In the realm of privacy, the digital explosion has left matters deeply unsettled.

## *Always On*

In *1984,* the pervasive, intrusive technology could be turned off:

> As O'Brien passed the telescreen a thought seemed to strike him. He stopped, turned aside and pressed a switch on the wall. There was a sharp snap. The voice had stopped.
>
> Julia uttered a tiny sound, a sort of squeak of surprise. Even in the midst of his panic, Winston was too much taken aback to be able to hold his tongue.
>
> "You can turn it off!" he said.
>
> "Yes," said O'Brien, "we can turn it off. We have that privilege. ...Yes, everything is turned off. We are alone."

Sometimes we can still turn it off today, and should. But mostly we don't want to. We don't want to be alone; we want to be connected. We find it convenient to leave it on, to leave our footprints and fingerprints everywhere, so we will be recognized when we come back. We don't want to have to keep retyping our name and address when we return to a web site. We like it when the restaurant remembers our name, perhaps because our phone number showed up on caller ID and was linked to our record in their database. We appreciate buying grapes for $1.95/lb instead of $3.49, just by letting the store know that we bought them. We may want to leave it on for ourselves because we know it is on for criminals. Being watched reminds us that they are watched as well. Being watched also means we are being watched over.

And perhaps we don't care that so much is known about us because that is the way human society used to be—kinship groups and small settlements, where knowing everything about everyone else was a matter of survival. Having it on all the time may resonate with inborn preferences we acquired millennia ago, before urban life made anonymity possible. Still today, privacy means something very different in a small rural town than it does on the Upper East Side of Manhattan.

We cannot know what the cost will be of having it on all the time. Just as troubling as the threat of authoritarian measures to restrict personal liberty is the threat of voluntary conformity. As Fano astutely observed, privacy allows limited social experimentation—the deviations from social norms that are much riskier to the individual in the glare of public exposure, but which can be, and often have been in the past, the leading edges of progressive social changes. With it always on, we may prefer not to try anything unconventional, and stagnate socially by collective inaction.

For the most part, it is too late, realistically, ever to turn it off. We may once have had the privilege of turning it off, but we have that privilege no more. We have to solve our privacy problems another way.

The digital explosion is shattering old assumptions about who knows what. Bits move quickly, cheaply, and in multiple perfect copies. Information that used to be public in principle—for example, records in a courthouse, the price you paid for your house, or stories in a small-town newspaper—is now available to everyone in the world. Information that used to be private and available to almost no one—medical records and personal snapshots, for example—can become equally widespread through carelessness or malice. The norms and business practices and laws of society have not caught up to the change.

The oldest durable communication medium is the written document. Paper documents have largely given way to electronic analogs, from which paper copies are produced. But are electronic documents really like paper documents? Yes and no, and misunderstanding the document metaphor can be costly. That is the story to which we now turn.

# CHAPTER 3

# Ghosts in the Machine

## *Secrets and Surprises of Electronic Documents*

## What You See Is Not What the Computer Knows

On March 4, 2005, Italian journalist Giuliana Sgrena was released from captivity in Baghdad, where she had been held hostage for a month. As the car conveying her to safety approached a checkpoint, it was struck with gunfire from American soldiers. The shots wounded Sgrena and her driver and killed an Italian intelligence agent, Nicola Calipari, who had helped engineer her release.

A fierce dispute ensued about why U.S soldiers had rained gunfire on a car carrying citizens of one of its Iraq war allies. The Americans claimed that the car was speeding and did not slow when warned. The Italians denied both claims. The issue caused diplomatic tension between the U.S. and Italy and was a significant political problem for the Italian prime minister.

The U.S. produced a 42-page report on the incident, exonerating the U.S. soldiers. The report enraged Italian officials. The Italians quickly released their own report, which differed from the U.S. report in crucial details.

Because the U.S. report included sensitive military information, it was heavily redacted before being shared outside military circles (see Figure 3.1). In another time, passages would have been blacked out with a felt marker, and the document would have been photocopied and given to reporters. But in the information age, the document was redacted and distributed electronically, not physically. The redacted report was posted on a web site the allies used to provide war information to the media. In an instant, it was visible to any of the world's hundreds of millions of Internet users.

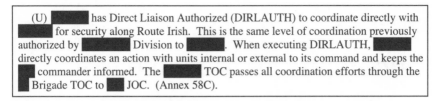

(U) ▆▆▆▆▆ has Direct Liaison Authorized (DIRLAUTH) to coordinate directly with ▆▆▆▆▆ for security along Route Irish. This is the same level of coordination previously authorized by ▆▆▆▆▆ Division to ▆▆▆▆▆. When executing DIRLAUTH, ▆▆▆▆▆ directly coordinates an action with units internal or external to its command and keeps the ▆ commander informed. The ▆▆▆▆▆ TOC passes all coordination efforts through the ▆ Brigade TOC to ▆ JOC. (Annex 58C).

Source: http://www.corriere.it/Media/Documenti/Classified.pdf, extract from page 10.

FIGURE 3.1    Section from page 10 of redacted U.S. report on the death of Italian journalist Nicola Calipari. Information that might have been useful to the enemy was blacked out.

One of those Internet users was an Italian blogger, who scrutinized the U.S. report and quickly recovered the redacted text using ordinary office software. The blogger posted the full text of the report (see Figure 3.2) on his own web site. The unredacted text disclosed positions of troops and equipment, rules of engagement, procedures followed by allied troops, and other information of interest to the enemy. The revelations were both dangerous to U.S. soldiers and acutely embarrassing to the U.S. government, at a moment when tempers were high among Italian and U.S. officials. In the middle of the most high-tech war in history, how could this fiasco have happened?

(U) 1-76 FA has Direct Liaison Authorized (DIRLAUTH) to coordinate directly with 1-69 IN for security along Route Irish. This is the same level of coordination previously authorized by 1st Cavalry Division to 2-82 FA. When executing DIRLAUTH, 1-76 FA directly coordinates an action with units internal or external to its command and keeps the 31D commander informed. The 1-76 FA TOC passes all coordination efforts through the 4th Brigade TOC to 31D JOC. (Annex 58C).

Source: http://www.corriere.it/Media/Documenti/Unclassified.doc.

FIGURE 3.2    The text of Figure 3.1 with the redaction bars electronically removed.

Paper documents and electronic documents are useful in many of the same ways. Both can be inspected, copied, and stored. But they are not equally useful for all purposes. Electronic documents are easier to change, but paper documents are easier to read in the bathtub. In fact, the metaphor of a series of bits as a "document" can be taken only so far. When stretched beyond its breaking point, the "document" metaphor can produce surprising and damaging results—as happened with the Calipari report.

Office workers love "WYSIWYG" interfaces—"What You See Is What You Get." They edit the electronic document on the screen, and when they print it, it looks just the same. They are deceived into thinking that what is in the computer is a sort of miniaturized duplicate of the image on the screen, instead of computer codes that produce the picture on the screen. In fact, the WYSIWYG metaphor is imperfect, and therefore risky. The report on the death of Nicola Calipari illustrates what can go wrong when users accept such a metaphor too literally. What the authors of the document saw was dramatically different from what they got.

The report had been prepared using software that creates PDF files. Such software often includes a "Highlighter Tool," meant to mimic the felt markers that leave a pale mark on ordinary paper, through which the underlying text is visible (see Figure 3.3). The software interface shows the tool's icon as a marker writing a yellow stripe, but the user can change the color of the stripe. Probably someone tried to turn the Highlighter Tool into a redaction tool by changing its color to black, unaware that what was visible on the screen was not the same as the contents of the electronic document.

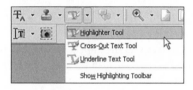

Reprinted with permission from Adobe Systems Incorporated.

FIGURE 3.3   Adobe Acrobat Highlighter Tool, just above the middle. On the screen, the "highlighter" is writing yellow ink, but with a menu command, it can be changed to any other color.

The Italian blogger guessed that the black bars were nothing more than overlays created using the Highlighter Tool, and that the ghostly traces of the invisible words were still part of the electronic document that was posted on the web. With that realization, he easily undid the black "highlighting" to reveal the text beneath.

Just as disturbing as this mistake is the fact that two major newspapers had quite publicly made the same mistake only a few years before. On April 16, 2000, the *New York Times* had detailed a secret CIA history of attempts by the U.S. to overthrow Iran's government in 1953. The newspaper reproduced sections of the CIA report, with black redaction bars to obscure the names of CIA operatives within Iran. The article was posted on the Web in mid-June, 2000, accompanied by PDFs of several pages of the CIA report. John Young, who administers a web site devoted to publishing government-restricted documents, removed the redaction bars and revealed the names of CIA agents. A controversy ensued about the ethics and legality of the disclosure, but the names are still available on the Web as of this writing.

The *Washington Post* made exactly the same mistake in 2002, when it published an article about a demand letter left by the Washington snipers, John Allen Muhammad and John Lee Malvo. As posted on the *Post*'s web site, certain information was redacted in a way that was easily reversed by an inquisitive reader of the online edition of the paper (see Figure 3.4). The paper fixed the problem quickly after its discovery, but not quickly enough to prevent copies from being saved.

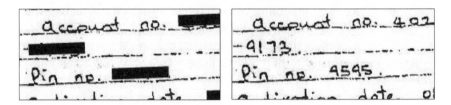

Source: Washington Post web site, transferred to web.bham.ac.uk/forensic/news/02/sniper2.html. Actual images taken from slide 29 of http://www.ccc.de/congress/2004/fahrplan/files/316-hidden-data-slides.pdf.

FIGURE 3.4   Letter from the Washington snipers. On the left, the redacted letter as posted on the *Washington Post* web site. On the right, the letter with the redaction bars electronically removed.

What might have been done in these cases, instead of posting the PDF with the redacted text hidden but discoverable? The Adobe Acrobat software has a security feature, which uses encryption (discussed in Chapter 5, "Secret Bits") to make it impossible for documents to be altered by unauthorized persons, while still enabling anyone to view them. Probably those who created these documents did not know about this feature, or about commercially available software called Redax, which government agencies use to redact text from documents created by Adobe Acrobat.

A clumsier, but effective, option would be to scan the printed page, complete with its redaction bars. The resulting file would record only a series of black and white dots, losing all the underlying typographical structure—font names and margins, for example. Whatever letters had once been "hidden" under the redaction bars could certainly not be recovered, yet this solution has an important disadvantage.

One of the merits of formatted text documents such as PDFs is that they can be "read" by a computer. They can be searched, and the text they contain can be copied. With the document reduced to a mass of black and white dots, it could no longer be manipulated as text.

A more important capability would be lost as well. The report would be unusable by programs that vocalize documents for visually impaired readers. A blind reader could "read" the U.S. report on the Calipari incident, because software is available that "speaks" the contents of PDF documents. A blind reader would find a scanned version of the same document useless.

## Tracking Changes—and Forgetting That They Are Remembered

In October, 2005, UN prosecutor Detlev Mehlis released to the media a report on the assassination of former Lebanese Prime Minister Rafik Hariri. Syria had been suspected of engineering the killing, but Syrian President Bashar al-Assad denied any involvement. The report was not final, Mehlis said, but there was "evidence of both Lebanese and Syrian involvement." Deleted, and yet uncovered by the reporters who were given the document, was an incendiary claim: that Assad's brother Maher, commander of the Republican Guard, was personally involved in the assassination.

Microsoft Word offers a "Track Changes" option. If enabled, every change made to the document is logged as part of the document itself—but ordinarily not shown. The document bears its entire creation history: who made each change, when, and what it was. Those editing the document can also add comments—which would not appear in the final document, but may help editors explain their thinking to their colleagues as the document moves around electronically within an office.

Of course, information about strategic planning is not meant for outsiders to see, and in the case of legal documents, can have catastrophic consequences if revealed. It is a simple matter to remove these notes about the document's history—but someone has to remember to do it! The UN prosecutor neglected to remove the change history from his Microsoft Word document, and a reporter discovered the deleted text (see Figure 3.5). (Of course, in Middle Eastern affairs, one cannot be too suspicious. Some thought that Mehlis had intentionally left the text in the document, as a warning to the Syrians that he knew more than he was yet prepared to acknowledge.)

A particularly negligent example of document editing involved SCO Corporation, which claimed that several corporations violated its intellectual property rights. In early 2004, SCO filed suit in a Michigan court against Daimler Chrysler, claiming Daimler had violated terms of its Unix software agreement with SCO. But the electronic version of its complaint carried its modification history with it, revealing a great deal of information about SCO's litigation planning. In particular, when the change history was revealed, it turned out that until exactly 11:10 a.m. on February 18, 2004, SCO had instead planned to sue a different company, Bank of America, in federal rather than state court, for copyright infringement rather than breach of contract!

> 96.    One witness of Syrian origin but resident in Lebanon, who claims to have worked for the Syrian intelligence services in Lebanon, has stated that approximately two weeks after the adoption of Security Council resolution 1559, senior Lebanese and Syrian officials decided to assassinate Rafik Hariri. He claimed that a senior Lebanese security official went several times to Syria to plan the crime, meeting once at the Meridian Hotel in Damascus and several times at the Presidential Place and the office of a senior Syrian security official. The last meeting was held in the house of the same senior Syrian

> Deleted: Maher Assad, Assef Shawkat, Hassan Khalil, Bahjat Suleyman and Jamil Al-Sayyed
> Deleted: Sayyed
> Deleted: Hotel
> Deleted: Shawkat

Source: Section of UN report, posted on Washington Post web site, www.washingtonpost.com/wp-srv/world/syria/mehlis.report.doc.

FIGURE 3.5    Section from the UN report on the assassination of Rafik Hariri. An earlier draft stated that Maher Assad and others were suspected of involvement in the killing, but in the document as it was released, their names were replaced with the phrase "senior Lebanese and Syrian officials."

## Saved Information About a Document

### FORGING METADATA

Metadata can help prove or refute claims. Suppose Sam emails his teacher a homework paper after the due date, with a plea that the work had been completed by the deadline, but was undeliverable due to a network failure. If Sam is a cheater, he could be exposed if he doesn't realize that the "last modified" date is part of the document. However, if Sam *is* aware of this, he could "stamp" the document with the right time by re-setting the computer's clock before saving the file. The name in which the computer is registered and other metadata are also forgeable, and therefore are of limited use as evidence in court cases.

An electronic document (for example, one produced by text-processing software) often includes information that is *about* the document—so-called *metadata*. The most obvious example is the name of the file itself. File names carry few risks. For example, when we send someone a file as an email attachment, we realize that the recipient is going to see the name of the file as well as its contents.

But the file is often tagged with much more information than just its name. The metadata generally includes the name associated with the owner of the computer, and the dates the file was created and last modified—often useful information, since the recipient can tell whether she is receiving an older or newer version than the version she already has. Some word processors include version information as well, a record of who changed what, when, and why. But the unaware can be trapped even by such innocent information, since it tends not to be visible unless the recipient asks to see it. In Figure 3.6, the metadata reveals the name of the military officer who created the redacted report on the death of Nicola Calipari.

| | |
|---|---|
| File name | sgrena_report.pdf |
| Document Type | PDF Document |
| File size | 251072 bytes |
| Page size | 8.5 x 11.0 inches |
| PDF version | 1.4 |
| Page count | 42 |
| Encryption | None |
| Modification Date | 04/30/05 |
| Title | I |
| Content Creator | Acrobat PDFMaker 6.0 for Word |
| PDF Producer | Acrobat Distiller 6.0 (Windows) |
| Creation Date | 04/30/05 |
| Author | richard.thelin |

Reprinted with permission from Adobe Systems Incorporated.

FIGURE 3.6    Part of the metadata of the Calipari report, as revealed by the "Properties" command of Adobe Acrobat Reader. The data shows that Richard Thelin was the author, and that he altered the file less than two minutes after creating it. Thelin was a Lieutenant Colonel in the U.S. Marine Corps at the time of the incident.

Authorship information leaked in this way can have real consequences. In 2003, the British government of Tony Blair released documentation of its case for joining the U.S. war effort in Iraq. The document had many problems—large parts of it turned out to have been plagiarized from a 13-year-old PhD thesis. Equally embarrassing was that the electronic fingerprints of four civil servants who created it were left on the document when it was released electronically on the No. 10 Downing Street web site. According to the *Evening Standard of London*, "All worked in propaganda units controlled by Alastair Campbell, Tony Blair's director of strategy and communications," although the report had supposedly been the work of the Foreign Office. The case of the "dodgy dossier" caused an uproar in Parliament.

You don't have to be a businessperson or government official to be victimized by documents bearing fingerprints. When you send someone a document as an attachment to an email, very likely the document's metadata shows who actually created it, and when. If you received it from someone else and then altered it, that may show as well. If you put the text of the document into the body of your email instead, the metadata won't be included; the message will be just the text you see on the screen. Be sure of what you are sending before you send it!

### Can the Leaks Be Stopped?

Even in the most professional organizations, and certainly in ordinary households, knowledge about technological dangers and risks does not spread instantaneously to everyone who should know it. The Calipari report was published five years after the *New York Times* had been embarrassed. How can users of modern information technology—today, almost all literate people—stay abreast of knowledge about when and how to protect their information?

It is not easy to prevent the leakage of sensitive information that is hidden in documents but forgotten by their creators, or that is captured as metadata. In principle, offices should have a check-out protocol so that documents are cleansed before release. But in a networked world, where email is a critical utility, how can offices enforce document release protocols without rendering simple tasks cumbersome? A rather harsh measure is to prohibit use of software that retains such information; that was the solution adopted by the British government in the aftermath of the "dodgy dossier" scandal. But the useful features of the software are then lost at the same time. A protocol can be established for converting "rich" document formats such as that of Microsoft Word to formats that retain less information, such as Adobe PDF. But it turns out that measures used to eradicate personally identifiable information from documents don't achieve as thorough a cleansing as is commonly assumed.

At a minimum, office workers need education. Their software has great capabilities they may find useful, but many of those useful features have risks as well. And we all just need to think about what we are doing with our documents. We all too mindlessly re-type keystrokes we have typed a hundred times in the past, not pausing to think that the hundred and first situation may be different in some critical way!

# Representation, Reality, and Illusion

René Magritte, in his famous painting of a pipe, said "This isn't a pipe" (see Figure 3.7). Of course it isn't; it's a painting of a pipe. The image is made out

of paint, and Magritte was making a metaphysical joke. The painting is entitled "The treachery of images," and the statement that the image isn't the
reality is part of the image itself.

Los Angeles County Museum of Art. Purchased with funds provided by the Mr. and Mrs. William
Preston Harrison Collection. Photograph © 2007 Museum Associates/LACMA.

FIGURE **3.7**    Painting by Magritte. The legend says "This isn't a pipe." Indeed, it's
only smudges of paint that make you think of a pipe, just as an electronic document
is only bits representing a document.

When you take a photograph, you capture inside the camera something
from which an image can be produced. In a digital camera, the bits in an electronic memory are altered according to some pattern. The image, we say, is
"represented" in the camera's memory. But if you took out the memory and
looked at it, you couldn't see the image. Even if you printed the pattern of 0s
and 1s stored in the memory, the image wouldn't appear. You'd have to know
*how* the bits represent the image in order to get at the image itself. In the
world of digital photography, the format of the bits has been standardized, so
that photographs taken on a variety of cameras can be displayed on a variety of computers and printed on a variety of printers.

The general process of digital photography is shown in Figure 3.8. Some
external reality—a scene viewed through a camera lens, for example—is
turned into a string of bits. The bits somehow capture useful information

about reality, but there is nothing "natural" about the way reality is captured. The representation is a sort of ghost of the original, not identical to the original and actually quite unlike it, but containing enough of the soul of the original to be useful later on. The representation follows rules. The rules are arbitrary conventions and the product of human invention, but they have been widely accepted so photographs can be exchanged.

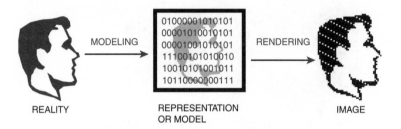

REALITY                    REPRESENTATION                    IMAGE
                           OR MODEL

FIGURE 3.8    Reproducing an image electronically is a two-stage process. First, the scene is translated into bits, creating a digital model. Then the model is rendered as a visible image. The model can be stored indefinitely, communicated from one place to another, or computationally analyzed and enhanced to produce a different model before it is rendered. The same basic structure applies to the reproduction of video and audio.

The representation of the photograph in bits is called a *model* and the process of capturing it is called *modeling*. The model is turned into an image by *rendering* the model; this is what happens when you transfer the bits representing a digital photograph to a computer screen or printer. Rendering brings the ghost back to life. The image resembles, to the human eye, the original reality—provided that the model is good enough. Typically, a model that is not good enough—has too few bits, for example—cannot produce an image that convincingly resembles the reality it was meant to capture.

Modeling always omits information. Magritte's painting doesn't smell like a pipe; it has a different patina than a pipe; and you can't turn it around to see what the other side of the pipe looks like. Whether the omitted information is irrelevant or essential can't be judged without knowing how the model is going to be used. Whoever creates the model and renders it has the power to shape the experience of the viewer.

The process of modeling followed by rendering applies to many situations other than digital photography. For example, the same transformations happen when music is captured on a CD or as an MP3. The rendering process produces audible music from a digital representation, via stereo speakers or a headset. CDs and MP3s use quite distinct modeling methods, with CDs generally capturing music more accurately, using a larger number of bits.

Knowing that digital representations don't resemble the things they represent explains the difference between the terms "analog" and "digital." An analog telephone uses a continuously varying electric signal to represent a continuously varying sound—the voltage of the telephone signal is an "analog" of the sound it resembles—in the same way that Magritte applied paint smoothly to canvas to mimic the shape of the pipe. The shift from analog to digital technologies, in telephones, televisions, cameras, X-ray machines, and many other devices, at first seems to lose the immediacy and simplicity of the old devices. But the enormous processing power of modern computers makes the digital representation far more flexible and useful.

Indeed, the same general processes are at work in situations where *there is no "reality" because the images are of things that have never existed.* Examples are video games, animated films, and virtual walk-throughs of unbuilt architecture. In these cases, the first step of Figure 3.8 is truncated. The "model" is created not by capturing reality in an approximate way, but by pure synthesis: as the strokes of an artist's electronic pen, or the output of computer-aided design software.

The severing of the immediate connection between representation and reality in the digital world has created opportunities, dangers, and puzzles. One of the earliest triumphs of "digital signal processing," the science of doing computations on the digital representations of reality, was to remove the scratches and noise from old recordings of the great singer Enrico Caruso. No amount of analog electronics could have cleaned up the old records and restored the clarity to Caruso's voice.

> ### CAN WE BE SURE A PHOTO IS UNRETOUCHED?
>
> Cryptographic methods (discussed in Chapter 5) can establish that a digital photograph has not been altered. A special camera gets a digital key from the "image verification system," attaches a "digital signature" (see Chapter 5) to the image and uploads the image and the signature to the verification system. The system processes the received image with the same key and verifies that the same signature results. The system is secure because it is impossible, with any reasonable amount of computation, to produce another image that would yield the same signature with this key.

And yet the growth of digital "editing" has its dark side as well. Photo-editing software such as Photoshop can be used to alter photographic evidence presented to courts of law.

The movie *Toy Story* and its descendants are unlikely to put human actors out of work in the near future, but how should society think about synthetic child pornography? "Kiddie porn" is absolutely illegal, unlike other forms of pornography, because of the harm done to the children who are abused to produce it. But what about pornographic images of children who do not exist and never have—who are simply the creation of a skilled graphic synthesizer? Congress outlawed such virtual kiddie porn in 1996, in a law that prohibited any image that "is, or appears to be, of a minor engaging in sexually explicit conduct." The Supreme Court overturned the law on First Amendment grounds. Prohibiting images that "appear to" depict children is going too far, the court ruled—such synthetic pictures, no matter how abhorrent, are constitutionally protected free speech.

---

*In the world of exploded assumptions about reality and artifice, laws that combat society's problems may also compromise rights of free expression.*

In this instance at least, reality matters, not what images appear to show. Chapter 7, "You Can't Say That on the Internet," discusses other cases in which society is struggling to control social evils that are facilitated by information technology. In the world of exploded assumptions about reality and artifice, laws that combat society's problems may also compromise rights of free expression.

## What Is the Right Representation?

### DIGITAL CAMERAS AND MEGAPIXELS

Megapixels—millions of pixels—are a standard figure of merit for digital cameras. If a camera captures too few pixels, it can't take good photographs. But no one should think that more pixels invariably yield a better image. If a digital camera has a low-quality lens, more pixels will simply produce a more precise representation of a blurry picture!

Figure 3.9 is a page from the Book of Kells, one of the masterpieces of medieval manuscript illumination, produced around A.D. 800 in an Irish monastery. The page contains a few words of Latin, portrayed in an astoundingly complex interwoven lacework of human and animal figures, whorls, and crosshatching. The book is hundreds of pages long, and in the entire work no two of the letters or decorative ornaments are drawn the same way. The elaborately ornate graphic shows just 21 letters (see Figure 3.10).

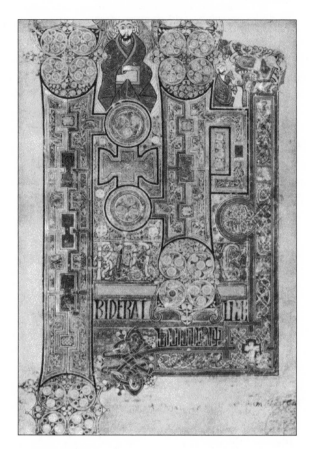

FIGURE 3.9   Opening page of the Gospel of St. John from the Book of Kells.

```
IN PRINCIPIO ERAT VERBUM
```

FIGURE 3.10   The words of the beginning of the gospel of St. John. In the book of Kells, the easiest word to spot is ERAT, just to the left of center about a quarter of the way up the page.

Do these two illustrations contain the same information? The answer depends on what information is meant to be recorded. If the only important thing were the Latin prose, then either representation might be equally good, though Figure 3.10 is easier to read. But the words themselves are far from the only important thing in the Book of Kells. It is one of the great works of Western art and craftsmanship.

A graphic image such as Figure 3.9 is represented as a rectangular grid of many rows and columns, by recording the color at each position in the grid (see Figure 3.11). To produce such a representation, the page itself is scanned, one narrow row after the next, and each row is divided horizontally into tiny square "picture elements" or *pixels*. An image representation based on a division into pixels is called a *raster* or *bitmap representation*. The representation corresponds to the structure of a computer screen (or a digital TV screen), which is also divided into a grid of individual pixels—how many pixels, and how small they are, affect the quality and price of the display.

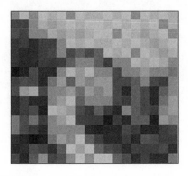

Copyright © Trinity College, Dublin.

FIGURE 3.11    A detail enlarged from the upper-right corner of the opening page of John from the Book of Kells.

What would be the computer representation of the mere Latin text, Figure 3.10? The standard code for the Roman alphabet, called ASCII for the American Standard Code for Information Interchange, assigns a different 8-bit code to each letter or symbol. ASCII uses one byte (8 bits) per character. For example, A = 01000001, a = 01100001, $ = 00100100, and 7 = 00110111. The equation 7 = 00110111 means that the bit pattern used to represent the symbol "7" in a string of text is 00110111. The space character has its own code, 00100000. Figure 3.12 shows the ASCII representation of the characters "IN PRINCIPIO ERAT VERBUM," a string of 24 bytes or 192 bits. We've separated the long string of bits into bytes to improve readability ever so slightly! But inside the computer, it would just be one bit after the next.

```
01001001 01001110 00100000 01010000
01010010 01001001 01001110 01000011
01001001 01010000 01001001 01001111
00100000 01000101 01010010 01000001
01010100 00100000 01010110 01000101
01010010 01000010 01010101 01001101
```

FIGURE 3.12   ASCII bit string for the characters of "IN PRINCIPIO ERAT VERBUM."

So 01001001 represents the letter I. But not always! Bit strings are used to represent many things other than characters. For example, the same bit string 01001001, if interpreted as the representation of a whole number in binary notation, represents 73. A computer cannot simply look at a bit string 01001001 and know whether it is supposed to represent the letter I or the number 73 or data of some other type, a color perhaps. A computer can interpret a bit string only if it knows the conventions that were used to create the document—the intended interpretation of the bits that make up the file.

The meaning of a bit string is a matter of convention. Such conventions are arbitrary at first. The code for the letter I could have been 11000101 or pretty much anything else. Once conventions have become accepted through a social process of agreement and economic incentive, they became nearly as inflexible as if they were physical laws. Today, millions of computers assume

---

**FILENAME EXTENSIONS**

The three letters after the dot at the end of a filename indicate how the contents are to be interpreted. Some examples are as follows:

| Extension | File Type |
| --- | --- |
| .doc | Microsoft Word document |
| .odt | OpenDocument text document |
| .ppt | Microsoft PowerPoint document |
| .ods | OpenDocument Spreadsheet |
| .pdf | Adobe Portable Document Format |
| .exe | Executable program |
| .gif | Graphics Interchange Format (uses 256-color palette) |
| .jpg | JPEG graphic file (Joint Photographic Experts Group) |
| .mpg | MPEG movie file (Moving Picture Experts Group) |

that 01001001, if interpreted as a character, represents the letter I, and the universal acceptance of such conventions is what makes worldwide information flows possible.

The document format is the key to turning the representation into a viewable document. If a program misinterprets a document as being in a different format from the one in which it was created, only nonsense will be rendered. Computers not equipped with software matching the program that created a document generally refuse to open it.

Which representation is "better," a raster image or ASCII? The answer depends on the use to which the document is to be put. For representation of freeform shapes in a great variety of shades and hues, a raster representation is unbeatable, provided the pixels are small enough and there are enough of them. But it is hard even for a trained human to find the individual letters within Figure 3.9, and it would be virtually impossible for a computer program. On the other hand, a document format based on ASCII codes for characters, such as the PDF format, can easily be searched for text strings.

The PDF format includes more than simply the ASCII codes for the text. PDF files include information about typefaces, the colors of the text and of the background, and the size and exact positions of the letters. Software that produces PDFs is used to typeset elegant documents such as this one. In other words, PDF is actually a *page description language* and describes visible features that are typographically meaningful. But for complicated pictures, a graphical format such as JPG must be used. A mixed document, such as these pages, includes graphics within PDF files.

## Reducing Data, Sometimes Without Losing Information

Let's take another look at the page from the Book of Kells, Figure 3.9, and the enlargement of a small detail of that image, Figure 3.11. The computer file from which Figure 3.9 was printed is 463 pixels wide and 651 pixels tall, for a total of about 300,000 individual pixels. The pages of the Book of Kells measure about 10 by 13 inches, so the raster image has only about 50 pixels per inch of the original work. That is too few to capture the rich detail of the original—Figure 3.11 actually shows one of the animal heads in the top-right corner of the page. A great deal of detail was lost when the original page was scanned and turned into pixels. The technical term for the problem is *undersampling*. The scanning device "samples" the color value of the original document at discrete points to create the representation of the document, and in this case, the samples are too far apart to preserve detail that is visible to the naked eye in the original.

The answer to undersampling is to increase the resolution of the scan—the number of samples per inch. Figure 3.13 shows how the quality of an image improves with the resolution. In each image, each pixel is colored with the "average" color of part of the original.

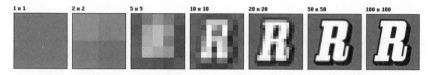

Credit as in Wikipedia, en.wikipedia.org/wiki/Image:Resolution_illustration.png.

FIGURE 3.13   A shape shown at various resolutions, from $1 \times 1$ to $100 \times 100$ pixels. A square block consisting of many pixels of a single shade can be represented much more compactly than by repeating the code for that shade as many times as there are pixels.

But, of course, a price is paid for increased resolution. The more pixels in the representation of an image, the more memory is needed to hold the representation. Double the resolution, and the memory needed goes up by a factor of four, since the resolution doubles both vertically and horizontally.

Standard software uses a variety of representational techniques to represent raster graphics more concisely. Compression techniques are of two kinds: "lossless" and "lossy." A *lossless* representation is one that allows exactly the same image to be rendered. A *lossy* representation allows an approximation to the same image to be rendered—an image that is different from the original in ways the human eye may or may not be able to discern.

One method used for lossless image compression takes advantage of the fact that in most images, the color doesn't change from pixel to pixel—the image has *spatial coherence*, to use the official term. Looking at the middle and rightmost images in Figure 3.13, for example, makes clear that in the $100 \times 100$ resolution image, the 100 pixels in a

### AUDIO COMPRESSION

MP3 is a lossy compression method for audio. It uses a variety of tricks to create small data files. For example, human ears are not far enough apart to hear low-frequency sounds stereophonically, so MP3s may record low frequencies in mono and play the same sound to both speakers, while recording and playing the higher frequencies in stereo! MP3s are "good enough" for many purposes, but a trained and sensitive ear can detect the loss of sound quality.

10 × 10 square in the top-left corner are all the same color; there is no need to repeat a 24-bit color value 100 times in the representation of the image.

Accordingly, graphic representations have ways of saying "all pixels in this block have the same color value." Doing so can reduce the number of bits significantly.

Depending on how an image will be used, a lossy compression method might be acceptable. What flashes on your TV is gone before you have time to scrutinize the individual pixels. But in some cases, only lossless compression is satisfactory. If you have the famous Zapruder film of the Kennedy assassination and want to preserve it in a digital archive, you want to use a lossless compression method once you have digitized it at a suitably fine resolution. But if you are just shipping off the image to a low-quality printer such as those used to print newspapers, lossy compression might be fine.

## Technological Birth and Death

The digital revolution was possible because the capacity of memory chips increased, relentlessly following Moore's Law. Eventually, it became possible to store digitized images and sounds at such high resolution that their quality was higher than analog representations. Moreover, the price became low enough that the storage chips could be included in consumer goods. But more than electrical engineering is involved. At more than a megabyte per image, digital cameras and HD televisions would still be exotic rarities. A *megabyte* is about a million bytes, and that is just too much data per image. The revolution also required better algorithms—better computational methods, not just better hardware—and fast, cheap processing chips to carry out those algorithms.

For example, digital video compression utilizes *temporal coherence* as well as spatial coherence. Any portion of the image is unlikely to change much in color from frame to frame, so large parts of a picture typically do not have to be retransmitted to the home when the frame changes after a thirtieth of a second. At least, that is true in principle. If a woman in a TV image walks across a fixed landscape, only her image, and a bit of landscape that newly appears from behind her once she passes it, needs be transmitted—*if* it is computationally feasible to compare the second frame to the first before it is transmitted and determine exactly where it differs from its predecessor. To keep up with the video speed, there is only a thirtieth of a second to do that computation. And a complementary computation has to be carried out at the other end—the previously transmitted frame must be modified to reflect the newly transmitted information about what part of it should change one frame time later.

Digital movies could not have happened without an extraordinary increase in speed and drop in price in computing power. Decompression algorithms are built into desktop photo printers and cable TV boxes, cast in silicon in chips more powerful than the fastest computers of only a few years ago. Such compact representations can be sent quickly through cables and as satellite signals. The computing power in the cable boxes and television sets is today powerful enough to reconstruct the image from the representation of what has changed. Processing is power.

By contrast, part of the reason the compact disk is dying as a medium for distributing music is that it doesn't hold enough data. At the time the CD format was adopted as a standard, decompression circuitry for CD players would have been too costly for use in homes and automobiles, so music could not be recorded in compressed form. The magic of Apple's iPod is not just the huge capacity and tiny physical size of its disk—it is the power of the processing chip that renders the stored model as music.

The birth of new technologies presage the death of old technologies. Digital cameras killed the silver halide film industry; analog television sets will soon be gone; phonograph records gave way to cassette tapes, which in turn gave way to compact disks, which are themselves now dying in favor of digital music players with their highly compressed data formats.

The periods of transition between technologies, when one emerges and threatens another that is already in wide use, are often marked by the exercise of power, not always progressively. Businesses that dominate old technologies are sometimes innovators, but often their past successes make them slow to change. At their worst, they may throw up roadblocks to progress in an attempt to hold their ground in the marketplace. Those roadblocks may include efforts to scare the public about potential disruptions to familiar practices, or about the dollar costs of progress.

Data formats, the mere conventions used to intercommunicate information, can be remarkably contentious, when a change threatens the business of an incumbent party, as the Commonwealth of Massachusetts learned when it tried to change its document formats. The tale of Massachusetts and OpenDocument illustrates how hard change can be in the digital world, although it sometimes seems to change on an almost daily basis.

## Data Formats as Public Property

No one owns the Internet, and everyone owns the Internet. No government controls the whole system, and in the U.S., the federal government controls only the computers of government agencies. If you download a web page to your home computer, it will reach you through the cooperation of several, perhaps dozens, of private companies between the web server and you.

**UPLOADING AND DOWNLOADING**

Historically, we thought of the Internet as consisting of powerful corporate "server" machines located "above" our little home computers. So when we retrieved material from a server, we were said to be "downloading," and when we transferred material from our machine to a server, we were "uploading." Many personal machines are now so powerful that the "up" and "down" metaphors are no longer descriptive, but the language is still with us. See the Appendix, and also the explanation of "peer-to-peer" in Chapter 6, "Balance Toppled."

This flexible and constantly changing configuration of computers and communication links developed because the Internet is in its essence not hardware, but protocols—the conventions that computers use for sending bits to each other (see the Appendix). The most basic Internet Protocol is known as IP. The Internet was a success because IP and the designs for the other protocols became public standards, available for anyone to use. Anyone could build on top of IP. Any proposed higher-level protocol could be adopted as a public standard if it met the approval of the networking community. The most important protocol exploiting IP is known as TCP. TCP is used by email and web software to ship messages reliably between computers, and the pair of protocols is known as TCP/IP. The Internet might not have developed that way had proprietary networking protocols taken hold in the early days of networking.

It was not always thus. Twenty to thirty years ago, all the major computer companies—IBM, DEC, Novell, and Apple—had their own networking protocols. The machines of different companies did not intercommunicate easily, and each company hoped that the rest of the world would adopt its protocols as standards. TCP/IP emerged as a standard because agencies of the U.S. government insisted on its use in research that it sponsored—the Defense Department for the ARPANET, and the National Science Foundation for NSFnet. TCP/IP was embedded in the Berkeley Unix operating system, which was developed under federal grants and came to be widely used in universities. Small companies quickly moved to use TCP/IP for their new products. The big companies moved to adopt it more slowly. The Internet, with all of its profusion of services and manufacturers, could not have come into existence had one of the incumbent manufacturers won the argument—and they failed even though their networking products were technologically superior to the early TCP/IP implementations.

File formats stand at a similar fork in the road today. There is increasing concern about the risks of commercial products evolving into standards. Society will be better served, goes the argument, if documents are stored in formats hammered out by standards organizations, rather than disseminated as part of commercial software packages. But consensus around one *de facto* commercial standard, the .doc format of Microsoft Word, is already well advanced.

Word's .doc format is proprietary, developed by Microsoft and owned by Microsoft. Its details are now public, but Microsoft can change them at any time, without consultation. Indeed, it does so regularly, in order to enhance the capabilities of its software—and new releases create incompatibilities with legacy documents. Some documents created with Word 2007 can't be opened in Word 2003 without a software add-on, so even all-Microsoft offices risk document incompatibilities if they don't adjust to Microsoft's format changes. Microsoft does not exclude competitors from adopting its format as their own document standard—but competitors would run great risks in building on a format they do not control.

In a large organization, the cost of licensing Microsoft Office products for thousands of machines can run into the millions of dollars. In an effort to create competition and to save money, in 2004 the European Union advanced the use of an "OpenDocument Format" for exchange of documents among EU businesses and governments. Using ODF, multiple companies could enter the market, all able to read documents produced using each other's software.

In September, 2005, the Commonwealth of Massachusetts decided to follow the EU initiative. Massachusetts announced that effective 15 months later, all the state's documents would have to be stored in OpenDocument Format. About 50,000 state-owned computers would be affected. State officials estimated the cost savings at about $45 million. But Eric Kriss, the state's secretary of administration and finance, said that more than software cost was at stake. Public documents were public property; access should never require the cooperation of a single private corporation. Peter Quinn, the state's Chief Information Officer, added, "The world is about open standards...I can't understand why anybody would want to continue making closed-format documents anymore."

Microsoft did not accept the state's decision without an argument. The company rallied advocates for the disabled to its side, claiming that no available OpenDocument software had the accessibility features Microsoft offered. Microsoft, which already had state contracts that extended beyond the switchover date, also argued that adopting the ODF standard would be unfair to Microsoft and costly to Massachusetts. "Were this proposal to be adopted, the significant costs incurred by the Commonwealth, its citizens, and the private sector would be matched only by the levels of confusion and incompatibility that would result...." Kriss replied, "The question is whether a sover-

## OPENDOCUMENT, OPEN SOURCE, FREE

These three distinct concepts all aim, at least in part, to slow the development of software monopolies. OpenDocument (opendocu ment.xml.org) is an open standard for file formats. Several major computer corporations have backed the effort, and have promised not to raise intellectual property issues that would inhibit the development of software meeting the standards. Open source (opensource.org) is a software development methodology emphasizing shared effort and peer review to improve quality. The site openoffice.org provides a full suite of open source office productivity tools, available without charge. Free software—"Free as in freedom, not free beer" (www.fsf.org, www.gnu.org)—"is a matter of the users' freedom to run, copy, distribute, study, change, and improve the software."

eign state has the obligation to ensure that its public documents remain forever free and unencumbered by patent, license, or other technical impediments. We say, yes, this is an imperative. Microsoft says they disagree and want the world to use their proprietary formats." The rhetoric quieted down, but the pressure increased. The stakes were high for Microsoft, since where Massachusetts went, other states might follow.

Three months later, neither Kriss nor Quinn was working for the state. The *Boston Globe* published an investigation of Quinn's travel expenses, but the state found him blameless. Tired of the mudslinging, under attack for his decision about open standards, and lacking Kriss's support, on December 24, Quinn announced his resignation. Quinn suspected "Microsoft money and its lobbyist machine" of being behind the *Globe* investigation and the legislature's resistance to his open standard initiative.

The deadline for Massachusetts to move to OpenDocuments has passed, and as of the fall of 2007, the state's web site still says the switchover will occur in the future. In the intervening months, the state explains, it became possible for Microsoft software to read and write OpenDocument formats, so the shift to OpenDocument would not eliminate Microsoft from the office software competition. Nonetheless, other software companies would not be allowed to compete for the state's office software business until "accessibility characteristics of the applications meet or exceed those of the currently deployed office suite"—i.e., Microsoft's. For the time being, Microsoft has the upper hand, despite the state's effort to wrest from private hands the formats of its public documents.

Which bits mean what in a document format is a multi-billion dollar business. As in any big business decisions, money and politics count, reason becomes entangled with rhetoric, and the public is only one of the stakeholders with an interest in the outcome.

# Hiding Information in Images

The surprises in text documents are mostly things of which the authors were ignorant or unaware. Image documents provide unlimited opportunities for hiding things intentionally—hiding secrets from casual human observers, and obscuring open messages destined for human recipients so anti-spam software won't filter them out.

## The Spam Wars

Many of us are used to receiving email pleas such as this one: *I am Miss Faatin Rahman the only child/daughter of late mrs helen rahman Address: Rue 142 Marcory Abidjan Cote d'ivoire west africa, I am 20 years old girl. I lost my parent, and I have an inheritance from my late mother, My parents were very wealthy farmers and cocoa merchant when they were alive, After the death of my father, long ago, my mother was controling his business untill she was poisoned by her business associates which she suffered and died, ... I am crying and seeking for your kind assistance in the following ways: To provide a safe bank account into where the money will be transferred for investment....*

If you get such a request, don't respond to it! Money will flow out of, not into, your bank account. Most people know not to comply. But mass emails are so cheap that getting one person out of a million to respond is enough to make the spammer financially successful.

"Spam filters" are programs that intercept email on its way into the in-box and delete messages like these before we read them. This kind of spam follows such a standard style that it is easy to spot automatically, with minimal risk that any real correspondence with banks or African friends will be filtered out by mistake.

But the spam artists have fought back. Many of us have received emails like the one in Figure 3.14. Why can't the spam filter catch things like this?

Word-processing software includes the name and size of the font in conjunction with the coded characters themselves, as well as other information, such as the color of the letters and the color of the background. Because the underlying text is represented as ASCII codes, however, it remains relatively easy to locate individual letters or substrings, to add or delete text, and to perform other such common text-processing operations. When a user positions a cursor over the letter on the screen, the program can figure out the location within the file of the character over which the cursor is positioned. Computer software can, in turn, render the character codes as images of characters.

WBRS WILL BLOW UP ON WEDNESDAY, AUGUST 30!

**Company: WILD BRUSH ENERGY (Other OTC:WBRS.PK)**
**Symbol: WBRS**
**Price: $0.051**
**1-day Target: $0.2**

## WILD BRUSH MAKES A MOVE!
Wild Brush Acquires Additional Powder River Oil & Gas Lease. Read More Online NOW!

## Who is Wild Brush?
*Wild Brush Energy is a diversified energy company whose primary goal is to identify and develop Oil &*
*Coalbed Methane sites within the State of Wyoming. In addition, Wild Brush Energy continues to evaluate*
*clean air alternative energy producing technologies such as Wind Power. Wild Brush trades in the U.S. under*
*the symbol "WBRS."*

*THE HURRICANE SEASON HAS BEGUN! AS HURRICANES THREATEN OIL*
*REFINERIES!*
*THE PRICE PER BARREL IS SOARING! GET IN NOW ON WBRS BEFORE*
*IT'S TOO LATE!*
*WATCH WBRS TRADE ON WEDNESDAY, AUGUST 30!*

FIGURE 3.14    Graphic spam received by one of the authors. Although it looks like text, the computer "sees" it as just an image, like a photograph. Because it doesn't realize that the pixels are forming letters, its spam filters cannot identify it as spam.

But just because a computer screen shows a recognizable letter of the alphabet, this does not mean that the underlying representation is by means of standard character codes. A digitized photograph of text may well look identical to an image rendered from a word-processing document—that is, the two utterly different representations may give rise to exactly the same image.

And that is one reason why, in the battle between spam producers and makers of spam filters, the spam producers currently have the upper hand. The spam of Figure 3.14 was produced in graphical form, even though what is represented is just text. As the underlying representation is pixels and not ASCII, spam like this makes it through all the filters we know about!

The problem of converting raster graphics to ASCII text is called *character recognition*. The term *optical character recognition*, or OCR, is used when the original document is a printed piece of paper. The raster graphic representation is the result of scanning the document, and then some character recognition algorithm is used to convert the image into a sequence of character codes. If the original document is printed in a standard typeface and is relatively free of smudges and smears, contemporary OCR software is quite accurate, and is now incorporated into commercially available scanners commonly packaged as multipurpose devices that also print, photocopy, and fax. Because OCR algorithms are now reasonably effective and widely available, the next generation of spam filters will likely classify emails such as Figure 3.14 as spam.

OCR and spam are merely an illustration of a larger point. Representation determines what can be done with data. In principle, many representations may be equivalent. But in practice, the secrecy of formatting information and the computation required to convert one format to another may limit the usefulness of the data itself.

## Hiding Information in Plain Sight

During World War I, the German Embassy in Washington, DC sent a message to Berlin that began thus: "PRESIDENT'S EMBARGO RULING SHOULD HAVE IMMEDIATE NOTICE." U.S. intelligence was reading all the German telegrams, and this one might have seemed innocuous enough. But the first letters of the words spelled out "PERSHING," the name of a U.S. Navy vessel. The entire telegram had nothing to do with embargoes. It was about U.S. ship movements, and the initial letters read in full, "PERSHING SAILS FROM N.Y. JUNE 1."

*Steganography* is the art of sending secret messages in imperceptible ways. Steganography is different from *cryptography*, which is the art of sending messages that are indecipherable. In a cryptographic communication, it is assumed that if Alice sends a message to Bob, an adversary may well intercept the message and recognize that it holds a secret. The objective is to make the message unreadable, except to Bob, if it falls into the hands of such an eavesdropper or enemy. In the world of electronic communication, sending an encrypted message is likely to arouse suspicion of electronic monitoring software. By contrast, in a steganographic message from Alice to Bob, the communication itself arouses no suspicion. It may even be posted on a web site and seem entirely innocent. Yet hidden in plain sight, in a way known only to Alice and Bob, is a coded message.

Steganography has been in use for a long time. The *Steganographia* of Johannes Trithemius (1462–1516) is an occult text that includes long conjurations of spirits. The first letters of the words of these mystic incantations encode other hidden messages, and the book was influential for a century after it was written. Computers have created enormous opportunities for steganographic communications. As a very simple example, consider an ordinary word-processing document—a simple love letter, for example. Print it out or view it on the screen, and it seems to be about Alice's sweet nothings to Bob, and nothing more. But perhaps Alice included a paragraph at the end *in which she changed the font color to white.* The software renders the white text on the white background, which looks exactly like the white background.

But Bob, if he knows what to look for, can make it visible—for example, by printing on black paper (just as the text could be recovered from the electronically redacted Calipari report).

If an adversary has any reason to think a trick like this might be in use, the adversary can inspect Alice's electronic letter using software that looks for messages hidden using just this technique. But there are many places to look for steganographic messages, and many ways to hide the information.

Since each Roman letter has an eight-bit ASCII code, a text can be hidden within another as long as there is an agreed-upon method for encoding 0s and 1s. For example, what letter is hidden in this sentence?

Steganographic algorithms hide messages inside photos, text, and other data.

The answer is "I," the letter whose ASCII character code is 01001001. In the first eight words of the sentence, words beginning with consonants encode 0 bits and words beginning with vowels encode 1s (see Figure 3.15).

```
Steganographic algorithms hide messages inside photos,  text,  and other data.
0               1          0    0        1      0        0     1
```

FIGURE 3.15   A steganographic encoding of text within text. Initial consonants encode 0, vowels encode 1, and the first eight words encode the 8-bit ASCII code for the letter "I."

A steganographic method that would seem to be all but undetectable involves varying ever so slightly the color values of individual pixels within a photograph. Red, green, and blue components of a color determine the color itself. A color is represented internally as one byte each for red, green, and blue. Each 8-bit string represents a numerical value between 0 and 255. Changing the rightmost bit from a 1 to a 0 (for example, changing 00110011 to 00110010), changes the numerical value by subtracting one—in this case, changing the color value from 51 to 50. That results in a change in color so insignificant that it would not be noticed, certainly not as a change in a single pixel. But the rightmost bits of the color values of pixels in the graphics files representing photographs can then carry quite large amounts of information, without raising any suspicions. The recipient decodes the message not by rendering the bits as visible images, but by inspecting the bits themselves, and picking out the significant 0s and 1s.

Who uses steganography today, if anyone? It is very hard to know. *USA Today* reported that terrorists were communicating using steganography in early 2001. A number of software tools are freely available that make steganography easy. Steganographic detectors—what are properly known as steganalysis tools—have also been developed, but their usefulness as yet seems to be limited. Both steganography and steganalysis software is freely available on the World Wide Web (see, for example, www.cotse.com/tools/stega.htm and www.outguess.org/detection.php).

The use of steganography to transmit secret messages is today easy, cheap, and all but undetectable. A foreign agent who wanted to communicate with parties abroad might well encode a bit string in the tonal values of an MP3 or the color values of pixels in a pornographic image on a web page. So much music and pornography flows between the U.S. and foreign countries that the uploads and downloads would arouse no suspicion!

## The Scary Secrets of Old Disks

By now, you may be tempted to delete all the files on your disk drive and throw it away, rather than run the risk that the files contain unknown secrets. That isn't the solution: Even deleted files hold secrets!

A few years ago, two MIT researchers bought 158 used disk drives, mostly from eBay, and recovered what data they could. Most of those who put the disks up for sale had made some effort to scrub the data. They had dragged files into the desktop trash can. Some had gone so far as to use the Microsoft Windows FORMAT command, which warns that it will destroy all data on the disk.

Yet only 12 of the 158 disk drives had truly been sanitized. Using several methods well within the technical capabilities of today's teenagers, the researchers were able to recover user data from most of the others. From 42 of the disks, they retrieved what appeared to be credit card numbers. One of the drives seemed to have come from an Illinois automatic teller machine and contained 2,868 bank account numbers and account balances. Such data from single business computers would be a treasure trove for criminals. But most of the drives from home computers also contained information that the owners would consider extremely sensitive: love letters, pornography, complaints about a child's cancer therapy, and grievances about pay disputes, for example. Many of the disks contained enough data to identify the primary user of the computer, so that the sensitive information could be tied back to an individual whom the researchers could contact.

## CLOUD COMPUTING

One way to avoid having problems with deleted disk files and expensive document-processing software is not to keep your files on your disks in the first place! In "cloud computing," the documents stay on the disks of a central service provider and are accessed through a web browser. "Google Docs" is one such service, which boasts very low software costs, but other major software companies are rumored to be exploring the market for cloud computing. If Google holds your documents, they are accessible from anywhere the Internet reaches, and you never have to worry about losing them—Google's backup procedures are better than yours could ever be. But there are potential disadvantages. Google's lawyers would decide whether to resist subpoenas. Federal investigators could inspect bits passing through the U.S., even on a trip between other countries.

The users of the computers had for the most part done what they thought they were supposed to do—they deleted their files or formatted their disks. They probably knew not to release toxic chemicals by dumping their old machines in a landfilll, but they did not realize that by dumping them on eBay, they might be releasing personal information into the digital environment. Anyone in the world could have bought the old disks for a few dollars, and all the data they contained. What is going on here, and is there anything to do about it?

Disks are divided into blocks, which are like the pages of a book—each has an identifying address, like a page number, and is able to hold a few hundred bytes of data, about the same amount as a page of text in a book. If a document is larger than one disk block, however, the document is typically not stored in consecutive disk blocks. Instead, each block includes a piece of the document, and the address of the block where the document is continued. So the entire document may be physically scattered about the disk, although logically it is held together as a chain of references of one block to another. Logically, the structure is that of a magazine, where articles do not necessarily occupy contiguous pages. Part of an article may end with "Continued on page 152," and the part of the article on page 152 may indicate the page on which it is continued from there, and so on.

Because the files on a disk begin at random places on disk, an *index* records which files begin where on the disk. The index is itself another disk file, but one whose location on the disk can be found quickly. A disk index is very much like the index of a book—which always appears at the end, so readers know where to look for it. Having found the index, they can quickly find the page number of any item listed in the index and flip to that page.

Why aren't disks themselves organized like books, with documents laid out on consecutive blocks? Because disks are different from books in two important respects. First, they are dynamic. The information on disks is constantly being altered, augmented, and removed. A disk is less like a book than like a three-ring binder, to which pages are regularly added and removed as information is gathered and discarded. Second, disks are perfectly re-writable. A disk block may contain one string of 0s and 1s at one moment, and as a result of a single writing operation, a different string of 0s and 1s a moment later. Once a 0 or a 1 has been written in a particular position on the disk, there is no way to tell whether the bit previously in that position was a 0 or a 1. There is nothing analogous to the faint traces of pencil marks on paper that are left after an erasure. In fact, there is no notion of "erasure" at all on a disk—all that ever happens is replacement of some bits by others.

Because disks are dynamic, there are many advantages to breaking the file into chained, noncontiguous blocks indexed in this way. For example, if the file contains a long text document and a user adds a few words to the middle of the text, only one or two blocks in the middle of the chain are affected. If enough text is added that those blocks must be replaced by five new ones, the new blocks can be logically threaded into the chain without altering any of the other blocks comprising the document. Similarly, if a section of text is deleted, the chain can be altered to "jump over" the blocks containing the deleted text.

Blocks that are no longer part of any file are added to a "pool" of available disk blocks. The computer's software keeps track of all the blocks in the pool. A block can wind up in the pool either because it has never been used or because it has been used but abandoned. A block may be abandoned because the entire file of which it was part has been deleted or because the file has been altered to exclude the block. When a fresh disk block is needed for any purpose—for example, to start a new file or to add to an existing file— a block is drawn from the pool of available blocks.

## What Happens to the Data in Deleted Files?

*Disk blocks are not re-written when they are abandoned and added to the pool.* When the block is withdrawn from the pool and put back to work as part of another file, it is overwritten and the old data is obliterated. But until then, the block retains its old pattern of zeroes and ones. The entire disk file may be intact—except that there is no easy way to find it. A look in the index will reveal nothing. But "deleting" a file in this way merely removes the index entry. The information is still there on the disk somewhere. It has no more been eradicated than the information in a book would be expunged by tearing out the index from the back of the volume. To find something in a book without an index, you just have to go through the book one page at a time looking for it—tedious and time-consuming, but not impossible.

And that is essentially what the MIT researchers did with the disks they bought off eBay—they went through the blocks, one at a time, looking for recognizable bit patterns. A sequence of sixteen ASCII character codes representing decimal digits, for example, looks suspiciously like a credit card number. Even if they were unable to recover an entire file, because some of the blocks comprising it had already been recycled, they could recognize significant short character strings such as account numbers.

Of course, there would be a simple way to prevent sensitive information from being preserved in fragments of "deleted" files. The computer could be programmed so that, instead of simply putting abandoned blocks into the pool, it actually over-wrote the blocks, perhaps by "zeroing" them—that is, writing a pattern of all 0s. Historically, computer and software manufacturers have thought the benefits of zeroing blocks far less than the costs. Society has not found "data leakage" to be a critical problem until recently—although that may be changing. And the costs of constantly zeroing disk blocks would be significant. Filling blocks with zeroes might take so much time that the users would complain about how slowly their machines were running

### THE LAW ADJUSTS

Awareness is increasing that deleted data can be recovered from disks. The Federal Trade Commission now requires "the destruction or erasure of electronic media containing consumer information so that the information cannot practicably be read or reconstructed," and a similar provision is in a 2007 Massachusetts Law about security breaches.

if every block were zeroed immediately. With some clever programming the process could be made unnoticeable, but so far neither Microsoft nor Apple has made the necessary software investment.

And who has not deleted a file and then immediately wished to recover it? Happily for all of us who have mistakenly dragged the wrong file into the trash can, as computers work today, deleted files are not immediately added to the pool—they can be dragged back out. Files can be removed only until you execute an "Empty trash" command, which puts the deleted blocks into the pool, although it does not zero them.

But what about the Windows "FORMAT" command, shown in Figure 3.16? It takes about 20 minutes to complete. Apparently it is destroying all the bits on the disk, as the warning message implies. But that is not what is happening. It is simply looking for faulty spots on the disk. Physical flaws in the magnetic surface can make individual disk blocks unusable, even though mechanically the disk is fine and most of the surface is flawless as well. The FORMAT command attempts to *read* every disk block in order to identify blocks that need to be avoided in the future. Reading every block takes a long time, but rewriting them all would take twice as long. The FORMAT command identifies the bad blocks and re-initializes the index, but leaves most of the data unaltered, ready to be recovered by an academic researcher—or an inventive snooper.

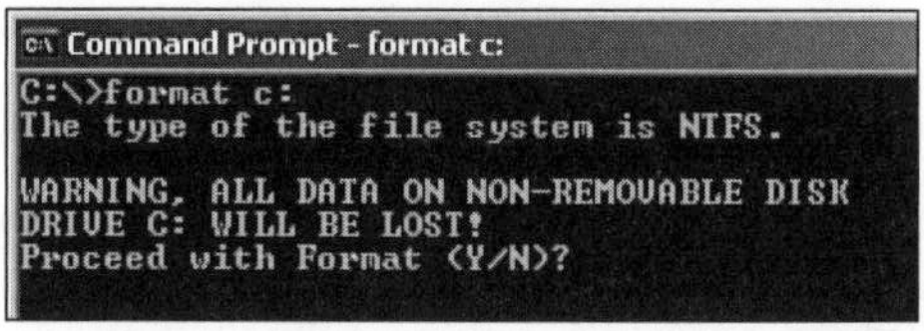

```
Command Prompt - format c:
C:\>format c:
The type of the file system is NTFS.

WARNING, ALL DATA ON NON-REMOVABLE DISK
DRIVE C: WILL BE LOST!
Proceed with Format (Y/N)?
```

FIGURE 3.16    Warning screen of Microsoft Windows FORMAT command. The statement that all the data will be lost is misleading—in fact, a great deal of it can be recovered.

As if the problems with disks were not troubling enough, exactly the same problems afflict the memory of cell phones. When people get rid of their old phones, they forget the call logs and email messages they contain. And if they do remember to delete them, using the awkward combinations of button-pushes described deep in the phone's documentation, they may not really have accomplished what they hoped. A researcher bought ten cell phones on eBay and recovered bank account numbers and passwords, corporate strategy plans, and an email exchange between a woman and her married boyfriend, whose wife was getting suspicious. Some of this information was recovered from phones whose previous owners had scrupulously followed the manufacturer's instructions for clearing the memory.

> **SOFTWARE TO SCRUB YOUR DISK**
>
> If you really want to get rid of all the data on your disk, a special "Secure empty trash" command is available on Macintosh computers. On Windows machines, DBAN is free software that really will zero your disk, available through dban.sourceforge.net, which has lots of other useful free software. Don't use DBAN on your disk until you are sure you don't want anything on it anymore!

In a global sense, bits turn out to be very hard to eradicate. And most of the time, that is exactly the way we want it. If our computer dies, we are glad that Google has copies of our data. When our cell phone dies, we are happy if our contact lists reappear, magically downloaded from our cellular service provider to our replacement phone. There are upsides and downsides to the persistence of bits.

Physical destruction always works as a method of data deletion. One of us uses a hammer; another of us prefers his axe. Alas, these methods, while effective, do not meet contemporary standards for recovery and recycling of potentially toxic materials.

## Can Data Be Deleted Permanently?

### COPIES MAKE DATA HARD TO DELETE

If your computer has ever been connected to a network, destroying its data will not get rid of copies of the same information that may exist on other machines. Your emails went to and from other people—who may have copies on their machines, and may have shared them with others. If you use Google's Gmail, Google may have copies of your emails even after you have deleted them. If you ordered some merchandise online, destroying the copy of the invoice on your personal computer certainly won't affect the store's records.

Rumors arise every now and then that engineers equipped with very sensitive devices can tell the difference between a 0 that was written over a 0 on a disk and a 0 that was written over a 1. The theory goes that successive writing operations are not perfectly aligned in physical space—a "bit" has width. When a bit is rewritten, its physical edges may slightly overlap or fall short of its previous position, potentially revealing the previous value. If such microscopic misalignments could be detected, it would be possible to see, even on a disk that has been zeroed, what the bits were *before* it was zeroed.

No credible authentication of such an achievement has ever been published, however, and as the density of hard disks continues to rise, the likelihood wanes that such data recovery can be accomplished. On the other hand, the places most likely to be able to achieve this feat are government intelligence agencies, which do not boast of their successes! So all that can be said for certain is that recovering overwritten data is within the capabilities of at most a handful of organizations—and if possible at all, is so difficult and costly that the data would have to be extraordinarily valuable to make the recovery attempt worthwhile.

## How Long Will Data Really Last?

As persistent as digital information seems to be, and as likely to disclose secrets unexpectedly, it also suffers from exactly the opposite problem. Sometimes electronic records become unavailable quite quickly, in spite of best efforts to save them permanently.

Figure 3.17 shows an early geopolitical and demographic database—the Domesday Book, an inventory of English lands compiled in 1086 by Norman monks at the behest of William the Conqueror. The Domesday Book is one of Britain's national treasures and rests in its archives, as readable today as it was in the eleventh century.

British National Archives.

FIGURE 3.17    The Domesday Book of 1086.

In honor of the 900th anniversary of the Domesday Book, the BBC issued a modern version, including photographs, text, and maps documenting how Britain looked in 1986. Instead of using vellum, or even paper, the material was assembled in digital formats and issued on 12-inch diameter video disks, which could be read only by specially equipped computers (see Figure 3.18). The project was meant to preserve forever a detailed snapshot of late twentieth-century Britain, and to make it available immediately to schools and libraries everywhere.

By 2001, the modern Domesday Book was unreadable. The computers and disk readers it required were obsolete and no longer manufactured. In 15 years, the memory even of how the information was formatted on the disks had been forgotten. Mocking the project's grand ambitions, a British newspaper exclaimed, "Digital Domesday Book lasts 15 years not 1000."

"Domesday Redux," from Ariadne, Issue 56.

FIGURE 3.18   A personal computer of the mid-1980s configured to read the 12-inch videodisks on which the modern "Domesday Book" was published.

Paper and papyrus thousands of years older even than the original Domesday Book are readable today. Electronic records become obsolete in a matter of years. Will the vast amounts of information now available because of the advances in storage and communication technology actually be usable a hundred or a thousand years in the future, or will the shift from paper to digital media mean the loss of history?

The particular story of the modern Domesday Book has a happy ending. The data was recovered, though just barely, thanks to a concerted effort by many technicians. Reconstructing the data formats required detective work on masses of computer codes (see Figure 3.19) and recourse to data structure books of the period—so that programmers in 2001 could imagine how others would have attacked the same data representation problems only 15 years earlier! In the world of computer science, "state of the art" expertise dies very quickly.

The recovered modern Domesday Book is accessible to anyone via the Internet. Even the data files of the original Domesday Book have been transferred to a web site that is accessible via the Internet.

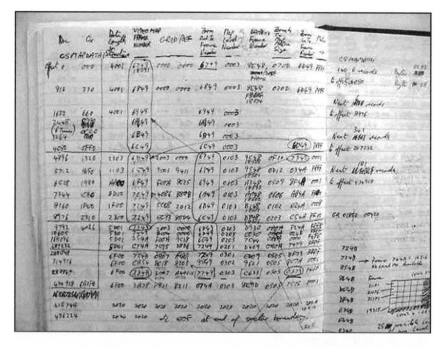

FIGURE 3.19 Efforts to reconstruct, shortly after the year 2000, the forgotten data formats for the modern "Domesday Book," designed less than 20 years earlier.

But there is a large moral for any office or library worker. We cannot assume that the back-ups and saved disks we create today will be useful even ten years from now for retrieving the vast quantities of information they contain. It is an open question whether digital archives—much less the box of disk drives under your bed in place of your grandmother's box of photographs—will be as permanent as the original Domesday Book. An extraordinary effort is underway to archive the entire World Wide Web, taking snapshots of every publicly accessible web page at period intervals. Can the effort succeed, and can the disks on which the archive is held

**PRESERVING THE WEB**

The Internet Archive (www.archive.org) periodically records "snapshots" of publicly accessible web pages and stores them away. Anyone can retrieve a page from the past, even if it no longer exists or has been altered. By installing a "Wayback" button (available from the Internet Archive) on your web browser, you can instantly see how any web page looked in the past—just go to the web page and click the Wayback button; you get a list of the archived copies of the page, and you can click on any of them to view it.

themselves be updated periodically so that the information will be with us forever?

Or would we be wisest to do the apparently Luddite thing: to print everything worth preserving for the long run—electronic journals, for example—so that documents will be preserved in the only form we are *certain* will remain readable for thousands of years?

The digital revolution put the power to document ideas into the hands of ordinary people. The technology shift eliminated many of the intermediaries once needed to produce office memoranda and books. Power over the thoughts in those documents shifted as well. The authority that once accompanied the physical control of written and printed works has passed into the hands of the individuals who write them. The production of information has been democratized—although not always with happy results, as the mishaps discussed in this chapter tellingly illustrate.

We now turn to the other half of the story: how we get the information that others have produced. When power over documents was more centralized, the authorities were those who could print books, those who had the keys to the file cabinets, and those with the most complete collections of documents and publications. Document collections were used both as information choke points and as instruments of public enlightenment. Libraries, for example, have been monuments to imperial power. University libraries have long been the central institutions of advanced learning, and local public libraries have been key democratizing forces in literate nations.

If everything is just bits and everyone can have as many bits as they want, the problem may not be having the information, but finding it. Having a fact on the disk in your computer, sitting a few inches from your eyes and brain, is irrelevant, if what you want to know is irretrievably mixed with billions of billions of other bits. Having the haystack does you no good if you can't find your precious needle within it. In the next chapter, we ask: Where does the power now go, in the new world where access to information means finding it, as well as having it?

# CHAPTER 4

# Needles in the Haystack

## *Google and Other Brokers in the Bits Bazaar*

## Found After Seventy Years

Rosalie Polotsky was 10 years old when she waved goodbye to her cousins, Sophia and Ossie, at the Moscow train station in 1937. The two sisters were fleeing the oppression of Soviet Russia to start a new life. Rosalie's family stayed behind. She grew up in Moscow, taught French, married Nariman Berkovich, and raised a family. In 1990, she emigrated to the U.S. and settled near her son, Sasha, in Massachusetts.

Rosalie, Nariman, and Sasha always wondered about the fate of Sophia and Ossie. The Iron Curtain had utterly severed communication among Jewish relatives. By the time Rosalie left for the U.S., her ties to Sophia and Ossie had been broken for so long that she had little hope of reconnecting with them—and, as the years wore on, less reason for optimism that her cousins were still alive. Although his grandfather dreamed of finding them, Sasha's search of immigrant records at Ellis Island and the International Red Cross provided no clues. Perhaps, traveling across wartime Europe, the little girls had never even made it to the U.S.

Then one day, Sasha's cousin typed "Polotsky" into Google's search window and found a clue. An entry on a genealogical web site mentioned "Minacker," the name of Sophia's and Ossie's father. In short order, Rosalie, Sophia, and Ossie were reunited in Florida, after 70 years apart. "All the time when he was alive, he asked me to do something to find them," said Sasha, recalling his grandfather's wish. "It's something magic."

The digital explosion has produced vast quantities of informative data, the Internet has scattered that data across the globe, and the World Wide Web has put it within reach of millions of ordinary people. But you can't reach for something if you don't know where it is. Most of that vast store of digital information might as well not exist without a way to find it. For most of us, the way to find things on the Web is with web search engines. Search is a wondrous, transformative technology, which both fulfills dreams and shapes human knowledge. The search tools that help us find needles in the digital haystack have become the lenses through which we view the digital landscape. Businesses and governments use them to distort our picture of reality.

# The Library and the Bazaar

In the beginning, the Web was a library. Information providers—mostly businesses and universities, which could afford to create web pages—posted information for others to see. Information consumers—mostly others in business and academia—found out where to get the information and downloaded it. They might know where to look because someone sent them the URL (the "Uniform Resource Locator"), such as mit.edu (the URL for MIT). Ordinary people didn't use the Web. Instead, they used services such as CompuServe for organized access to databases of various kinds of information.

As the Web went commercial, directories began to appear, including printed "Yellow Pages." These directories listed places to go on the Web for various products and services. If you wanted to buy a car, you looked in one place, and you looked in another place to find a job. These lists resembled the categories AOL and CompuServe provided in the days before consumers could connect directly to the Internet. Human beings constructed these lists—editors decided what went in each category, and what got left out entirely.

The Web has changed drastically since the mid-1990s. First, it is no

> ## WEB 1.0 VS. WEB 2.0
>
> In contemporary jargon, the newer, more participatory web sites to which users can contribute are dubbed "Web 2.0." The older, more passive web sites are now called "Web 1.0." These look like software release numbers, but "Web 2.0" describes something subtler and more complex. Web 2.0 sites—Facebook and Wikipedia, for example—exploit what economists call "network effects." Because users are contributing information as well as utilizing information others supply, these sites become more valuable the more people are using them. See http://www.oreillynet.com/lpt/a/6228 for a fuller explanation of Web 2.0.

longer a passive information resource. Blogs, Wikipedia, and Facebook are contributory structures, where peer involvement makes the information useful. Web sites are cheap and easy to create; ordinary individuals and even the smallest of organizations can now have them. As a result, the content and connectedness of the Web are changing all the time.

Second, the Web has gotten so big and so unstructured that it is not humanly possible to split it up into neat categories. Web pages simply don't lend themselves to organization in a nice structure, like an outline. There is no master plan for the Web—vast numbers of new pages are added daily in an utterly unstructured way. You certainly can't tell what a web page contains by looking at its URL.

Moreover, hierarchical organization is useless in helping you find information if you can't tell where in the hierarchy it might belong. You don't usually go to the Web to look for a web page. You go to look for *information*, and are glad to get it wherever you can find it. Often, you can't even guess where to look for what you want to know, and a nice, structured organization of knowledge would do you no good. For example, any sensible organization of human knowledge, such as an encyclopedia, would have a section on cows and a section on the moon. But if you didn't know that there was a nursery rhyme about the cow jumping over the moon, neither the "cow" nor the "moon" entry would help you figure out what the cow supposedly did to the moon. If you typed both words into a search engine, however, you would find out in the blink of an eye.

Search is the new paradigm for finding information—and not just on the Web as a whole. If you go to Wal-Mart's web site, you can trace through its hierarchical organization. At the top level, you get to choose between "accessories," "baby," "boys," "girls," and so on. If you click "baby," your next click takes you to "infant boys," "toddler girls," and so on. There is also a search window at the top. Type whatever you want, and you may be taken directly to what you are looking for—but only on Wal-Mart's site. Such limited search engines help us share photos, read newspapers, buy books online from Amazon or Barnes and Noble, and even find old email on our own laptops.

Search makes it possible to find things in vast digital repositories. But search is more than a quick form of look-up in a digital library. *Search is a new form of control over information.*

> *Search is a new form of control over information.*

Information retrieval tools such as Google are extraordinarily democratizing—Rosalie and Sasha Berkovich did not need to hire a professional people-finder. But the power that has been vested in individuals is not the only kind that search has created. We have given search engines control over where we get reliable information—the same control we used to assign to authoritative sources, such as encyclopedias and "newspapers of record." If we place absolute trust in a search engine to find things for us, we are giving the search engine the power to make it hard or impossible for us to know things. Use Google in China, and your searches will "find" very different information about democracy than they will "find" if you use Google in the United States. Search for "401(K)" on John Hancock's web site, and Fidelity's 401(K) plans will seem not to exist.

For the user, search is the power to find things, and for whoever controls the engine, search is the power to shape what you see. Search is also power of a third kind. Because the search company records all our search queries, we are giving the search company the power that comes with knowing what we want to know. In its annual "Zeitgeist" report, Google takes the pulse of the population by revealing the questions its search engine is most often asked. It was amusing to know that of the most popular "Who is ...?" searches of 2007, "God" was #1 and "Satan" was #10, with "Buckethead" beating "Satan" at #6. Search engines also gather similar information about each one of us individually. For example, as discussed in Chapter 2, Amazon uses the information to suggest books you might like to read once you have used its web site for a bit.

> Here are some interesting Google Zeitgeist results from 2007: among "What is" questions, "love" was #1 and "gout" was #10; among "How to" queries, "kiss" was #1 and "skateboard" was #10.

The Web is no longer a library. It is a chaotic marketplace of the billions of ideas and facts cast up by the bits explosion. Information consumers and information producers constantly seek out each other and morph into each other's roles. In this shadowy bits bazaar, with all its whispers and its couriers running to and fro, search engines are brokers. Their job is not to supply the undisputed truth, nor even to judge the accuracy of material that others provide. Search engines connect willing producers of information to willing consumers. They succeed or fail not on the quality of the information they provide, because they do not produce content at all. They only make connections. Search engines succeed or fail depending on whether we are happy with the connections they make, and nothing more. In the bazaar, it is not always the knowledgeable broker who makes the most deals. To stay in business, a broker just has to give most people what they want, consistently over time.

Search does more than find things for us. Search helps us discover things we did not know existed. By searching, we can all be armchair bits detectives, finding surprises in the book *next* to the one we were pulling off the digital bookshelf, and sniffing out curious information fragments cast far and wide by the digital explosion.

## *Forbidden Knowledge Is Only a Click Away*

Schizophrenia is a terrible brain disease, afflicting millions of people. If you wanted to know about the latest treatment options, you might try to find some web sites and read the information they contain.

Some people already know where they think they can good find medical information—they have bookmarked a site they trust, such as WebMD.com or DrKoop.com. If you were like us, however, you'd use a search engine—Google.com, Yahoo.com, or Ask.com, for example. You'd type in a description of what you were looking for and start to click links and read. Of course, you should *not* believe uncritically anything you read from a source you don't know anything about—or act on the medical information you got through your browsing, without checking with a physician.

When we tried searching for "schizophrenia drugs" using Google, we got the results shown in Figure 4.1. The top line tells us that if we don't like these results, there are a quarter-million more that Google would be glad to show us. It also says that it took six-hundredths of a second to get these results for us—we didn't sense that it took even that long. Three "Sponsored Links" appear to the right. A link is "sponsored" if someone has paid Google to have it put there—in other words, it's an advertisement. To the left is a variety of ordinary links that Google's information retrieval algorithms decided were most likely to be useful to someone wanting information about "schizophrenia drugs." Those ordinary links are called the search engine's *organic* results, as opposed to the sponsored results.

Google ™ is a registered trademark of Google, Inc. Reprinted by permission.

FIGURE 4.1   Google's results from a search for "schizophrenia drugs."

---

**THOSE FUNNY NAMES**

Yahoo! is an acronym—it stands for "Yet Another Hierarchical Officious Oracle" (docs.yahoo.com/info/misc/history.html). "Google" comes from "googol," which is the number represented by a 1 followed by 100 zeroes. The Google founders were evidently thinking big!

---

Just looking at this window raises a series of important questions:

- The Web is enormous. How can a search engine find those results so fast? Is it finding every appropriate link?

- How did Google decide what is search result number 1 and what is number 283,000?

- If you try another search engine instead of Google, you'll get different results. Which is right? Which is better? Which is more authoritative?

- Are the sponsored links supposed to be better links than the organic links, or worse? Is the advertising really necessary?

- How much of this does the government oversee? If a TV station kept reporting lies as the truth, the government would get after them. Does it do anything with search engines?

We shall take up each of these questions in due course, but for the time being, let's just pursue our medical adventure.

When we clicked on the first organic link, it took us to a page from the web site of a distinguished Swedish university. That page contained some information about the different kinds of schizophrenia drugs. One of the drugs it mentioned was "olanzapin (Zyprexa)." The trade name rang a bell for some reason, so we started over and searched for "Zyprexa."

The first of the organic links we got back was to www.zyprexa.com, which described itself as "The Official ZYPREXA Olanzapine Site." The page was clearly marked as maintained by Eli Lilly and Company, the drug's manufacturer. It provided a great deal of information about the drug, as well as photographs of smiling people—satisfied patients, presumably—and slogans such as "There is Hope" and "Opening the Door to Possibility." The next few links on our page of search results were to the medical information sites drugs.com, rxlist.com, webmd.com, and askapatient.com.

Just below these was a link that took us in a different direction: "ZyprexaKills wiki." The drug was associated with some serious side effects, it seems, and Lilly allegedly kept these side effects secret for a long time. At the very top of that page of search results, as the only sponsored link, was the following: "Prescription Drug Lawsuit. Zyprexa-olanzapine-lawyer.com. Pancreatitis & diabetes caused by this drug? Get legal help today." That link took us to a web form where a Houston attorney offered to represent us against Lilly.

It took only a few more mouse clicks before a document appeared that was entitled "Olanzapine—Blood glucose changes" (see Figure 4.2). It was an internal Lilly memorandum, never meant to be seen outside the company, and marked as a confidential exhibit in a court case. Some patients who had developed diabetes while using Zyprexa had sued Lilly, claiming that the drug had caused the disease. In the course of that lawsuit, this memo and other confidential materials were shared with the plaintiffs' lawyers under a standard discovery protocol. Through a series of improper actions by several lawyers, a *New York Times* reporter procured these documents. The reporter then published an exposé of Lilly's slowness to acknowledge the drug's side effects. The documents themselves appeared on a variety of web sites.

---

# OLANZAPINE - BLOOD GLUCOSE CHANGES

## SUMMARY

### OLANZAPINE AND GLYCEMIA

Zyprexa MDL 1596    Confidential-Subject to Protective Order
## Zyprexa MDL Plaintiffs' Exhibit No.00916

---

Source: www.furiousseasons.com/zyprexa%20documents/ZY1%20%20%2000008758.pdf.

FIGURE 4.2    Top and bottom lines of a document filed in a court case. It was supposed to be kept secret, but once on the Web, anyone searching for "Zyprexa documents" finds it easily.

Lilly demanded that the documents be returned, that all copies be destroyed, and that the web sites that had posted them be required to take them down. A legal battle ensued. On February 13, 2007, Judge Jack B. Weinstein of the U.S. District Court in New York issued his judgment, order, and injunction. Yes, what had been done with the documents was grievously wrong and contrary to earlier court orders. The lawyers and the journalist had cooked up a scam on the legal system, involving collusion with an Alaska lawyer who had nothing to do with the case, in order to spring the documents. The lawyers who conspired to get the documents had to give them back and not keep any copies. They were enjoined against giving any copies to anyone else.

But, concluded Judge Weinstein, the web sites were another matter. The judge would not order the web sites to take down their copies. Lilly was entitled to the paper documents, but the bits had escaped and could not be recaptured. As of this writing, the documents are still viewable. We quickly found them directly by searching for "zyprexa documents."

The world is a different place from a time when the judge could have ordered the return of *all* copies of offending materials. Even if there were hundreds of copies in file cabinets and desk drawers, he might have been able to insist on their return, under threat of harsh penalties. But the Web is not a file cabinet or a desk drawer. "Web sites," wrote Judge Weinstein, "are primarily fora for speech." Lilly had asked for an injunction against five web sites that had posted the documents, but millions of others could post them in the future. "Limiting the fora available to would-be disseminators by such an infinitesimal percentage would be a fruitless exercise," the judge concluded. It probably would not be effective to issue a broader injunction, and even if it were, "the risk of unlimited inhibitions of free speech should be avoided when practicable."

The judge understood the gravity of the issue he was deciding. Fundamentally, he was reluctant to use the authority of the government in a futile attempt to prevent people from saying what they wanted to say and finding out what they wanted to know. Even if the documents had been visible only for a short time period, unknown numbers of copies might be circulating privately among interested parties. Grasping for an analogy, the judge suggested that God Himself had failed in His attempt to enjoin Adam and Eve from their pursuit of the truth!

Two sponsored links appeared when we did the search for "zyprexa documents." One was for another lawyer offering his services for Zyprexa-related lawsuits against Lilly. The other, triggered by the word "documents" in our search term, was for Google itself: "Online Documents. Easily share & edit documents online for free. Learn more today. docs.google.com." This was an ironic reminder that the bits are out there, and the tools to spread them are there too, for anyone to use. Thanks to search engines, anyone can find the information they want. Information has exploded out of the shells that used to contain it.

In fact, the architecture of human knowledge has changed as a result of search. In a single decade, we have been liberated from information straightjackets that have been with us since the dawn of recorded history. And many who should understand what has happened, do not. In February 2008, a San Francisco judge tried to shut down the Wikileaks web site, which posts leaked confidential documents anonymously as an aid to whistleblowers. The judge ordered the name "Wikileaks" removed from DNS servers, so the URL "Wikileaks.org" would no longer correspond to the correct IP address. (In the guts of the Internet, DNS servers provide the service of translating URLs into IP addresses. See the Appendix.) The publicity that resulted from this censorship attempt made it easy to find various "mirrors"–identical twins, located elsewhere on the Web–by searching for "Wikileaks."

# The Fall of Hierarchy

For a very long time, people have been organizing things by putting them into categories and dividing those categories into subcategories. Aristotle tried to classify everything. Living things, for example, were either plants or animals. Animals either had red blood or did not; red-blooded animals were either live-bearers or egg-bearers; live-bearers were either humans or other mammals; egg-bearers either swam or flew; and so on. Sponges, bats, and whales all presented classification enigmas, on which Aristotle did not think he had the last word. At the dawn of the Enlightenment, Linnaeus provided a more useful way of classifying living things, using an approach that gained intrinsic scientific validity once it reflected evolutionary lines of descent.

Our traditions of hierarchical classification are evident everywhere. We just love outline structures. The law against cracking copyright protection (discussed in Chapter 6, "Balance Toppled") is Title 17, Section 1201, paragraph (a), part (1), subpart (A). In the Library of Congress system, every book is in one of 26 major categories, designated by a Roman letter, and these major categories are internally divided in a similar way—B is philosophy, for example, and BQ is Buddhism.

If the categories are clear, it may be possible to use the *organizing* hierarchy to *locate* what you are looking for. That requires that the person doing the searching not only know the classification system, but be skilled at making all the necessary decisions. For example, if knowledge about living things was organized as Aristotle had it, anyone wanting to know about whales would have to know *already* whether a whale was a fish or a mammal in order to go down the proper branch of the classification tree. As more and more knowledge has to be stuffed into the tree, the tree grows and sprouts twigs, which over time become branches sprouting more twigs. The classification problem becomes unwieldy, and the retrieval problem becomes practically impossible.

The system of Web URLs started out as such a classification tree. The site www.physics.harvard.edu is a web server, of the physics department, within Harvard University, which is an educational institution. But with the profusion of the Web, this system of domain names is now useless as a way of finding anything whose URL you do not already know.

In 1991, when the Internet was barely known outside academic and government circles, some academic researchers offered a program called "Gopher." This program provided a hierarchical directory of many web sites, by organizing the directories provided by the individual sites into one big outline.

"Gopher" was a pun—it was software you could use to "go for" information on the Web. It was also the mascot of the University of Minnesota, where the software was first developed.

Finding things using Gopher was tedious by today's standards, and was dependent on the organizational skills of the contributors. Yahoo! was founded in 1994 as an online Internet directory, with human editors placing products and services in categories, making recommendations, and generally trying to make the Internet accessible to non-techies. Although Yahoo! has long since added a search window, it retains its basic directory function to the present day.

The practical limitations of hierarchical organization trees were foreseen sixty years ago. During World War II, President Franklin Roosevelt appointed Vannevar Bush of MIT to serve as Director of the Office of Strategic Research and Development (OSRD). The OSRD coordinated scientific research in support of the war effort. It was a large effort—30,000 people and hundreds of projects covered the spectrum of science and engineering. The Manhattan Project, which produced the atomic bomb, was just a small piece of it.

From this vantage point, Bush saw a major obstacle to continued scientific progress. We were producing information faster than it could be consumed, or even classified. Decades before computers became commonplace, he wrote about this problem in a visionary article, "As We May Think." It appeared in the *Atlantic Monthly*—a popular magazine, not a technical journal. As Bush saw it,

> The difficulty seems to be, not so much that we publish unduly ... but rather that publication has been extended far beyond our present ability to make real use of the record. The summation of human experience is being expanded at a prodigious rate, and the means we use for threading through the consequent maze to the momentarily important item is the same as was used in the days of square-rigged ships. ...
> Our ineptitude in getting at the record is largely caused by the artificiality of systems of indexing.

The dawn of the digital era was at this time barely a glimmer on the horizon. But Bush imagined a machine, which he called a "memex," that would augment human memory by storing and retrieving all the information needed. It would be an "enlarged intimate supplement" to human memory, which can be "consulted with exceeding speed and flexibility."

Bush clearly perceived the problem, but the technologies available at the time, microfilm and vacuum tubes, could not solve it. He understood that the problem of finding information would eventually overwhelm the progress of science in creating and recording knowledge. Bush was intensely aware that civilization itself had been imperiled in the war, but thought we must proceed with optimism about what the record of our vast knowledge might bring us. Man "may perish in conflict before he learns to wield that record for his true good. Yet, in the application of science to the needs and desires of man, it would seem to be a singularly unfortunate stage at which to terminate the process, or to lose hope as to the outcome."

### A Futurist Precedent

In 1937, H. G. Wells anticipated Vannevar Bush's 1945 vision of a "memex." Wells wrote even more clearly about the possibility of indexing everything, and what that would mean for civilization:

> There is no practical obstacle whatever now to the creation of an efficient index to all human knowledge, ideas and achievements, to the creation, that is, of a complete planetary memory for all mankind. And not simply an index; the direct reproduction of the thing itself can be summoned to any properly prepared spot. ... This in itself is a fact of tremendous significance. It foreshadows a real intellectual unification of our race. The whole human memory can be, and probably in a short time will be, made accessible to every individual. ... This is no remote dream, no fantasy.

Capabilities that were inconceivable then are commonplace now. Digital computers, vast storage, and high-speed networks make information search and retrieval necessary. They also make it possible. The Web is a realization of Bush's memex, and search is key to making it useful.

# It Matters How It Works

How can Google or Yahoo! possibly take a question it may never have been asked before and, in a split second, deliver results from machines around the world? The search engine doesn't "search" the entire World Wide Web in response to your question. That couldn't possibly work quickly enough—it would take more than a tenth of a second just for bits to move around the earth at the speed of light. Instead, the search engine has *already* built up an index of web sites. The search engine does the best it can to find an answer to your query using its index, and then sends its answer right back to you.

To avoid suggesting that there is anything unique about Google or Yahoo!, let's name our generic search engine Jen. Jen integrates several different processes to create the illusion that you simply ask her a question and she gives back good answers. The first three steps have nothing to do with your particular query. They are going on repeatedly and all the time, whether anyone is posing any queries or not. In computer speak, these steps are happening in the *background*:

1. **Gather information.** Jen explores the Web, visiting many sites on a regular basis to learn what they contain. Jen revisits old pages because their contents may have changed, and they may contain links to new pages that have never been visited.

2. **Keep copies.** Jen retains copies of many of the web pages she visits. Jen actually has a duplicate copy of a large part of the Web stored on her computers.

3. **Build an index.** Jen constructs a huge index that shows, at a minimum, which words appear on which web pages.

When you make a query, Jen goes through four more steps, in the *foreground*:

4. **Understand the query.** English has lots of ambiguities. A query like "red sox pitchers" is fairly challenging if you haven't grown up with baseball!

5. **Determine the relevance of each possible result to the query.** Does the web page contain information the query asks about?

6. **Determine the ranking of the relevant results.** Of all the relevant answers, which are the "best"?

7. **Present the results.** The results need not only to be "good"; they have to be shown to you in a form you find useful, and perhaps also in a form that serves some of Jen's other purposes—selling more advertising, for example.

Each of these seven steps involves technical challenges that computer scientists love to solve. Jen's financial backers hope that her engineers solve them better than the engineers of competing search engines.

We'll go through each step in more detail, as it is important to understand what is going on—at every step, more than technology is involved. Each step also presents opportunities for Jen to use her information-gathering and editorial powers in ways you may not have expected—ways that shape your view of the world through the lens of Jen's search results.

The background processing is like the set-building and rehearsals for a theatrical production. You couldn't have a show without it, but none of it happens while the audience is watching, and it doesn't even need to happen on any particular schedule.

## *Step 1: Gather Information*

Search engines don't index everything. The ones we think of as general utilities, such as Google, Yahoo!, and Ask, find information rather indiscrimi-
nately throughout the Web. Other search engines are domain-specific. For
example, Medline searches only through medical literature. ArtCylopedia
indexes 2,600 art sites. The FindLaw LawCrawler searches only legal web
sites. Right from the start, with any search engine, some things are in the
index and some are out, because some sites are visited during the gathering
step and others are not. Someone decides what is worth remembering and
what isn't. If something is left out in Step 1, there is no possibility that you
will see it in Step 7.

Speaking to the Association of National Advertisers in October 2005, Eric
Schmidt, Google's CEO, observed that of the 5,000 terabytes of information
in the world, only 170 terabytes had been indexed. (A *terabyte* is about a trillion bytes.) That's just a bit more than 3%, so 97% was not included. Another
estimate puts the amount of indexed information at only .02% of the size of
the databases and documents reachable via the Web. Even in the limited context of the World Wide Web, Jen needs to decide what to look at, and how
frequently. These decisions implicitly define what is important and what is
not, and will limit what Jen's users can find.

How *often* Jen visits web pages to index them is one of her precious trade
secrets. She probably pays daily visits to news sites such as CNN.com, so that
if you ask tonight about something that happened this morning, Jen may
point you to CNN's story. In fact, there is most likely a master list of sites to
be visited frequently, such as whitehouse.gov—sites that change regularly
and are the object of much public interest. On the other hand, Jen probably
has learned from her repeated visits that some sites don't change at all. For
example, the Web version of a paper published ten years ago doesn't change.
After a few visits, Jen may decide to revisit it once a year, just in case. Other
pages may not be posted long enough to get indexed at all. If you post a
futon for sale on Craigslist.com, the ad will become accessible to potential
buyers in just a few minutes. If it sells quickly, however, Jen may never see
it. Even if the ad stays up for a while, you probably won't be able to find it
with most search engines for several days.

Jen is clever about how often she revisits pages—but her cleverness also
codifies some judgments, some priorities—some *control*. The more important
Jen judges your page to be, the less time it will take for your new content to
show up as responses to queries to Jen's search engine.

Jen roams the Web to gather information by following links from the
pages she visits. Software that crawls around the Web is (in typical geek

## How a Spider Explores the Web

Search engines gather information by wandering through the World Wide Web. For example, when a spider visits the main URL of the publisher of this book, www.pearson.com, it retrieves a page of text, of which this is a fragment:

```
<div id="subsidiary">
<h2 class="hide">Subsidiary sites links</h2>
<label for="subsidiarySites" class="hide">Available
sites</label>
<select name="subsidiarySites" id="subsidiarySites" size="1">
<option value="">Browse sites</option>
<optgroup label="FT Group">
<option value="http://www.ftchinese.com/sc/index.jsp">
  Chinese.FT.com</option>
<option value="http://ftd.de/">FT Deutschland</option>
```

This text is actually a computer program written in a special programming language called HTML ("HyperText Markup Language"). Your web browser renders the web page by executing this little program. But the spider is retrieving this text not to render it, but to index the information it contains. "FT Deutschland" is text that appears on the screen when the page is rendered; such terms should go into the index. The spider recognizes other links, such as www.ftchinese.com or ftd.de, as URLs of pages it needs to visit in turn. In the process of visiting those pages, it indexes them and identifies yet more links to visit, and so on!

A spider, or web crawler, is a particular kind of *bot*. A bot (as in "robot") is a program that endlessly performs some intrinsically repetitive task, often an information-gathering task.

irony) called a "spider." Because the spidering process takes days or even weeks, Jen will not know immediately if a web page is taken down—she will find out only when her spider next visits the place where it used to be. At that point, she will remove it from her index, but in the meantime, she may respond to queries with links to pages that no longer exist. Click on such a link, and you will get a message such as "Page not found" or "Can't find the server."

Because the Web is unstructured, there is no inherently "correct" order in which to visit the pages, and no obvious way to know when to stop. Page A may contain references to page B, and also page B to page A, so the spider has to be careful not to go around in circles. Jen must organize her crawl of the Web to visit as much as she chooses without wasting time revisiting sections she has already seen.

A web site may stipulate that it does not want spiders to visit it too frequently or to index certain kinds of information. The site's designer simply puts that information in a file named robots.txt, and virtually all web-crawling software will respect what it says. Of course, pages that are inaccessible without a login cannot be crawled at all. So, the results from Step 7 may be influenced by what the sites want Jen to know about them, as well as by what Jen thinks is worth knowing. For example, Sasha Berkovich was fortunate that the Polotsky family tree had been posted to part of the genealogy.com web site that was open to the public—otherwise, Google's spider could not have indexed it.

Finally, spidering is not cost free. Jen's "visits" are really requests to web sites that they send their pages back to her. Spidering creates Internet traffic and also imposes a load on the web server. This part of search engines' background processing, in other words, has unintended effects on the experience of the entire Internet. Spiders consume network bandwidth, and they may tie up servers, which are busy responding to spider requests while their ordinary users are trying to view their pages. Commercial search engines attempt to schedule their web crawling in ways that won't overload the servers they visit.

## Step 2: Keep Copies

Jen downloads a copy of every web page her spider visits—this is what it means to "visit" a page. Instead of rendering the page on the screen as a web browser would, Jen indexes it. If she wishes, she can retain the copy after she has finished indexing it, storing it on her own disks. Such a copy is said to be "cached," after the French word for "hidden." Ordinarily Jen would not do anything with her cached copy; it may quickly become out of date. But caching web pages makes it possible for Jen to have a page that no longer exists at its original source, or a version of a page older than the current one. This is the flip side of Jen never knowing about certain pages because their owners took them down before she had a chance to index them. With a cached page, Jen knows what used to be on the page even after the owner intended it to disappear.

Caching is another blow to the Web-as-library metaphor, because removing information from the bookshelf doesn't necessarily get rid of it. Efforts to scrub even dangerous information are beyond the capability of those who posted it. For example, after 9/11, a lot of information that was once available on the Web was pulled. Among the pages that disappeared overnight were reports on government vulnerabilities, sensitive security information, and even a Center for Disease Control chemical terrorism report that revealed industry shortcomings. Because the pages had been cached, however, the bits lived on at Google and other search engine companies.

Not only did those pages of dangerous information survive, but anyone could find them. Anytime you do a search with one of the major search engines, you are offered access to the cached copy, as well as the link to where the page came from, whether or not it still exists. Click on the link for the "Cached" page, and you see something that looks very much like what you might see if you clicked on the main link instead. The cached copy is identified as such (see Figure 4.3).

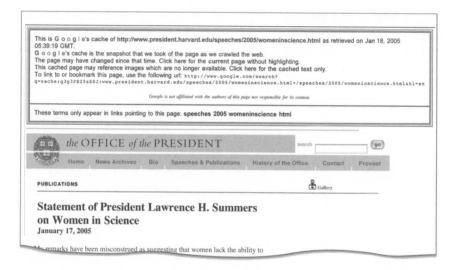

FIGURE 4.3   Part of a cached web page, Google's copy of an official statement made by Harvard's president and replaced two days later after negative public reaction. This copy was retrieved from Google after the statement disappeared from the university's web site. Harvard, which holds the copyright on this once-public statement, refused to allow it to be printed in this book (see Conclusion).

This is an actual example; it was the statement Lawrence Summers released on January 17, 2005, after word of his remarks about women in science became public. As reported in *Harvard Magazine* in March–April 2005, the statement began, "My remarks have been misconstrued as suggesting that women lack the ability to succeed at the highest levels of math and science. I did not say that, nor do I believe it." This unapologetic denial stayed on the

*The digital explosion grants the power of both instant communication and instant retraction—but almost every digital action leaves digital fingerprints.*

Harvard web site for only a few days. In the face of a national firestorm of protest, Summers issued a new statement on January 19, 2005, reading, in part, "I deeply regret the impact of my comments and apologize for not having weighed them more carefully." Those searching for the President's statement were then led to the contrite new statement—but for a time, the original, defiant version remained visible to those who clicked on the link to Google's cached copy.

---

**FINDING DELETED PAGES**

An easy experiment on finding deleted pages is to search using Google for an item that was sold on craigslist. You can use the "site" modifier in the Google search box to limit your search to the craigslist web site, by including a "modifier":

`futon site:craigslist.com`

The results will likely return pages for items that are no longer available, but for which the cached pages will still exist.

---

The digital explosion grants the power of both instant communication and instant retraction—but almost every digital action leaves digital fingerprints. Bits do not die easily, and digital words, once said, are hard to retract.

If Jen caches web pages, it may be possible for you to get information that was retracted after it was discovered to be in error or embarrassing. Something about this doesn't feel quite right, though—is the information on those pages really Jen's to do with as she wishes? If the material is copyrighted—a published paper from ten years ago, for example—what right does Jen have to show you her cached copy? For that matter, what right did she have to keep a copy in the first place? If you have copyrighted something, don't you have some authority over who can make copies of it?

This enigma is an early introduction to the confused state of copyright law in the digital era, to which we return in Chapter 6. Jen cannot index my web page without receiving a copy of it. In the most literal sense, any time you "view" or "visit" a web page, you are actually copying it, and then your web browser renders the copy on the screen. A metaphorical failure once again: The Web is *not a library*. Viewing is an exchange of bits, not a passive activity, as far as the web site is concerned. If "copying" copyrighted materials was totally prohibited, neither search engines nor the Web itself could work, so some sort of copying must be permissible. On the other hand, when Jen caches the material she indexes—perhaps an entire book, in the case of the

Google Books project—the legal controversies become more highly contested. Indeed, as we discuss in Chapter 6, the Association of American Publishers and Google are locked in a lawsuit over what Google is and is not allowed to do with the digital images of books that Google has scanned.

## Step 3: Build an Index

When we searched the Web for "Zyprexa," Jen consulted her index, which has the same basic structure as the index of a book: a list of terms followed by the places they occur. Just as a book's index lists page numbers, Jen's index lists URLs of web pages. To help the search engine give the most useful responses to queries, the index may record other information as well: the size of the font in which the term appears, for example, and where on the page it appears.

Indexes are critical because having the index in order—like the index

> **INDEXES AND CONCORDANCES**
>
> The information structure used by search engines is technically known as an *inverted index*—that is, an index of the words in a document or a set of documents, and the places where those words appear. Inverted indexes are not a new idea; the biblical concordances laboriously constructed by medieval monks were inverted indexes. Constructing concordances was one of the earliest applications of computer technology to a nonmathematical problem.

of a book, which is in alphabetical order—makes it possible to find things much faster than with sequential searching. This is where Jen's computer scientists really earn their salaries, by devising clever ways of storing indexed information so it can be retrieved quickly. Moore's Law also played a big role in the creation of web indexes—until computer memories got fast enough, cheap enough, and big enough, even the cleverest computer scientists could not program machines to respond instantly to arbitrary English queries.

When Jen wants to find a term in her index, she does not start at the beginning and go through it one entry at a time until she finds what she is looking for. That is not the way you would look up something in the index of a book; you would use the fact that the index is in order alphabetically. A very simple strategy to look up something in a big ordered index, such as a phone book, is just to open the book in the middle and see if the item you are looking for belongs in the first half or the second. Then you can ignore half the phone book and use the same strategy to subdivide the remaining half. The number of steps it takes to get down to a single page in a phone book with $n$ pages using this method is the number of times you have to divide $n$ by 2 to get down to 1. So if $n$ is 1000, it takes only 10 of these probing steps to find any item using *binary search*, as this method is known.

In general, the number of steps needed to search an index of $n$ things using binary search is proportional, not to $n$, but to the number of digits in $n$. That means that binary search is exponentially faster than linear search—searching through a million items would take only 20 steps, and through a billion items would take 30 steps. And binary search is fairly dumb by comparison with what people actually do—if you were looking for "Ledeen" in the phone book, you might open it in the middle, but if you were looking for "Abelson," you'd open it near the front. That strategy can be reduced to an even better computer algorithm, exponentially faster than binary search.

How big is Jen's index, in fact? To begin with, how many terms does Jen index? That is another of her trade secrets. Jen's index could be useful with a few tens of millions of entries. There are fewer than half a million words in the English language, but Jen probably wants to index some numbers too (try searching for a number such as 327 using your search engine). Proper names and at least some words in foreign languages are also important. The list of web pages associated with a term is probably on disk in most cases, with only the information about *where* on the disk kept with the term itself in main memory. Even if storing the term and the location on disk of the list of associated URLs takes 100 bytes per entry, with 25 million entries, the table of index entries would occupy 2.5 gigabytes (about 2.5 billion bytes) of main memory. A few years ago, that amount of memory was unimaginable; today, you get that on a laptop from Wal-Mart. The index can be searched quickly—using binary search, for example—although retrieving the list of URLs might require going to disk. If Jen has Google's resources, she can speed up her query response by keeping URLs in main memory too, and she can split the search process across multiple computers to make it even faster.

Now that the preparations have been made, we can watch the performance itself—what happens when you give Jen a query.

## Step 4: Understand the Query

When we asked Google the query *Yankees beat Red Sox*, only one of the top five results was about the Yankees beating the Red Sox (see Figure 4.4). The others reported instead on the Red Sox beating the Yankees. Because English is hard for computers to understand and is often ambiguous, the simplest form of query analysis ignores syntax, and treats the query as simply a list of keywords. Just looking up a series of words in an index is computationally easy, even if it often misses the intended meaning of the query.

To help users reduce the ambiguity of their keyword queries, search engines support "advanced queries" with more powerful features. Even the simplest, putting a phrase in quotes, is used by fewer than 10% of search engine users. Typing the quotation marks in the query "Red Sox beat Yankees" produces more appropriate results. You can use "~" to tell Google to find synonyms, "-" to exclude certain terms, or cryptic commands such as "allinurl:" or "inanchor:" to limit the part of the Web to search. Arguably we didn't ask our question the right way, but most of us don't bother; in general, people just type in the words they want and take the answers they get.

Often they get back quite a lot. Ask Yahoo! for the words "allergy" and "treatment," and you find more than 20,000,000 references. If you ask for "allergy treatment"—that is, if you just put quotes around the two words—you get 628,000 entries, and quite different top choices. If you ask for "treating allergies," the list shrinks to 95,000. The difference between these queries may have been unintentional, but the search engine thought they were drastically different. It's remarkable that human-computer communication through the lens of the search engine is so useful, given its obvious imperfections!

Google ™ is a registered trademark of Google, Inc. Reprinted by permission.

FIGURE 4.4   Keyword search misses the meaning of English-language query. Most of the results for the query "Yankees beat Red Sox" are about the Red Sox beating the Yankees.

## NATURAL LANGUAGE QUERIES

Query-understanding technology is improving. The experimental site www.digger.com, for example, tells you when your query is ambiguous and helps you clarify what you are asking. If you ask Digger for information about "java," it realizes that you might mean the beverage, the island, or the programming language, and helps get the right interpretation if it guessed wrong the first time.

Powerset (www.powerset.com) uses natural language software to disambiguate queries based on their English syntax, and answers based on what web pages actually say. That would resolve the misunderstanding of "Yankees beat Red Sox."

Ongoing research promises to transfer the burden of disambiguating queries to the software, where it belongs, rather than forcing users to twist their brains around computerese. Natural language understanding seems to be on its way, but not in the immediate future. We may need a hundred-fold increase in computing power to make semantic analysis of web pages accurate enough so that search engines no longer give boneheaded answers to simple English queries.

Today, users tend to be tolerant when search engines misunderstand their meaning. They blame themselves and revise their queries to produce better results. This may be because we are still amazed that search engines work at all. In part, we may be tolerant of error because in web search, the cost to the user of an inappropriate answer is very low. As the technology improves, users will expect more, and will become less tolerant of wasting their time sorting through useless answers.

## Step 5: Determine Relevance

A search engine's job is to provide results that match the intent of the query. In technical jargon, this criterion is called "relevance." Relevance has an objective component—a story about the Red Sox beating the Yankees is only marginally responsive to a query about the Yankees beating the Red Sox. But relevance is also inherently subjective. Only the person who posed the query can be the final judge of the relevance of the answers returned. In typing my query, I probably meant the New York Yankees beating the Boston Red Sox of Major League Baseball, but I didn't say that—maybe I meant the Flagstaff Yankees and the Continental Red Sox of Arizona Little League Baseball.

Finding all the relevant documents is referred to as "recall." Because the World Wide Web is so vast, there is no reasonable way to determine if the search engine is finding everything that is relevant. Total recall is unachievable—but it is also unimportant. Jen could give us thousands or even millions more responses that she judges to be relevant, but we are unlikely to look beyond the first page or two. Degree of relevance always trumps level of recall. Users want to find a few good results, not all possible results.

The science of measuring relevance is much older than the Web; it goes back to work by Gerald Salton in the 1960s, first at Harvard and later at Cornell. The trick is to automate a task when what counts as success has such a large subjective component. We want the computer to scan the document, look at the query, do a few calculations, and come up with a number suggesting how relevant the document is to the query.

As a very simple example of how we might calculate the relevance of a document to a query, suppose there are 500,000 words in the English language. Construct two lists of 500,000 numbers: one for the document and one for the query. Each position in the lists corresponds to one of the 500,000 words—for example, position #3682 might be for the word "drugs." For the document, each position contains a count of the number of times the corresponding word occurs in the document. Do the same thing for the query—unless it contains repeated words, each position will be 1 or 0. Multiply the lists for the document and the query, position by position, and add up the 500,000 results. If no word in the query appears in the document, you'll get a result of 0; otherwise, you will get a result greater than 0. The more frequently words from the query appear in the document, the larger the results will be.

> ### SEARCH ENGINES AND INFORMATION RETRIEVAL
>
> Three articles offer interesting insights into how search engines and information retrieval work:
>
> "The Anatomy of a Large-Scale Hypertextual Web Search Engine" by Sergey Brin and Larry Page was written in 2000 and gives a clear description of how the original Google worked, what the goal was, and how it was differentiated from earlier search engines.
>
> "Modern Information Retrieval: A Brief Overview" by Amit Singhal was written in 2001 and surveys the IR scene. Singhal was a student of Gerry Salton and is now a Google Fellow.
>
> "The Most Influential Paper Gerald Salton Never Wrote" by David Dubin presents an interesting look at some of the origins of the science.

Figure 4.5 shows how the relevance calculation might proceed for the query "Yankees beat Red Sox" and the visible part of the third document of Figure 4.4, which begins, "Red Sox rout Yankees ...." (The others probably contain more of the keywords later in the full document.) The positions in the two lists correspond to words in a dictionary in alphabetical order, from "ant" to "zebra." The words "red" and "sox" appear two times each in the snippet of the story, and the word "Yankees" appears three times.

| Lexicon: ant, ..., beat, ..., defeating, ..., new, ..., patriots, ..., red, ..., sox, ..., Yankees, ..., zebra, ... | | | | | | | | |
|---|---|---|---|---|---|---|---|---|
| Doc: | 0, ..., | 1, ..., | 2, ..., | 1, ..., | 0, ..., | 2, ..., | 2, ..., | 3, ..., | 0, ... |
| Query: | 0, ..., | 1, ..., | 0, ..., | 0, ..., | 0, ..., | 1, ..., | 1, ..., | 1, ..., | 0, ... |

| Doc × Query | 0, ..., | 1, ..., | 0, ..., | 0, ..., | 0, ..., | 2, ..., | 2, ..., | 3, ..., | 0, ... |
|---|---|---|---|---|---|---|---|---|---|

Sum of elements of Doc × Query = 1+2+2+3 = 8 = "relevance" of document to query

FIGURE 4.5   Document and query lists for relevance calculation.

That is a very crude relevance calculation—problems with it are easy to spot. Long documents tend to be measured as more relevant than short documents, because they have more word repetitions. Uninteresting words such as "from" add as much to the relevance score as more significant terms such as "Yankees." Web search engines such as Google, Yahoo!, MSN, and Ask.com consider many other factors in addition to which words occur and how often. In the list for the document, perhaps the entries are not word counts, but another number, adjusted so words in the title of the page get greater weight. Words in a larger font might also count more heavily. In a query, users tend to type more important terms first, so maybe the weights should depend on where words appear in the query.

## Step 6: Determine Ranking

Once Jen has selected the relevant documents—perhaps she's chosen all the documents whose relevance score is above a certain threshold—she "ranks" the search results (that is, puts them in order). Ranking is critical in making the search useful. A search may return thousands of relevant results, and users want to see only a few of them. The simplest ranking is by relevance—putting the page with the highest relevance score first. That doesn't work well, however. For one thing, with short queries, many of the results will have approximately the same relevance.

More fundamentally, the documents Jen returns should be considered "good results" not just because they have high relevance to the query, but also because the documents themselves have high quality. Alas, it is hard to say what "quality" means in the search context, when the ultimate test of success is providing what people want. In the example of the earlier sidebar, who is to judge whether the many links to material about Britney Spears are really "better" answers to the "spears" query than the link to Professor Spears? And whatever "quality" may be, the ranking process for the major web search engines takes place automatically, without human intervention. There is no way to include protocols for checking professional licenses and past convictions for criminal fraud—not in the current state of the Web, at least.

Even though quality can't be measured automatically, something like "importance" or "reputation" can be extracted from the structure of linkages that holds the Web together. To take a crude analogy, if you think of web pages as scientific publications, the reputations of scientists tend to rise if their work is widely cited in the work of other scientists. That's far from a

## WHAT MAKES A PAGE SEARCHABLE

No search provider discloses the full details of its relevance and ranking algorithm. The formulas remain secret because they offer competitive advantages, and because knowing what gives a page high rank makes abuse easier. But here are some of the factors that might be taken into account:

- Whether a keyword is used in the title of the web page, a major heading, or a second-level heading
- Whether it appears only in the body text, and if so, how "prominently"
- Whether the web site is considered "trustworthy"
- Whether the pages linked to from within the page are themselves relevant
- Whether the pages that link to this page are relevant
- Whether the page is old or young
- Whether the pages it links to are old or young
- Whether it passes some objective quality metric—for example, not containing any misspellings

Once you go to the trouble of crawling the Web, there is plenty to analyze, if you have the computing power to do it!

perfect system for judging the importance of scientific work—junk science journals do exist, and sometimes small groups of marginal scientists form mutual admiration societies. But for the Web, looking at the linkage structure is a place to start to measure the significance of pages.

One of Google's innovations was to enhance the relevance metric with another numerical value called "PageRank." PageRank is a measure of the "importance" of each a page that takes into account the external references to it—a World Wide Web popularity contest. If more web pages link to a particular page, goes the logic, it must be more important. In fact, a page should be judged more important if a lot of *important* pages link to it than if the same number of unimportant pages link to it. That seems to create a circular definition of importance, but the circularity can be resolved—with a bit of mathematics and a lot of computing power.

This way of ranking the search results seems to reward reputation and to be devoid of judgment—it is a mechanized way of aggregating mutual opinions. For example, when we searched using Google for "schizophrenia drugs," the top result was part of the site of a Swedish university. Relevance was certainly part of the reason that page came up first; the page was specifically about drugs used to treat schizophrenia, and the words "schizophrenia" and "drugs" both appeared in the title of the page. Our choice of words affected the relevance of the page—had we gone to the trouble to type "medicines" instead of "drugs," this link wouldn't even have made it to the first page of search results. Word order matters, too—Google returns different results for "drugs schizophrenia" than for "schizophrenia drugs."

Sergey Brin and Larry Page, Google's founders, were graduate students at Stanford when they developed the company's early technologies. The "Page" in "PageRank" refers not to web pages, but to Larry Page.

This page may also have been ranked high because many other web pages contained references to it, particularly if many of those pages were themselves judged to be important. Other pages about schizophrenia drugs may have used better English prose style, may have been written by more respected scientific authorities, and may have contained more up-to-date information and fewer factual errors. The ranking algorithm has no way to judge any of that, and no one at Google reads every page to make such judgments.

Google, and other search engines that rank pages automatically, use a secret recipe for ranking—a pinch of this and a dash of that. Like the formula for Coca-Cola, only a few people know the details of commercial ranking algorithms. Google's algorithm is patented, so anyone can read a description. Figure 4.6 is an illustration from that patent, showing several pages with links to each other. This illustration suggests that both the documents themselves and the links between them might be assigned varying numbers as measures of their importance. But the description omits many details and, as actually implemented, has been adjusted countless times to improve its performance. A company's only real claim for the validity of its ranking formula is that people like the results it delivers—if they did not, they would shift to one of the competing search engines.

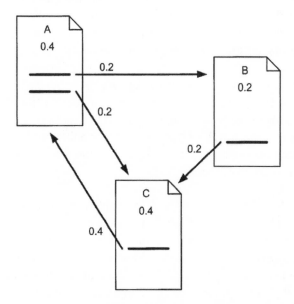

FIGURE 4.6   A figure from the PageRank patent (U.S. Patent #6285999), showing how links between documents might receive different weights.

It may be that one of the things people like about their favored search engine is consistently getting what they believe to be unbiased, useful, and even truthful information. But "telling the truth" in search results is ultimately only a means to an end—the end being greater profits for the search company.

Ranking is a matter of opinion. But a lot hangs on those opinions. For a user, it usually does not matter very much which answer comes up first or whether any result presented is even appropriate to the query. But for a company offering a product, where it appears in the search engine results *can* be a matter of life and death.

KinderStart (www.kinderstart.com) runs a web site that includes a directory and search engine focused on products and services for young children. On March 19, 2005, visits to its site declined by 70% when Google lowered its PageRank to zero (on a scale of 0 to 10). Google may have deemed KinderStart's page to be low quality because its ranking algorithm found the page to consist mostly of links to other sites. Google's public description of its criteria warns about pages with "little or no original content." KinderStart saw matters differently and mounted a class action lawsuit against Google, claiming, among other things, that Google had violated its rights to free speech under the First Amendment by making its web site effectively invisible. Google countered that KinderStart's low PageRank was just Google's opinion, and opinions were not matters to be settled in court:

> Google, like every other search engine operator, has made that determination for its users, exercising its judgment and expressing its opinion about the relative significance of web sites in a manner that has made it the search engine of choice for millions. Plaintiff KinderStart contends that the judiciary should have the final say over that editorial process.

## SEEING A PAGE'S PAGERANK

Google has a toolbar you can add to certain browsers, so you can see PageRanks of web pages. It is downloadable from toolbar. google.com. You can also use the site www.iwebtool.com/ pagerank_checker to enter a URL in a window and check its PageRank.

No fair, countered KinderStart to Google's claim to be just expressing an opinion. "PageRank," claimed KinderStart, "is not a mere statement of opinion of the innate value or human appeal of a given web site and its web pages," but instead is "a mathematically-generated product of measuring and assessing the quantity and depth of all the hyperlinks on the Web that tie into PageRanked web site, under programmatic determination by Defendant Google."

The judge rejected every one of KinderStart's contentions—and not just the claim that KinderStart had a free speech right to be more visible in Google searches. The judge also rejected claims that Google was a monopoly guilty of antitrust violations, and that KinderStart's PageRank of zero amounted to a defamatory statement about the company.

Whether it's a matter of opinion or manipulation, KinderStart is certainly much easier to find using Yahoo! than Google. Using Yahoo!, `kinderstart.com` is the top item returned when searching for "kinderstart." When we used Google, however, it did not appear until the twelfth page of results.

A similar fate befell `bmw.de`, the German web page of automaker BMW. The page Google indexed was straight text, containing the words "gebrauchtwagen" and "neuwagen" ("used car" and "new car") dozens of times. But a coding trick caused viewers instead to see a more conventional page with few words and many pictures. The effect was to raise BMW's position in searches for "new car" and "used car," but the means violated Google's clear instructions to web site designers: "Make pages for users, not for search engines. Don't deceive your users or present different content to search engines than you display to users, which is commonly referred to as 'cloaking.'" Google responded with a "death penalty"–removing `bmw.de` from its index. For a time, the page simply ceased to exist in Google's universe. The punitive measure showed that Google was prepared to act harshly against sites attempting to gain rank in ways it deemed consumers would not find helpful–and at the same time, it also made clear that Google was prepared to take *ad hoc* actions against individual sites.

## Step 7: Presenting Results

After all the marvelous hard work of Steps 1–6, search engines typically provide the results in a format that is older than Aristotle–the simple, top-to-bottom list. There are less primitive ways of displaying the information.

If you search for something ambiguous like "washer" with a major web search engine, you will be presented with a million results, ranging from clothes washers to software packages that remove viruses. If you search Home Depot's web site for "washer," you will get a set of automatically generated choices to assist you in narrowing the search: a set of categories, price ranges, brand names, and more, complete with pictures (see Figure 4.7).

Alternatives to the simple rank-ordered list for presenting results better utilize the visual system. Introducing these new forms of navigation may shift the balance of power in the search equation. Being at the top of the list may no longer have the same economic value, but something else may replace the currently all-important rank of results–quality of the graphics, for example.

No matter how the results are presented, something else appears alongside them, and probably always will. It is time to talk about those words from the sponsors.

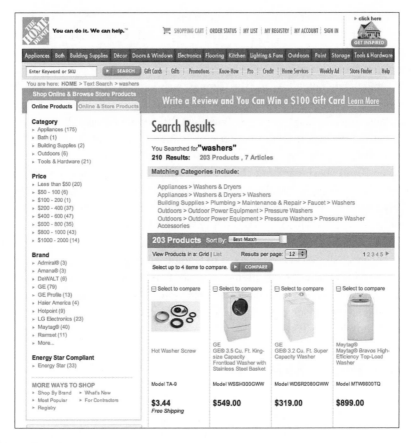

Source: Home Depot.

FIGURE 4.7   Results page from a search for "washers" on the Home Depot web site.

# Who Pays, and for What?

Web search is one of the most widely used functions of computers. More than 90% of online adults use search engines, and more than 40% use them on a typical day. The popularity of search engines is not hard to explain. Search engines are generally free for anyone to use. There are no logins, no fine print to agree to, no connection speed parameters to set up, and no personal information to be supplied that you'd rather not give away. If you have an Internet connection, then you almost certainly have a web browser, and it probably comes with a web search engine on its startup screen. There are no directions to read, at least to get started. Just type some words and answers come back. You can't do anyone any harm by typing random queries and seeing what happens. It's even fun.

Perhaps because search is so useful and easy, we are likely to think of our search engine as something like a public utility—a combination of an encyclopedia and a streetlamp, a single source supplying endless amounts of information to anyone. In economic terms, that is a poor analogy. Utilities charge for whatever they provide—water, gas, or electricity—and search firms don't. Utilities typically don't have much competition, and search firms do. Yet we trust search engines as though they were public utilities because their results just flow to us, and because the results seem consistent with our expectations. If we ask for American Airlines, we find its web site, and if we ask for "the price of tea in China," we find both the actual price ($1.84 for 25 tea bags) and an explanation of the phrase. And perhaps we trust them because we assume that machines are neutral and not making value judgments. The fact that our expectations are rarely disappointed does not, however, mean that our intuitions are correct.

Who pays for all this? There are four possibilities:

- The users could pay, perhaps as subscribers to a service.

- Web sites could pay for the privilege of being discovered.

- The government or some nonprofit entity could pay.

- Advertisers could pay.

All four business models have all been tried.

## Commercial-Free Search

In the very beginning, universities and the government paid, as a great deal of information retrieval research was conducted in universities under federal grants and contracts. WebCrawler, one of the first efforts to crawl the Web in order to produce an index of terms found on web pages, was Brian Pinkerton's research project at the University of Washington. He published a paper about it in 1994, at an early conference on the World Wide Web. The 1997 academic research paper by Google's founders, explaining PageRank, acknowledges support by the National Science Foundation, the Defense Advanced Research Projects Agency, and the National Aeronautics and Space Administration, as well as several industrial supporters of Stanford's computer science research programs. To this day, Stanford University owns the patent on the PageRank algorithm—Google is merely the exclusive licensee.

Academia and government were the wellsprings of search technology, but that was before the Web became big business. Search needed money to grow. Some subscription service web sites, such as AOL, offered search engines. Banner ads appeared on web sites even before search engines became the way to find things, so it was natural to offer advertising to pay for search engine sites. Banner ads are the equivalent of billboards or displayed ads in newspapers. The advertiser buys some space on a page thought promising to bring in some business for the advertiser, and displays an eye-catching come-on.

With the advent of search, it was possible to sell advertising space depending on what was searched for—"targeted advertising" that would be seen only by viewers who might have an interest in the product. To advertise cell phones, for example, ads might be posted only on the result pages of searches involving the term "phone." Like billboards, banner ads bring in revenue. And also like billboards, posting too many of them, with too much distracting imagery, can annoy the viewer!

*There was a presumed, generally acknowledged ethical line. Payola was a no-no.*

Whichever business model was in use, there was a presumed, generally acknowledged ethical line. If you were providing a search engine, you were not supposed to accept payments to alter the presentation of your results. If you asked for information, you expected the results to be impartial, even if they were subjective. Payola was a no-no. But there was a very fine line between partiality and subjectivity, and the line was drawn in largely unexplored territory. That territory was expanding rapidly, as the Web moved out of the academic and research setting and entered the world of retail stores, real estate brokers, and impotence cures.

Holding a line against commercialism posed a dilemma—what Brin and Page, in their original paper, termed the "mixed motives" of advertising-based search engines. How would advertisers respond if the engine provided highly ranked pages that were unfriendly to their product? Brin and Page noted that a search for "cell phones" on their prototype search engine returned an article about the dangers of talking on cell phones while driving. Would cell phone companies really pay to appear on the same page with information that might discourage people from buying cell phones? Because of such conflicts, Google's founders predicted "that advertising funded search engines will be inherently biased toward the advertisers and away from the needs of the consumers." They noted that one search engine, Open Text, had already gotten out of the search engine business after it was reported to be selling rank for money.

## Placements, Clicks, and Auctions

Only a year later, the world had changed. Starting in 1998, Overture (originally named GoTo.com) made a healthy living by leaping with gusto over the presumed ethical line. That line turned out to have been a chasm mainly in the minds of academics. Overture simply charged advertisers to be searchable, and charged them more for higher rankings in the search results. The argument in favor of this simple commercialism was that if you could afford to pay to be seen, then your capacity to spend money on advertising probably reflected the usefulness of your web page. It mattered not whether this was logical, nor whether it offended purists. It seemed to make people happy. Overture's CEO explained the company's rationale in simple terms. Sounding every bit like a broker in the bazaar arguing with the authorities, Jeffrey Brewer explained, "Quite frankly, there's no understanding of how any service provides results. If consumers are satisfied, they really are not interested in the mechanism."

Customers were indeed satisfied. In the heady Internet bubble of the late 1990s, commercial sites were eager to make themselves visible, and users were eager to find products and services. Overture introduced a second innovation, one that expanded its market beyond the sites able to pay the substantial up-front fees that AOL and Yahoo! charged for banner ads. Overture charged advertisers nothing to have their links posted—it assessed fees only if users clicked on those links from Overture's search results page. A click was only a penny to start, making it easy for small-budget Web companies to buy advertising. Advertisers were eager to sign up for this "pay-per-click" (PPC) service. They might not get a sale on every click, but at least they were paying only for viewers who took the trouble to learn a little bit more than what was in the advertisement.

As a search term became popular, the price for links under that term went up. The method of setting prices was Overture's third innovation. If several advertisers competed for the limited real estate on a search results page, Overture held an auction among them and charged as much as a dollar a click. The cost per click adjusted up and down, depending on how many other customers were competing for use of the same keyword. If a lot of advertisers wanted links to their sites to appear when you searched for "camera," the price per click would rise. Real estate on the screen was a finite resource, and the market would determine the going rates. Auctioning keywords was simple, sensible, and hugely profitable.

Ironically, the bursting of the Internet bubble in 2000 only made Overture's pay-for-ranking, pay-per-click, keyword auction model more attractive. As profits and capital dried up, Internet businesses could no longer afford up-front capital to buy banner ads, some of which seemed to yield meager results. As a result, many companies shifted their advertising budgets to Overture and other services that adopted some of Overture's innovations. The bursting bubble affected the hundreds of early search companies as well. As competition took its toll, Yahoo! and AOL both started accepting payment for search listings.

## Uncle Sam Takes Note

Different search engines offered different levels of disclosure about the pay-for-placement practice. Yahoo! labeled the paid results with the word "Sponsored," the term today generally accepted as the correct euphemism for "paid advertisement." Others used vaguer terms such as "partner results" or "featured listings." Microsoft's MSN offered a creative justification for its use of the term "featured" with no other explanation: MSN's surveys showed that consumers already assumed that search results were for sale—so there was no need to tell them! With the information superhighway becoming littered with roadkill, business was less fun, and business tactics became less grounded in the utopian spirit that had given birth to the Internet. "We can't afford to have ideological debates anymore," said Evan Thornley, CEO of one startup. "We're a public company."

At first, the government stayed out of all this, but in 2001, Ralph Nader's watchdog organization, Consumer Alert, got involved. Consumer Alert filed a complaint with the Federal Trade Commission alleging that eight search engine vendors were deceiving consumers by intermingling "paid inclusion" and "paid placement" results along with those that were found by the search engine algorithm. Consumer Alert's Executive Director, Gary Ruskin, was direct in his accusation: "These search engines have chosen crass commercialism over editorial integrity. We are asking the FTC to make sure that no one is tricked by the search engines' descent into commercial deception. If they are going to stuff ads into search results, they should be required to say that the ads are ads."

The FTC agreed, and requested search engines to clarify the distinction between organic results and sponsored results. At the same time, the FTC issued a consumer alert to advise and inform consumers of the practice (see Figure 4.8). Google shows its "sponsored links" to the right, as in Figure 4.1, or slightly indented. Yahoo! shows its "sponsor results" on a colored background.

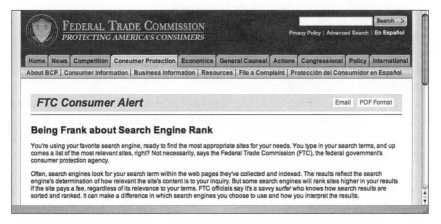

Source: Federal Trade Commission.

FIGURE **4.8**   FTC Consumer Alert about paid ranking of search results.

## Google Finds Balance Without Compromise

As the search engine industry was struggling with its ethical and fiscal problems in 2000, Google hit a vein of gold.

Google already had the PageRank algorithm, which produced results widely considered superior to those of other search engines. Google was fast, in part because its engineers had figured out how to split both background and foreground processing across many machines operating in parallel. Google's vast data storage was so redundant that you could pull out a disk drive anywhere and the engine didn't miss a beat. Google was not suspected of taking payments for rankings. And Google's interface was not annoying— no flashy banner ads (no banner ads at all, in fact) on either the home page or the search results page. Google's home page was a model of understatement. There was almost nothing on it except for the word "Google," the search window, and the option of getting a page of search results or of "feeling lucky" and going directly to the top hit (an option that was more valuable when many users had slow dialup Internet connections).

There were two other important facts about Google in early 2000: Google was expanding, and Google was not making much money. Its technology was successful, and lots of people were using its search engine. It just didn't have a viable business model—until AdWords.

Google's AdWords allows advertisers to participate in an auction of keywords, like Overture's auction for search result placement. But when you win an AdWords auction, you simply get the privilege of posting a small text advertisement on Google's search results pages under certain circumstances—not the right to have your web site come up as an organic search result. The beauty of the system was that it didn't interfere with the search results, was relatively unobtrusive, was keyed to the specific search, and did not mess up the screen with irritating banner ads.

At first, Google charged by the "impression"—that is, the price of your AdWords advertisement simply paid for having it shown, whether or not anyone clicked on it. AdWords switched to Overture's pay-per-click business model in 2002. Initially, the advertisements were sold one at a time, through a human agent at Google. AdWords took off when the process of placing an advertisement was automated. To place an ad today, you simply fill out a web form with information about what search terms you want to target, what few words you want as the text of your ad—and what credit card number Google can use to charge its fee.

Google's technology was brilliant, but none of the elements of its business model was original. With the combination, Google took off and became a giant. The advertising had no effect on the search results, so confidence in the quality of Google's search results was undiminished. AdWords enabled Google to achieve the balance Brin and Page had predicted would be impossible: commercial sponsorship without distorted results. Google emerged—from this dilemma, at least—with its pocketbooks overflowing and its principles intact.

## Banned Ads

Targeted ads, such as Google's AdWords, are changing the advertising industry. Online ads are more cost-effective because the advertiser can control who sees them. The Internet makes it possible to target advertisements not just by search term, but geographically—to show different ads in California than in Massachusetts, for example. The success of web advertising has blown to bits a major revenue source for newspapers and television. The media and communications industries have not yet caught up with the sudden reallocation of money and power.

*The success of web advertising has blown to bits a major revenue source for newspapers and television.*

As search companies accumulate vast advertising portfolios, they control what products, legal or illegal, may be promoted. Their lists result from a combination of legal requirements, market demands, and corporate philosophy. The combined effect of these decisions represents a kind of soft censorship—with which newspapers have long been familiar, but which acquires new significance as search sites become a dominant advertising engine. Among the items and services for which Google will not accept advertisements are fake designer goods, child pornography (some adult material is permitted in the U.S., but not if the models *might* be underage), term paper writing services, illegal drugs and some legal herbal substances, drug paraphernalia, fireworks, online gambling, miracle cures, political attack ads (although political advertising is allowed in general), prostitution, traffic radar jammers, guns, and brass knuckles. The list paints a striking portrait of what Joe and Mary Ordinary want to see, should see, or will tolerate seeing—and perhaps also how Google prudentially restrains the use of its powerfully liberating product for illegal activities.

# Search Is Power

At every step of the search process, individuals and institutions are working hard to control what we see and what we find—not to do us ill, but to help us. Helpful as search engines are, they don't have panels of neutral experts deciding what is true or false, or what is important or irrelevant. Instead, there are powerful economic and social motivations to present information that is to our liking. And because the inner workings of the search engines are not visible, those controlling what we see are themselves subject to few controls.

## *Algorithmic Does Not Mean Unbiased*

Because search engines compute relevance and ranking, because they are "algorithmic" in their choices, we often assume that they, unlike human researchers, are immune to bias. But bias can be coded into a computer program, introduced by small changes in the weights of the various factors that go into the ranking recipe or the spidering selection algorithm. And even what *counts* as bias is a matter of human judgment.

Having a lot of money will not buy you a high rank by paying that money to Google. Google's PageRank algorithm nonetheless incorporates something of a bias in favor of the already rich and powerful. If your business has become successful, a lot of other web pages are likely to point to yours, and that increases your PageRank. This makes sense and tends to produce the results that most people feel are correct. But the degree to which power should beget more power is a matter over which powerful and marginal businesses might have different views. Whether the results "seem right," or the search algorithm's parameters need adjusting, is a matter only humans can judge.

For a time, Amazon customers searching for books about abortion would get back results including the question, "Did you mean adoption?" When a pro-choice group complained, Amazon responded that the suggestion was automatically generated, a consequence of the similarity of the words. The search engine had noticed, over time, that many people who searched for "abortion" also searched for "adoption." But Amazon agreed to make the *ad hoc* change to its search algorithm to treat the term "abortion" as a special case. In so doing, the company unintentionally confirmed that its algorithms sometimes incorporate elements of human bias.

Market forces are likely to drive commercially viable search engines toward the bias of the majority, and also to respond to minority interests only in proportion to their political power. Search engines are likely to favor fresh items over older and perhaps more comprehensive sources, because their users go to the Internet to get the latest information. If you rely on a search engine to discover information, you need to remember that others are making judgment calls for you about what you are being shown.

## Not All Search Engines Are Equal

When we use a search engine, we may think that what we are getting is a representative sample of what's available. If so, what we get from one search engine should be pretty close to what we get from another. This is very far from reality.

A study comparing queries to Google, Yahoo!, ASK, and MSN showed that the results returned on the first page were unique 88% percent of the time. Only 12% of the first-page results were in common to even two of these four search engines. If you stick with one search engine, you could be missing what you're looking for. The tool ranking.thumbshots.com provides vivid graphic representations of the level of overlap between the results of different search engines, or different searches using the same search engine. For example, Figure 4.9 shows how little overlap exists between Google and Yahoo! search results for "boston florist."

Each of the hundred dots in the top row represents a result of the Google search, with the highest-ranked result at the left. The bottom row represents Yahoo!'s results. A line connects each pair of identical search results—in this case, only 11% of the results were in common. Boston Rose Florist, which is Yahoo's number-one response, doesn't turn up in Google's search at all—not in the top 100, or even in the first 30 pages Google returns.

Ranking determines visibility. An industry research study found that 62% of search users click on a result from the first page, and 90% click on a result within the first three pages. If they don't find what they are looking for, more than 80% start the search over with the same search engine, changing the keywords—as though confident that the search engine "knows" the right answer, but they haven't asked the right question. A study of queries to the Excite search engine found that more than 90% of queries were resolved in the first three pages. Google's experience is even more concentrated on the first page.

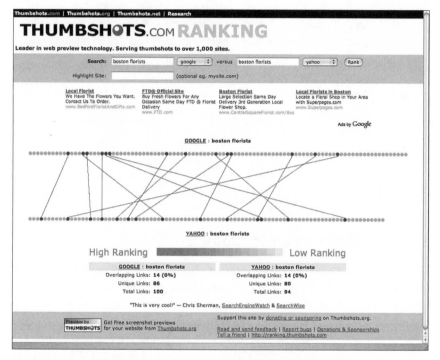

Reprinted with permission of SmartDevil, Inc.

FIGURE 4.9    Thumbshots comparison of Google and Yahoo! search results for "boston florists."

Search engine users have great confidence that they are being given results that are not only useful but authoritative. 36% of users thought seeing a company listed among the top search results indicated that it was a top company in its field; only 25% said that seeing a company ranked high in search results would not lead them to think that it was a leader in its field. There is, in general, no reason for such confidence that search ranking corresponds to corporate quality.

## CAT AND MOUSE WITH BLOG SPAMMERS

You may see comments on a blog consisting of nothing but random words and a URL. A malicious bot is posting these messages in the hope that Google's spider will index the blog page, including the spam URL. With more pages linking to the URL, perhaps its PageRank will increase and it will turn up in searches. Blogs counter by forcing you to type some distorted letters—a so-called *captcha* ("Completely Automated Public Turing test to tell Computers and Humans Apart"), a test to determine if the party posting the comment is really a person and not a bot. Spammers counter by having their bot take a copy of the captcha and show it to human volunteers. The spam bot then takes what the volunteers type and uses it to gain entry to the blog site. The volunteers are recruited by being given access to free pornography if they type the captcha's text correctly! Here is a sample captcha:

This image has been released into the public domain by its author, Kruglov at the wikipedia project. This applies worldwide.

## Search Results Can Be Manipulated

Search is a remarkable business. Internet users put a lot of confidence in the results they get back from commercial search engines. Buyers tend to click on the first link, or at least a link on the first page, even though those links may depend heavily on the search engine they happen to be using, based on complex technical details that hardly anyone understands. For many students, for example, the library is an information source of last resort, if that. They do research as though whatever their search engine turns up must be a link to the truth. If people don't get helpful answers, they tend to blame themselves and change the question, rather than try a different search engine—even though the answers they get can be inexplicable and capricious, as anyone googling "kinderstart" to find kinderstart.com will discover.

Under these circumstances, anyone putting up a web site to get a message out to the world would draw an obvious conclusion. Coming out near the top of the search list is too important to leave to chance. Because ranking is algorithmic, a set of rules followed with diligence and precision, it must be possible to manipulate the results. The Search Engine Optimization industry (SEO) is based on that demand.

Search Engine Optimization is an activity that seeks to improve how particular web pages rank within major search engines, with the intent of increasing the traffic that will come to those web sites. Legitimate businesses try to optimize their sites so they will rank higher than their competitors. Pranksters and pornographers try to optimize their sites, too, by fooling the search engine algorithms into including them as legitimate results, even though their trappings of legitimacy are mere disguises. The search engine companies tweak their algorithms in order to see through the disguises, but their tweaks sometimes have unintended effects on legitimate businesses. And the tweaking is largely done in secret, to avoid giving the manipulators any ideas about countermeasures. The result is a chaotic battle, with innocent bystanders, who have become reliant on high search engine rankings, sometimes injured as the rules of engagement keep changing.

Google proclaims of its PageRank algorithm that "Democracy on the web works," comparing the ranking-by-inbound-links to a public election. But the analogy is limited—there are many ways to manipulate the "election," and the voting rules are not fully disclosed.

The key to search engine optimization is to understand how particular engines do their ranking—what factors are considered, and what weights they are given—and then to change your web site to improve your score. For example, if a search engine gives greater weight to key words that appear in the title, and you want your web page to rank more highly when someone searches for "cameras," you should put the word "cameras" in the title. The weighting factors may be complex and depend on factors external to your own web page—for example, external links that point to your page, the age of the link, or the prestige of the site from which it is linked. So significant time, effort, and cost must be expended in order to have a meaningful impact on results.

Then there are techniques that are sneaky at best—and "dirty tricks" at worst. Suppose, for example, that you are the web site designer for Abelson's, a new store that wants to compete with Bloomingdale's. How would you entice people to visit Abelson's site when they would ordinarily go to Bloomingdale's? If you put "We're better than Bloomingdale's!" on your web page, Abelson's page might appear in the search results for "Bloomingdale's." But you might not be willing to pay the price of mentioning the competition on Abelson's page. On the other hand, if you just put the word "Bloomingdale's" *in white text on a white background* on Abelson's page, a human viewer wouldn't see it—but the indexing software might index it anyway. The indexer is working with the HTML code that generates the page, not the visible page itself. The software might not be clever enough to realize that the word "Bloomingdale's" in the HTML code for Abelson's web page would not actually appear on the screen.

A huge industry has developed around SEO, rather like the business that has arisen around getting high school students packaged for application to college. A Google search for "search engine optimization" returned 11 sponsored links, including some with ads reading "Page 1 Rankings Guarantee" and "Get Top Rankings Today."

Is the search world more ethical because the commercial rank-improving transactions are indirect, hidden from the public, and going to the optimization firms rather than to the search firms? After all, it is only logical that if you have an important message to get out, you would optimize your site to do so. And you probably wouldn't have a web site at all if you thought you had nothing important to say. Search engine companies tend to advise their web site designers just to create better, more substantive web pages, in much the same way that college admissions officials urge high school students just to learn more in school. Neither of the dependent third-party "optimization" industries is likely to disappear anytime soon because of such principled advice.

And what's "best"—for society in general, not just for the profits of the search companies or the companies that rely on them—can be very hard to say. In his book, *Ambient Findability*, Peter Morville describes the impact of search engine optimization on the National Cancer Institute's site, www. cancer.gov. The goal of the National Cancer Institute is to provide the most reliable and the highest-quality information to people who need it the most,

## GOOGLE BOMBING

A "Google bomb" is a prank that causes a particular search to return mischievous results, often with political content. For example, if you searched for "miserable failure" after the 2000 U.S. presidential election, you got taken to the White House biography of George Bush. The libertarian Liberty Round Table mounted an effort against the Center for Science in the Public Interest, among others. In early 2008, www.libertyroundtable.org read, "Have you joined the Google-bombing fun yet? Lob your volleys at the food nazis and organized crime. Your participation can really make the difference with this one—read on and join the fun! Current Target: Verizon Communications, for civil rights violations." The site explains what HTML code to include in your web page, supposedly to trick Google's algorithms.

Marek W., a 23-year-old programmer from Cieszyn, Poland, "Google bombed" the country's president, Lech Kaczyński. Searches for "kutas" using Google (it's the Polish word for "penis") returned the president's web site as the first choice. Mr. Kaczyński was not pleased, and insulting the president is a crime in Poland. Marek is now facing three years in prison.

often cancer sufferers and their families. Search for "cancer," and the NCI site was "findable" because it appeared near the topic of the search page results. That wasn't the case, though, when you looked for specific cancers, yet that's exactly what the majority of the intended users did. NCI called in search engine optimization experts, and all that is now changed. If we search for "colon cancer," the specific page on the NCI site about this particular form of cancer appears among the top search results.

Is this good? Perhaps—if you can't trust the National Cancer Institute, who *can* you trust? But WebMD and other commercial sites fighting for the top position might not agree. And a legitimate coalition, the National Colorectal Cancer Roundtable, doesn't appear until page 7, too deep to be noticed by almost any user.

Optimization is a constant game of cat and mouse. The optimizers look for better ways to optimize, and the search engine folks look for ways to produce more reliable results. The game occasionally claims collateral victims. Neil Montcrief, an online seller of large-sized shoes, prospered for a while because searches for "big feet" brought his store, 2bigfeet.com, to the top of the list. One day, Google tweaked its algorithm to combat manipulation. Montcrief's innocent site fell to the twenty-fifth page, with disastrous consequences for his economically marginal and totally web-dependent business.

Manipulating the ranking of search results is one battleground where the power struggle is played out. Because search is the portal to web-based information, controlling the search results allows you, perhaps, to control what people think. So even governments get involved.

## Search Engines Don't See Everything

Standard search engines fail to index a great deal of information that is accessible via the Web. Spiders may not penetrate into databases, read the contents of PDF or other document formats, or search useful sites that require a simple, free registration. With a little more effort than just typing into the search window of Google or Yahoo!, you may be able to find exactly what you are looking for. It is a serious failure to assume that something is unimportant or nonexistent simply because a search engine does not return it. A good overview of resources for finding things in the "deep web" is at Robert Lackie's web site, www.robertlackie.com.

## Search Control and Mind Control

To make a book disappear from a library, you don't have to remove it from the bookshelf. All you need to do is to remove its entry from the library catalog—if there is no record of where to find it, it does not matter if the book actually still exists.

When we search for something, we have an unconfirmed confidence that what the search engine returns is what exists. A search tool is a lens through which we view information. We count on the lens not to distort the scene, although we know it can't show us the entire landscape at once. Like the book gone from the catalog, information that cannot be found may as well not exist. So removing information in the digital world does not require removing the documents themselves. You can make things disappear by banishing them into the un-indexed darkness.

*You can make things disappear by banishing them into the un-indexed darkness.*

By controlling "findability," search tools can be used to hide as well as to reveal. They have become a tool of governments seeking to control what their people know about the world, a theme to which we return in Chapter 7, "You Can't Say That on the Internet." When the Internet came to China, previously unavailable information began pouring into the country. The government responded by starting to erect "the great firewall of China," which filtered out information the government did not want seen. But bits poured in more quickly than offending web sites could be blocked. One of the government's counter-measures, in advance of a Communist Party congress in 2002, was simply to close down certain search engines. "Obviously there is some harmful information on the Internet," said a Chinese spokesman by way of explanation. "Not everyone should have access to this harmful information." Google in particular was unavailable—it may have been targeted because people could sometimes use it to access a cached copy of a site to which the government had blocked direct access.

Search was already too important to the Chinese economy to leave the ban in place for very long. The firewall builders got better, and it became harder to reach banned sites. But such a site might still turn up in Google's search results. You could not access it when you clicked on the link, but you could see what you were missing.

In 2004, under another threat of being cut off from China, Google agreed to censor its news service, which provides access to online newspapers. The company reluctantly decided not to provide any information at all about those stories, reasoning that "simply showing these headlines would likely result in Google News being blocked altogether in China." But the government was not done yet.

The really hard choice came a year later. Google's search engine was available inside China, but because Google's servers were located outside the country, responses were sluggish. And because many of the links that were returned did not work, Google's search engine was, if not useless, at least uncompetitive. A Chinese search engine, Baidu, was getting most of the business.

Google had a yes-or-no decision: to cooperate with the government's web site censorship or to lose the Chinese market. How would it balance its responsibilities to its shareholders to grow internationally with its corporate mission: "to organize the world's information and make it universally accessible and useful"?

> **GOOGLE U.S. VS. GOOGLE CHINA**
> You can try some searches yourself:
> - www.google.com is the version available in the United States.
> - www.google.cn is the version available in China.

Would the company co-founded by an émigré from the Soviet Union make peace with Chinese censorship?

Completely universal accessibility was already more than Google could lawfully accomplish, even in the U.S. If a copyright holder complained that Google was making copyrighted material improperly accessible, Google would respond by removing the link to it from search results. And there were other U.S. laws about web content, such as the Communications Decency Act, which we discuss in Chapter 7.

Google's accommodation to Chinese authorities was, in a sense, nothing more than the normal practice of any company: You have to obey the local laws anywhere you are doing business. China threw U.S. laws back at U.S. critics. "After studying internet legislation in the West, I've found we basically have identical legislative objectives and principles," said Mr. Liu Zhengrong, deputy chief of the Internet Affairs Bureau of the State Council Information Office. "It is unfair and smacks of double standards when (foreigners) criticize China for deleting illegal and harmful messages, while it is legal for U.S. web sites to do so."

And so, when Google agreed in early 2006 to censor its Chinese search results, some were awakened from their dreams of a global information utopia. "While removing search results is inconsistent with Google's mission, providing no information (or a heavily degraded user experience that amounts to no information) is more inconsistent with our mission," a Google statement read. That excuse seemed weak-kneed to some. A disappointed libertarian commentator countered, "The evil of the world is made possible by the sanction that you give it." (This is apparently an allusion to another Google maxim, "Don't be evil"—now revised to read, "You can make money without doing evil.") The U.S. Congress called Google and other search companies on the carpet. "Your abhorrent activities in China are a disgrace," said

California Representative Tom Lantos. "I cannot understand how your corporate executives sleep at night."

The results of Google's humiliating compromise are striking, and anyone can see them. Figure 4.10 shows the top search results returned by the U.S. version of Google in response to the query "falun gong."

Google ™ is a registered trademark of Google, Inc. Reprinted by permission.

FIGURE 4.10    Search results for "falun gong" provided by Google U.S.

By contrast, Figure 4.11 shows the first few results in response to the same query if the Chinese version of Google is used instead. All the results are negative information about the practice, or reports of actions taken against its followers.

Most of the time, whether you use the U.S. or Chinese version of Google, you will get similar results. In particular, if you search for "shoes," you get sponsored links to online shoe stores so Google can pay its bills.

But there are many exceptions. One researcher tested the Chinese version of Google for 10,000 English words and found that roughly 9% resulted in censored responses. Various versions of the list of blocked words exist, and the specifics are certainly subject to change without notice. Recent versions contained such entries as "crime against humanity," "oppression," and "genocide," as well as lists of dissidents and politicians.

Google ™ is a registered trademark of Google, Inc. Reprinted by permission.

FIGURE **4.11**    Results of "falun gong" search returned by Google China.

The search engine lens is not impartial. At this scale, search can be an effective tool of thought control. A Google executive told Congress, "In an imperfect world, we had to make an imperfect choice"—which is surely the truth. But business is business. As Google CEO Eric Schmidt said of the company's practices, "There are

The home page of the OpenNet Initiative at the Berkman Center for Internet and Society, opennet. net, has a tool with which you can check which countries block access to your favorite (or least favorite) web site. A summary of findings appears as the book *Access Denied* (MIT Press, 2008).

many, many ways to run the world, run your company ... If you don't like it, *don't participate*. You're here as a volunteer; we didn't force you to come."

## You Searched for WHAT? Tracking Searches

> **IMAGE SEARCH**
>
> There are search engines for pictures, and searching for faces presents a different kind of privacy threat. Face recognition by computer has recently become quick and reliable. Computers are now better than people at figuring out which photos are of the same person. With millions of photographs publicly accessible on the Web, all that's needed is a single photo tagged with your name to find others in which you appear. Similar technology makes it possible to find products online using images of similar items. Public image-matching services include riya.com, polarrose.com, and like.com.

Search engine companies can store everything you look for, and everything you click on. In the world of limitless storage capacity, it pays for search companies to keep that data—it might come in handy some day, and it is an important part of the search process. But holding search histories also raises legal and ethical questions. The capacity to retain and analyze query history is another power point—only now the power comes from knowledge about what interests you as an individual, and what interests the population as a whole.

But why would search companies bother to keep every keystroke and click? There are good reasons not to—personal privacy is endangered when such data is retained, as we discuss in Chapter 2. For example, under the USA PATRIOT Act, the federal government could, under certain circumstances, require your search company to reveal what you've been searching for, without ever informing you that it is getting that data. Similar conditions are even easier to imagine in more oppressive countries. Chinese dissidents were imprisoned when Yahoo! turned over their email to the government—in compliance with local laws. Representative Chris Smith asked, "If the secret police a half century ago asked where Anne Frank was hiding, would the correct answer be to hand over the information in order to comply with local laws?" What if the data was not email, but search queries?

From the point of view of the search company, it is easy to understand the reason for retaining your every click. Google founder Sergey Brin says it all on the company's "Philosophy" page: "The perfect search engine would understand exactly what you mean and give back exactly what you want." Your search history is revealing—and Jen can read your mind much better if she knows what you have been thinking about in the past.

Search quality can improve if search histories are retained. We may prefer, for privacy reasons, that search engines forget everything that has happened, but there would be a price to pay for that—a price in performance to us, and a consequent price in competitiveness to the search company. There is no free lunch, and whatever we may think in theory about Jen keeping track of our search queries, in practice we don't worry about it very much, even when we know.

Even without tying search data to our personal identity, the aggregated search results over time provide valuable data for marketing and economic analysis. Figure 4.12 shows the pattern of Google searches for "iPhone" alongside the identity of certain news stories. The graph shows the number of news stories (among

> You can track trends yourself at www.google.com/trends.

those Google indexes) that mentioned Apple's iPhone. Search has created a new asset: billions of bits of information about *what* people want to know.

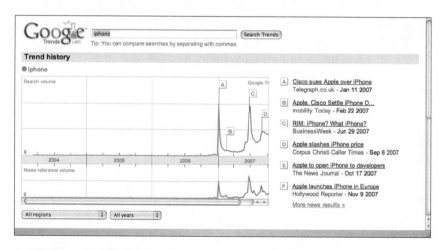

Google ™ is a registered trademark of Google, Inc. Reprinted by permission.

FIGURE 4.12   The top line shows the number of Google searches for "iphone," and the bottom line shows the number of times the iPhone was mentioned in the news sources Google indexes.

# Regulating or Replacing the Brokers

Search engines have become a central point of control in a digital world once imagined as a centerless, utopian universe of free-flowing information. The important part of the search story is not about technology or money, although there is plenty of both. It is about power—the power to make things visible, to cause them to exist or to make them disappear, and to control information and access to information.

*Search engines have become a central point of control in a digital world once imagined as a centerless, utopian universe of free-flowing information.*

Search engines create commercial value not by creating information, but by helping people find it, by understanding what people are interested in finding, and by targeting advertising based on that understanding. Some critics unfairly label this activity "freeloading," as though they themselves could have created a Google had they not preferred to do something more creative (see Chapter 6). It is a remarkable phenomenon: *Information access has greater market value than information creation.* The market capitalization of Google ($157 billion) is more than 50% larger than the combined capitalization of the *New York Times* ($3 billion), Pearson Publishing ($13 billion), eBay ($45 billion), and Macy's ($15 billion). A company providing access to information it did not create has greater market value than those that did the creating. In the bits bazaar, more money is going to the brokers than to the booths.

---

### OPEN ALTERNATIVES

There are hundreds of open source search projects. Because the source of these engines is open, anyone can look at the code and see how it works. Most do not index the whole Web, just a limited piece, because the infrastructure needed for indexing the Web as a whole is too vast. Nutch (`lucene.apache.org/nutch`, `wiki.apache.org/nutch`) is still under development, but already in use for a variety of specialized information domains. Wikia Search, an evolving project of Wikipedia founder Jimmy Wales (`search.wikia.com/wiki/Search_Wikia`), uses Nutch as an engine and promises to draw on community involvement to improve search quality. Moreover, privacy is a founding principle—no identifying data is retained.

The creation and redistribution of power is an unexpected side effect of the search industry. Should any controls be in place, and should anyone (other than services such as searchenginewatch.com) watch over the industry? There have been a few proposals for required disclosure of search engine selection and ranking algorithms, but as long as competition remains in the market, such regulation is unlikely to gain traction in the U.S. And competition there is—although Microsoft pled to the FTC that Google was close to "controlling a virtual monopoly share" of Internet advertising. That charge, rejected by the FTC, brought much merriment to some who recalled Microsoft's stout resistance a few years earlier to charges that it had gained monopoly status in desktop software. Things change quickly in the digital world.

> **METASEARCH**
>
> Tools such as copernic.com, surfwax.com, and dogpile.com are *metasearch engines*—they query various search engines and report results back to the user on the basis of their own ranking algorithms. On the freeloading theory of search, they would be freeloading on the freeloaders!

We rely on search engines. But we don't know what they are doing, and there are no easy answers to the question of what to do about it.

French President Jacques Chirac was horrified that the whole world might rely on American search engines as information brokers. To counter the American hegemony, France and Germany announced plans for a state-sponsored search engine in early 2006. As Chirac put it, "We must take up the challenge posed by the American giants Google and Yahoo. For that, we will launch a European search engine, Quaero." The European governments, he explained, would enter this hitherto private-industry sphere "in the image of the magnificent success of Airbus. ... Culture is not merchandise and cannot be left to blind market forces." A year later, Germany dropped out of the alliance, because, according to one industry source, the "Germans apparently got tired of French America-bashing and the idea of developing an alternative to Google."

So for the time being at least, the search engine market rules, and the buyer must beware. And probably that is as it should be. Too often, well-intentioned efforts to regulate technology are far worse than the imagined evils they were intended to prevent. We shall see several examples in the coming chapters.

———— ✳ ————

Search technology, combined with the World Wide Web, has had an astonishing effect on global access to information. The opportunities it presents for limiting information do not overshadow its capacity to enlighten. Things unimaginable barely a decade ago are simple today. We can all find our lost relatives. We can all find new support groups and the latest medical information for our ailments, no matter how obscure. We can even find facts in books we have never held in our hands. Search shines the light of the digital explosion on things we want to make visible.

Encryption technology has the opposite purpose: to make information secret, even though it is communicated over open, public networks. That paradoxical story of politics and mathematics is the subject of the next chapter.

# CHAPTER 5

# Secret Bits

## How Codes Became Unbreakable

## Encryption in the Hands of Terrorists, and Everyone Else

September 13, 2001. Fires were still smoldering in the wreckage of the World Trade Center when Judd Gregg of New Hampshire rose to tell the Senate what had to happen. He recalled the warnings issued by the FBI years before the country had been attacked: the FBI's most serious problem was "the encryption capability of the people who have an intention to hurt America." "It used to be," the senator went on, "that we had the capability to break most codes because of our sophistication." No more. "The technology has outstripped the code breakers," he warned. Even civil libertarian cryptographer Phil Zimmermann, whose encryption software appeared on the Internet in 1991 for use by human rights workers world-wide, agreed that the terrorists were probably encoding their messages. "I just assumed," he said, "somebody planning something so diabolical would want to hide their activities using encryption."

*Encryption* is the art of encoding messages so they can't be understood by eavesdroppers or adversaries into whose hands the messages might fall. De-scrambling an encrypted message requires knowing the sequence of symbols—the "key"—that was used to encrypt it. An encrypted message may be visible to the world, but without the key, it may as well be hidden in a locked box. Without the key—exactly the right key—the contents of the box, or the message, remains secret.

What was needed, Senator Gregg asserted, was "the cooperation of the community that is building the software, producing the software, and building the equipment that creates the encoding technology"—cooperation, that is, enforced by legislation. The makers of encryption software would have to enable the government to bypass the locks and retrieve the decrypted messages. And what about encryption programs written abroad, which could be shared around the world in the blink of an eye, as Zimmermann's had been? The U.S. should use "the market of the United States as leverage" in getting foreign manufacturers to follow U.S. requirements for "back doors" that could be used by the U.S. government.

By September 27, Gregg's legislation was beginning to take shape. The keys used to encrypt messages would be held in escrow by the government under tight security. There would be a "quasi-judicial entity," appointed by the Supreme Court, which would decide when law enforcement had made its case for release of the keys. Civil libertarians squawked, and doubts were raised as to whether the key escrow idea could actually work. No matter, opined the Senator in late September. "Nothing's ever perfect. If you don't try, you're never going to accomplish it. If you do try, you've at least got some opportunity for accomplishing it."

Abruptly, three weeks later, Senator Gregg dropped his legislative plan. "We are not working on an encryption bill and have no intention to," said the Senator's spokesman on October 17.

On October 24, 2001, Congress passed the USA PATRIOT Act, which gave the FBI sweeping new powers to combat terrorism. But the PATRIOT Act does not mention encryption. U.S. authorities have made no serious attempt to legislate control over cryptographic software since Gregg's proposal.

## *Why Not Regulate Encryption?*

Throughout the 1990s, the FBI had made control of encryption its top legislative priority. Senator Gregg's proposal was a milder form of a bill, drafted by the FBI and reported out favorably by the House Select Committee on Intelligence in 1997, which would have mandated a five-year prison sentence for selling encryption products unless they enabled immediate decryption by authorized officials.

How could regulatory measures that law enforcement deemed critical in 1997 for fighting terrorism drop off the legislative agenda four years later, in the aftermath of the worst terrorist attack ever suffered by the United States of America?

No technological breakthrough in cryptography in the fall of 2001 had legislative significance. There also weren't any relevant diplomatic breakthroughs.

No other circumstances conspired to make the use of encryption by terrorists and criminals an unimportant problem. It was just that something else about encryption had become accepted as more important: the explosion of commercial transactions over the Internet. Congress suddenly realized that it had to allow banks and their customers to use encryption tools, as well as airlines and their customers, and eBay and Amazon and their customers. Anyone using the Internet for commerce needed the protection that encryption provided. Very suddenly, there were millions of such people, so many that the entire U.S. and world economy depended on public confidence in the security of electronic transactions.

The tension between enabling secure conduct of electronic commerce and preventing secret communication among outlaws had been in the air for a decade. Senator Gregg was but the last of the voices calling for restrictions on encryption. The National Research Council had issued a report of nearly 700 pages in 1996 that weighed the alternatives. The report concluded that on balance, efforts to control encryption would be ineffective, and that their costs would exceed any imaginable benefit. The intelligence and defense establishment was not persuaded. FBI Director Louis Freeh testified before Congress in 1997 that "Law enforcement is in unanimous agreement that the widespread use of robust non-key recovery [i.e., non-escrowed] encryption ultimately will devastate our ability to fight crime and prevent terrorism."

Yet only four years later, even in the face of the September 11th attack, the needs of commerce admitted no alternative to widespread dissemination of encryption software to every business in the country, as well as to every home computer from which a commercial transaction might take place. In 1997, average citizens, including elected officials, might never have bought anything online. Congress members' families might not have been regular computer users. By 2001, all that had changed—the digital explosion was happening. Computers had become consumer appliances, Internet connections were common in American homes—and awareness of electronic fraud had become widespread. Consumers did not want their credit card numbers, birthdates, and Social Security numbers exposed on the Internet.

Why is encryption so important to Internet communications that Congress was willing to risk terrorists using encryption, so that American businesses and consumers could use it too? After all, information security is not a new need. People communicating by postal mail, for example, have reasonable assurances of privacy without any use of encryption.

The answer lies in the Internet's open architecture. Bits move through the Internet not in a continuous stream, but in discrete blocks, called *packets*. A packet consists of about 1500 bytes, no more (see the Appendix). Data packets are not like envelopes sent through postal mail, with an address on the outside and contents hidden. They are like postcards, with everything exposed for anyone to see. As the packets move through the Internet, they are steered on their way by computers called *routers,* which are located at the switching points. Every data packet gets handled at every router: stored, examined, checked, analyzed, and sent on its way. Even if all the fibers and wires could be secured, wireless networks would allow bits to be grabbed out of the air without detection.

If you send your credit card number to a store in an ordinary email, you might as well stand in Times Square and shout it at the top of your lungs. By 2001, a lot of credit card numbers were traveling as bits though glass fibers and through the air, and it was impossible to prevent snoopers from looking at them.

The way to make Internet communications secure—to make sure that no one but the intended recipient knows what is in a message—is for the sender to encrypt the information so that only the recipient can decrypt it. If that can be accomplished, then eavesdroppers along the route from sender to receiver can examine the packets all they want. All they will find is an undecipherable scramble of bits.

In a world awakening to Internet commerce, encryption could no longer be thought of as it had been from ancient times until the turn of the third millennium: as armor used by generals and diplomats to protect information critical to national security. Even in the early 1990s, the State Department demanded that an encryption researcher register as an international arms dealer. Now suddenly, encryption was less like a weapon and more like the armored cars used to transport cash on city streets, except that these armored cars were needed by everyone. Encryption was no longer a munition; it was money.

The commoditization of a critical military tool was more than a technology shift. It sparked, and continues to spark, a rethinking of fundamental notions of privacy and of the balance between security and freedom in a democratic society.

"The question," posed MIT's Ron Rivest, one of the world's leading cryptographers, during one of the many debates over encryption policy that occurred during the 1990s, "is whether people should be able to conduct private conversations, immune from government surveillance, even when that surveillance is fully authorized by a Court order." In the post-2001 atmosphere that produced the PATRIOT Act, it's far from certain that Congress would have responded to Rivest's question with a resounding "Yes." But by 2001, commercial realities had overtaken the debates.

To fit the needs of electronic commerce, encryption software had to be widely available. It had to work perfectly and quickly, with no chance of anyone cracking the codes. And there was more: Although encryption had been used for more than four millennia, no method known until the late twentieth century would have worked well enough for Internet commerce. But in 1976, two young mathematicians, operating outside the intelligence community that was the center of cryptography research, published a paper that made a reality out of a seemingly absurd scenario: Two parties work out a secret key that enables them to exchange messages securely—even if they have never met and all their messages to each other are in the open, for anyone to hear. With the invention of *public-key cryptography*, it became possible for every man, woman, and child to transmit credit card numbers to Amazon more securely than any general had been able to communicate military orders fifty years earlier, orders on which the fate of nations depended.

# Historical Cryptography

Cryptography—"secret writing"—has been around almost as long as writing itself. Ciphers have been found in Egyptian hieroglyphics from as early as 2000 B.C. A *cipher* is a method for transforming a message into an obscured form, together with a way of undoing the transformation to recover the message. Suetonius, the biographer of the Caesars, describes Julius Caesar's use of a cipher in his letters to the orator Cicero, with whom he was planning and plotting in the dying days of the Roman Republic: "... if he [Caesar] had anything confidential to say, he wrote it in cipher, that is, by so changing the order of the letters of the alphabet, that not a word could be made out. If anyone wishes to decipher these, and get at their meaning, he must substitute the fourth letter of the alphabet, namely D, for A, and so with the others." In other words, Caesar used a letter-by-letter translation to encrypt his messages:

```
ABCDEFGHIJKLMNOPQRSTUVWXYZ

DEFGHIJKLMNOPQRSTUVWXYZABC
```

To encrypt a message with Caesar's method, replace each letter in the top row by the corresponding letter in the bottom row. For example, the opening of Caesar's Commentaries "Gallia est omnis divisa in partes tres" would be encrypted as:

Plaintext: GALLIA EST OMNIS DIVISA IN PARTES TRES

Ciphertext: JDOOLD HVW RPQLV GLYLVD LQ SDUWHV WUHV

The original message is called the *plaintext* and the encoded message is called the *ciphertext*. Messages are decrypted by doing the reverse substitutions.

This method is called the *Caesar shift* or the *Caesar cipher*. The encryption/decryption rule is easy to remember: "Shift the alphabet three places." Of course, the same idea would work if the alphabet were shifted more than three places, or fewer. The Caesar cipher is really a family of ciphers, with 25 possible variations, one for each different amount of shifting.

Caesar ciphers are very simple, and an enemy who knew that Caesar was simply shifting the plaintext could easily try all the 25 possible shifts of the alphabet to decrypt the message. But Caesar's method is a representative of a larger class of ciphers, called *substitution ciphers*, in which one symbol is substituted for another according to a uniform rule (the same letter is always translated the same way).

There are a great many more substitution ciphers than just shifts. For example, we could scramble the letters according to the rule

```
ABCDEFGHIJKLMNOPQRSTUVWXYZ

XAPZRDWIBMQEOFTYCGSHULJVKN
```

so that A becomes X, B becomes A, C becomes P, and so on. There is a similar substitution for every way of reordering the letters of the alphabet. The number of different reorderings is

$$26 \times 25 \times 24 \times \cdots \times 3 \times 2$$

which is about $4 \times 10^{26}$ different methods—ten thousand times the number of stars in the universe! It would be impossible to try them all. General substitution ciphers must be secure—or so it might seem.

## Breaking Substitution Ciphers

In about 1392, an English author—once thought to be the great English poet Geoffrey Chaucer, although that is now disputed—wrote a manual for use of an astronomical instrument. Parts of this manual, which was entitled *The Equatorie of the Planetis*, were written in a substitution cipher (see Figure 5.1). This puzzle is not as hard as it looks, even though there is very little ciphertext with which to work. We know it is written in English—Middle English, actually—but let's see how far we can get thinking of it as encrypted English.

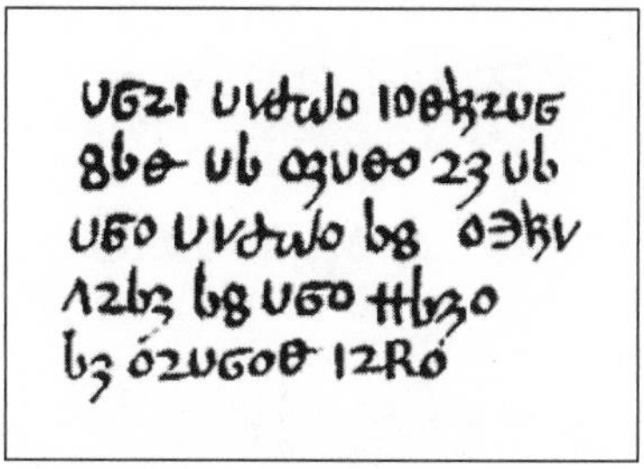

Folio 30v of Peterson MS 75.1, *The Equatorie of Planetis*, a 14th century manuscript held at University of Cambridge.

FIGURE 5.1   Ciphertext in *The Equatorie of Planetis* (1392).

Although this looks like gibberish, it contains some patterns that may be clues. For example, certain symbols occur more frequently than others. There are twelve **♂**s and ten **♄** s, and no other symbol occurs as frequently as these. In ordinary English texts, the two most frequently occurring letters are E and T, so a fair guess is that these two symbols correspond to these two letters. Figure 5.2 shows what happens if we assume that **♂** = E and **♄** = T. The pattern **♄♂** appears twice and apparently represents a three-letter word beginning with T and ending with E. It could be TIE or TOE, but THE seems more likely, so a reasonable assumption is that **♅** = H. If that is true, what is the four-letter word at the beginning of the text, which begins with TH? Not THAT, because it ends with a new symbol, nor THEN, because the third letter is also new. Perhaps THIS. And there is a two-letter word beginning with T that appears twice in the second line—that must be TO. Filling in the equivalencies for H, I, S, and O yields Figure 5.3.

FIGURE 5.2   *Equatorie* ciphertext, with the two most common symbols assumed to stand for E and T.

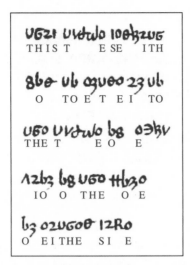

FIGURE 5.3   *Equatorie* ciphertext, with more conjectural decodings.

At this point, the guessing gets easier—probably the last two words are EITHER SIDE—and the last few symbols can be inferred with a knowledge of Middle English and some idea of what the text is about. The complete plaintext is: *This table servith for to entre in to the table of equacion of the mone on either side* (see Figure 5.4).

FIGURE 5.4   *Equatorie* ciphertext, fully decoded.

The technique used to crack the code is *frequency analysis*: If the cipher is a simple substitution of symbols for letters, then crucial information about which symbols represent which letters can be gathered from how often the various symbols appear in the ciphertext. This idea was first described by the Arabic philosopher and mathematician Al-Kindi, who lived in Baghdad in the ninth century.

By the Renaissance, this kind of informed guesswork had been reduced to a fine art that was well known to European governments. In a famous example of the insecurity of substitution ciphers, Mary Queen of Scots was beheaded in 1587 due to her misplaced reliance on a substitution cipher to conceal her correspondence with plotters against Queen Elizabeth I. She was not the last to have put too much confidence in an encryption scheme that looked hard to crack, but wasn't. Substitution ciphers were in common use as late as the 1800s, even though they had been insecure for a millennium by that time! Edgar Allen Poe's mystery story *The Gold Bug* (1843) and A. Conan Doyle's Sherlock Holmes mystery *Adventure of the Dancing Men* (1903) both turn on the decryption of substitution ciphers.

## Secret Keys and One-Time Pads

In cryptography, every advance in code-breaking yields an innovation in code-making. Seeing how easily the *Equatorie* code was broken, what could we do to make it more secure, or *stronger*, as cryptographers would say? We might use more than one symbol to represent the same plaintext letter. A method named for the sixteenth-century French diplomat Blaise de Vigenère uses multiple Caesar ciphers. For example, we can pick twelve Caesar ciphers and use the first cipher for encrypting the 1st, 13th, and 25th letters of the plaintext; the second cipher for encrypting the 2nd, 14th, and 26th plaintext letters; and so on. Figure 5.5 shows such a Vigenère cipher. A plaintext message beginning SECURE... would be encrypted to produce the ciphertext *llqgrw*..., as indicated by the boxed characters in the figure—S is encrypted using the first row, E is encrypted using the second row, and so on. After we use the bottom row of the table, we start again at the top row, and repeat the process over and over.

We can use the cipher of Figure 5.5 without having to send our correspondent the entire table. Scanning down the first column spells out *thomasbbryan*, which is the key for the message. To communicate using Vigenère encryption, the correspondents must first agree on a key. They then use the key to construct a substitution table for encrypting and decrypting messages.

When SECURE was encrypted as *llqgrw*, the two occurrences of E at the second and sixth positions in the plaintext were represented by different ciphertext letters, and the two occurrences of the ciphertext letter *l* represented different plaintext letters. This illustrates how the Vigenère cipher confounds simple frequency analysis, which was the main tool of cryptanalysts at the time. Although the idea may seem simple, the discovery of the Vigenère cipher is regarded as a fundamental advance in cryptography, and the method was considered to be unbreakable for hundreds of years.

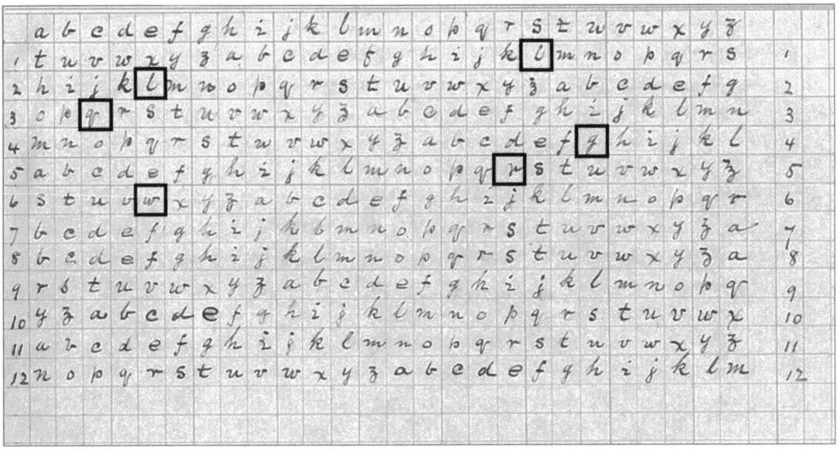

Harvard University Archives.

FIGURE 5.5 A Vigenère cipher. The key, *thomasbbryan*, runs down the second column. Each row represents a Caesar cipher in which the shift amount is determined by a letter of the key. (Thomas B. Bryan was an attorney who used this code for communicating with a client, Gordon McKay, in 1894.)

## CRYPTOGRAPHY AND HISTORY

Cryptography (code-making) and cryptanalysis (code-breaking) have been at the heart of many momentous events in human history. The intertwined stories of diplomacy, war, and coding technology are told beautifully in two books: *The Code-Breakers*, revised edition, by David Kahn (Scribner's, 1996) and *The Code Book* by Simon Singh (Anchor paperback, 2000).

Cryptographers use stock figures for describing encryption scenarios: Alice wants to send a message to Bob, and Eve is an adversary who may be eavesdropping.

Suppose Alice wants to send Bob a message (see Figure 5.6). The lock-and-key metaphor goes this way: Alice puts the message in a box and locks the box, using a key that only she and Bob possess. (Imagine that the lock on Alice's box is the kind that needs the key to lock it as well as to open it.) If Eve intercepts the box in transit, she has no way to figure out what key to use to open it. When Bob receives the box, he uses his copy of the key to open it. As long as the key is kept secret, it doesn't matter that others can see that there is a box with something in it, and even what kind of lock is on the box. In the same way, even if an encrypted message comes with an announcement that it is encrypted using a Vigenère cipher, it will not be easy to decrypt, except by someone who has the key.

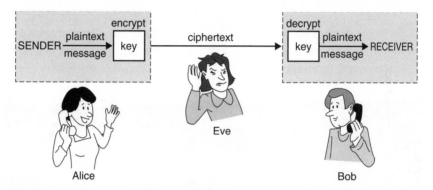

FIGURE 5.6   Standard cryptographic scenario. Alice wants to send a message to Bob. She encrypts it using a secret key. Bob decrypts it using his copy of the key. Eve is an eavesdropper. She intercepts the coded message in transit, and tries to decrypt it.

Or at least that's the idea. The Vigenère cipher was actually broken in the mid 1800s by the English mathematician Charles Babbage, who is now recognized as a founding figure in the field of computing. Babbage recognized that if someone could guess or otherwise deduce the length of the key, and hence the length of the cycle on which the Vigenère cipher was repeated, the problem was reduced to breaking several simple substitutions. He then used a brilliant extension of frequency analysis to discover the length of the key. Babbage never published his technique, perhaps at the request of British Intelligence. A Prussian Army officer, William Kasiski, independently figured out how to break the Vigenère code and published the method in 1863. The Vigenère cipher has been insecure ever since.

The sure way to beat this attack is to use a key that is as long as the plaintext, so that there are no repetitions. If we wanted to encrypt a message of length 100, we might use 100 Caesar ciphers in an arrangement like that of Figure 5.5, extended to 100 rows. Every table row would be used only once. A code like this is known as a *Vernam cipher*, after its World War I-era inventor, AT&T telegraph engineer Gilbert Vernam, and is more commonly referred to as a *one-time pad*.

The term "one-time pad" is based on a particular physical implementation of the cipher. Let's again imagine that Alice wants to get a message to Bob. Alice and Bob have identical pads of paper. Each page of the pad has a key written on it. Alice uses the top page to encrypt a message. When Bob receives it, he uses the top page of his pad to decrypt the message. Both Alice and Bob tear off and destroy the top page of the pad when they have used it. It is essential that the pages not be re-used, as doing so could create patterns like those exploited in cracking the Vigenère cipher.

One-time pads were used during the Second World War and the Cold War in the form of booklets filled with digits (see Figure 5.7). Governments still use one-time pads today for sensitive communications, with large amounts of keying material carefully generated and distributed on CDs or DVDs.

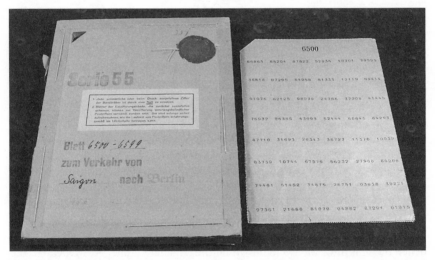

National Security Agency.

FIGURE 5.7    German one-time pad used for communication between Berlin and Saigon during the 1940s. Encrypted messages identified the page to be used in decryption. The cover warns, "Sheets of this encryption book that seem to be unused could contain codes for messages that are still on their way. They should be kept safe for the longest time a message might need for delivery."

A one-time pad, if used correctly, cannot be broken by cryptanalysis. There are simply no patterns to be found in the ciphertext. There is a deep relation between information theory and cryptography, which Shannon explored in 1949. (In fact, it was probably his wartime research on this sensitive subject that gave birth to his brilliant discoveries about communication in general.) Shannon proved mathematically what is obvious intuitively: The one-time pad is, in principle, as good as it gets in cryptography. It is absolutely unbreakable—in theory.

But as Yogi Berra said, "In theory, there is no difference between theory and practice. In practice, there is." Good one-time pads are hard to produce. If the pad contains repetitions or other patterns, Shannon's proof that one-time pads are uncrackable no longer holds. More seriously, transmitting a pad between the parties without loss or interception is likely to be just as difficult as communicating the plaintext of the message itself without detection. Typically, the parties would share a pad ahead of time and hope to conceal it in their travels. Big pads are harder to conceal than small pads, however, so the temptation arises to re-use pages—the kiss of death for security.

The Soviet KGB fell victim to exactly this temptation, which led to the partial or complete decryption of over 3000 diplomatic and espionage messages by U.S. and British intelligence during the years 1942–1946. The National Security Agency's VENONA project, publicly revealed only in 1995, was responsible for exposing major KGB agents such as Klaus Fuchs and Kim Philby. The Soviet messages were doubly encrypted, using a one-time pad on top of other techniques; this made the code-breaking project enormously difficult. It was successful only because, as World War II wore on and material conditions deteriorated, the Soviets re-used the pads.

Because one-time pads are impractical, almost all encryption uses relatively short keys. Some methods are more secure than others, however. Computer programs that break Vigenère encryption are readily available on the Internet, and no professional would use a Vigenère cipher today. Today's sophisticated ciphers are the distant descendents of the old substitution methods. Rather than substituting message texts letter for letter, computers divide the ASCII-encoded plaintext message into blocks. They then transform the bits in the block according to some method that depends on a key. The key itself is a sequence of bits on which Alice and Bob must agree and keep secret from Eve. Unlike the Vigenère cipher, there are no known shortcuts for breaking these ciphers (or at least none known publicly). The best method to decrypt a ciphertext without knowing the secret key seems to be brute-force exhaustive search, trying all possible keys.

The amount of computation required to break a cipher by exhaustive search grows exponentially in the size of the key. Increasing the key length by one bit doubles the amount of work required to break the cipher, but only slightly increases the work required to encrypt and decrypt. This is what makes these ciphers so useful: Computers may keep getting faster—even at an exponential rate—but the work required to break the cipher can also be made to grow exponentially by picking longer and longer keys.

# Lessons for the Internet Age

Let's pause for a moment to consider some of the lessons of cryptographic history—morals that were well-understood by the early twentieth century. In the late twentieth century, cryptography changed drastically because of modern computer technology and new cryptographic algorithms, but these lessons are still true today. They are too often forgotten.

## Breakthroughs Happen, but News Travels Slowly

Mary Stuart was beheaded when her letters plotting against Elizabeth were deciphered by frequency analysis, which Al-Kindi had described nine centuries earlier. Older methods have also remained in use to the present day, even for high-stakes communications. Suetonius explained the Caesar cipher in the first century A.D. Yet two millennia later, the Sicilian Mafia was still using the code. Bernardo Provenzano was a notorious Mafia boss who managed to stay on the run from Italian police for 43 years. But in 2002, some *pizzini*—ciphertexts typed on small pieces of paper—were found in the possession of one of his associates. The messages included correspondence between Bernardo and his son Angelo, written in a Caesar cipher—with a shift of three, exactly as Suetonius had described it. Bernardo switched to a more secure code, but the dominos started to topple. He was finally traced to a farmhouse and arrested in April 2006.

Even scientists are not immune from such follies. Although Babbage and Kasiski had broken the Vigenère cipher in the mid-nineteenth century, *Scientific American* 50 years later described the Vigenère method as "impossible of translation."

Encoded messages tend to look indecipherable. The incautious, whether naïve or sophisticated, are lulled into a false sense of security when they look at apparently unintelligible jumbles of numbers and letters. Cryptography is a science, and the experts know a lot about code-breaking.

## Confidence Is Good, but Certainty Would Be Better

There are no guarantees that even the best contemporary ciphers won't be broken, or haven't been broken already. Some of the ciphers have the potential to be validated by mathematical proofs, but actually providing those proofs will require deep mathematical breakthroughs. If anyone knows how to break modern codes, it is probably someone in the National Security

Agency or a comparable agency of a foreign government, and those folks don't tend to say much publicly.

In the absence of a formal proof of security, all one can do is to rely on what has been dubbed the Fundamental Tenet of Cryptography: *If lots of smart people have failed to solve a problem, then it probably won't be solved (soon).*

Of course, that is not a very useful principle in practice—by definition, breakthroughs are unlikely to happen "soon." But they do happen, and when they do, indigestion among cryptographers is widespread. In August 2004, at an annual cryptography conference, researchers announced that they had been able to break a popular algorithm (MD5) for computing cryptographic operations called *message digests*, which are fundamental security elements in almost all web servers, password programs, and office products. Cryptographers recommended switching to a stronger algorithm (SHA-1) but within a year, weaknesses were uncovered in this method as well.

A provably secure encryption algorithm is one of the holy grails of computer science. Every weakness exposed in proposed algorithms yields new ideas about how to make them stronger. We aren't there yet, but progress is being made.

> *A provably secure encryption algorithm is one of the holy grails of computer science.*

## Having a Good System Doesn't Mean People Will Use It

Before we explain that unbreakable encryption may finally be possible, we need to caution that even mathematical certainty would not suffice to create perfect security, if people don't change their behavior.

Vigenère published his encryption method in 1586. But foreign-office cipher secretaries commonly avoided the Vigenère cipher because it was cumbersome to use. They stayed with simple substitution ciphers—even though it was well-known that these ciphers were readily broken—and they hoped for the best. By the eighteenth century, most European governments had skilled "Black Chambers" through which all mail to and from foreign embassies was routed for decryption. Finally, the embassies switched to Vigenère ciphers, which themselves continued to be used after information about how to crack them had become widely known.

And so it is today. Technological inventions, no matter how solid in theory, will not be used for everyday purposes if they are inconvenient or expensive. The risks of weak systems are often rationalized in attempts to avoid the trouble of switching to more secure alternatives.

In 1999, an encryption standard known as WEP (Wired Equivalent Privacy) was introduced for home and office wireless connections. In 2001, however, WEP was found to have serious flaws that made it easy to eavesdrop on wireless networks, a fact that became widely known in the security community. Despite this, wireless equipment companies continued to sell WEP products, while industry pundits comforted people that "WEP is better than nothing." A new standard (WPA—Wi-Fi Protected Access) was finally introduced in 2002, but it wasn't until September 2003 that products were required to use the new standard in order to be certified. Hackers were able to steal more than 45 million credit and debit card records from TJX, the parent company of several major retail store chains, because the company was still using WEP encryption as late as 2005. That was long after WEP's insecurities were known and WPA was available as a replacement. The cost of that security breach has reached the hundreds of millions of dollars.

Similarly, many of today's "smart card" systems that use RFID (Radio Frequency Identification) tags are insecure. In January 2005, computer scientists from Johns Hopkins University and RSA Data Security announced that they had cracked an RFID-based automobile anti-theft and electronic payment system built into millions of automobile key tags. They demonstrated this by making multiple gasoline purchases at an Exxon/Mobile station. A spokesman for Texas Instruments, which developed the system, countered that the methods the team used were "wildly beyond the reach of most researchers," saying "I don't see any reason to change this approach."

When encryption was a military monopoly, it was possible in principle for a commander to order everyone to start using a new code if he suspected that the enemy had cracked the old one. The risks of insecure encryption today arise from three forces acting in consort: the high speed at which news of insecurities travels among experts, the slow speed at which the inexpert recognize their vulnerabilities, and the massive scale at which cryptographic software is deployed. When a university researcher discovers a tiny hole in an algorithm, computers everywhere become vulnerable, and there is no central authority to give the command for software upgrades everywhere.

## The Enemy Knows Your System

The last lesson from history may seem counterintuitive. It is that a cryptographic method, especially one designed for widespread use, should be regarded as more reliable if it is widely known and seems not to have been broken, rather than if the method itself has been kept secret.

The Flemish linguist Auguste Kerckhoffs articulated this principle in an 1883 essay on military cryptography. As he explained it,

> The system must not require secrecy, and it could fall into the hands of the enemy without causing trouble.... Here I mean by system, not the key itself, but the material part of the system: tables, dictionaries, or whatever mechanical apparatus is needed to apply it. Indeed, it's not necessary to create imaginary phantoms or to suspect the integrity of employees or subordinates, in order to understand that, if a system requiring secrecy were to find itself in the hands of too many individuals, it could be compromised upon each engagement in which any of them take part.

In other words, if a cryptographic method is put in widespread use, it is unrealistic to expect that the method can remain secret for long. Thus, it should be designed so that it will remain secure, even if everything but a small amount of information (the key) becomes exposed.

Claude Shannon restated Kerckhoffs's Principle in his paper on systems for secret communication: "... we shall assume that *the enemy knows the system being used.*" He went on to write:

> The assumption is actually the one ordinarily used in cryptographic studies. It is pessimistic and hence safe, but in the long run realistic, since one must expect his system to be found out eventually.

Kerckhoffs's Principle is frequently violated in modern Internet security practice. Internet start-up companies routinely make bold announcements about new breakthrough proprietary encryption methods, which they refuse to subject to public scrutiny, explaining that the method must be kept secret in order to protect its security. Cryptographers generally regard such "security through obscurity" claims with extreme skepticism.

Even well-established organizations run afoul of Kerckhoffs's Principle. The Content Scrambling System (CSS) used on DVDs (Digital Versatile Disks) was developed by a consortium of motion picture studios and consumer electronics companies in 1996. It encrypts DVD contents in order to limit unauthorized copying. The method was kept secret to prevent the manufacture of unlicensed DVD players. The encryption algorithm, which consequently was never widely analyzed by experts, turned out to be weak and was cracked within three years after it was announced. Today, CSS decryption programs, together with numerous unauthorized "ripped" DVD contents, circulate widely on the Internet (see Chapter 6, "Balance Toppled" for a more detailed discussion of copy protection).

Kerckhoffs's Principle has been institutionalized in the form of encryption standards. The *Data Encryption Standard* (DES) was adopted as a national standard in the 1970s and is widely used in the worlds of business and finance. It has pretty much survived all attempts at cracking, although the inexorable progress of Moore's Law has made exhaustive searching through all possible keys more feasible in recent years. A newer standard, Advanced Encryption Standard (AES), was adopted in 2002 after a thorough and public review. It is precisely because these encryption methods are so widely known that confidence in them can be high. They have been subjected to both professional analysis and amateur experimentation, and no serious deficiencies have been discovered.

These lessons are as true today as they ever were. And yet, something else, something fundamental about cryptography, is different today. In the late twentieth century, cryptographic methods stopped being state secrets and became consumer goods.

## Secrecy Changes Forever

For four thousand years, cryptography was about making sure Eve could not read Alice's message to Bob if Eve intercepted the message *en route*. Nothing could be done if the key itself was somehow discovered. Keeping the key secret was therefore of inestimable importance, and was a very uncertain business.

If Alice and Bob worked out the key when they met, how could Bob keep the key secret during the dangers of travel? Protecting keys was a military and diplomatic priority of supreme importance. Pilots and soldiers were instructed that, even in the face of certain death from enemy attack, their first responsibility was to destroy their codebooks. Discovery of the codes could cost thousands of lives. The secrecy of the codes was everything.

And if Alice and Bob never met, then how could they agree on a key without *already* having a secure method for transmitting the key? That seemed like a fundamental limitation: Secure communication was practical only for people who could arrange to meet beforehand, or who had access to a prior method of secure communication (such as military couriers) for carrying the key between them. If Internet communications had to proceed on this assumption, electronic commerce never could have gotten off the ground. Bit packets racing through the network are completely unprotected from eavesdropping.

And then, in the 1970s, everything changed. Whitfield Diffie was a 32-year-old mathematical free spirit who had been obsessed with cryptography since his years as an MIT undergraduate. 31-year-old Martin Hellman was a hard-nosed graduate of the Bronx High School of Science and an Assistant Professor at Stanford. Diffie had traveled the length of the country in search of collaborators on the mathematics of secret communication. This was not an easy field to enter, since most serious work in this area was being done behind the firmly locked doors of the National Security Agency. Ralph Merkle, a 24-year-old computer science graduate student, was exploring a new approach to secure communication. In the most important discovery in the entire history of cryptography, Diffie and Hellman found a practical realization of Merkle's ideas, which they presented in a paper entitled "New Directions in Cryptography." This is what the paper described:

> *A way for Alice and Bob, without any prior arrangement, to agree on a secret key, known only to the two of them, by using messages between them that are not secret at all.*

In other words, as long as Alice and Bob can communicate with each other, they can establish a secret key. It does not matter if Eve or anyone else can hear everything they say. Alice and Bob can come to a consensus on a secret key, and there is no way for Eve to use what she overhears to figure out what that secret key is. This is true even if Alice and Bob have never met before and have never made any prior agreements.

It was revealed in 1997 that the same public-key techniques had been developed within the British secret Government Communication Headquarters (GCHQ) two years before Diffie and Hellman's work, by James Ellis, Clifford Cocks, and Malcolm Williamson.

The impact of this discovery cannot be overstated. The art of secret communication was a government monopoly, and had been since the dawn of writing—governments had the largest interests in secrets, and the smartest scientists worked for governments. But there was another reason why governments had done all the serious cryptography. Only governments had the wherewithal to assure the production, protection, and distribution of the keys on which secret communication depended. If the secret keys could be produced by public communication, everyone could use cryptography. They just had to know how; they did not need armies or brave couriers to transmit and protect the keys.

Diffie, Hellman, and Merkle dubbed their discovery "public-key cryptography." Although its significance was not recognized at the time, it is the invention that made electronic commerce possible. If Alice is you and Bob is Amazon, there is no possibility of a meeting—how could you physically go to Amazon to procure a key? Does Amazon even *have* a physical location? If Alice is to send her credit card number to Amazon securely, the encryption has to be worked out on the spot, or rather, on the two separate spots separated by the Internet. Diffie-Hellman-Merkle, and a suite of related methods that followed, made secure Internet transactions possible. If you have ever ordered anything from an online store, you have been a cryptographer without realizing it. Your computer and the store's computer played the roles of Alice and Bob.

It seems wildly counterintuitive that Alice and Bob could agree on a secret key over a public communication channel. It was not so much that the scientific community had tried and failed to do what Diffie, Hellman, and Merkle did. It never occurred to them to try, because it seemed so obvious that Alice had to give Bob the keys somehow.

Even the great Shannon missed this possibility. In his 1949 paper that brought all known cryptographic methods under a unified framework, he did not realize that there might be an alternative. "The key must be transmitted by non-interceptable means from transmitting to receiving points," he wrote. Not true. Alice and Bob can get the same secret key, even though all their messages are intercepted.

*Alice and Bob can get the same secret key, even though all their messages are intercepted.*

The basic picture of how Alice communicates her secret to Bob remains as shown in Figure 5.6. Alice sends Bob a coded message, and Bob uses a secret key to decrypt it. Eve may intercept the ciphertext *en route*.

The goal is for Alice to do the encryption in such a way that it is *impossible* for Eve to decrypt the message in any way other than a brute-force search through all possible keys. If the decryption problem is "hard" in this sense, then the phenomenon of exponential growth becomes the friend of Alice and Bob. For example, suppose they are using ordinary decimal numerals as keys, and their keys are ten digits long. If they suspect that Eve's computers are getting powerful enough to search through all possible keys, they can switch to 20-digit keys. The amount of time Eve would require goes up by a factor of $10^{10}$ = 10,000,000,000. Even if Eve's computers were powerful enough to crack any 10-digit key in a second, it would then take her more than 300 years to crack a 20-digit key!

Exhaustive search is always *one* way for Eve to discover the key. But if Alice encrypts her message using a substitution or Vigenère cipher, the encrypted message will have patterns that enable Eve to find the key far more quickly. The trick is to find a means of encrypting the message so that the ciphertext reveals no patterns from which the key could be inferred.

## The Key Agreement Protocol

The crucial invention was the concept of a *one-way computation*—a computation with two important properties: It can be done quickly, but it can't be undone quickly. To be more precise, the computation quickly combines two numbers $x$ and $y$ to produce a third number, which we'll call $x * y$. If you know the value of $x * y$, there is no quick way to figure out what value of $y$ was used to produce it, even if you also know the value of $x$. That is, if you know the values of $x$ and the result $z$, the only way to find a value of $y$ so that $z = x * y$ is trial and error search. Such an exhaustive search would take time that grows exponentially with the number of digits of $z$—practically impossible, for numbers of a few hundred digits. Diffie and Hellman's one-way computation also has an important third property: $(x * y) * z$ always produces the same result as $(x * z) * y$.

The key agreement protocol starts from a base of public knowledge: how to do the computation $x * y$, and also the value of a particular large number $g$. (See the Endnotes for the details.) All this information is available to the entire world. Knowing it, here is how Alice and Bob proceed.

1. Alice and Bob each choose a random number. We'll call Alice's number $a$ and Bob's number $b$. We'll refer to $a$ and $b$ as Alice and Bob's *secret keys*. Alice and Bob keep their secret keys secret. *No one except Alice knows the value of $a$, and no one except Bob knows the value of $b$.*

2. Alice calculates $g * a$ and Bob calculates $g * b$. (Not hard to do.) The results are called their *public keys* $A$ and $B$, respectively.

3. Alice sends Bob the value of $A$ and Bob sends Alice the value of $B$. It doesn't matter if Eve overhears these communications; $A$ and $B$ are not secret numbers.

4. When she has received Bob's public key $B$, Alice computes $B * a$, using her secret key $a$ as well as Bob's public key $B$. Likewise, when Bob receives $A$ from Alice, he computes $A * b$.

Even though Alice and Bob have done different computations, they have ended up with the same value. Bob computes $A * b$, that is, $(g * a) * b$ (see Step 2—$A$ is $g * a$). Alice computes $B * a$, that is, $(g * b) * a$. Because of the

## ARE WE SURE NO ONE CAN CRACK THE CODE?

No one has proved mathematically that the public-key encryption algorithms are unbreakable, in spite of determined efforts by top mathematicians and computer scientists to provide absolute proof of their security. So our confidence in them rests on the Fundamental Tenet: *No one has broken them so far.* If anyone knows a fast method, it's probably the National Security Agency, which operates in an environment of extreme secrecy. Maybe the NSA knows how and isn't telling. Or maybe some inventive loner has cracked the code but prefers profit to celebrity, and is quietly socking away huge profits from decoding messages about financial transactions. Our bet is that no one knows how and no one will.

third property of the one-way computation, that number is $(g * a) * b$ once again—the same value, arrived at in a different way!

This shared value, call it $K$, is the key Alice and Bob will use for encrypting and decrypting their subsequent messages, using whatever standard method of encryption they choose.

Now here's the crucial point. Suppose Eve has been listening to Alice and Bob's communications. Can she do anything with all the information she has? She has overheard $A$ and $B$, and she knows $g$ because it is an industry standard. She knows all the algorithms and protocols that Alice and Bob are using; Eve has read Diffie and Hellman's paper too! But to compute the key $K$, Eve would have to know one of the secret keys, either $a$ or $b$. She doesn't—only Alice knows $a$ and only Bob knows $b$. On numbers of a few hundred digits, no one knows how to find $a$ or $b$ from $g$, $A$, and $B$ without searching through impossibly many trial values.

Alice and Bob can carry out their computations with personal computers or simple special-purpose hardware. But even the most powerful computers aren't remotely fast enough to let Eve break the system, at least not by any method known.

Exploiting this difference in computational effort was Diffie, Hellman, and Merkle's breakthrough. They showed how to create shared secret keys, without requiring secure channels.

## Public Keys for Private Messages

Suppose Alice wants to have a way for anyone in the world to send her encrypted messages that only she can decrypt. She can do this with a small variation of the key-agreement protocol. All the computations are the same as in the key agreement protocol, except they take place in a slightly different order.

Alice picks a secret key $a$ and computes the corresponding public key $A$. She publishes $A$ in a directory.

If Bob (or anyone) now wants to send Alice an encrypted message, he gets Alice's public key from the directory. Next, he picks his own secret key $b$ and computes $B$ as before. He also uses Alice's public key $A$ from the directory to compute an encryption key $K$ just as with the key-agreement protocol: $K = A * b$. Bob uses $K$ as a key to encrypt a message to Alice, and he sends Alice the ciphertext, along with $B$. Because he uses $K$ only once, $K$ is like a one-time pad.

When Alice receives Bob's encrypted message, she takes the $B$ that came with message, together with her secret key $a$, just as in the key agreement protocol, and computes the same $K = B * a$. Alice now uses $K$ as the key for decrypting the message. Eve can't decrypt it, because she doesn't know the secret keys.

*With public-key encryption, anyone can send encrypted mail to anyone over an insecure, publicly exposed communication path.*

This might seem like just a simple variant of key agreement, but it results in a major conceptual change in how we think about secure communication. With public-key encryption, *anyone* can send encrypted mail to *anyone* over an insecure, publicly exposed communication path. The only thing on which they need to agree is to use the Diffie-Hellman-Merkle method—and knowing that is of no use to an adversary trying to decipher an intercepted message.

## Digital Signatures

In addition to secret communication, a second breakthrough achievement of public-key cryptography is preventing forgeries and impersonations in electronic transactions.

Suppose Alice wants to create a public announcement. How can people who see the announcement be sure that it really comes from Alice—that it's not a forgery? What's required is a method for marking Alice's public message in such a way that anyone can easily verify that the mark is Alice's and no one can forge it. Such a mark is called a *digital signature*.

To build on the drama we have used already, we'll continue to talk about Alice sending a message to Bob, with Eve trying to do something evil while the message is in transit. In this case, however, we are not concerned with the secrecy of Alice's message—only with assuring Bob that what he receives is really what Alice sent. In other words, the message may not be secret—perhaps it is an important public announcement. Bob needs to be confident that the signature he sees on the message is Alice's and that the message could not have been tampered with before he received it.

Digital signature protocols use public keys and secret keys, but in a different way. The protocol consists of two computations: one Alice uses to process her message to create the signature, and one Bob uses to verify the signature. Alice uses her secret key and the message itself to create the signature. Anyone can then use Alice's public key to verify the signature. The point is that everyone can know the public key and thus verify the signature, but only the person who knows the secret key could have produced the signature. This is the reverse of the scenario of the previous section, where anyone can encrypt a message, but only the person with the secret key can decrypt it.

A digital signature scheme requires a computational method that makes signing easy if you have the secret key and verifying easy if you have the public key—and yet makes it computationally infeasible to produce a verifiable signature if you don't know the secret key. Moreover, the signature depends on the message as well as on the secret key of the person signing it. Thus, the digital signature protocol attests to the *integrity* of the message—that it was not tampered with in transit—as well as to its *authenticity*—that the person who sent it really is Alice.

In typical real systems, used to sign unencrypted email, for example, Alice doesn't encrypt the message itself. Instead, to speed up the signature computation, she first computes a compressed version of the message, called a *message digest*, which is much shorter than the message itself. It requires less computation to produce the signature for the digest than for the full message. How message digests are computed is public knowledge. When Bob receives Alice's signed message, he computes the digest of the message and verifies that it is identical to what he gets by decrypting the attached signature using Alice's public key.

The digesting process needs to produce a kind of fingerprint—something small that is nonetheless virtually unique to the original. This compression process must avoid a risk associated with using digests. If Eve could produce a different message with the same digest, then she could attach Alice's signature to Eve's message. Bob would not realize that someone had tampered with the message before he received it. When he went through the verification process, he would compute the digest of Eve's message, compare it to the result of decrypting the signature that Alice attached to Alice's message, and find them identical. This risk is the source of the insecurity of the message digest function MD5 mentioned earlier in this chapter, which is making the cryptographic community wary about the use of message digests.

## RSA

Diffie and Hellman introduced the concept of digital signatures in their 1976 paper. They suggested an approach to designing signatures, but they did not present a concrete method. The problem of devising a practical digital signature scheme was left as a challenge to the computer science community.

The challenge was met in 1977 by Ron Rivest, Adi Shamir, and Len Adleman of the MIT Laboratory for Computer Science. Not only was the RSA (Rivest-Shamir-Adleman) algorithm a practical digital signature scheme, but it could also be used for confidential messaging. With RSA, each person generates a pair of keys—a public key and a secret key. We'll again call Alice's public key $A$ and her secret key $a$. The public and private keys are inverses: If you transform a value with $a$, then transforming the result with $A$ recovers the original value. If you transform a value with $A$, then transforming the result with $a$ recovers the original value.

Here's how RSA key pairs are used. People publish their public keys and keep their secret keys to themselves. If Bob wants to send Alice a message, he picks a standard algorithm such as DES and a key $K$, and transforms $K$ using Alice's public key $A$. Alice transforms the result using her secret key $a$ to recover $K$. As with all public-key encryption, only Alice knows her secret key, so only Alice can recover $K$ and decrypt the message.

To produce a digital signature, Alice transforms the message using her secret key $a$ and uses the result as the signature to be sent along with the message. Anyone can then check the signature by transforming it with Alice's public key $A$ to verify that this matches the original message. Because only Alice knows her secret key, only Alice could have produced something that, when transformed with her public key, will reproduce the original message.

It seems to be infeasible in the RSA cryptosystem—as in the Diffie-Hellman-Merkle system—to compute a secret key corresponding to a public key. RSA uses a different one-way computation than the one used by the Diffie-Hellman-Merkle system. RSA is secure only if it takes much longer to factor an $n$-digit number than to multiply two $n/2$-digit numbers. RSA's reliance on the difficulty of factoring has engendered enormous interest in finding fast ways to factor numbers. Until the 1970s, this was a mathematical pastime of theoretical interest only. One can multiply numbers in time comparable to *the number of digits*, while factoring a number requires effort

*A breakthrough in factoring would render RSA useless and would undermine many of the current standards for Internet security.*

comparable to *the value of the number itself*, as far as anyone knows. A breakthrough in factoring would render RSA useless and would undermine many of the current standards for Internet security.

## Certificates and Certification Authorities

There's a problem with the public-key methods we've described so far. How can Bob know that the "Alice" he's communicating with really is Alice? Anyone could be at the other end of the key-agreement communication pretending to be Alice. Or, for secure messaging, after Alice places her public key in the directory, Eve might tamper with the directory, substituting her own key in place of Alice's. Then, anyone who tries to use the key to create secret messages intended for Alice, will actually be creating messages that Eve, not Alice, can read. If "Bob" is you and "Alice" is the mayor ordering an evacuation of the city, some impostor could be trying to create a panic. If "Bob" is your computer and "Alice" is your bank's, "Eve" could be trying to steal your money!

This is where digital signatures can help. Alice goes to a trusted authority, to which she presents her public key together with proof of her identity. The authority digitally signs Alice's key—producing a signed key called a *certificate*. Now, instead of just presenting her key when she wants to communicate, Alice presents the certificate. Anyone who wants to use the key to communicate with Alice first checks the authority's signature to see that the key is legitimate.

People check a certificate by checking the trusted authority's signature. How do they know that the signature on the certificate really is the trusted authority's signature, and not some fraud that Eve set up for the purpose of issuing fake certificates? The authority's signature is itself guaranteed by another certificate, signed by another authority, and so on, until we reach an authority whose certificate is

**COMMERCIAL CERTIFICATES**

VeriSign, which is currently the major commercial certification authority, issues three classes of personal certificates. Class 1 is for assuring that a browser is associated with a particular email address and makes no claims about anyone's real identity. Class 2 provides a modest level of identity checking. Organizations issuing them should require an application with information that can be checked against employee records or credit records. Class 3 certificates require applying in person for verification of identity.

well-known. In this way, Alice's public key is vouched for, not only by a certificate and a single signature, but by a chain of certificates, each one with a signature guaranteed by the next certificate.

Organizations that issue certificates are called *certification authorities.* Certification authorities can be set up for limited use (for example, a corporation might serve as a certification authority that issues certificates for use on its corporate network). There are also companies that make a business of selling certificates for public use. The trust you should put in a certificate depends on two things: your assessment of the reliability of the signature on the certificate and *also* your assessment of the certification authority's policy in being willing to sign things.

# Cryptography for Everyone

In real life, none of us is aware that we are carrying out one-way computations while we are browsing the Web. But every time we order a book from Amazon, check our bank or credit card balance, or pay for a purchase using PayPal, that is exactly what happens. The tell-tale sign that an encrypted web transaction is taking place is that the URL of the web site begins with "https" (the "s" is for "secure") instead of "http." The consumer's computer and the computer of the store or the bank negotiate the encryption, using public key cryptography—unbeknownst to the human beings involved in the transaction. The store attests to its identity by presenting a certificate signed by a Certification authority that the consumer's computer has been preconfigured to recognize. New keys are generated for each new transaction. Keys are cheap. Secret messages are everywhere on the Internet. We are all cryptographers now.

*We are all cryptographers now.*

At first, public-key encryption was treated as a mathematical curiosity. Len Adleman, one of the inventors of RSA, thought that the RSA paper would be "the least interesting paper I would ever be on." Even the National Security Agency, as late as 1977, was not overly concerned about the spread of these methods. They simply did not appreciate how the personal computer revolution, just a few years away, would enable anyone with a home PC to exchange encrypted messages that even NSA could not decipher.

But as the 1980s progressed, and Internet use increased, the potential of ubiquitous cryptography began to become apparent. Intelligence agencies became increasingly concerned, and law enforcement feared that encrypted communications could put an end to government wiretapping, one of its most powerful tools. On the commercial side, industry was beginning to appreciate that customers would want private communication, especially in an era of electronic commerce. In the late 1980s and early 1990s, the Bush and the Clinton administrations were floating proposals to control the spread of cryptographic systems.

In 1994, the Clinton administration unveiled a plan for an "Escrowed Encryption Standard" that would be used on telephones that provided encrypted communications. The technology, dubbed "Clipper," was an encryption chip developed by the NSA that included a *back door*–an extra key held by the government, which would let law enforcement and intelligence agencies decrypt the phone communications. According to the proposal, the government would purchase only Clipper phones for secure communication. Anyone wanting to do business with the government over a secure telephone would also have to use a Clipper phone. Industry reception was cold, however (see Figure 5.8), and the plan was dropped. But in a sequence of modified proposals beginning in 1995, the White House attempted to convince industry to create encryption products that had similar back doors. The carrot here, and the stick, was export control law. Under U.S. law, cryptographic products could not be exported without a license, and violating export controls could result in severe criminal penalties. The administration proposed that encryption software would receive export licenses only if it contained back doors.

The ensuing, often heated negotiations, sometimes referred to as the "crypto wars," played out over the remainder of the 1990s. Law enforcement and national security argued the need for encryption controls. On the other side of the debate were the technology companies, who did not want government regulation, and civil liberties groups, who warned against the potential for growing communication surveillance. In essence, policymakers could not come to grips with the transformation of a major military technology into an everyday personal tool.

We met Phil Zimmermann at the beginning of this chapter, and his career now becomes a central part of the story. Zimmermann was a journeyman programmer and civil libertarian who had been interested in cryptography since his youth. He had read a *Scientific American* column about RSA encryption in 1977, but did not have access to the kinds of computers that would be needed to implement arithmetic on huge integers, as the RSA algorithms demanded. But computers will get powerful enough if you wait. As the 1980s progressed, it became possible to implement RSA on home computers. Zimmermann set about to produce encryption software for the people, to counter the threat of increased government surveillance. As he later testified before Congress:

On April 16, 1993, the New York Times broke the story of the Clipper Chip, an encryption technology developed by the National Security Agency that allows government to eavesdrop on the communications of criminals, suspects, and unfortunately, law-abiding citizens alike.

On February 9, 1994, the U.S. Department of Commerce and Vice President of the United States summarily announced that the Clipper Chip is the U.S. Government standard, and that the Government will do everything in its power to encourage its use in the private sector and the international community.

They'll excuse us if we don't wish them luck.

## SINK CLIPPER!

Because some things are better left unread. RSA

Reprinted with permission of RSA Security, Inc.

FIGURE 5.8 Part of the "crypto wars," the furious industry reaction against the Clinton Administration's "Clipper chip" proposal.

The power of computers had shifted the balance towards ease of surveillance. In the past, if the government wanted to violate the privacy of ordinary citizens, it had to expend a certain amount of effort to intercept and steam open and read paper mail, or listen to and possibly transcribe spoken telephone conversations. This is analogous to catching fish with a hook and a line, one fish at a time. Fortunately for freedom and democracy, this kind of labor-intensive monitoring is not practical on a large scale. Today, electronic mail is gradually replacing conventional paper mail, and is soon to be the norm for everyone, not the novelty it is today. Unlike paper mail, e-mail messages are just too easy to intercept and scan for interesting keywords. This can be done easily, routinely, automatically, and undetectable on a grand scale. This is analogous to driftnet fishing—making a quantitative and qualitative Orwellian difference to the health of democracy.

Cryptography was the answer. If governments were to have unlimited surveillance powers over electronic communications, people everywhere needed easy-to-use, cheap, uncrackable cryptography so they could communicate without governments being able to understand them.

Zimmermann faced obstacles that would have stopped less-zealous souls. RSA was a patented invention. MIT had licensed it exclusively to the RSA Data Security Company, which produced commercial encryption software for corporations, and RSA Data Security had no interest in granting Zimmermann the license he would need to distribute his RSA code freely, as he wished to do.

And there was government policy, which was, of course, exactly the problem to which Zimmermann felt his encryption software was the solution. On January 24, 1991, Senator Joseph Biden, a co-sponsor of antiterrorist legislation Senate Bill 266, inserted some new language into the bill:

> It is the sense of Congress that providers of electronic communications services and manufacturers of electronic communications service equipment shall ensure that communications systems permit the government to obtain the plaintext contents of voice, data, and other communications when appropriate authorized by law.

This language received a furious reaction from civil liberties groups and wound up not surviving, but Zimmermann decided to take matters into his own hands.

By June of 1991, Zimmermann had completed a working version of his software. He named it PGP for "Pretty Good Privacy," after Ralph's mythical Pretty Good Groceries that sponsored Garrison Keillor's *Prairie Home Companion*. The software mysteriously appeared on several U.S. computers, available for anyone in the world to download. Soon copies were everywhere—not just in the U.S., but all over the world. In Zimmermann's own words: "This technology belongs to everybody." The genie was out of the bottle and was not going back in.

Zimmermann paid a price for his libertarian gesture. First, RSA Data Security was confident that this technology belonged to *it*, not to "everybody." The company was enraged that its patented technology was being given away. Second, the government was furious. It instituted a criminal investigation for violation of the export control laws, although it was not clear what laws, if any, Zimmermann had violated. Eventually MIT brokered an agreement that let Zimmermann use the RSA patent, and devised a way to put PGP on the Internet for use in the U.S., and in conformance with export controls.

By the end of the decade, the progress of electronic commerce had overtaken the key escrow debate, and the government had ended its criminal investigation without an indictment. Zimmermann built a business around PGP (see www.pgp.com), while still allowing free downloads for individuals. His web site contains testimonials from human rights groups in Eastern Europe and Guatemala attesting to the liberating force of secret communication among individuals and agencies working against oppressive regimes. Zimmermann had won.

Sort of.

> **ENCRYPTION REGULATION ABROAD**
>
> Some countries have adjusted to multiple uses of the same encryption algorithms, for commercial, military, and conspiratorial purposes. For example, the Chinese government strictly regulates the sale of encryption products, "to protect information safety, to safeguard the legal interests of citizens and organizations, and to ensure the safety and interests of the nation." In 2007, the United Kingdom enacted laws requiring the disclosure of encryption keys to government authorities investigating criminal or terror investigations, on penalty of up to five years in prison.

## Cryptography Unsettled

Today, every banking and credit card transaction over the Web is encrypted. There is widespread concern about information security, identity theft, and degradation of personal privacy. PGP and other high-quality email encryption programs are widely available—many for free.

But very little email is encrypted today. Human rights groups use encrypted email. People with something to hide probably encrypt their email. But most of us don't bother encrypting our email. In fact, millions of people use Gmail, willingly trading their privacy for the benefits of free, reliable service. Google's computers scan every email, and supply advertisements related to the subject matter. Google might turn over email to the government in response to a court order, without challenging the demand. Why are we so unconcerned about email privacy?

*Why are we so unconcerned about email privacy?*

First, there is still little awareness of how easily our email can be captured as the packets flow through the Internet. The password requests needed to get our email out of the mail server may provide the

## SPYING ON CITIZENS

Historically, spying on citizens required a warrant (since citizens have an expectation of privacy), but spying on foreigners did not. A series of executive orders and laws intended to combat terrorism allow the government to inspect bits that are on their way into or out of the country. (Perhaps even a phone call to an airline, if it is answered by a call center in India.) Also excluded from judicial oversight is any "surveillance directed at a person reasonably believed to be located outside of the United States," whether that person is a U.S. citizen or not. Such developments may stimulate encryption of electronic communications, and hence in the end prove to be counterproductive. That in turn might renew efforts to criminalize encryption of email and telephone communications in the U.S.

illusion of security, but they do nothing to protect the messages themselves from being sniffed as they float through fibers, wires, and the air. The world's biggest eavesdropping enterprise is very poorly known. It is the international ECHELON system, which automatically monitors data communications to and from satellites that relay Internet traffic. ECHELON is a cooperative project of the U.S. and several of its allies, and is the descendant of communications intelligence systems from the time of the Second World War. But it is up-to-date technologically. If your email messages use words that turn up in ECHELON's dictionary, they may get a close look.

Second, there is little concern because most ordinary citizens feel they have little to hide, so why would anyone bother looking? They are not considering the vastly increased capacity for automatic monitoring that governments now possess—the driftnet monitoring of which Zimmermann warned.

Finally, encrypted email is not built into the Internet infrastructure in the way encrypted web browsing is. You have to use nonstandard software, and the people you communicate with have to use some compatible software. In commercial settings, companies may not want to make encryption easy for office workers. They have an interest—and in many cases, regulatory requirements—to watch out for criminal activities. And they may not want to suggest that email is being kept private if they are unable to make that guarantee, out of fear of liability if unsecured email falls into the wrong hands.

It is not just email and credit card numbers that might be encrypted. Instant Messaging and VoIP telephone conversations are just packets flowing through the Internet that can be encrypted like anything else. Some Internet phone software (such as Skype) encrypts conversations, and there are several other products under development—including one led by Zimmermann himself—to create easy-to-use encryption software for Internet telephone conversations. But for the most part, digital communications are open, and Eve the evil eavesdropper, or anyone else, can listen in.

Overall, the public seems unconcerned about privacy of communication today, and the privacy fervor that permeated the crypto wars a decade ago is nowhere to be seen. In a very real sense, the dystopian predictions of both sides of that debate are being realized: On the one hand, encryption technology is readily available around the world, and people can hide the contents of their messages, just as law enforcement feared—there is widespread speculation about Al Qaeda's use of PGP, for example. At the same time, the spread of the Internet has been accompanied by an increase in surveillance, just as the opponents of encryption regulation feared.

So although outright prohibitions on encryption are now impossible, the social and systems aspects of encryption remain in an unstable equilibrium. Will some information privacy catastrophe spark a massive re-education of the Internet-using public, or massive regulatory changes to corporate practice? Will some major supplier of email services and software, responding to consumers wary of information theft and government surveillance, make encrypted email the default option?

The bottom-line question is this: As encryption becomes as ordinary a tool for personal messages as it already is for commercial transactions, will the benefits to personal privacy, free expression, and human liberty outweigh the costs to law enforcement and national intelligence, whose capacity to eavesdrop and wiretap will be at an end?

Whatever the future of encrypted communication, encryption technology has another use. Perfect copies and instant communication have blown the legal notion of "intellectual property" into billions of bits of teenage movie and music downloads. Encryption is the tool used to lock movies so only certain people can see them and to lock songs so only certain people can hear them—to put a hard shell around this part of the digital explosion. The changed meaning of copyright is the next stop on our tour of the exploded landscape.

# CHAPTER 6

# Balance Toppled

## *Who Owns the Bits?*

## Automated Crimes—Automated Justice

Tanya Andersen was home having dinner with her eight-year-old daughter in December 2005 when they were interrupted by a knock at the door. It was a legal process server, armed with a lawsuit from the Recording Industry Association of America (RIAA), a trade organization representing half a dozen music publishers that together control over 90% of music distribution in the U.S. The RIAA claimed that the Oregon single mother surviving on disability payments owed them close to a million dollars for illegally downloading 1,200 tracks of gangsta rap and other copyrighted music.

Andersen's run-in with the RIAA had begun nine months previously with a "demand letter" from a Los Angeles law firm. The letter stated that "a number of record companies" had sued her for copyright infringement and that she could settle for $4,000–$5,000 or face the consequences. She suspected the letter was a scam, and protested to the RIAA that she had never downloaded any music. Andersen repeatedly offered to let the record companies verify this for themselves by inspecting her computer's hard drive, but the RIAA refused the offers. At one point, an RIAA representative admitted to her that he believed she was probably innocent. But, he warned, once the RIAA starts a lawsuit, they don't drop it, because doing so would encourage other people to defend themselves against the recording industry's claims.

Andersen found a lawyer after the December lawsuit was served, and they convinced a judge to order an inspection of the hard drive. The RIAA's own expert determined that Andersen's computer had never been used for illegal downloading. But instead of dropping the suit, the RIAA increased the pressure on Andersen to settle. They demanded that their lawyers be allowed to take a deposition from Andersen's daughter, and even tried to reach the child directly by calling the apartment. An unknown woman phoned her elementary school principal falsely claiming to be her grandmother and asking about the girl's attendance. RIAA lawyers contacted Andersen's friends and relatives, telling them that Andersen was a thief who collected violent, racist music. The pressure on the 41-year-old Andersen, who suffered from a painful illness and emotional problems, forced her to abandon her hope of entering a back-to-work program. Instead, she sought additional psychiatric care. Finally, after two years, Andersen was able to file a motion for summary judgment, which required the RIAA to come to court with proof of their claims. When they could not produce proof, the case was dismissed. Andersen is currently suing the RIAA for fraud and malicious prosecution.

> A great deal of information about digital copyright issues can be found at www.chillingeffects.org, a joint project of the Electronic Frontier Foundation and of several university law clinics.

## 26,000 Lawsuits in Five Years

The RIAA has filed more than 26,000 lawsuits against individuals for illegal downloading since 2003. The process begins when MediaSentry, RIAA's investigative company, logs into a file-sharing network in search of computers hosting music for download. MediaSentry connects to these computers and scans them for music files. When it finds something suspicious, it sends the computer's IP address to the RIAA's Anti-Piracy group, together with a list of the files it found. RIAA staff members download and listen to a few of these to verify that they are in fact copyrighted songs. Then they file a lawsuit against "John Doe," the person who uses the computer at the offending IP address. (See the Appendix for an explanation of IP addresses and other aspects of Internet structure.) With the lawsuit as a legal basis, they subpoena the computer's Internet Service Provider, forcing disclosure of the real name of the John Doe user at that IP address. The RIAA sends the user its demand letter, naming the songs that were verified and citing the total number of songs found as the basis for damages. The letter offers an opportunity to settle; the average settlement demand is about $4,000, non-negotiable. There's even a web site, p2plawsuits.com, which users can visit to pay conveniently.

It's an automated sort of justice for the digital age. But these are automated sorts of crimes. File-sharing programs are commonly configured to start up and run automatically, exchanging files without human intervention.

The computer's owner may not even be aware that it has been configured to upload files in the background.

It's also an error-prone form of justice. Matching names to IP addresses is unreliable—several computers on the same wireless network might share the same IP address. An Internet Service Provider allocating IP addresses might shift them around, so that a computer with a particular IP address today might not be the same computer that was file sharing from that IP address last week. Even if it is the same computer, there's no way to prove who was using it at the time. And maybe there was a clerical error in reporting.

The RIAA knows that the process is flawed, but given their stake in stopping downloading, they see no choice. Not only are they seeing their products being distributed for free, but they themselves might be liable to lawsuits from artists for neglecting to protect the artists' copyrights. Explains Amy Weiss, RIAA Senior Vice President for Communications, "When you fish with a net, you sometimes are going to catch a few dolphin.... But we also realize that this cybershoplifting needs to stop." Besides Andersen, other snared "dolphin" included a Georgia family that didn't own a computer, a paralyzed stroke victim in Florida sued for files downloaded in Michigan, and an 83-year-old West Virginia woman who hated computers and who, as it turned out, was deceased.

## The High Stakes for Infringement

Error or not, most people choose to pay when they get the demand letter. The cost of settling is less than the legal fees for contesting, and the cost of losing the lawsuit is staggering: damages of at least $750 for each song downloaded. The 4,000-song contents of a 20GB iPod would be grounds for minimum damages of $3 million—a thousand times the cost of purchasing those songs on iTunes. (A GB, or *gigabyte*, is about a billion bytes.)

Driftnet justice, automated policing of automated crimes, and three million dollars minimum damages for an iPod's worth of music are consequences of policies honed for

> ### $750 A SONG
>
> The minimum damages that the court *must* award for infringement is $750 per infringing act. In cases where the infringement can be shown to be "willful," damages could be as high as $150,000 per infringement, or $600 million for the 4,000 songs on an iPod. For defendants who can prove that they weren't even aware of the infringement, the court still *must* award at least $200 per infringement—a "mere" $800,000 for 4,000 songs.

a pre-networked world colliding with the exponentials of the digital explosion. Take the $3-million iPod. This traces to the Copyright Act of 1976, which introduced a provision letting copyright holders sue for minimum *statutory damages* of $750 per infringement.

The rationale for statutory damages is to ensure that the penalty is sufficient to deter infringement even when actual damages to the copyright holder are small. The scale of the damages has dreadful consequences in the age of digital reproduction, because each time a song is copied (uploaded or downloaded), it counts as a *separate* infringement. That way of reckoning "acts of infringement" may have seemed reasonable when the standards were set in pre-Internet 1976—when people could make only a few unauthorized copies, one by one. But the damage calculations balloon into unreality when a thousand songs can be downloaded to a home computer in a few hours over a high-speed network connection.

Although the digital explosion may have blown the legal penalties for infringement out of realistic proportion to the offense, it has also brought a more fundamental change: that the public is now concerned with copyright at all. Before the Internet, what could an ordinary person do to infringe copyright—make fifty photocopies of a book and sell them on the street corner? That would surely be infringement. But it would also be a lot of work, and the financial loss to the copyright holder would be insignificant.

Of all the dislocations of the digital explosion, the loss of the copyright balance is the most rancorous. Ordinary people can now effortlessly copy and distribute information on a massive scale. Listeners clash with a content industry whose economics relies on ordinary people not doing precisely that. As a

---

### SENDING A MESSAGE

In October 2007, Jammie Thomas, a Minnesota single mother of two who earns $36,000 a year, was found guilty of sharing 24 songs on the Kazaa file-sharing network ... and fined $222,000: $9,250 per song. This was the first of the RIAA's 16,000 lawsuits that went all the way to a jury trial. In the others, people settled or, as with Tanya Andersen, the case was dismissed or dropped. Given the legal statutory damages for infringement, Thomas's fine for 24 songs could have been anywhere between $18,000 and $3.6 million.

A juror interviewed afterward reported that there were people advocating for fines at both ends of that spectrum during deliberation: "We wanted to send a message that you don't do this, that you have been warned."

Said the RIAA's lawyer after the verdict was read, "This is what can happen if you don't settle."

result, millions of people are today vilified as "pirates" and "thieves," while content providers are demonized as subverters of innovation and consumer freedom trying to protect their outdated business models.

*Of all the dislocations of the digital explosion, the loss of the copyright balance is the most rancorous.*

The war over copyright and the Internet has been escalating for more than 15 years. It is a spiral of more and more technology that makes it ever easier for more and more people to share more and more information. This explosion is countered by a legislative response that brings more and more acts within the scope of copyright enforcement, subject to punishments that grow ever more severe. Regulation tries to keep pace by banning technology, sometimes even before the technology exists. Single mothers facing mind-numbing lawsuits are merely collateral damage in that war today. If we cannot slow the arms race, tomorrow's casualties may come to include the open Internet and dynamic of innovation that fuels the information revolution.

# NET Act Makes Sharing a Crime

Copyright infringement was not even a criminal matter in the U.S. until the turn of the twentieth century, although an infringer could be sued for civil damages. Infringement with a profit motive first became a crime in 1897. The maximum punishment was then a year in prison and a $1,000 fine. Things stayed that way until 1976, when Congress started enacting a series of laws that repeatedly increased the penalties, motivated largely by prompting from the RIAA and the MPAA (Motion Picture Association of America). By 1992, an infringement conviction could result in a ten-year prison sentence and stiff fines, but only if the infringement was done "for the purpose of commercial advantage or private financial gain." Without a commercial motive, there was no crime.

That changed in 1994.

During the 1980s, MIT became one of the first universities to deploy large numbers of computer workstations connected to the Internet and open to anyone on campus. Even several years later, public clusters of networked powerful computers were not very common. In December 1993, some students in one of the clusters noticed a machine that was strangely unresponsive and was strenuously exercising its disk drive. When the computer staff examined this "bug," they discovered that the machine was acting as a file-server bulletin board—a relay point where people around the Internet were uploading and downloading files. Most of the files were computer games, and there was also some word-processing software.

MIT, like most universities, prefers to handle matters like this internally, but in this case there was a complication: The FBI had asked about this very same machine only a few days earlier. Federal agents had been investigating some crackers in Denmark who were trying to use MIT machines to break into National Weather Service computers. While measuring network traffic into and out of MIT, the Bureau had noticed a lot of activity coming from this particular machine. The bulletin board had nothing to do with the Denmark operation, but MIT felt that it had to tell the FBI what was happening. An agent staked out the machine and identified an MIT undergraduate, accusing him of operating the bulletin board.

The Justice Department seized on the case. The software industry was growing rapidly in 1994, and the Internet was just starting to enter the public eye—and here was the power of the Internet being turned to "piracy." The Boston U.S. Attorney issued a statement claiming that the MIT bulletin board was responsible for more than a million dollars in monetary losses, adding "We need to respond to the culture that no one is hurt by these thefts and that there is nothing wrong with pirating software."

What had occurred at MIT involved copyright infringement to be sure, but there was no commercial motive and hence no crime—no basis on which the Justice Department could act. There might have been grounds for a civil suit, but the companies whose software was involved were not interested in suing. Instead, the Boston U.S. Attorney's office, after checking with their superiors in Washington, brought a charge of wire fraud against the student, on the grounds that his acts constituted interstate transmission of stolen property.

At the trial, Federal District Judge Stearns dismissed the case, citing a Supreme Court ruling that bootleg copies do not qualify as stolen property. Stearns chastised the student, describing his behavior as "heedlessly irresponsible." The judge suggested that Congress could modify the copyright law to permit criminal prosecutions in cases like this if it so wished. But he emphasized that changing the rules should be up to Congress, not the courts. To accept the prosecution's claim, he warned, would "serve to criminalize the conduct ... of the myriad of home computer users who succumb to the temptation to copy even a single software program for private use." He cited Congressional testimony from the software industry that even the industry would not consider such an outcome desirable.

Two years later, Congress responded by passing the 1997 No Electronic Theft (NET) Act. Described by its supporters as "closing the loophole" demonstrated by the MIT bulletin board, NET criminalized any unauthorized copying with retail value over $1000, commercially motivated or not. This addressed Judge Stearns's suggestion, but it did not heed his caution: From now on, anyone making unauthorized copies at home, even a single copy of an expensive computer program, was risking a year in prison. After only two more years, Congress was back with the Digital Theft Deterrence and Copyright Damages Improvement Act of 1999. Its supporters argued that NET had been ineffective in stopping "piracy," and that penalties needed to be increased. The copyright arms race was in full swing.

## The Peer-to-Peer Upheaval

The NET Act marked the first time that the Internet had triggered a significant expansion of liability for copyright infringement. It would hardly be the last.

In the summer of 1999, Sean Fanning, a student at Northeastern University, began distributing a new file-sharing program and joined his uncle in forming a company around it: Napster. Napster made it easy to share files, especially music tracks, over the Internet, and to share them on a scale never before seen.

Here is how the system worked: Suppose Napster user Mary wants to share her computer file copy of Sarah McLachlan's 1999 hit *Angel*. She tells the Napster service, which adds "Angel; Sarah McLachlan" to its directory, together with an ID for Mary's computer. Any other Napster user who would like to get a copy of *Angel*, say Beth, can query the Napster directory to learn that Mary has a copy. Beth's computer then connects directly to Mary's computer and downloads the song without any further involvement from the Napster service. The connecting and downloading are done transparently by Napster-supplied software running on Mary's and Beth's computers.

The key point is that previous file-sharing set-ups like the MIT bulletin board were so-called *centralized systems*. They collected files at a central computer for people to download. Napster, in contrast, maintained only a central directory showing where files on other computers could be found. The individual computers passed the files among themselves directly. This kind of system organization is called a *peer-to-peer* architecture.

Peer-to-peer architectures make vastly more efficient use of the network than centralized systems, as Figure 6.1 indicates. In a centralized system, if many users want to download files, they must all get the files from the central server, whose connection to the Internet would consequently become a bottleneck as the number of users grows. In a peer-to-peer system, the central server itself need communicate only a tiny amount of directory information, while the large network load for transmitting the files is distributed over

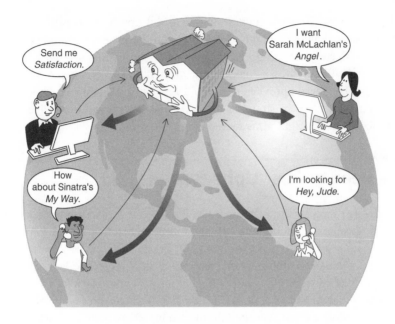

FIGURE 6.1   Underlying organization of traditional and peer-to-peer client-server network architectures. On the top, a traditional centralized file distribution architecture, in which files are downloaded to clients from a central server. On the bottom, a Napster-style peer-to-peer architecture in which the central server holds only directory information and the actual files are transmitted directly between clients without passing through the server.

the Internet connections of all the users. Even the slow connections common with personal computers in 1999 were enough for Napster's peer-to-peer system to let millions of users share music files ... which they did. By early 2001, two years after Napster appeared, there were more than 26 million registered Napster users. At some colleges, more than 80% of the on-campus network traffic could be traced to Napster. Students held Napster parties. You hooked up a computer to some speakers and to the Internet, invited your friends over—and for any song title requested, there it was. Someone among those millions of Napster users had the song available for downloading. This was the endless cornucopia of music; the universal jukebox.

## The Specter of Secondary Liability

Universal though it may have been, this jukebox was collecting no quarters for the music industry. Previous escapades in file sharing, usually done on a small scale among friends, were barely annoyances from an economic perspective. Even the MIT bulletin board that engendered the No Electronic Theft Act had perhaps a few hundred users altogether. Napster was on a completely different scale, where anyone could readily share music files with a few hundred thousand "friends." The recording industry recognized this immediately, and in December 1999, just a few months after Napster appeared, the RIAA sued it for more than $100 million in damages.

Napster protested that it had no liability. After all, Napster itself wasn't copying any files. It was merely providing a directory service. How could you hold a company liable for simply publishing the locations of items on the Internet? Wasn't that publication just exercising freedom of speech? Unfortunately for Napster, the California Federal District Court didn't agree, and in July 2000, found Napster guilty of secondary copyright infringement (enabling others to infringe, and profiting from the infringement). A year later, after an unsuccessful appeal to the Ninth Circuit, the court ordered Napster's file-sharing service to shut down.

Napster was dead, but it had captured the imagination of the technical community as a striking demonstration of the power of the

> **SECONDARY INFRINGEMENT**
>
> Copyright law distinguishes between two kinds of secondary infringement. The first is *contributory infringement*—i.e., knowingly providing tools that enable others to infringe. The second is *vicarious infringement*—i.e., profiting from the infringement of others that one is in a position to control, and not preventing it. Napster was found guilty of both contributory and vicarious infringement.

Internet's fundamental architecture. No central machine controls the network; every machine in the network has equal rights to send any other machine a message. Machines connected to the Internet are, as the lingo has it, *peers*. The notion of the Internet as a network of peer machines communicating with each other directly—as opposed to a network of client machines mediated by central servers—was hardly new. Even the very first Internet technical specification, published in 1969, described the network architecture in terms of machines interacting as a network of peers. Systems incorporating peer-to-peer communication between larger computers had been in wide use since the early 1980s.

Napster showed that the same principle remained valid when the peers were millions of personal computers controlled by ordinary people. Napster's use of peer-to-peer was illegal, but it demonstrated the potential of the idea. Research and development in distributed computing took off. In 2000 and 2001, more than $500 million was invested in companies building peer-to-peer applications. And transcending its roots as a technical network architecture, "P2P" became enshrined in techno-pop-culture-speak as a catchword for organizations of all types—including social, corporate, and political—that harness the power of myriad cooperating individuals without reliance on central authorities. As one 2001 review gushed, "P2P is a mindset, not a particular technology or industry."

Napster had also given an entire generation a taste of the Internet as universal jukebox for which people would clamor. Yet the recording companies, who worked together to combat illegal downloading, failed to collaborate to create a legal and profitable Internet music service to fill the vacuum left by Napster. Instead of capitalizing on file-sharing technology, they demonized it as a threat to their business. That technological rejectionism ratcheted up the rancor in the arms race, but it also did something even more short-sighted. The music companies surrendered a vast business opportunity to the profit of more imaginative entrepreneurs. Two years later, Apple would launch its iTunes music store, the first commercially successful music downloading service.

## Sharing Goes Decentralized

In the meantime, new file-sharing schemes sprouted up that explored new technical architectures in attempts to tiptoe around liability for secondary infringement. Napster's legal Achilles's heel had been its central directory. As the court had ruled, control of the directory amounted to control of the file-sharing activity, and Napster was consequently liable for that activity. The new architectures got rid of central directories entirely. One of the simplest methods, called *flooding*, works like this: Each computer in the file-sharing network maintains a list of other computers in the network. When file-sharer

Beth wants to find a copy of *Angel*, her computer asks all the computers in its list. Each of those computers offers to send Beth a copy of *Angel* if it has one, and otherwise relays Beth's request to all the computers on *its* list, and so on, until the request eventually reaches a computer that has the file. Figure 6.2 illustrates the process. In contrast to the Napster-style architecture in Figure 6.1, there's no central directory. Distributed architectures like

**CONTENT-DISTRIBUTION NETWORKS**
The bare-bones flooding method sketched here is too simple to support practical large networks. But the success of decentralized peer-to-peer architectures has stimulated research into practical *content-distribution network* architectures that exploit the efficiency and robustness of peer-to-peer methods.

this are powerful because they can be extremely robust. The network will keep working even if many individual computers fail or go offline, as long as enough computers remain to propagate the requests.

FIGURE 6.2   In contrast to Napster-style peer-to-peer systems illustrated earlier, decentralized file-sharing systems such as Grokster have no central directories.

## No Safe Harbors

The companies building the new generation of file-sharing systems hoped these distributed architectures would also immunize them against liability for secondary copyright infringement. After all, once users had the software, what they did with it was beyond the companies' knowledge or control. So, how could the companies be held liable for what users did? To the recording industry, however, this was just Napster all over again: exploiting the Internet to promote copyright infringement on a massive scale. In October 2001, the RIAA sued the makers of three of the most popular systems—Grokster, Morpheus, and Kazaa—for damages of $150,000 per infringement.

The three companies responded that they had no control over the users' actions. Moreover, their software was only one piece of the infrastructure that enabled file-sharing, and there were many other pieces. If the three software companies were liable, wouldn't makers of the other pieces be liable as well? What about Microsoft, whose operating system lets users of one computer copy files from other computers? What about Cisco, whose routers relay the unlicensed copyrighted material? What about the computer manufacturers, whose machines run the software? Wouldn't a ruling against the file-sharing network software companies expose the entire industry to liability?

The Supreme Court had provided guidance for navigating these waters with the landmark 1984 case *Sony v. Universal Studios*. In an episode that foreshadowed the *Grokster* suit 17 years later, the MPAA had sued Sony Corporation, charging Sony with secondary infringement for selling a device that was threatening to ruin the motion picture industry: the video cassette recorder. As the President of the MPAA thundered before Congress in 1982: "I say to you that the VCR is to the American film producer and the American public as the Boston strangler is to the woman home alone."

In a narrow 5 to 4 decision, the Supreme Court ruled in Sony's favor, holding that even though there was widespread infringement from people using VCRs

> ... the sale of copying equipment, like the sale of other articles of commerce, does not constitute contributory infringement if the product is widely used for legitimate, unobjectionable purposes. Indeed, it need merely be capable of substantial noninfringing uses.

The technology industries applauded. Here was a reasonably clear criterion they could rely on in evaluating the risk in bringing new products to market. Showing that a product was capable of substantial noninfringing uses would provide a "safe harbor" against allegations of secondary infringement.

This 1984 scenario—a new technology, a threatened business model—was now being replayed in the 2001 *Grokster* suit. The file-sharing companies were quick to cite the *Sony* ruling in their defense, explaining that there were many noninfringing uses of file sharing.

In April 2003, the Central California Federal District Court agreed that this case was different from Napster, and dismissed the suit, citing the *Sony* decision and commenting that the RIAA was asking the court to "expand existing copyright law beyond its well-drawn boundaries." In reaction, the RIAA immediately began its campaign of suing individual users of the file-sharing software—the campaign that would later snag Tanya Andersen and Jammie Thomas.

The District Court's ruling was appealed, and it was upheld by the Ninth Circuit, the same court that had ruled against Napster three years earlier:

> In short, from the evidence presented, the district court quite correctly concluded that the software was capable of substantial noninfringing uses and, therefore, that the *Sony-Betamax* doctrine applied.

The RIAA naturally appealed, and when the Supreme Court agreed to review the decision, the entire networked world held its breath. Were content publishers to have no legal recourse against massive file-sharing? Would the *Sony* safe harbor be overturned? In June 2005, the Court returned a unanimous verdict in favor of the RIAA:

> We hold that one who distributes a device with the object of promoting its use to infringe copyright, as shown by clear expression or other affirmative steps taken to foster infringement, is liable for the resulting acts of infringement by third parties.

## A Question of Intent

The content industry had won, although it ended up with less than it had hoped for. The MPAA wanted the court to be explicit in weakening the *Sony* "substantial noninfringing use" standard. Instead, the court declared that the *Sony* case was not at issue here, and it would not revisit that standard. The file-sharing companies' liability, the court said, stemmed not from the capabilities of the software, but from the companies' intent in distributing it.

The technology industries (other than the three defendants, who were driven out of business) breathed an immediate sigh of relief that *Sony* had been left intact. But this was quickly followed by second thoughts. The

*Grokster* decision had opened up an entirely new set of grounds on which one could be held liable for secondary infringement. As the court ruled: "Nothing in *Sony* requires courts to ignore evidence of intent to promote infringement if such evidence exists."

But what evidence? If someone accuses your company of secondary infringement, how confidently can you defend yourself against accusations of bad intent? The *Sony* safe harbor doesn't seem so safe any more.

Take an example: The *Grokster* ruling cited "advertising an infringing use" as evidence of an active step taken to encourage infringement. Apple introduced the iTunes desktop with its CD-copying software in 2001. Early advertisements heavily promoted the product with the slogan "Rip, Mix, Burn." Was that a demonstration of Apple's bad intent? Many people certainly thought so, including the Chairman of Walt Disney when he told Congress in 2002, "There are computer companies, that their ads, full-page ads, billboards up and down San Francisco and L.A., that say—what do they say?—'rip, mix, burn' to kids to buy the computer."

Can your company risk introducing a product with that slogan in the post-*Grokster* era? You might expect that you would have every chance of winning an "intent" fight in court, but the risks of losing are catastrophic. In personal infringement cases like Tanya Andersen's, even the minimum statutory damage penalties of $750 per infringement could have meant a million dollar claim over the (falsely alleged) songs on her hard drive—a staggering burden for an individual. But a technology company could conceivably be liable for damages based on *every* song illegally copied by *every* user of a device. Say you sell 14 million iPods (the number Apple sold in 2006) times 100 songs allegedly copied per iPod times $750 per song. That's more than a trillion dollars in damages—more than 100 times the *total* retail revenues of the recording industry worldwide in 2006! Liability like that might seem ridiculous, but that's the law. It means that guessing wrong is a bet-the-company mistake.

> ### No Commercial Skipping
>
> In 2001, ReplayTV Network introduced a digital video recorder for television programs that included the ability to skip commercials automatically. It also permitted people to move recorded shows from one ReplayTV machine to another. The company was sued for secondary infringement by the major movie studios and television networks, and driven into bankruptcy before the case was concluded. The company that bought Replay's assets settled the case, promising not to include these features in its future models.

Better to be conservative and not introduce products with features that might prompt a lawsuit, even if you are reasonably sure that your products are legal.

We can speculate about products and features that are unavailable today due to the uncertainties in *Grokster's* "intent" standard, coupled with penalties for secondary infringement penalties that could lead to nightmarish fines. Companies are naturally reluctant to give examples, but one might ask why songs shared wirelessly with Microsoft Zune players self-destruct after three plays, or why Tivo recorders don't have automatic commercial skipping or let you move recorded movies to a PC. Non-coincidentally, in 2002, the CEO of a major cable network characterized skipping commercials while watching TV as theft, although he allowed that "I guess there could be a certain amount of tolerance for going to the bathroom."

But speculating about the consequences of liability alone is largely pointless, because these liability risks have not been increasing in a vacuum. A second front has opened up in the copyright wars. Here, the weapons are not lawsuits, but technology.

# Authorized Use Only

Computers process information by copying bits—between disk and memory, between memory and networks, from one part of memory to another. Actually, most computers are able to "keep" bits in memory only by recopying them over and over, thousands of times a second. (Ordinary computers use what is called Dynamic Random Access Memory, or DRAM. The copying is what makes it "dynamic.") The relation of all this essential copying to the kind of copying governed by copyright law has been intellectual fodder for legal scholars—and for lawyers looking for new grounds on which to sue.

Computers cannot run programs stored on disk without copying the program code to memory. The copyright law explicitly permits this copying for the purpose of running the program. But suppose someone wants simply to *look at* the code in memory, not to run it. Does that require explicit permission from the copyright holder? In 1993, a U.S. Federal Circuit Court ruled that it does.

Going further, computers cannot display images on the screen without copying them to a special part of memory called a display buffer. Does this mean that, even if you purchase a computer graphic image, you can't view the image without explicit permission from the copyright holder each time? A 1995 report from the Department of Commerce argued that it does mean exactly this, and went on to imply that almost any use of a digital work involves making a copy and therefore requires explicit permission.

## Digital Rights and Trusted Systems

Legal scholars can debate whether copyright law mandates a future of "authorized use only" for digital information. The answer may not matter much, because that future is coming to pass through the technologies of digital rights management and trusted systems.

The core idea is straightforward. If computers are making it easy to copy and distribute information without permission, then *change computers* so that copying or distributing without permission is difficult or impossible. This is not an easy change to make; perhaps it cannot be done at all without sacrificing the computer's ability to function as a general-purpose device. But it's a change that's underway nonetheless.

Here is the issue: Suppose (fictitious) Fortress Publishers is in the business of selling content over the Web. They'd like the only people getting their content to be those whose pay. Fortress can start by restricting access on their web site to registered users only, by requiring passwords. Much web content is sold like this today—for instance, *Wall Street Digest* or *Safari Books Online*. The method works well (or at least has worked well so far) for this type of material, but there's a problem with higher-value content. How does Fortress prevent people who've bought its material from copying and redistributing it?

One thing Fortress can do is to distribute their material in encrypted form, in such a way that it can be decrypted and processed only by programs that obey certain rules. For instance, if Fortress distributes PDF documents created with Adobe Acrobat, it can use Adobe LiveCycle Enterprise Suite to control whether people reading the PDF file with Adobe Reader are allowed to print it, modify it, or copy portions of it. Fortress can even arrange to make a document "phone home" over the Internet—i.e., to notify Fortress whenever it is opened and report the IP address of the computer that is opening it. Similarly, if Fortress prepares music files for use with Windows Media Player, it can use Microsoft Windows Media Rights Manager to limit the number of times the music can be played, to control whether it can be copied to a portable player or a CD, force it to expire after a certain period of time, or make it phone home for permission each time it's played so that the Fortress web server can check a license and require payment if necessary.

The general technique of distributing content together with control information that restricts its use is called *digital rights management* (DRM). DRM systems are widely used today, and there are industry specifications (called *rights expression languages*) that detail a wide range of restrictions that can be imposed.

DRM might appear to solve Fortress's problem, but the approach is far from airtight. How can Fortress be confident that people using their material are using it with the intended programs, the ones that obey the DRM restrictions? Encrypting the files helps, but as explained in Chapter 5, attackers break that kind of encryption all the time—it happens regularly with PDF and Windows Media. More simply, someone could modify the document reader or the media player program to save unencrypted copies of the material as they are running, and then distribute those copies all over the Internet for anyone's use.

To prevent this, Fortress could rely on the computer operating system to require that any program manipulating their content must be certified. Before a program is run, the operating system checks a digital

> ### ENCRYPTION AND DRM
>
> Chapter 5 explains public-key encryption and digital signatures—the technologies that make public distribution of encrypted material possible. The "messages" that Alice and Bob are exchanging might be not text messages, but rather music, videos, illustrated documents, or anything at all. As the first koan says, "it's all just bits." Thus, the encryption technologies that Alice and Bob use for secret communication can be used by content suppliers to control the conditions under which consumers can watch movies or listen to songs.

signature for the program to verify that the program is approved and has not been altered. That's better, but a really clever attacker might alter the operating system so that it will run the modified program anyway. How could anyone prevent that? The answer is to build a chip into every computer that checks the operating system each time the machine is turned on. If the operating system has been modified, the computer will not boot. The chip should be tamper-proof so that any attempt to disable it will render the machine inoperable.

This basic technique was worked out during the 1980s and demonstrated in several research and advanced development projects, but only since 2006 has it been ready for wide deployment in consumer-grade computers. The required chip, called a *Trusted Platform Module* (TPM), was designed by the *Trusted Computing Group*, a consortium of hardware and software companies formed in 1999. More than half of the computers shipped worldwide today contain TPMs. Popular operating systems, including Microsoft Windows Vista and several versions of GNU/Linux, can use them for security applications. One application, *trusted boot*, prevents the computer from booting if the operating system has been modified (for example, by a virus). Another application, called *sealed storage*, lets you encrypt files in such a way that they can be decrypted only on particular computers that you specify. Given today's concerns over viruses and Internet security, it's a safe bet that TPMs will become pervasive. One industry estimate shows that more than 80% of laptop PCs will include TPMs by 2009.

## Asserting Control Beyond the Bounds of Copyright

Fortress Publishers' problem could be solved in a world of digital rights management reinforced by trusted computing, but is that something we should welcome?

For one thing, it gives Fortress a level of control over use of its material that goes far beyond the bounds of copyright law. When we buy a book today, we take for granted that we have the right to read it whenever we like and as many times as we like; read it from cover to cover or skip around; lend it to a friend; resell it; copy out a paragraph for use in a book report; donate it to a school library; open it without "phoning home" to tell Fortress we are doing so. We need no permission to do any of these things. Are we willing to give up these rights when books are digital computer files? How about music? Videos? Software? Should we care?

Now leave to one side, for a moment, the dispute between music companies and listeners. DRM and trusted computing technologies, once standard in personal computers, will have other uses. The same methods that, in one country, prohibit people from playing unlicensed songs can, in another country, prevent people from listening to unapproved political speeches or reading unapproved newspapers. Developers of DRM and trusted platforms may be creating effective technologies to control the use of information, but no one has yet devised effective methods to circumscribe the limits of that control. As one security researcher warned: "Trusted computing" means that "third parties can trust that your computer will disobey your wishes."

> *The same methods that, in one country, prohibit people from playing unlicensed songs can, in another country, prevent people from listening to unapproved political speeches or reading unapproved newspapers.*

Another concern with DRM is that it increases opportunities for technology lock-in and anticompetitive mischief. It is tempting to design operating systems that run only certified applications in order to protect against viruses or bogus document readers and media players. But this can easily turn into an environment where no one can market a new media player without publishers' approval, or where no one can deploy *any* application without first having it registered and approved by Microsoft, HP, or IBM. A software company that poses a competitive threat to established interests, like publishers, operating system vendors, or computer manufacturers, might suddenly encounter "complications" in getting its products certified. One reason innovation has been so rapid in information technology is that the infrastructure is open: You don't need permission to introduce new programs and devices on the Internet. A world of trusted systems could easily jeopardize this.

A third DRM difficulty is that, in the name of security and virus protection, we could easily slip into an unwinnable arms race of increasing technology lock-down that provides no real gain for content owners. As soon as attackers anywhere bypass the DRM to produce an unencrypted copy, they can distribute it—and they might be willing to go to a lot of effort to be able to do that.

Think, for example, about making unauthorized copies of movies. Very sophisticated attackers might modify the TPM hardware on their computers, putting a lot of effort into bypassing the tamper-proof chip. Here's an even easier method: let the TPM system operate normally, but hook up a video recorder in place of the computer display. That particular attack has been anticipated by the industry with a standard that requires all high-definition video to be transmitted between devices in encrypted form. Windows Vista implements this in its *Output Protection Management* subsystem, out of concern that otherwise the movie studios would not permit high-definition video to be played on PCs at all. Even that protection scheme is vulnerable—you could simply point a video recorder at the screen. The result would not be high-definition quality, but once it has been digitized, it could be sent around the Internet without any further degradation.

Content owners worried about these sorts of attacks refer to them as the *analog hole*, and there seems to be no technological way to prevent them. J.K. Rowling tried to prevent unauthorized Internet copies of *Harry Potter and the Deathly Hallows* by not releasing an electronic version of the book at all. That did not stop the zealous fan mentioned in Chapter 2 from simply photographing every page and posting the entire book on the Web even before it was in bookstores.

In the words of one computer security expert, "Digital files cannot be made uncopyable, any more than water can be made not wet." There is one thing for certain: The DRM approach to copyright control is difficult, frustrating, and potentially fraught with unintended consequences. Out of that frustration has emerged a third response—along with liability and DRM—to the increasing levels of copying on the Internet: outright criminalization of technology.

## Forbidden Technology

The lines of text following this paragraph might be illegal to print in a book sold in the United States. We've omitted the middle four lines to protect ourselves and our publisher. Had we left them in, this would be a computer program, written in the Perl computer language, to unscramble encrypted DVDs. Informing you how to break DVD encryption so you could copy your DVDs would be a violation of 17 USC §1201, the *anti-circumvention* provision of the 1998 Digital Millennium Copyright Act (DMCA). This section of the DMCA outlaws technology for bypassing copyright protection. Don't bother turning to the back of the book for a note telling you where to find the missing four lines. A New York U.S. District Judge ruled in 2000 that even providing so much as a web link to the code was a DMCA violation in itself, and the Appeals Court agreed.

```
s''$/=\\2048;while(<>){G=29;R=142;if((@a=unqT="C*",_)[20]&48){D=89;_unqb24.qT.@

. . . (four lines suppressed) . . .

)+=P+( F&E))for@a[128..$#a]\\}print+qT.@a}';s/[D-HO-U_]/\\$$&/g;s/q/pack+/g;eval
```

The DMCA's anti-circumvention rules do more than stop people from printing gibberish in books. They outlaw a broad class of technologies—outlaw manufacturing them, selling them, writing about them, and even talking about them. That Congress took such a step shows the depth of the alarm and frustration at how easily DRM is bypassed. With §1201, Congress legislated, not against copyright infringement, but against bypassing itself, whether or not anything is copied afterwards. If you find an encrypted web page that contains the raw text of the Bible and break the encryption order to read Genesis, that's not copyright infringement—but it *is* circumvention. Circumvention is its own offense, subject to many of the same penalties as copyright infringement: statutory damages and, in some cases, imprisonment. Congress intentionally chose to make the offense independent of actual infringement. Alternative proposals that would have limited the prohibition to circumvention for the purpose of copyright infringement were considered and defeated.

The DMCA prohibition goes further. As §1201(a)(2) decrees:

> No person shall manufacture, import, offer to the public, provide, or otherwise traffic in any technology, product, service, device, component, or part thereof, that ... is primarily designed or produced for the purpose of circumventing a technological measure that effectively controls access to a work protected under [copyright].

Here the law passes from regulating behavior (circumvention) to regulating technology itself. It's a big step, but in the words of one of the bill's supporters at the time, "I continue to believe that we must ban devices whose major purpose is circumvention because I do not think it will work from the enforcement standpoint. That is, allowing anti-circumvention devices to proliferate freely, and outlaw only the inappropriate use of them, seems to me unlikely to deter much."

In the arena of security, there is an odd asymmetry between the world of atoms and the world of bits. There are many published explanations of how to crack mechanical combination locks, and even of how to construct a physical master key for a building from a key to a single lock in the set. But if the lock is digital, and what is behind it is *Pirates of the Caribbean*, the rules are different. Federal law prohibits publication of any explanation of how to reverse-engineer that kind of lock.

Legislators may not have seen an effective alternative, but they crafted an awkward form of regulation that begins with a broad prohibition and then grants exemptions on a case-by-case basis. The need for exemptions became apparent even as the DMCA was being drafted. A few exemptions got written into the statute. These included permission for intelligence and law enforcement agents to break encryption during the course of investigations and permission for non-profit libraries to break the encryption on a work, but only for the purpose of deciding whether to buy it. The law also included a complex rule that allows certain types of encryption research under certain circumstances. Recognizing that needs for new exemptions would continue to arise, Congress charged the Librarian of Congress to conduct hearings to review the exemptions every three years and grant new ones if appropriate.

For instance, in November 2006, after a year-long hearing process, a new exemption gave Americans the right to undo the lock-in on their mobile phones for the purpose of shifting to a new cellular service provider. The ruling had a big impact nine months later in August 2007, when Apple released its iPhone, locked to the AT&T cellular network. Users clamored to unlock their iPhones so they could be used on other networks, and several companies began selling unlocking services. But the language of the DMCA and the exemption is so murky that, while unlocking your *own* phone is legal, distributing unlocking software or even *telling* other people how to unlock their phones might still be a DMCA violation. Indeed, AT&T threatened legal action against at least one unlocking company.

## Copyright Protection or Competition Avoidance?

The DMCA's framework for regulation is a poor match to technology innovation, because the lack of an appropriate exemption can stymie the deployment of a new device or a new application. Given the ferocity of industry competition, there's the constant temptation to exploit the broad language of the prohibition as grounds for lawsuits against competitors.

In 2002, the Chamberlain garage-door company sued a maker of universal electronic garage-door openers, claiming that the universal transmitters circumvented access controls when they sent radio signals to open and close the doors. It took two years for the case to finally die at the appeals court. That same year, Lexmark International sued a company that made replacement toner cartridges for Lexmark printers, charging that the cartridges circumvented access controls in order to function with the printer. The District Court agreed. The ruling was overturned on appeal in 2004, but in the meantime, the alternative cartridges were kept off the market for a year and a half. In 2004, the Storage Technology Corporation successfully convinced the Boston District Court that it was a DMCA violation for third-party vendors to service its systems. Had the appeals court not overturned the ruling, we might now be in a situation where no independent company could service computer hardware. It would be as if Ford Tauruses came with their hoods sealed, and it was illegal for any mechanic not licensed by Ford to service them.

Lawsuits like these earned the DMCA the epithet "Digital Millennium Competition Avoidance." Fortunately, none of the lawsuits were ultimately successful, because the courts ruled that the underlying disputes weren't sufficiently related to copyrighted material—it's unlikely that Congress intended the DMCA to apply to garage doors. But in areas where copyright enters, the anti-competitive impact of the DMCA emerges in full force.

Imagine that the 1984 Supreme Court ruling in the *Sony* case had gone the other way, and the Court had declared Sony liable for copyright infringement for selling VCRs. Would VCRs have disappeared? Almost certainly not—consumers wanted them. More likely, the electronics industry would have cut a deal with the motion picture industry, giving them control over the capabilities of VCRs. VCRs would have become highly regulated machines, regulated to meet the demands of the motion picture industry. All new VCR features would need to be approved, and any feature the MPAA didn't like would be kept off the market. The capabilities of the VCR would be under the control of the content industry.

That's the kind of world we are living in today when it comes to digital media. If a company manufactures a product that processes digital information, it needs to be concerned about copyright infringement, even without the DMCA. This is a big concern, especially after *Grokster*. But suppose the device could not be used for copyright infringement. Even then, if the digital information is restricted by DRM, the product must abide by the terms of the DRM restrictions. Otherwise, that would be circumvention, so the product couldn't be legally manufactured at all. The terms of the DRM restrictions are completely at the whim of the content provider. Once Fortress Publishers installs DRM, they get to dictate the behavior of any device that accesses their material.

In the case of DVDs, DVD content is encrypted with an algorithm called the Content Scrambling System (CSS), developed by Matsushita and Toshiba and first introduced in 1996. As mentioned in Chapter 5, that algorithm was quickly broken—a textbook violation of Kerckhoffs's Principle—and underground decryption programs are today readily found on the Internet. The censored six lines of text earlier in this chapter is one such program.

Although CSS is useless for realistic copy protection, it is invaluable as an enabler of anti-competitive technology regulation. Any company marketing a product that decrypts DVDs needs a license from the DVD Copy Control Association (DVD CCA), an organization formed in 1999. The license conditions are determined by whatever the CCA decides. For example, all DVD players must obey "region coding," which limits them to playing DVDs made for one part of the world only, and an individual player's region can be changed no more than five times. Region coding has nothing to do with copyright. It is there to support a motion picture industry marketing strategy of releasing movies in different parts of the world at different times. The varied license restrictions include some that companies are not even permitted to see until after they have signed the license.

## The Face of Technology Lock-in

Suppose you are a company with an idea for an innovative DVD product. Maybe it is a home entertainment system that lets people copy and store DVDs for later watching, and you have worked out a way to do this without encouraging copyright infringement. This is an actual product. Kaleidescape, the California start-up that makes it, was sued by the DVD CCA in 2004 for violating a provision of the CSS license that forces DVD players to be designed to work only when there is a physical disk present. In March 2007, a California court ruled in Kaleidescape's favor, on the grounds that the license wasn't clear enough, but the case is being appealed. In any case, the CCA can change the license at any time. The legal wrangling has kept the company under a cloud for three years. Another start-up working on a similar product at the same time folded when it failed to get venture funding, "in part due to the threat of legal action from the DVD CCA."

The DVD technology lock-in has been in place since 2000. A similar lock-in is being implemented for high-definition cable TV. A campaign to extend the lock-in to all consumer media technology is being promoted in Washington as the *broadcast flag initiative*. And more trial balloons keep being floated in the name of protecting copyright. A bill was introduced in Congress to ban home recording of satellite radio. NBC urged the Federal Communications Commission to force Internet service providers to filter all Internet traffic for copyright infringement (that is, to compel ISPs to check packets as they are passed around the Internet and to discard packets deemed to contain unauthorized material). In 2002, Congress considered a breathtakingly broad prohibition against *any* communications device that does not implement copyright control—a bill that had to be redrafted after it became apparent that the first draft would have banned heart pacemakers and hearing aids.

So, in the United States today, a technology company is free to invent a new garage-door opener without needing its design approved by the garage-door makers. It can manufacture cheaper replacement toner cartridges without approval from the printer companies. It cannot, however, create new software applications that manipulate video from Hollywood movie DVDs without permission from the DVD CCA. It cannot in principle create *any* new product or service around DRM-restricted digital content without getting permission, often from the very people who might regard that new product as a competitive threat.

This is the regulatory posture at the present juncture in the copyright wars. People can debate the merits of this position. Some say that the DMCA is necessary. Others claim that it has been largely ineffective in curtailing infringement, as the continuing calls for ever more severe copyright penalties demonstrate.

*The anti-circumvention approach is poisonous to the innovation that drives the digital age.*

But whatever its merits, the anti-circumvention approach is poisonous to the innovation that drives the digital age. It hobbles the rapid deployment of new products and services that interoperate with existing infrastructure. The uncertain legal risks drive away the venture capital needed to bring innovations to market.

In essence, the DMCA has enlisted the force of criminal law in the service of the lock-in shenanigans invited by DRM. It has introduced anti-competitive regulation under the guise of copyright protection. By outlawing technology for circumventing DRM, the law has, in the words of one critic, become a tool for "circumventing competition."

Public Knowledge (`publicknowledge.org`) is a Washington DC public-interest group that focuses on policy issues concerning digital information. See their "issues" and "policy" blogs to stay current on the latest happenings in Washington.

# Copyright Koyaanisqatsi: Life Out of Balance

1982 marked the release of an astonishing film called *Koyaanisqatsi*. The title is a Hopi Indian word meaning "life out of balance." The film, which has no dialogue or narration, barrages viewers with images at once hauntingly beautiful and deeply disturbing, images that juxtapose the world of nature with the world of cities. The relentless message is that technology is destroying our ability to live harmonious, balanced lives.

In the first decade of the twenty-first century, we inhabit a world of copyright koyaanisqatsi. Virtually every salvo in the copyright war, Congressional bill introduced, lawsuit filed, court ruling issued, or advocacy piece trumpeted, pays homage to the "traditional balance of copyright" and the need to preserve it. The truth is that the balance is gone, toppled in the digital explosion, which is likewise shattering the framework for any civil consensus over the disposition of information. The balance is gone for good reason.

Copyright (at least in the United States) is supposedly a deal the government strikes between the creator of a work and the public. The creator gets limited monopoly control over the work, for limited times, which provides the opportunity to benefit commercially. The public gets the benefit of having the work, and also gets to use it without restriction after the monopoly has expired. The parameters of the deal have evolved over the years, generally in the direction of a stronger monopoly. Under the first U.S. copyright law, enacted in 1790, copyright lasted a maximum of 28 years. Today, it lasts until 70 years after the author's death. In principle, however, it's still a deal.

It is an enormously complex deal, and it is easy see why. Today's copyright law is the outcome of 200 years of wrangling, negotiating, and compromising. The first copyright statute was printed in its entirety in two newspaper columns of the *Columbian Centinel*, shown in Figure 6.3. As the enlarged text insert shows, the law covered only maps, charts, and books, and granted exclusive rights to "print, reprint, publish, or vend." The period of copyright was 14 years (with a 14-year renewal). Today's statute runs to more than 200 pages. It's a Byzantine stew peppered with exceptions, qualifications, and arcane provisions. You can't make a public performance of a musical work unless you're an

> ### DIGITAL COPYRIGHT
>
> *Digital Copyright* by Jessica Litman (Prometheus Books, 2001) recounts the evolution of U.S. copyright law as a series of negotiated compromises. The Citizen Media Law Project (www.citmedialaw.org) offers useful information to online publishers—not just about copyright, but other legal matters as well.

agricultural society at an agricultural fair. You can't freely copy written works, but you can if you're an association for the blind and you're making an edition of the work in Braille (but not if the work is a standardized test). A radio station can't broadcast a recording without a license from the music publisher, but it doesn't need a license from the record company—but that's only if it's an analog broadcast. For digital satellite radio, you need licenses from both (but there are exceptions).

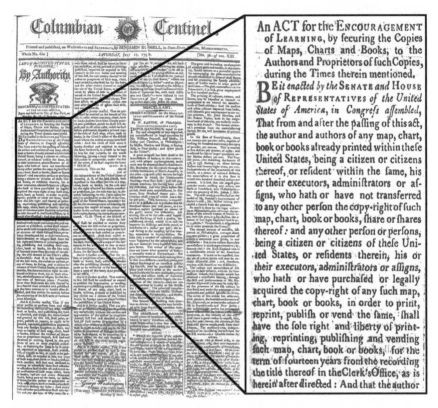

FIGURE 6.3    The first U.S. copyright law—"An Act for the Encouragement of Learning." It was printed as the first two columns of the July 17, 1790 edition of the *Columbian Centinel*. Note George Washington's signature on the bill at the bottom of the second column.

It is a law written for specialists, not for ordinary people. Even ordinary lawyers have trouble interpreting it. But that never mattered, because the copyright deal never was about ordinary people. The so-called "copyright balance" was largely a balancing act among competing business interests. The evolution of copyright law has been a story of the relevant players sitting down at the table and working things out, with Congress generally following suit. Ordinary people were not involved, because ordinary people had no real ability to publish, and they had nothing to bring to the table.

## Late to the Table

The digital explosion has changed all that by making it easy for anyone to copy and distribute information on a world-wide scale. We can all be publishers now. The public is now a party to the copyright deal—but the game has been going on for 200 years, and the hands were dealt long ago.

When people come to the table with their new publishing power, expecting to take full advantage of information technology, they find that there are possibilities that seem attractive, easy, and natural, but for which the public's rights have already been "balanced" away. Among the lost opportunities are copying a DVD to a portable player, making the video clip equivalent of an audio mixtape, placing a favorite cartoon or a favorite song on a Facebook page, or adding your own creative input to a work of art you love and sharing that with the world.

People resent it when acts like these are denounced as theft and piracy. As a contributor to a computer bulletin board quipped, "My first-grade teacher told me I should share, and now they're telling me it's illegal."

### CAN YOU COPY MUSIC CDS TO YOUR COMPUTER?

Of course, you *can* easily copy CDs to your computer hard drive: There are dozens of software packages designed to do just that, and millions of people do it regularly. Yet the legal issues in CD copying are both murky and confusing—a striking example of the mismatch of copyright law and public understanding.

In testimony at the Jammie Thomas trial in October 2007 (see the sidebar earlier this chapter), Jennifer Pariser, the head of litigation for Sony BMG, suggested that ripping your own legally purchased CD, even for personal use, is illegal, asserting that making a copy of a purchased song is just "a nice way of saying 'steals just one copy'." The RIAA web site specifically states that there is no legal right to copy music CDs, although it allows that copying music "usually won't raise concerns" so long as the copy is for personal use, and it warns that it's illegal to give your copy away or lend it to others to copy.

In contrast, in an October 2006 poll of Los Angeles teenagers, 69% believed that it *is* legal to copy a CD from a friend who had purchased it.

That resentment can easily grow to a sense of moral outrage. In the words of Electronic Frontier Foundation founder, John Gilmore:

> What is wrong is that we have invented the technology to eliminate scarcity, but we are deliberately throwing it away to benefit those who profit from scarcity. We now have the means to duplicate any kind of information that can be compactly represented in digital media.... We should be rejoicing in mutually creating a heaven on earth! Instead, those crabbed souls who make their living from perpetuating scarcity are sneaking around, convincing co-conspirators to chain our cheap duplication technology so that it *won't* make copies—at least not of the kind of goods *they* want to sell us. This is the worst sort of economic protectionism—beggaring your own society for the benefit of an inefficient local industry.

But one person's sharing can be another person's theft, and the other side in the copyright war has no shortage of its own moral outrage. The motion picture industry estimates that the retail value of unauthorized movie copies floating around the Internet is more than $7 billion. As the president of the MPAA puts it:

> We will not welcome ... theft masquerading as technology. No business, including the movies, can keep its doors open, its employees paid, and its customers satisfied if pirates and thieves are allowed to run ramshackle over this country's basic protection of the right of individuals to the ownership of their creative expressions, and to benefit from those expressions and that ownership.

This is not "balance." It's a nasty firefight filled with indignation, recriminations, and a path of escalating punishments and anticompetitive regulation in the name of copyright law. As collateral damage of the battle, innovation is being held hostage.

## Toward De-Escalation

Getting off that path requires freeing ourselves of old ideas and perspectives. Difficult as that seems, there are grounds for optimism. During 2007, the recording industry made a major shift away from reliance on digital rights management. In addition to restraints it imposes on technology, DRM is an inconvenience both for consumers and publishers. There has been an increasing public acknowledgement of the downsides of DRM, not only by consumer groups, but by the industry itself.

One of the first visible moves was an announcement in February 2007 by Apple's Steve Jobs, in the form of an open letter to recording industry executives asking them to relax the licensing restrictions that required Apple to implement DRM on iTunes music. In Jobs's view, a world of online stores selling DRM-free music that could play on any player would be "clearly the best alternative for consumers, and Apple would embrace it in a heartbeat." The industry reacted coldly, but other groups chimed in to agree with Jobs. In March, Musicload, one of Europe's largest online music retailers, came out against DRM, noting that 75% of its customer service calls were due to DRM. Musicload asserted that DRM makes using music difficult for consumers and hinders the development of a mass market for legal downloads. In November, the British Entertainment Retailers Association also came out against DRM. Its director general claimed that copy protection mechanisms were "stifling growth and working against the consumer interest."

By the summer of 2007, Apple iTunes and (separately) Universal Music Group began releasing music tracks that could be freely copied. The iTunes tracks contained information ("watermarks") identifying the original purchaser from iTunes. That way, if large numbers of unauthorized copies would appear on the Internet, the original purchaser could be traced and held accountable.

A few months later, even that level of restriction was vanishing. By the beginning of 2008, all four major music labels—Universal, EMI, Warner, and Sony/BMG—were releasing music for sale through Amazon without watermarks that identified individual buyers. It was a remarkable about-face over the course of a year. When Jobs made his February 2007 proposal, Warner Music CEO Edgar Bronfman flat-out rejected the idea as "completely without logic or merit." Before the end of the year, Warner was announcing that it would

> **USING WATERMARKING**
>
> Using watermarking rather than copy restrictions and access control is an example of a general approach to regulation through *accountability*, rather than *restriction*. Don't try to prohibit violations in advance, but make it possible to identify violations when they occur and deal with them then. The same perspective can apply in privacy, as mentioned in Chapter 2, where one can focus on the appropriate use of personal information rather than restricting access to it.

sell DRM-free music on Amazon, with Bronfman explaining in a note to
employees:

> By removing a barrier to the sale and enjoyment of audio downloads,
> we bring an energy-sapping debate to a close and allow ourselves to
> refocus on opportunities and products that will benefit not only
> WMG, but our artists and our consumers as well.

The increasing recognition that the DRM approach is failing is sparking
experiments with other models for distributing music on the Internet.
Universal has been talking to Sony and other labels about a subscription service, where users would pay a fixed fee and then get as much music as they
want. One plan links the service to a new hardware device, here the price of
the service would be folded into the price of the hardware.

A related idea is to distribute music through blanket licenses with mobile
carriers or ISPs. New companies are emerging that offer this kind of service
on college computer networks. Another variant is the idea of *unlimited content networks*. These are networks that give access to music or video that
floats around the network with no restrictions. People can make unlimited use
of the material—downloading, copying, moving it to portable devices, sharing with others—as long as they keep it within the network.

A complementary approach promotes sharing of music and other creative
works in a way that enriches the common culture, by making it easy for creators to distribute their own work and to build on each other's work. One
organization that provides technical and legal tools to encourage this is
*Creative Commons*. This organization distributes a family of copyright
licenses that creators can use for publishing their works on the Internet,
including licenses that permit open sharing. The licenses are expressed both
as legal documents and as computer code that can support new applications.
If a work appears on the Web with the appropriate Creative Commons code,
for example, search engines might return references to it when asked to find
material that can be used under specified licensing conditions. Stimulating
open sharing on the Internet is an example of moving toward a *commons*—
that is, a system of sharing that minimizes the need for fine-grained property
restrictions (Chapter 8, "Bits in the Air" includes more on the notion of a
commons).

Experience with these and other approaches will show whether there are
economically viable models for distributing music that do not rely upon

DRM. Success could pave the way for the motion picture industry and other publishers to get off the anti-circumvention path—a dead end that has been more effective at harming innovation than at stopping infringement, and which even some of the original architects of the policy are now acknowledging as a failed approach.

> **CREATIVE COMMONS LICENSES**
>
> If you've created works that you want to publish on the Internet, you can use the Creative Commons license generator at `creativecommons.org` to obtain a license tailored to your needs. With the license, you can retain specified rights of your choice while granting blanket permission for other uses.

Even then, however, the larger problems created by the DMCA would not fade away, since policies locked into law are not easily unlocked. If the content industry moves to better business models and the DRM battles subside, the DMCA's anticircumvention provisions may continue to be anti-consumer, anti-competitive blots on the digital landscape. Unless repealed from the legal code, they would remain as battlefield relics of a war that was settled by peaceful means—unexploded ordnance that a litigious business could still use in ways unrelated to the law's original intent.

# The Limits of Property

For 15 years, the fights over digital music and digital video have been the front line of the copyright wars. Perhaps innovations and experiments that are already underway will help defuse those battles. The enormous potential of the Internet for good—and for profit—need not be sacrificed to combat its abuse. If you do not like what others are doing with the Internet, the Internet does not have to become your enemy—unless you make it your enemy.

The indignation over copyright is intense. The interest in new approaches, such as accountability and commons, suggests the deeper source of the discomfort with the metaphors of property and theft when applied to words and music. The copyright balance that is being toppled by digitization is not just the traditional tension between creator and the public. It is the balance between the individual and society that underlies our notions of property itself. Accountability and commons are attempts to find substitutes for the ever-expanding property restrictions imposed in the name of digital copyright law.

**FREE CULTURE**

Lawrence Lessig's *Free Culture: How Big Media Uses Technology and the Law to Lock Down Culture and Control Creativity* (Penguin, 2004) compellingly traces the story of how overbroad copyright restrictions are jeopardizing the future of a robust and vibrant public culture.

When we characterize movies, songs, and books as "property," we evoke visceral metaphors of freedom and independence: "my parcel of land versus your parcel of land." But the digital explosion is fracturing these property metaphors. "My parcel of land" might be different from "your parcel of land," but when both parcels are blown to clouds of bits, the clouds swirl together. The property lines that would separate them vanish in a fog of network packets.

## Learning To Fly Through the Digital Clouds

In 2004, Google embarked on a project, mentioned in Chapter 4, to index the book collections of several large libraries for Google's search engine. The idea is that when you search on the Web, you'll be able to find books relevant to your search query, together with a snippet of text from the book. As Google describes it, they are creating "an enhanced card catalog of the world's books," and this should be no more controversial than any card catalog.

The Association of American Publishers (AAP) and the Authors' Guild object to the Google book project, and they are suing Google for copyright infringement. In the words of the AAP President Patricia Schroeder, "Google is seeking to make millions of dollars by freeloading on the talent and property of authors and publishers." The president of the Authors' Guild equates including a book in the project with stealing the work. At issue is the fact that Google is scanning the books and making copies in order to create the search index, and the case is being debated on legal technicalities about whether this scanning constitutes copyright infringement.

The library project will certainly be beneficial to Google by making its search engine more valuable, and Google is indeed scanning the books without permission from the copyright holders. Are they "appropriating property" and extracting value from it without compensating the owners, not even asking for permission? Should Google be permitted to do that? If you write a book, and that's "property" that you "own," how far should the limits of your ownership extend?

As a society, we have faced this kind of question before. If a stream runs through your land, do you own the water in the stream? Are there limits to your ownership? Can you pump out that water and sell it—even if that would

### COPYRIGHT AND WEB SEARCHING

If you believe that the Google library project violates copyright, you might wonder whether search engines themselves infringe copyright by caching and indexing web sites and providing links. This claim has been the source of lawsuits, but the courts have been rejecting it. In *Field v. Google* (January 2006), a Nevada District Court ruled that Google's caching and indexing of web sites is permissible. One of the factors in the ruling was that Google stores web pages in its cache only temporarily. In *Perfect 10 v. Google* (May 2007), the Ninth Circuit Court denied an adult magazine's request for a preliminary injunction to prevent Google from linking to its site and posting thumbnail images from it.

cause water shortages downstream? What about the obligations of landowners upstream from you? These were major controversial issues in the western U.S. in the nineteenth century, which eventually resulted in codifying a system of limited property rights that landowners have to the water running through their land.

Suppose an airplane flies over your land. Is that trespassing? Suppose the plane is flying very low. How far upward does your property right extend? From ancient times, property rights were held to reach upward indefinitely. Perhaps airlines should be required to seek permission from every landowner whose property their planes traverse. Imagine being faced with that regulatory question at the dawn of the Aviation Age. Should we require airlines to obtain that permission out of respect for property and ownership? That might have seemed reasonable at a time when planes flew at only a few thousand feet. But had society done that, what would have been the implications for innovation in air travel? Would we ever have seen the emergence of transcontinental flight, or would the path to that technology have been blocked by thickets of regulation? Congress forestalled the growth of those thickets by nationalizing the navigable airspace in 1926.

Similarly, should we require Google to get permission from every book's copyright holder before including it in the index? It seems perfectly reasonable—and in fact other book indexing projects are underway that do seek that permission. Yet perhaps book search is the fledging digital equivalent of the low-flying aircraft. Can we envision the future transcontinental flights, where books, music, images, and videos are automatically extracted, sampled, mixed, and remixed; fed into massive automated reasoning engines; assimilated into the core software of every personal computer and every cell phone—and thousands of other things for which the words don't even exist yet?

What's the proper balance? How far "upward" into the bursting information space should property rights extend? What should ownership even mean when we're talking about bits? We don't know, and finding answers won't be easy. But somehow, we must learn to fly.

The digital explosion casts information every which way, breaching established boundaries of property. Technologies have confounded copyright—the rules that would regulate and restrain bits in their flight. Technological solutions have been brought to bear on the problems technology created. Those solutions created *de facto* policies of their own, bypassing the considerations of public interest on which copyright was balanced.

Property lines are not the only boundaries the explosion is breaching, and copyright is not the only arena in which information regulation is challenged. Bits fly across national borders. They fly into private homes and public places carrying content that is unwanted, even harmful—content that has historically been restricted, not by copyright, but by regulations against defamation and pornography. Yet the bits fly anyway, and that is the conundrum to which we now turn.

CHAPTER 7

# You Can't Say That on the Internet

*Guarding the Frontiers of Digital Expression*

## Do You Know Where Your Child Is on the Web Tonight?

It was every parent's worst nightmare. Katherine Lester, a 16-year-old honors student from Fairgrove, Michigan, went missing in June 2006. Her parents had no idea what had happened to her; she had never given them a moment's worry. They called the police. Then federal authorities got involved.

After three days of terrifying absence, she was found, safe—in Amman, Jordan.

Fairgrove is too small to have a post office, and the Lesters lived in the last house on a dead-end street. In another time, Katherine's school, six miles away, might have been the outer limit of her universe. But through the Internet, her universe was—the whole world. Katherine met a Palestinian man, Abdullah Jimzawi, from Jericho on the West Bank. She found his profile on the social networking web site, MySpace, and sent him a message: "u r cute." They quickly learned everything about each other through online messages. Lester tricked her mother into getting her a passport, and then took off for the Middle East. When U.S. authorities met her plane in Amman, she agreed to return home, and apologized to her parents for the distress she had caused them.

A month later, Representative Judy Biggert of Illinois rose in the House to co-sponsor the Deleting Online Predators Act (DOPA). "MySpace.com and other networking web sites have become new hunting grounds for child predators," she said, noting that "we were all horrified" by the story of Katherine Lester. "At least let's give parents some comfort that their children won't fall prey while using the Internet at schools and libraries that receive federal funding for Internet services." The law would require those institutions to prevent children from using on-location computers to access chat rooms and social networking web sites without adult supervision.

Speaker after speaker rose in the House to stress the importance of protecting children from online predators, but not all supported the bill. The language was "overbroad and ambiguous," said one. As originally drafted, it seemed to cover not just MySpace, but sites such as Amazon and Wikipedia. These sites possess some of the same characteristics as MySpace—users can create personal profiles and continually share information with each other using the Web. Although the law might block children in schools and libraries from "places" where they meet friends (and sometimes predators), it would also prevent access to online encyclopedias and bookstores, which rely on content posted by users.

Instead of taking the time to develop a sharper definition of what exactly was to be prohibited, DOPA's sponsors hastily redrafted the law to omit the definition, leaving it to the Federal Communications Commission to decide later just what the law would cover. Some murmured that the upcoming midterm elections were motivating the sponsors to put forward an ill-considered and showy effort to protect children—an effort that would likely be ineffective and so vague as to be unconstitutional.

Children use computers in lots of places; restricting what happens in schools and libraries would hardly discourage determined teenagers from sneaking onto MySpace. Only the most overbearing parents could honestly answer the question *USA Today* asked in its article about "cyber-predators": "It's 11 p.m. Do you know where your child is on the Web tonight?"

The statistics about what can go wrong were surely terrifying. The Justice Department has made thousands of arrests for "cyber enticement"—almost always older men using social networking web sites to lure teenagers into meetings, some of which end very badly. Yet, as the American Library Association stated in opposition to DOPA, education, not prohibition, is the "key to safe use of the Internet." Students have to learn to cooperate online, because network use, and all the human interactions it enables, are basic tools of the new, globally interconnected world of business, education, and citizenship.

And perhaps even the globally interconnected world of true love. The tale of Katherine Lester took an unexpected turn. From the moment she was found in Jordan, Lester steadily insisted that she intended to marry Jimzawi.

Jimzawi, who was 20 when he and Lester first made contact, claimed to be in love with her—and his mother agreed. Jimzawi begged Lester to tell her parents the truth before she headed off to meet him, but she refused. Upon her return, authorities charged Lester as a runaway child and took her passport away from her. But on September 12, 2007, having attained legal independence by turning 18, she again boarded a plane to the Middle East, finally to meet her beloved face to face. The affair finally ended a few weeks later in an exchange of accusations and denials, and a hint that a third party had attracted Lester's attentions. There was no high-tech drama to the breakup—except that it was televised on *Dr. Phil*.

The explosion in digital communications has confounded long-held assumptions about human relationships—how people meet, how they come to know each other, and how they decide if they can trust each other. At the same time, the explosion in digital information, in the form of web pages and downloadable photographs, has put at the fingertips of millions material that only a few years ago no one could have found without great effort and expense. Political dissidents in Chinese Internet cafés can (if they dare) read pro-democracy blogs. People all around the world who are ashamed about their illness, starved for information about their sexual identity, or eager to connect with others of their minority faith can find facts, opinion, advice, and companionship. And children too small to leave home by themselves can see lurid pornography on their families' home computers. Can societies anymore control what their members see and to whom they talk?

## Metaphors for Something Unlike Anything Else

DOPA, which has not been passed into law, is the latest battle in a long war between conflicting values. On the one hand, society has an interest in keeping unwanted information away from children. On the other hand, society as a whole has an interest in maximizing open communication. The U.S. Constitution largely protects the freedom to speak and the right to hear. Over and over, society has struggled to find a metaphor for electronic communication that captures the ways in which it is the same as the media of the past and the ways in which it is different. Laws and regulations are built on traditions; only by understanding the analogies can the speech principles of the past be extended to the changed circumstances of the present—or be consciously transcended.

What laws should apply? The Internet is not exactly like anything else. If you put up a web site, that is something like publishing a book, so perhaps the laws about books should apply. But that was Web 1.0—a way for "publishers" to publish and viewers to view. In the dynamic and participatory Web 2.0, sites such as MySpace change constantly in response to user postings. If you send an email, or contribute to a blog, that is something like placing a telephone call, or maybe a conference call, so maybe laws about telephones should be the starting point. Neither metaphor is perfect. Maybe television is a better analogy, since browsing the Web is like channel surfing—except that the Internet is two-way, and there is no limit to the number of "channels."

Underneath the web software and the email software is the Internet itself. The Internet just delivers packets of bits, not knowing or caring whether they are parts of books, movies, text messages, or voices, nor whether the bits will wind up in a web browser, a telephone, or a movie projector. John Perry Barlow, former lyricist for the Grateful Dead and co-founder of the Electronic Frontier Foundation, used a striking metaphor to describe the Internet as it burst into public consciousness in the mid-1990s. The world's regulation of the flow of information, he said, had long controlled the transport of wine bottles. In "meatspace," the physical world, different rules applied to books, postal mail, radio broadcasts, and telephone calls—different kinds of bottles. Now the wine itself flowed freely through the network, nothing but bits freed from their packaging. Anything could be put in, and the same kind of thing would come out. But in between, it was all the same stuff—just bits. What are the rules of Cyberspace—what are the rules for the bits themselves?

When information is transmitted between two parties, whether the information is spoken words, written words, pictures, or movies, there is a source and a destination. There may also be some intermediaries. In a lecture hall, the listeners hear the speaker directly, although whoever provided the hall also played an important role in making the communication possible. Books have authors and readers, but also publishers and booksellers in between. It is natural to ascribe similar roles to the various parties in an Internet communication, and, when things go wrong, to hold any and all of the parties responsible. For example, when Pete Solis contacted a 14-year-old girl ("Jane Doe") through her MySpace profile and allegedly sexually assaulted her when they met in person, the girl's parents sued MySpace for $30 million for enabling the assault.

The Internet has a complex structure. The source and destination may be friends emailing each other, they may be a commercial web site and a residential customer, or they may be one office of a company sending a mockup of an advertising brochure to another office halfway around the world. The source and destination each has an ISP. Connecting the ISPs are routing switches, fiber optic cables, satellite links, and so on. A packet that flows through the Internet may pass through devices and communication links owned by dozens of different parties. For convenience (and in the style of Jonathan Zittrain), we'll call the collection of devices that connect the ISPs to each other *the cloud*. As shown in Figure 7.1, speech on the Internet goes from the source to an ISP, into the cloud, out of the cloud to another ISP, and to its destination (see the sidebar, "Cloud Computing," in Chapter 3 for additional information about this).

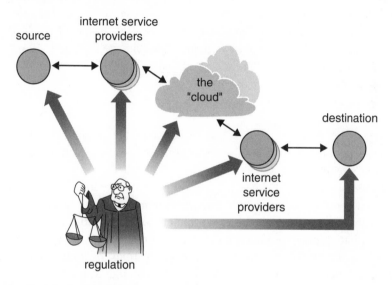

Based on figure by Jonathan Zittrain

FIGURE **7.1**   Where to regulate the Internet?

If a government seeks to control speech, it can attack at several different points. It can try to control the speaker or the speaker's ISP, by criminalizing certain kinds of speech. But that won't work if the speaker isn't in the same country as the listener. It can try to control the listener, by prohibiting possession of certain kinds of materials. In the U.S., possession of copyrighted software without an appropriate license is illegal, as is possession of other copyrighted material with the intent to profit from redistributing it. If citizens have reasonable privacy rights, however, it is hard for the government to know what its citizens possess. In a society such as the U.S., where citizens have reasonable rights of due process, one-at-a-time prosecutions for possession are unwieldy. As a final alternative, the government can try to control the intermediaries.

There are parallels in civil law. The parents of the Jane Doe sued MySpace because it was in the communication path between Mr. Solis and their daughter, even though MySpace was not the alleged assailant.

---

### DEFAMING PUBLIC FIGURES

Damaging statements about public figures, even if false, are not defamatory unless they were made with malicious intent. This extra clause protects news media against libel claims by celebrities who are offended by the way the press depicts them. It was not always so, however. The pivotal case was *New York Times Co. v. Sullivan*, 376 U.S. 254 (1964), in which the newspaper was sued by officials in Alabama on the basis of a pro-civil-rights advertisement it published. The story is detailed, along with a readable history of the First Amendment, in *Make No Law* by Anthony Lewis (Vintage Paperback, 1992). For a later account of First Amendment struggles, see Lewis's *Freedom for the Thought That We Hate* (Basic Books, 2008).

---

Very early, defamation laws had to adapt to the Internet. In the U.S., speech is defamatory if it is false, communicated to third parties, and damages one's reputation.

In the physical world, when the speaker defames someone, the intermediaries between the speaker and the listener sometimes share responsibility with the speaker—and sometimes not. If we defame someone in this book, we may be sued, but so may the book's publisher, who might have known that what we were writing was false. On the other hand, the trucker who transported the book to the bookstore probably isn't liable, even though he too helped get our words from us to our readers. Are the various electronic intermediaries more like publishers, or truckers? Do the parents of Jane Doe have a case against MySpace?

Society has struggled to identify the right metaphors to describe the parties to an electronic communication. To understand this part of the story of electronic information, we have to go back to pre-Internet electronic communication.

## Publisher or Distributor?

CompuServe was an early provider of computer services, including bulletin boards and other electronic communities users could join for a fee. One of these fora, Rumorville USA, provided a daily newsletter of reports about broadcast journalism and journalists. CompuServe didn't screen or even collect the rumors posted on Rumorville. It contracted with a third party, Don Fitzpatrick Associates (DFA), to provide the content. CompuServe simply posted whatever DFA provided without reviewing it. And for a long time, no one complained.

In 1990, a company called Cubby, Inc. started a competing service, Skuttlebut, which also reported gossip about TV and radio broadcasting. Items appeared on Rumorville describing Skuttlebut as a "new start-up scam" and alleging that its material was being stolen from Rumorville. Cubby cried foul and went after CompuServe, claiming defamation. CompuServe acknowledged that the postings were defamatory, but claimed it was not acting as a publisher of the information—just a distributor. It simply was sending on to subscribers what other people gave it. It wasn't responsible for the contents, any more than a trucker is responsible for libel that might appear in the magazines he handles.

What was the right analogy? Was CompuServe more like a newspaper, or more like the trucker who transports the newspaper to its readers?

More like the trucker, ruled the court. A long legal tradition held distributors blameless for the content of the publications they delivered. Distributors can't be expected to have read all the books on their trucks. Grasping for a better analogy, the court described CompuServe as "an electronic for-profit library." Distributor or library, CompuServe was independent of DFA and couldn't be held responsible for libelous statements in what DFA provided. The case of *Cubby v. CompuServe* was settled decisively in CompuServe's favor. Cubby might go after the source, but that wasn't CompuServe. CompuServe was a blameless intermediary. So was MySpace, years later, when Jane Doe's parents sought redress for Mr. Solis's alleged assault of their daughter. In a ruling building on the *Cubby* decision, MySpace was absolved of responsibility for what Solis had posted.

When *Cubby v. CompuServe* was decided, providers of computer services everywhere exhaled. If the decision had gone the other way, electronic distribution of information might have become a risky business that few dared to enter. Computer networks created an information infrastructure unprecedented in its low overhead. A few people could connect tens of thousands, even millions, to each other at very low cost. If everything disseminated had to be reviewed by human readers before it was posted, to ensure that any damaging statements were truthful, its potential use for participatory democracy would be severely limited. For a time, a spirit of freedom ruled.

## Neither Liberty nor Security

"The law often demands that we sacrifice some liberty for greater security. Sometimes, though, it takes away our liberty to provide us less security." So wrote law professor Eugene Volokh in the fall of 1995, commenting on a court case that looked similar to *Cubby v. CompuServe*, but wasn't.

Eugene Volokh has a blog, volokh.com, in which he comments regularly on information freedom issues and many other things.

Prodigy was a provider of computer services, much like CompuServe. But in the early 1990s, as worries began to rise about the sexual content of materials available online, Prodigy sought to distinguish itself as a family-oriented service. It pledged to exercise editorial control over the postings on its bulletin boards. "We make no apology," Prodigy stated, "for pursuing a value system that reflects the culture of the millions of American families we aspire to serve. Certainly no responsible newspaper does less...." Prodigy's success in the market was due in no small measure to the security families felt in accessing its fora, rather than the anything-goes sites offered by other services.

One of Prodigy's bulletin boards, called "Money Talk," was devoted to financial services. In October 1994, someone anonymously posted comments on Money Talk about the securities investment firm Stratton Oakmont. The firm, said the unidentified poster, was involved in "major criminal fraud." Its president was "soon to be proven criminal." The whole company was a "cult of brokers who either lie for a living or get fired."

Stratton Oakmont sued Prodigy for libel, claiming that Prodigy should be regarded as the publisher of these defamatory comments. It asked for $200 million in damages. Prodigy countered that it had zero responsibility for what its posters said. The matter had been settled several years earlier by the *Cubby v. CompuServe* decision. Prodigy wasn't the publisher of the comments, just the distributor.

In a decision that stunned the Internet community, a New York court ruled otherwise. By exercising editorial control in support of its family-friendly image, said the court, Prodigy became a publisher, with the attendant responsibilities and risks. Indeed, Prodigy had likened itself to a newspaper publisher, and could not at trial claim to be something less.

It was all quite logical, as long as the choice was between two metaphors: distributor or newspaper. In reality, though, a service provider wasn't exactly like either. Monitoring for bad language was a pretty minor form of editorial work. That was a far cry from checking everything for truthfulness.

Be that as it may, the court's finding undercut efforts to create safe districts in Cyberspace. After the decision, the obvious advice went out to bulletin board operators: Don't even consider editing or censoring. If you do, *Stratton Oakmont v. Prodigy* means you may be legally liable for any malicious falsehood that slips by your review. If you don't even try, *Cubby v. CompuServe* means you are completely immune from liability.

This was fine for the safety of the site operators, but what about the public interest? Freedom of expression was threatened, since fewer families would be willing to roam freely through the smut that would be posted. At the same time, security would not be improved, since defamers could always post their lies on the remaining services with their all-welcome policies.

## The Nastiest Place on Earth

Every communication technology has been used to control, as well as to facilitate, the flow of ideas. Barely a century after the publication of the Gutenberg Bible, Pope Paul IV issued a list of 500 banned authors. In the United States, the First Amendment protects authors and speakers from government interference: *Congress shall make no law ... abridging the freedom of speech, or of the press* .... But First Amendment protections are not absolute. No one has the right to publish obscene materials. The government can destroy materials it judges to be obscene, as postal authorities did in 1918 when they burned magazines containing excerpts of James Joyce's *Ulysses.*

What exactly counts as obscene has been a matter of much legal wrangling over the course of U.S. history. The prevailing standard today is the one the Supreme Court used in 1973 in deciding the case of *Miller v. California*, and is therefore called the *Miller Test*. To determine whether material is obscene, a court must consider the following:

1. Whether the average person, applying contemporary community standards, would find that the work, taken as a whole, appeals to the prurient interest.

2. Whether the work depicts or describes, in a patently offensive way, sexual conduct specifically defined by the applicable state law.

3. Whether the work, taken as a whole, lacks serious literary, artistic, political, or scientific value.

Only if the answer to each part is "yes" does the work qualify as obscene. The Miller decision was a landmark, because it established that there were no national standards for obscenity. There were only "community" standards, which could be different in Mississippi than in New York City. But there were no computer networks in 1973. What is a "community" in Cyberspace?

**What is a "community" in Cyberspace?**

In 1992, the infant World Wide Web was hardly world-wide, but many Americans were using dial-up connections to access information on centralized, electronic bulletin boards. Some bulletin boards were free and united communities of interest—lovers of baseball or birds, for example. Others distributed free software. Bob and Carleen Thomas of Milpitas, California, ran a different kind of bulletin board, called Amateur Action. In their advertising, they described it as "The Nastiest Place on Earth."

For a fee, anyone could download images from Amateur Action. The pictures were of a kind not usually shown in polite company, but readily available in magazines sold in the nearby cities of San Francisco and San Jose. The Thomases were raided by the San Jose police, who thought they might have been distributing obscene materials. After looking at their pictures, the police decided that the images were not obscene by local standards.

Bob and Carleen were not indicted, and they added this notice to their bulletin board: "The San Jose Police Department as well as the Santa Clara County District Attorney's Office and the State of California agree that Amateur Action BBS is operating in a legal manner."

Two years later, in February 1994, the Thomases were raided again, and their computer was seized. This time, the complaint came from Agent David Dirmeyer, a postal inspector—in *western Tennessee*. Using an assumed name, Dirmeyer had paid $55 and had downloaded images to his computer in Memphis. Nasty stuff indeed, particularly for Memphis: bestiality, incest, and sado-masochism. The Thomases were arrested. They stood trial in Memphis on federal charges of transporting obscene material via common carrier, and via interstate commerce. They were convicted by a Tennessee jury, which concluded that their Milpitas bulletin board violated the community standards of Memphis. Bob was sentenced to 37 months incarceration and Carleen to 30.

The Thomases appealed their conviction, on the grounds that they could not have known where the bits were going, and that the relevant community, if not San Jose, was a community of Cyberspace. The appeals court did not agree. Dirmeyer had supplied a Tennessee postal address when he applied for membership in Amateur Action. The Thomases had called him at his Memphis telephone number to give him the password—they had known where he was. The Thomases, concluded the court, should have been more careful where they sent their bits, once they started selling them out of state. Shipping the bits was just like shipping a videotape by UPS (a charge of which the Thomases were also convicted). The laws of meatspace applied to Cyberspace—and one city's legal standards sometimes applied thousands of miles away.

# The Most Participatory Form of Mass Speech

Pornography was part of the electronic world from the moment it was possible to store and transmit words and images. The Thomases learned that bits were like books, and the same obscenity standards applied.

In the mid-1990s, something else happened. The spread of computers and networks vastly increased the number of digital images available and the number of people viewing them. Digital pornography became not just the same old thing in a new form—it seemed to be a brand-new thing, because there was so much of it and it was so easy to get in the privacy of the home. Nebraska Senator James Exon attached an anti-Internet-pornography amendment to a telecommunications bill, but it seemed destined for defeat on civil liberties grounds. And then all hell broke loose.

On July 3, 1995, *Time Magazine* blasted "CYBERPORN" across its cover. The accompanying story, based largely a single university report, stated:

> *What the Carnegie Mellon researchers discovered was: THERE'S AN AWFUL LOT OF PORN ONLINE. In an 18-month study, the team surveyed 917,410 sexually explicit pictures, descriptions, short stories, and film clips. On those Usenet newsgroups where digitized images are stored, 83.5% of the pictures were pornographic.*

The article later noted that this statistic referred to only a small fraction of all data traffic, but failed to explain that the offending images were mostly on limited-access bulletin boards, not openly available to children or anyone else. It mentioned the issue of government censorship, and it quoted John Perry Barlow on the critical role of parents. Nonetheless, when Senator Grassley of Iowa read the *Time Magazine* story into the Congressional Record, attributing its conclusions to a study by the well-respected Georgetown University Law School, he called on Congress to "help parents who are under assault in this day and age" and to "help stem this growing tide."

Grassley's speech, and the circulation in the Capitol building of dirty pictures downloaded by a friend of Senator Exon, galvanized the Congress to save the children of America. In February 1996, the Communications Decency Act, or CDA, passed almost unanimously and was signed into law by President Clinton.

The CDA made it a crime to use "any interactive computer service to display in a manner available to a person under 18 years of age, any comment, request, suggestion, proposal, image, or other communication that, in context, depicts or describes, in terms patently offensive as measured by contemporary community standards, sexual or excretory activities or organs." Criminal penalties would also fall on anyone who "knowingly permits any telecommunications facility under such person's control to be used" for such prohibited activities. And finally, it criminalized the transmission of materials that were "obscene or indecent" to persons known to be under 18.

These "display provisions" of the CDA vastly extended existing antiobscenity laws, which already applied to the Internet. The dual prohibitions against *making offensive images available to a person under 18*, and against transmitting *indecent materials to persons known to be under 18*, were unlike anything that applied to print publications. "Indecency," whatever it meant, was something short of obscenity, and only obscene materials had been illegal prior to the CDA. A newsstand could tell the difference between a 12-year-old customer and a 20-year-old, but how could anyone check ages in Cyberspace?

When the CDA was enacted, John Perry Barlow saw the potential of the Internet for the free flow of information challenged. He issued a now-classic manifesto against the government's effort to regulate speech:

> Governments of the Industrial World, you weary giants of flesh and steel, I come from Cyberspace, the new home of Mind. On behalf of the future, I ask you of the past to leave us alone. You have no sovereignty where we gather.... We are creating a world that all may enter without privilege or prejudice accorded by race, economic power, military force, or station of birth. We are creating a world where anyone, anywhere may express his or her beliefs, no matter how singular, without fear of being coerced into silence or conformity.... In our world, all the sentiments and expressions of humanity, from the debasing to the angelic, are parts of a seamless whole, the global conversation of bits.... [Y]ou are trying to ward off the virus of liberty by erecting guard posts at the frontiers of Cyberspace.

Brave and stirring words, even if the notion of Cyberspace as a "seamless whole" had already been rendered doubtful. At a minimum, bits had to meet different obscenity standards in Memphis than in Milpitas, as the Thomases had learned. In fact, the entire metaphor of the Internet as a "space" with "frontiers" was fatally flawed, and misuse of that metaphor continues to plague laws and policies to this day.

Civil libertarians joined the chorus challenging the Communications Decency Act. In short order, a federal court and the U.S. Supreme Court ruled in the momentous case of *ACLU v. Reno*. The display provisions of the CDA were unconstitutional. "The Government may only regulate free speech for a compelling reason," wrote Judge Dalzell in the district court decision, "and in the least restrictive manner." It would chill discourse unacceptably to demand age verification over the Internet from every person who might see material that any adult has a legal right to see.

The government had argued that the authority of the Federal Communications Commission (FCC) to regulate the content of TV and radio broadcasts, which are required not to be "indecent," provided an analogy for government oversight of Internet communications.

The courts disagreed. The FCC analogy was wrong, they ruled, because the Internet was far more open than broadcast media. Different media required different kinds of laws, and the TV and radio laws were more restrictive than laws were for print media, or should be for the Internet. "I have no doubt" wrote Judge Dalzell, "that a Newspaper Decency Act, passed because Congress discovered that young girls had read a front page article in the *New York Times* on female genital mutilation in Africa, would be unconstitutional.... The Internet may fairly be regarded as a never-ending worldwide conversation. The Government may not, through the CDA, interrupt that conversation. As the most participatory form of mass speech yet developed, the Internet deserves the highest protection from governmental intrusion." The CDA's display provisions were dead.

In essence, the court was unwilling to risk the entire Internet's promise as a vigorous marketplace of ideas to serve the narrow purpose of protecting children from indecency. Instead, it transferred the burden of blocking unwanted communications from source ISPs to the destination. The DOPA's proposed burden on libraries and schools is heir to the court's ruling overturning the CDA. Legally, there seemed to be nowhere else to control speech except at the point where it came out of the cloud and was delivered to the listener.

Lost in the 1995–96 Internet indecency hysteria was the fact that the "Carnegie Mellon report" that started the legislative ball rolling had been discredited almost as soon as the *Time Magazine* story appeared. The report's author, Martin Rimm, was an Electrical Engineering undergraduate. His

**DEFENDING ELECTRONIC FREEDOMS**

The Electronic Frontier Foundation, www.eff.org, is the leading public advocacy group defending First Amendment and other personal rights in Cyberspace. Ironically, it often finds itself in opposition with media and telecommunications companies. In principle, communications companies should have the greatest interest in unfettered exchange of information. In actual practice, they often benefit financially from policies that limit consumer choice or expand surveillance and data-gathering about private citizens. The EFF was among the plaintiffs bringing suit in the case that overturned the CDA.

study's methodology was flawed, and perhaps fraudulent. For example, he told adult bulletin board operators that he was studying how best to market pornography online, and that he would repay them for their cooperation by sharing his tips. His conclusions were unreliable. Why hadn't that been caught when his article was published? Because the article was not a product of Georgetown University, as Senator Grassley had said. Rather, it appeared in the *Georgetown Law Review*, a student publication that used neither peer nor professional reviewers. Three weeks after publishing the "Cyberporn" article, *Time* acknowledged that Rimm's study was untrustworthy. In spite of this repudiation, Rimm salvaged something from his efforts: He published a book called *The Pornographer's Handbook: How to Exploit Women, Dupe Men, & Make Lots of Money.*

## Protecting Good Samaritans—and a Few Bad Ones

The *Stratton Oakmont v. Prodigy* decision, which discouraged ISPs from exercising any editorial judgment, had been handed down in 1995, just as Congress was preparing to enact the Communications Decency Act to protect children from Internet porn. Congress recognized that the consequences of *Stratton Oakmont* would be fewer voluntary efforts by ISPs to screen their sites for offensive content. So, the bill's sponsors added a "Good Samaritan" provision to the CDA.

The intent was to allow ISPs to act as editors without running the risk that they would be held responsible for the edited content, thus putting themselves in the jam in which Prodigy had found itself. So the CDA included a provision absolving ISPs of liability on account of anything they did, in good faith, to filter out "obscene, lewd, lascivious, filthy, excessively violent, harassing, or otherwise objectionable" material. For good measure, the CDA pushed the *Cubby* court's "distributor" metaphor to the limit, and beyond. ISPs should *not* be thought of as publishers, or as sources either. "No provider or user of an interactive computer service shall be treated as the publisher or speaker of any information provided by another information content provider." This was the bottom line of §230 of the CDA, and it meant that there would be no more *Stratton Oakmont v. Prodigy* Catch-22s.

When the U.S. Supreme Court struck down the CDA in 1996, it negated only the display provisions, the clauses that threatened the providers of "indecent" content. The Good Samaritan clause was allowed to stand and remains the law today. ISPs can do as much as they want to filter or censor their content, without any risk that they will assume publishers' liabilities in the process.

Or as little as they choose, as Ken Zeran learned to his sorrow a few years later.

---

### THE CDA AND DISCRIMINATION

The "Good Samaritan" clause envisioned a sharp line between "service providers" (which got immunity) and "content providers" (which did not). But as the technology world evolved, the distinction became fuzzy. A roommate-matching service was sued in California, on the basis that it invited users to discriminate by categorizing their roommate preferences (women only, for example). A court ruled that the operators of the web site were immune as service providers. An appeals court reversed the decision, on the basis that the web site became a content provider by filtering the information applicants provided—people seeking female roommates would not learn about men looking for roommates. There was nothing wrong with *that*, but the principle that the roommate service had *blanket* protection, under the CDA, to filter as it wished would mean that with equal impunity, it could ask about racial preferences and honor them. That form of discrimination would be illegal in newspaper ads. "We doubt," wrote the appeals court judge, "this is what Congress had in mind when it passed the CDA."

The worst terrorist attack in history on U.S. soil prior to the 2001 destruction of New York's World Trade Center was the bombing of the Alfred P. Murrah Federal building in Oklahoma City on April 19, 1995. 168 people were killed, some of them children in a day care center. Hundreds more were injured when the building collapsed around them and glass and rubble rained down on the neighborhood. One man who made it out alive likened the event to the detonation of an atomic bomb.

Less than a week later, someone with screen name "Ken ZZ03" posted an advertisement on an America On Line (AOL) bulletin board. Ken had "Naughty Oklahoma T-Shirts" for sale. Among the available slogans were "Visit Oklahoma—it's a Blast" and "Rack'em, Stack'em, and Pack'em—Oklahoma 1995." Others were even cruder and more tasteless. To get your T-shirt, said the ads, you should call Ken. The posting gave Ken's phone number.

The number belonged to Ken Zeran, an artist and filmmaker in Seattle, Washington. Zeran had nothing to do with the posting on AOL. It was a hoax.

Ken Zeran started to receive calls. Angry, insulting calls. Then death threats.

Zeran called AOL and asked them to take down the posting and issue a retraction. An AOL employee promised to take down the original posting, but said retractions were against company policy.

The next day, an anonymous poster with a slightly different screen name offered more T-shirts for sale, with even more offensive slogans.

*Call Ken.* And by the way—there's high demand. So if the phone is busy, call back.

Zeran kept calling AOL to ask that the postings be removed and that further postings be prevented. AOL kept promising to close down the accounts and remove the postings, but didn't. By April 30, Ken was receiving a phone call every two minutes. Ken's art business depended on that phone number—he couldn't change it or fail to answer it, without losing his livelihood.

About this time, Shannon Fullerton, the host of a morning drive-time radio talk show on KRXO in Seattle, received by email a copy of one of the postings. Usually his show was full of light-hearted foolishness, but after the bombing, Fullerton and his radio partner had devoted several shows to sharing community grief about the Oklahoma City tragedy. Fullerton read Ken's T-shirt slogans over the air. And he read Ken's telephone number and told his listeners to call Ken and tell him what they thought of him.

Zeran got even more calls, and more death threats. Fearing for his safety, he obtained police surveillance of his home. Most callers were not interested in hearing what Ken had to say when he answered the phone, but he managed to keep one on the line long enough to learn about the KRXO broadcast. Zeran contacted the radio station. KRXO issued a retraction, after which the number of calls Ken received dropped to fifteen per day. Eventually, a newspaper exposed the hoax. AOL finally removed the postings, after leaving them visible for a week. Ken's life began to return to normal.

> **WAS THE RADIO STATION LIABLE?**
>
> Zeran sued the radio station separately, but failed in that effort as well. Much as he may have suffered, reasoned the court, it wasn't defamation, because none of the people who called him even knew who Ken Zeran was—so his reputation couldn't possibly have been damaged when the radio station spoke ill of "Ken"!

Zeran sued AOL, claiming defamation, among other things. By putting up the postings, and leaving them up long after it had been informed that they were false, AOL had damaged him severely.

The decision went against Zeran, and the lower court's decision held up on appeal. AOL certainly had behaved like a publisher, by communicating the postings in the first place and by choosing not to remove them when informed that they were fraudulent. Unlike the defendant in the *Cubby v. CompuServe* case, AOL knew exactly what it was publishing. But the Good Samaritan provision of the CDA specifically stated that AOL should not legally be *treated* as a publisher. AOL had no liability for Zeran's woes.

Zeran's only recourse was to identify the actual speaker, the pseudonymous Ken ZZ03 who made the postings. And AOL would not help him do that. Everyone felt sorry for Ken, but the system gave him no help.

The posters could evade responsibility as long as they remained anonymous, as they easily could on the Internet. And Congress had given the ISPs a complete waiver of responsibility for the consequences of false and damaging statements, even when the ISP knew they were false. Had anyone in Congress thought through the implications of the Good Samaritan clause?

# Laws of Unintended Consequences

The Good Samaritan provision of the CDA has been the friend of free speech, and a great relief to Internet Service Providers. Yet its application has defied logical connection to the spirit that created it.

Sidney Blumenthal was a Clinton aide whose job it was to dish dirt on the president's enemies. On August 11, 1997, conservative online columnist Matt Drudge reported, "Sidney Blumenthal has a spousal abuse past that has been effectively covered up." The White House denied it, and the next day Drudge withdrew the claim. The Blumenthals sued AOL, which had a deal with Drudge. And had deeper pockets—the Blumenthals asked for $630,000,021. AOL was as responsible for the libel as Drudge, claimed the Blumenthals, because AOL could edit what Drudge supplied. AOL could even insist that Drudge delete items AOL did not want posted. The court sided with AOL, and cited the Good Samaritan clause of the CDA. AOL couldn't be treated like a publisher, so it couldn't be held liable for Drudge's falsehoods. Case closed.

*The Communications Decency Act has been used to protect an ISP whose chat room was being used to peddle child pornography.*

Even more strangely, the Good Samaritan clause of the Communications Decency Act has been used to protect an ISP whose chat room was being used to peddle child pornography.

In 1998, Jane and John Doe, a mother and her minor son, sued AOL for harm inflicted on the son. The Does alleged that AOL chat rooms were used to sell pornographic images of the boy made when he was 11 years old. They claimed that in 1997, Richard Lee Russell had lured John and two other boys to engage in sexual activities with each other and with Russell. Russell then used AOL chat rooms to market photographs and videotapes of these sexual encounters.

Jane Doe complained to AOL. Under the terms of its agreement with its users, AOL specifically reserved the right to terminate the service of anyone engaged in such improper activities. And yet AOL did not suspend Russell's service, or even warn him to stop what he was doing. The Does wanted compensation from AOL for its role in John Doe's sexual abuse.

The Does lost. Citing the Good Samaritan clause, and the precedent of the *Zeran* decision, the Florida courts held AOL blameless. Online service providers who knowingly allow child pornography to be marketed on their bulletin boards could not be treated as though they had published ads for kiddie porn.

The Does appealed and lost again. The decision in AOL's favor was 4-3 at the Florida Supreme Court. Judge J. Lewis fairly exploded in his dissenting opinion. The Good Samaritan clause was an attempt to remove disincentives from the development of filtering and blocking technologies, which would assist parents in their efforts to protect children. "[I]t is inconceivable that Congress intended the CDA to shield from potential liability an ISP alleged to have taken absolutely no actions to curtail illicit activities ... while profiting from its customer's continued use of the service." The law had been transformed into one "which both condones and exonerates a flagrant and reprehensible failure to act by an ISP in the face of ... material unquestionably harmful to children." This made no sense. The sequence of decisions "thrusts Congress into the unlikely position of having enacted legislation that encourages and protects the involvement of ISPs as silent partners in criminal enterprises for profit."

The problem, as Judge Lewis saw it, was that it wasn't enough to say that ISPs were not like publishers. They really were more like distributors—as Ken Zeran had tried to argue—and distributors are not *entirely* without responsibility for what they distribute. A trucker who knows he is carrying child pornography, and is getting a cut of the profits, has *some* legal liability for his complicity in illegal commerce. His role is not that of a publisher, but it is not nothing either. The *Zeran* court had created a muddle by using the wrong analogy. Congress had made the muddle possible by saying nothing about the right analogy after saying that publishing was the wrong one.

# Can the Internet Be Like a Magazine Store?

After the display provision of the CDA was ruled unconstitutional in 1997, Congress went back to work to protect America's children. The Child Online Protection Act (COPA), passed into law in 1998, contained many of the key elements of the CDA, but sought to avoid the CDA's constitutional problems by narrowing it. It applied only to "commercial" speech, and criminalized knowingly making available to minors "material harmful to minors." For the purposes of this law, a "minor" was anyone under 17. The statute extended the Miller Test for obscenity to create a definition of material that was not obscene but was "harmful to minors:"

> The term "material that is harmful to minors" means any communication ... that — (A) the average person, applying contemporary community standards, would find, taking the material as a whole and with respect to minors, is designed to appeal to ... the prurient interest; (B) depicts, describes, or represents, in a manner patently offensive with respect to minors, ... [a] sexual act, or a lewd exhibition of the genitals or post-pubescent female breast; and (C) taken as a whole, lacks serious literary, artistic, political, or scientific value for minors.

COPA was challenged immediately and never took effect. A federal judge enjoined the government from enforcing it, ruling that it was likely to be unconstitutional. The matter bounced between courts through two presidencies. The case started out as *ACLU v. Reno*, for a time was known as *ACLU v. Ashcroft*, and was decided as *ACLU v. Gonzalez*. The judges were uniformly sympathetic to the intent of Congress to protect children from material they should not see. But in March 2007, the ax finally fell on COPA. Judge Lowell A. Reed, Jr., of U.S. District Court for the Eastern District of Pennsylvania, confirmed that the law went too far in restricting speech.

Part of the problem was with the vague definition of material "harmful to minors." The prurient interests of a 16-year-old were not the same as those of an 8-year-old; and what had literary value for a teenager might be valueless for a younger child. How would a web site designer know which standard he should use to avoid the risk of imprisonment?

But there was an even more basic problem. COPA was all about keeping away from minors material that would be perfectly legal for adults to have. It put a burden on information distributors to ensure that recipients of such information were of age. COPA provided a "safe harbor" against prosecution for those who in good faith checked the ages of their customers. Congress imagined a magazine store where the clerks wouldn't sell dirty magazines to children who could not reach the countertop, and might ask for identification of any who appeared to be of borderline age. The law envisioned that something similar would happen in Cyberspace:

> It is an affirmative defense to prosecution under this section that the defendant, in good faith, has restricted access by minors to material that is harmful to minors (A) by requiring use of a credit card, debit account, adult access code, or adult personal identification number; (B) by accepting a digital certificate that verifies age; or (C) by any other reasonable measures that are feasible under available technology.

The big problem was that these methods either didn't work or didn't even exist. Not every adult has a credit card, and credit card companies don't want their databases used to check customers' ages. And if you don't know what is meant by an "adult personal identification number" or a "digital certificate that verifies age," don't feel badly—neither do we. Clauses (B) and (C) were basically a plea from Congress for the industry to come up with some technical magic for determining age at a distance.

In the state of the art, however, computers can't reliably tell if the party on the other end of a communications link is human or is another computer. For a computer to tell whether a human is over or under the age of 17, even imperfectly, would be very hard indeed. Mischievous 15-year-olds could get around any simple screening system that could be used in the home. The Internet just isn't like a magazine store.

Even if credit card numbers or personal identification systems could distinguish children from adults, Judge Reed reasoned, such methods would intimidate computer users. Fearful of identity theft or government surveillance, many computer users would refuse interrogation and would not reveal personal identifying information as the price for visiting web sites deemed "harmful to minors." The vast electronic library would, in practice, fall into disuse and start to close down, just as an ordinary library would become useless if everyone venturing beyond the children's section had to endure a background check.

Congress's safe harbor recommendations, concluded Judge Reed, if they worked at all, would limit Internet speech drastically. Information adults had a right to see would, realistically, become unavailable to them. The filtering technologies noted when the CDA was struck down had improved, so the government could not credibly claim that limiting speech was the only possible approach to protecting children. And even if the free expression concerns were calmed or ignored, and even if everything COPA suggested worked perfectly, plenty of smut would still be available to children. The Internet was borderless, and COPA's reach ended at the U.S. frontier. COPA couldn't stop the flood of harmful bits from abroad.

Summing up, Reed quoted the thoughts of Supreme Court Justice Kennedy about a flag-burning case. "The hard fact is that sometimes we must make decisions we do not like. We make them because they are right, right in the sense that the law and the Constitution, as we see them, compel the result." Much as he was sympathetic to the end of protecting children from harmful communications, Judge Reed concluded, "perhaps we do the minors of this country harm if First Amendment protections, which they will with age inherit fully, are chipped away in the name of their protection."

# Let Your Fingers Do the Stalking

Newsgroups for sharing sexual information and experiences started in the early 1980s. By the mid-90s, there were specialty sites for every orientation and inclination. So when a 28-year-old woman entered an Internet chat room in 1998 to share her sexual fantasies, she was doing nothing out of the ordinary. She longed to be assaulted, she said, and invited men reading her email to make her fantasy a reality. "I want you to break down my door and rape me," she wrote.

What *was* unusual was that she gave her name and address—and instructions about how to get past her building's security system. Over a period of several weeks, nine men took up her invitation and showed up at her door, often in the middle of the night. When she sent them away, she followed up with a further email to the chat room, explaining that her rejections were just part of the fantasy.

In fact, the "woman" sending the emails was Gary Dellapenta, a 50-year-old security guard whose attentions the actual woman had rebuffed. The victim of this terrifying hoax did not even own a computer. Dellapenta was caught because he responded directly to emails sent to entrap him. He was convicted and imprisoned under a recently enacted California anti-"cyberstalking" statute. The case was notable not because the events were unusual, but because it resulted in a prosecution and conviction. Most victims are not so successful in seeking redress. Most states lacked appropriate laws, and most victims could not identify their stalkers. Sometimes the stalker did not even know the victim—but simply found her contact information somewhere in Cyberspace.

Speeches and publications with frightening messages have long received First Amendment protections in the U.S., especially when their subject is political. Only when a message is likely to incite "imminent lawless action" (in the words of a 1969 Supreme Court decision) does speech become illegal—a test rarely met by printed words. This high threshold for government intervention builds on a "clear and present danger" standard explained most eloquently by Justice Louis Brandeis in a 1927 opinion. "Fear of serious injury cannot alone justify suppression of free speech .... No danger flowing from speech can be deemed clear and present, unless the incidence of the evil apprehended is so imminent that it may befall before there is opportunity for full discussion."

Courts apply the same standard to web sites. An anti-abortion group listed the names, addresses, and license plate numbers of doctors performing abortions on a web site called the "Nuremberg Files." It suggested stalking the doctors, and updated the site by graying out the names of those who had been wounded and crossing off those who had been murdered. The web site's creators acknowledged that abortion was legal, and claimed not to be threatening anyone, only collecting dossiers in the hope that the doctors could at some point in the future be held accountable for "crimes against humanity."

The anti-abortion group was taken to court in a civil action. After a long legal process, the group was found liable for damages because "true threats of violence were made with the intent to intimidate."

The courts had a very difficult time with the question of whether the Nuremberg Files web site was threatening or not, but there was nothing intrinsic to the mode of publication that complicated that decision. In fact, the same group had issued paper "WANTED" posters, which were equally part of the materials at issue. Reasonable jurists could, and did, come to different conclusions about whether the text on the Nuremberg Files web site met the judicial threshold.

But the situation of Dellapenta's victim, and other women in similar situations, seemed to be different. The scores being settled at their expense had no political dimensions. There were already laws against stalking and telephone harassment; the Internet was being used to recruit proxy stalkers and harassers. Following the lead of California and other states, Congress passed a federal anti-cyberstalking law.

## Like an Annoying Telephone Call?

The "2005 Violence Against Women and Department of Justice Reauthorization Act" (signed into law in early 2006) assigned criminal penalties to anyone who "utilizes any device or software that can be used to originate telecommunications or other types of communications that are transmitted, in whole or in part, by the Internet ... without disclosing his identity and with intent to annoy, abuse, threaten, or harass any person...." The clause was little noticed when the Act was passed in the House on a voice vote and in the Senate unanimously.

Civil libertarians again howled, this time about a single word in the legislation. It was fine to outlaw abuse, threats, and harassment by Internet. Those terms had some legal history. Although it was not always easy to tell whether the facts fit the definitions, at least the courts had standards for judging what these words meant.

But "annoy"? People put lots of annoying things on web sites and say lots of annoying things in chat rooms. There is even a web site, annoy.com, devoted to posting annoying political messages anonymously. Could Congress really have intended to ban the use of the Internet to annoy people?

Congress had extended telephone law to the Internet, on the principle that harassing VoIP calls should not receive more protection than harassing landline telephone calls. In using broad language for electronic communications, however, it created another in the series of legal muddles about the aptness of a metaphor.

The Telecommunications Act of 1934 made it a criminal offense for anyone to make "a telephone call, whether or not conversation ensues, without disclosing his identity and with intent to annoy, abuse, threaten, or harass any person at the called number." In the world of telephones, the ban posed no threat to free speech, because a telephone call is one-to-one communication. If the person you are talking to doesn't want to listen, your free speech rights are not infringed. The First Amendment gives you no right to be sure anyone in particular hears you. If your phone call is unwelcome, you can easily find another forum in which to be annoying. The CDA, in a clause that was not struck down along with the display provisions, extended the prohibition to faxes and emails—still, basically, person-to-person communications. But harassing VoIP calls were not criminal under the Telecommunications Act. In an effort to capture all telephone-like technologies under the same regulation, the same clause was extended to all forms of electronic communication, including the vast "electronic library" and "most participatory form of mass speech" that is the Internet.

Defenders of the law assured alarmed bloggers that "annoying" sites would not be prosecuted unless they also were personally threatening, abusive, or harassing. This was an anti-cyberstalking provision, they argued, not a censorship law. Speech protected by the First Amendment would certainly be safe. Online publishers, on the other hand, were reluctant to trust prosecutors' judgment about where the broadly written statute would be applied. And based on the bizarre and unexpected uses to which the CDA's Good Samaritan provisions had been put, there was little reason for confidence that the legislative context for the law would restrict its application to one corner of Cyberspace.

The law was challenged by The Suggestion Box, which describes itself as helping people send anonymous emails for reasons such as to "report sensitive information to the media" and to "send crime tips to law enforcement agencies anonymously." The law, as the complaint argued, might criminalize the sort of employee whistle-blowing that Congress encouraged in the aftermath of scandals about corporate accounting practices. The Suggestion Box dropped its challenge when the Government stated that mere annoyances would not be prosecuted, only communications meant "to instill fear in the victim." So the law is in force, with many left wishing that Congress would be more precise with its language!

Which brings us to the present. The "annoyance" clause of the Violence Against Women Act stands, but only because the Government says that it doesn't mean what it says. DOPA, with which this chapter began, remains stuck in Congress. Like the CDA and COPA, DOPA has worthy goals. The measures it proposes would, however, probably do more harm than good. In requiring libraries to monitor the computer use of children using sites such as MySpace, it would likely make those sites inaccessible through public libraries, while having little impact on child predators. The congressional sponsors have succumbed to a well-intentioned but misguided urge to control a social problem by restricting the technology that assists it.

## Digital Protection, Digital Censorship—and Self-Censorship

The First Amendment's ban on government censorship complicates government efforts to protect the safety and security of U.S. citizens. Given a choice between protection from personal harm and some fool's need to spout profanities, most of us would opt for safety. Security is immediate and freedom is long-term, and most people are short-range thinkers. And most people think of security as a personal thing, and gladly leave it to the government to worry about the survival of the nation.

> *Given a choice between protection from personal harm and some fool's need to spout profanities, most of us would opt for safety.*

But in the words of one scholar, the bottom line on the First Amendment is that "in a society pledged to self-government, it is never true that, in the long run, the security of the nation is endangered by the freedom of the people." The Internet censorship bills have passed Congress by wide margins because members of Congress dare not be on record as voting against the safety of their constituents—and especially against the safety of children. Relatively isolated from political pressure, the courts have repeatedly undone speech-restricting legislation passed by elected officials.

Free speech precedes the other freedoms enumerated in the Bill of Rights, but not just numerically. In a sense, it precedes them logically as well. In the words of Supreme Court Justice Benjamin Cardozo, it is "the matrix, the indispensable condition, of nearly every other form of freedom."

For most governments, the misgivings about censoring electronic information are less profound.

In Saudi Arabia, you can't get to www.sex.com. In fact, *every* web access in Saudi Arabia goes through government computers to make sure the URL isn't

## INTERNET FREEDOM

A great many organizations devote significant effort to maintaining the Internet's potential as a free marketplace of ideas. In addition to EFF, already mentioned earlier in this chapter, some others include: the Electronic Privacy Information Network, www.epic.org; The Free Expression Network, freeexpression.org, which is actually a coalition; the American Civil Liberties Union, www.aclu.org; and the Chilling Effects Clearinghouse, www.chillingeffects.org. The OpenNet Initiative, opennet.net, monitors Internet censorship around the world. OpenNet's findings are presented in *Access Denied: The Practice and Policy of Global Internet Filtering*, by Ronald J. Deibert, John G. Palfrey, Rafal Rohozinski, and Jonathan Zittrain (eds.), MIT Press, 2008.

on the government's blacklist. In Thailand, www.stayinvisible.com is blocked; that's a source of information about Internet privacy and tools to assist in anonymous web surfing.

The disparity of information freedom standards between the U.S. and other countries creates conflicts when electronic transactions involve two nations. As discussed in Chapter 4, China insists that Google not help its citizens get information the government does not want them to have. If you try to get to certain web sites from your hotel room in Shanghai, you suddenly lose your Internet connection, with no explanation. You might think there was a glitch in the network somewhere, except that you can reconnect and visit other sites with no problems.

Self-censorship by Internet companies is also increasing—the price they pay for doing business in certain countries. Thailand and Turkey blocked the video-sharing site YouTube after it carried clips lampooning (and, as those governments saw it, insulting) their current or former rulers. A Google official described censorship as the company's "No. 1 barrier to trade." Stirred by the potential costs in lost business and legal battles, Internet companies have become outspoken information libertarians, even as they do what must be done to meet the requirements of foreign governments. Google has even hired a Washington lobbyist to seek help from the U.S. government in its efforts to resist censorship abroad.

It is easy for Americans to shrug their isolationist shoulders over such problems. As long as all the information is available in the U.S., one might reason, who cares what version of Google or YouTube runs in totalitarian regimes abroad? That is for those countries to sort out.

But the free flow of information into the U.S. is threatened by the laws of other nations about the operation of the press. Consider the case of Joseph Gutnick and *Barron's* magazine.

On October 30, 2000, the financial weekly *Barron's* published an article suggesting that Australian businessman Joseph Gutnick was involved in money-laundering and tax evasion. Gutnick sued Dow Jones Co., the publisher of *Barron's*, for defamation. The suit was filed in an Australian court. Gutnick maintained that the online edition of the magazine, available in Australia for a fee, was in effect published in Australia. Dow Jones countered that the place of "publication" of the online magazine was New Jersey, where its web servers were located. The suit, it argued, should have been brought in a U.S. court and judged by the standards of U.S. libel law, which are far more favorable to the free speech rights of the press. The Australian court agreed with Gutnick, and the suit went forward. Gutnick ultimately won an apology from Dow Jones and $580,000 in fines and legal costs.

The implications seem staggering. Americans on American soil expect to be able to speak very freely, but the Australian court claimed that the global Internet made Australia's laws applicable wherever the bits reaching Australian soil may have originated. The Amateur Action conundrum about what community standards apply to the borderless Internet had been translated to the world of global journalism. Will the freedom of the Internet press henceforth be the minimum applying to any of the nations of the earth? Is it possible that a rogue nation could cripple the global Internet press by extorting large sums of money from alleged defamers, or by imposing death sentences on reporters it claimed had insulted their leaders?

The American press tends to fight hard for its right to publish the truth, but the censorship problems reach into Western democracies more insidiously for global corporations not in the news business. It is sometimes easier for American companies to meet the minimum "world" standards of information freedom than to keep different information available in the U.S. There may even be reasons in international law and trade agreements that make such accommodations to censorship more likely. Consider the trials of Yahoo! France.

In May 2000, the League Against Racism and Anti-Semitism (LICRA, in its French acronym) and the Union of French Jewish Students (UEJF) demanded to a French court that Yahoo! stop making Nazi paraphernalia available for online auction, stop showing pictures of Nazi memorabilia, and prohibit the dissemination of anti-Semitic hate speech on discussion groups available in France. Pursuant to the laws of France, where the sale and display of Nazi items is illegal, the court concluded that what Yahoo! was doing was an offense to the "collective memory" of the country and a violation of Article R654 of the Penal Code. It told Yahoo! that the company was a threat to "internal public order" and that it had to make sure no one in France could view such items.

Yahoo! removed the items from the yahoo.fr site ordinarily available in France. LICRA and UEJF then discovered that from within France, they could also get to the American site, yahoo.com, by slightly indirect means. Reaching across the ocean in a manner reminiscent of the Australian court's defamation action, the French court demanded that the offending items, images, and words be removed from the American web site as well.

Yahoo! resisted for a time, claiming it couldn't tell where the bits were going—an assertion somewhat lacking in credibility since the company tended to attach French-language advertising to web pages if they were dispatched to locations in France. Eventually, Yahoo! made a drastic revision of its standards for the U.S. site. Hate speech was prohibited under Yahoo's revised service terms with its users, and most of the Nazi memorabilia disappeared. But Nazi stamps and coins were still available for auction on the U.S. site, as were copies of *Mein Kampf*. In November 2000, the French court affirmed and extended its order: *Mein Kampf* could not be offered for sale in France. The fines were adding up.

Yahoo! sought help in U.S. courts. It had committed no crime in the U.S., it stated. French law could not leap the Atlantic and trump U.S. First Amendment protections. Enforcement of the French order would have a chilling effect on speech in the United States. A U.S. district court agreed, and the decision was upheld on appeal by a three-judge panel of the Court of Appeals for the Ninth Circuit (Northern California).

But in 2006, the full 11-member court of appeals reversed the decision and found against Yahoo!. The company had not suffered enough, according to the majority opinion, nor tried long enough to have the French change their minds, for appeal to First Amendment protections to be appropriate. A dissenting opinion spoke plainly about what the court seemed to be doing. "We should not allow a foreign court order," wrote Judge William Fletcher, "to be used as leverage to quash constitutionally protected speech...."

*It would be a sad irony if information liberty, so stoutly defended for centuries in the U.S., would fall in the twenty-first century to a combination of domestic child protection laws and international money-making opportunities.*

Such conflicts will be more common in the future, as more bits flow across national borders. The laws, trade agreements, and court decisions of the next few years, many of them regulating the flow of "intellectual property," will shape the world of the future. It would be a sad irony if information liberty, so stoutly defended for centuries in the U.S., would fall in the twenty-first century to a combination of domestic child protection laws and international money-making opportunities. But as one British commentator said when the photo-hosting site Flickr removed photos to conform with orders from Singapore, Germany, Hong Kong, and Korea, "Libertarianism is all very well when you're a hacker. But business is business."

Information freedom on the Internet is a tricky business. Technological changes happen faster than legal changes. When a technology shift alarms the populace, legislators respond with overly broad laws. By the time challenges have worked their way through the courts, another cycle of technology changes has happened, and the slow heartbeat of lawmaking pumps out another poorly drafted statute.

The technology of radio and television has also challenged the legislative process, but in a different way. In the broadcast world, strong commercial forces are arrayed in support of speech-restricting laws that have long since outgrown the technology that gave birth to them. We now turn to those changes in the radio world.

# CHAPTER 8

# Bits in the Air

## *Old Metaphors, New Technologies, and Free Speech*

## Censoring the President

On July 17, 2006, U.S. President George Bush and British Prime Minister Tony Blair were chatting at the G-8 summit in St. Petersburg, Russia. The event was a photo opportunity, but the two leaders did not realize that a microphone was on. They were discussing what the UN might do to quell the conflict between Israel and militant forces in Lebanon. "See the irony is," said Bush, "what they need to do is get Syria to get Hezbollah to stop doing this shit and it's over."

The cable network CNN carried the clip in full and posted it on the Web, but most broadcast stations bleeped out the expletive. They were aware of the fines, as much as $325,000, that the Federal Communications Commission might impose for airing the word "shit."

The FCC had long regulated speech over the public airways, but had raised its decency standards after the 2002 "Golden Globes" awards presentation. Singer Bono had won the "Best Original Song" award. In his acceptance speech, broadcast live on NBC, he said, "This is really, really, fucking brilliant." The FCC ruled that this remark was "patently offensive under contemporary community standards for the broadcast medium." It promised to fine and even pull the licenses of stations broadcasting such remarks.

In 2006, the Commission extended the principle from the F-word to the S-word. Nicole Richie, referring to a reality TV show on which she had done some farm work, said to Paris Hilton, "Why do they even call it *The Simple Life*? Have you ever tried to get cow shit out of a Prada purse? It's not so fucking simple." The FCC's ruling on Richie's use of the excrement metaphor implied that Bush's use would be "presumptively profane" in the eyes of the FCC.

A federal court reversed the FCC's policy against such "fleeting" expletives—an expansion of indecency policies that had been in place for decades. Congress quickly introduced legislation to restore the FCC's new and strict standard, and the whole matter was to be argued before the U.S. Supreme Court in the spring of 2008. The FCC had adopted its new standards after complaints about broadcast indecency rose from fewer than 50 to about 1.4 million in the period from 2000 to 2004. Congress may have thought that the new speech code reflected a public mandate.

Under the First Amendment, the government is generally not in the speech-restricting business. It can't force its editorial judgments on newspapers, even to increase the range of information available to readers. The Supreme Court struck down as unconstitutional a Florida law assuring political candidates a simple "right to reply" to newspaper attacks on them.

Nonetheless, in 2006, an agency of the federal government was trying to keep words off television, using rules that "presumptively" covered even a candid conversation about war and peace between leaders of the free world. Dozens of newspapers printed Bush's remark in full, and anyone with an Internet connection could hear the audio. In spite of the spike in indecency complaints to the FCC, Americans are generally opposed to having the government nanny their television shows.

# How Broadcasting Became Regulated

The FCC gained its authority over what is said on radio and TV broadcasts when there were fewer ways to distribute information. The public airways were scarce, went the theory, and the government had to make sure they were used in the public interest. As radio and television became universally accessible, a second rationale emerged for government regulation of broadcast speech. Because the broadcast media have "a uniquely pervasive presence in the lives of all Americans," as the Supreme Court put it in 1978, the government had a special interest in protecting a defenseless public from objectionable radio and television content.

The explosion in communications technologies has confused both rationales. In the digital era, there are far more ways for bits to reach the consumer, so broadcast radio and television are hardly unique in their pervasiveness.

With minimal technology, anyone can sit at home or in Starbucks and choose from among billions of web pages and tens of millions of blogs. Shock jock Howard Stern left broadcast radio for satellite radio, where the FCC has no authority to regulate what he says.

More than 90% of American television viewers get their TV signal through similarly unregulated cable or satellite, not through broadcasts from rooftop antennas. RSS feeds supply up-to-date information to millions of on-the-go cell phone users. Radio stations and television channels are today neither scarce nor uniquely pervasive.

*In the digital era, there are far more ways for bits to reach the consumer, so broadcast radio and television are hardly unique in their pervasiveness.*

For the government to protect children from all offensive information arriving through any communication medium, its authority would have to be expanded greatly and updated continuously. Indeed, federal legislation has been introduced to do exactly that–to extend FCC indecency regulations for broadcast media to satellite and cable television as well.

The explosion in communications raises another possibility, however. If almost anyone can now send information that many people can receive, perhaps the government's interest in restricting transmissions should be less than what it once was, not greater. In the absence of scarcity, perhaps the government should have no more authority over what gets said on radio and TV than it does over what gets printed in newspapers. In that case, rather than expanding the FCC's censorship authority, Congress should eliminate it entirely, just as the Supreme Court ended Florida's regulation of newspaper content.

Parties who already have spots on the radio dial and the TV channel lineup respond that the spectrum–the public airwaves–should remain a limited resource, requiring government protection. No one is making any more radio spectrum, goes the theory, and it needs to be used in the public interest.

But look around you. There are still only a few stations on the AM and FM radio dials. But thousands, maybe tens of thousands, of radio communications are passing through the air around you. Most Americans walk around with two-way radios in their pockets–devices we call cell phones–and most of the nation's teenagers seem to be talking on them simultaneously. Radios and television sets could be much, much smarter than they now are and could make better use of the airwaves, just as cell phones do.

Engineering developments have vitiated the government's override of the First Amendment on radio and television. The Constitution demands, under these changed circumstances, that the government stop its verbal policing.

**SURVIVING ON WIRELESS**

A dramatic example of the pervasiveness of wireless networks, in spite of the limits on spectrum where they are allowed to operate, was provided in the aftermath of the destruction of the World Trade Center on September 11, 2001. Lower Manhattan communicated for several days largely on the strength of wireless. Something similar happened after the December 2006 earthquake that severed undersea communications cables in southeast Asia.

As a scientific argument, the claim that the spectrum is necessarily scarce is now very weak. Yet that view is still forcefully advanced by the very industry that is being regulated. The incumbent license holders—existing broadcast stations and networks—have an incentive to protect their "turf" in the spectrum against any risk, real or imagined, that their signals might be corrupted. By deterring technological innovation, incumbents can limit competition and avoid capital investments. These oddly intertwined strands—the government's interest in artificial scarcity to justify speech regulation and the incumbents' interest in artificial scarcity to limit competition and costs—today impair both cultural and technological creativity, to the detriment of society.

To understand the confluent forces that have created the world of today's radio and television censorship, we have to go back to the inventors of the technology.

## From Wireless Telegraph to Wireless Chaos

Red, orange, yellow, green, blue—the colors of the rainbow—are all different and yet are all the same. Any child with a crayon box knows that they are all different. They are the same because they are all the result of electromagnetic radiation striking our eyes. The radiation travels in waves that oscillate very quickly. The only physical difference between red and blue is that red waves oscillate around 450,000,000,000,000 times per second, and blue waves about 50% faster.

Because the spectrum of visible light is continuous, an infinity of colors exists between red and blue. Mixing light of different frequencies creates other colors—for example, half blue waves and half red creates a shade of pink known as magenta, which does not appear in the rainbow.

In the 1860s, British physicist James Clerk Maxwell realized that light consists of electromagnetic waves. His equations predicted that there might be waves of other frequencies—waves that people couldn't sense. Indeed, such waves have been passing right through us from the beginning of time. They shower down invisibly from the sun and the stars, and they radiate when lightning strikes. No one suspected they existed until Maxwell's equations said they should. Indeed, there should be a whole spectrum of invisible waves of different frequencies, all traveling at the same great speed as visible light.

In 1887, the radio era began with a demonstration by Henrich Hertz. He bent a wire into a circle, leaving a small gap between the two ends. When he set off a big electric spark a few feet away, a tiny spark jumped the gap of the almost-completely-circular wire. The big spark had set off a shower of unseen electromagnetic waves, which had traveled through space and caused electric current to flow in the other wire. The tiny spark was the current completing the circuit. Hertz had created the first antenna, and had revealed the radio waves that struck it. The unit of frequency is named in his honor: One cycle per second is 1 hertz, or Hz for short. A kHz (kilohertz) is a thousand cycles per second, and a MHz (megahertz) is a million cycles per second. These are the units on the AM and FM radio dials.

Gugliemo Marconi was neither a mathematician nor a scientist. He was an inventive tinkerer. Only 13 years old at the time of Hertz's experiment, Marconi spent the next decade developing, by trial and error, better ways of creating bursts of radio waves, and antennas for detecting them over greater distances.

In 1901, Marconi stood in Newfoundland and received a single Morse code letter transmitted from England. On the strength of this success, the Marconi Wireless Telegraph Company was soon enabling ships to communicate with each other and with the shore. When the *Titanic* left on its fateful voyage in 1912, it was equipped with Marconi equipment. The main job of the ship's radio operators was to relay personal messages to and from passengers, but they also received at least 20 warnings from other ships about the icebergs that lay ahead.

The words "Wireless Telegraph" in the name of Marconi's company suggest the greatest limitation of early radio. The technology was conceived as a device for point-to-point communication. Radio solved the worst problem of telegraphy. No calamity, sabotage, or war could stop wireless transmissions by severing cables. But there was a compensating disadvantage: Anyone could listen in. The enormous power of broadcasting to reach thousands of people at once was at first seen as a liability. Who would pay to send a message to another person when anyone could hear it?

As wireless telegraphy became popular, another problem emerged—one that has shaped the development of radio and television ever since. If several people were transmitting simultaneously in the same geographic area, their signals couldn't be kept apart. The *Titanic* disaster demonstrated the confusion that could result. The morning after the ship hit the iceberg, American newspapers reported excitedly that all passengers had been saved and the ship was being towed to shore. The mistake resulted from a radio operator's garbled merger of two unrelated segments of Morse code. One ship inquired if "all Titanic passengers safe?" A completely different ship reported that it was "300 miles west of the Titanic and towing an oil tank to Halifax." All the ships had radios and radio operators. But there were no rules or conventions about whether, how, or when to use them.

Listeners to Marconi's early transmitters were easily confused because they had no way to "tune in" a particular communication. For all of Marconi's genius in extending the range of transmission, he was using essentially Hertz's method for generating radio waves: big sparks. The sparks splattered electromagnetic energy across the radio spectrum. The energy could be stopped and started to turn it into dots and dashes, but there was nothing else to control. One radio operator's noise was like any other's. When several transmitted simultaneously, chaos resulted.

The many colors of visible light look white if all blended together. A color filter lets through some frequencies of visible light but not others. If you look at the world through a red filter, everything is a lighter or darker shade of red, because only the red light comes through. What radio needed was something similar for the radio spectrum: a way to produce radio waves of a single frequency, or at least a narrow range of frequencies, and a receiver that could let through those frequencies and screen out the rest. Indeed, that technology already existed.

In 1907, Lee De Forest patented a key technology for the De Forest Radio Telephone Company—dedicated to sending voice and even music over the radio waves. When he broadcast Enrico Caruso from the Metropolitan Opera House on January 13, 1910, the singing reached ships at sea. Amateurs huddled over receivers in New York and New Jersey. The effect was sensational. Hundreds of amateur broadcasters sprang into action over the next few years, eagerly saying whatever they wanted, and playing whatever music they could, to anyone who happened to be listening.

*With no clear understanding about what frequencies to use, radio communication was a hit-or-miss affair.*

But with no clear understanding about what frequencies to use, radio communication was a hit-or-miss affair. Even what the *New York Times* described as the "homeless song waves" of the Caruso broadcast clashed with another station that, "despite all entreaties," insisted on broadcasting at the identical 350kHz frequency. Some people could "catch the ecstasy" of Caruso's voice, but others got only some annoying Morse code: "I took a beer just now."

## Radio Waves in Their Channels

The emerging radio industry could not grow under such conditions. Commercial interests complemented the concerns of the U.S. Navy about amateur interference with its ship communications. The *Titanic* disaster, although it owed little to the failures of radio, catalyzed government action. On May 12, 1912, William Alden Smith called for radio regulation on the floor of the U.S. Senate. "When the world weeps together over a common loss...," proclaimed the Senator, "why should not the nations clear the sea of its conflicting idioms and wisely regulate this new servant of humanity?"

The Radio Act of 1912 limited broadcasting to license holders. Radio licenses were to be "granted by the Secretary of Commerce and Labor upon application therefor." In granting the license, the Secretary would stipulate the frequencies "authorized for use by the station for the prevention of interference and the hours for which the station is licensed for work." The Act reserved for government use the choice frequencies between about 200 and 500kHz, which permitted the clearest communications over long distances. Amateurs were pushed off to "short wave" frequencies above 1500kHz, considered useless for technological reasons. The frequency 1000kHz was reserved for distress calls, and licensed stations were required to listen to it every 15 minutes (the one provision that

> ### HIGH FREQUENCIES
>
> Over the years, technological improvements have made it possible to use higher and higher frequencies. Early TV was broadcast at what were then considered "Very High Frequencies" (VHF) because they were higher than AM radio. Technology improved again, and more stations appeared at "Ultra High Frequencies" (UHF). The highest frequency in commercial use today is 77GHz—77 gigahertz, that is, 77,000MHz. In general, high frequency signals fade with distance more than low signals, and are therefore mainly useful for localized or urban environments. Short waves correspond to high frequencies because all radio waves travel at the same speed, which is the speed of light.

might have helped the *Titanic*, since the radio operators of a nearby ship had gone off-duty and missed the *Titanic's* rescue pleas). The rest of the spectrum the Secretary could assign to commercial radio stations and private businesses. Emphasizing the nature of radio as "wireless telegraphy," the Act made it a crime for anyone hearing a radio message to divulge it to anyone except its intended recipient.

Much has changed since 1912. The uses of radio waves have become more varied, the allocation of spectrum blocks has changed, and the range of usable frequencies has grown. The current spectrum allocation picture has grown into a dense, disorganized quilt, the product of decades of Solomonic FCC judgments (see Figure 8.1). But still, the U.S. government stipulates what parts of the spectrum can be used for what purposes. It prevents users from interfering with each other and with government communications by demanding that they broadcast at limited power and only at their assigned frequencies. As long as there weren't many radio stations, the implied

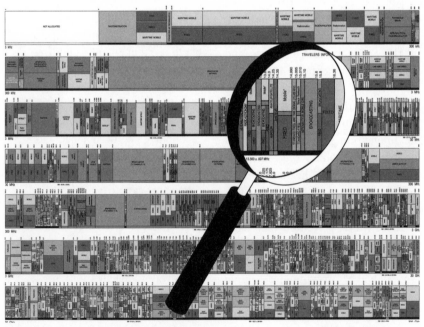

Source: www.ntia.doc.gov/osmhome/allochrt.pdf.

FIGURE **8.1**    Frequency allocation of the U.S. radio spectrum. The spectrum from 3kHz to 300GHz is laid out from left to right and top to bottom, with the scale 10 times denser in each successive row. For example, the large block in the second row is the AM radio dial, about 1MHz wide. The same amount of spectrum would be about .00002 of an inch wide in the bottom row.

promise in the Act of 1912 that licenses would be granted "upon application therefor" caused no problems. With the gossip of the pesky amateurs pushed into remote radio territory, there was plenty of spectrum for commercial, military, and safety use.

Within a decade, that picture had changed dramatically. On November 2, 1920, a Detroit station broadcast the election of Warren Harding as President of the United States, relaying to its tiny radio audience the returns it was receiving by telegraph. Radio was no longer just point-to-point communication. A year later, a New York station broadcast the World Series between the Giants and the Yankees, pitch by pitch. Sports broadcasting was born with a broadcaster drearily repeating the ball and strike information telephoned by a newspaper reporter at the ballpark.

Public understanding of the possibilities grew rapidly. The first five radio stations were licensed for broadcasting in 1921. Within a year, there were 670. The number of radio receivers jumped in a year from less than 50,000 to more than 600,000, perhaps a million. Stations using the same frequency in the same city divided up the hours of the day. As radio broadcasting became a profitable business, the growth could not go on forever.

On November 12, 1921, the New York City broadcast license of Intercity Radio Co. expired. Herbert Hoover, then the Secretary of Commerce, refused to renew it, on the grounds that there was no frequency on which Intercity could broadcast in the city's airspace without interfering with government or other private stations. Intercity sued Hoover to have its license restored, and won. Hoover, said the court, could choose the frequency, but he had no discretion to deny the license. As the congressional committee proposing the 1912 Radio Act had put it, the licensing system was "substantially the same as that in use for the documenting upward of 25,000 merchant vessels." The implied metaphor was that Hoover should keep track of the stations like ships in the ocean. He could tell them what shipping lanes to use, but he couldn't keep them out of the water.

The radio industry begged for order. Hoover convened a National Radio Conference in 1922 in an attempt to achieve consensus on new regulations before chaos set in. The spectrum was "a great national asset," he said, and "it becomes of primary public interest to say who is to do the broadcasting, under what circumstances, and with what type of material." "[T]he large mass of subscribers need protection as to the noises which fill their instruments," and the airwaves need "a policeman" to detect "hogs that are endangering the traffic."

Hoover divided the spectrum from 550kHz to 1350kHz in 10kHz bands—called "channels," consistent with the nautical metaphor—to squeeze in more stations. Empty "guard bands" were left on each side of allocated bands because broadcast signals inevitably spread out, reducing the amount of usable spectrum. Persuasion and voluntary compliance helped Hoover limit interference. As stations became established, they found it advantageous to comply with Hoover's prescriptions. Start-ups had a harder time breaking in. Hoover convinced representatives of a religious group that to warn of the coming apocalypse, they should buy time on existing stations rather than build one of their own. After all, their money would go farther that way—in six months, after the world had ended, they would have no further use for a transmitter. Hoover's effectiveness made Congress complacent—the system was working well enough without laws.

But as the slicing got finer, the troubles got worse. WLW and WMH in Cincinnati broadcast on the same frequency in 1924 until Hoover brokered a deal for three stations to share two frequencies in rotating time slots. Finally, the system broke down. In 1925, Zenith Radio Corporation was granted a license to use 930kHz in Chicago, but only on Thursday nights, only from 10 p.m. to midnight, and only if a Denver station didn't wish to broadcast then. Without permission, Zenith started broadcasting at 910kHz, a frequency that was more open because it had been ceded by treaty to Canada. Hoover fined Zenith; Zenith challenged Hoover's authority to regulate frequencies, and won in court. The Secretary then got even worse news from the U.S. Attorney General: The 1912 Act, drafted before broadcasting was even a concept, was so ambiguous that it probably gave Hoover no authority to regulate anything about broadcast radio—frequency, power, or time of day.

Hoover threw up his hands. Anyone could start a station and choose a frequency—there were 600 applications pending—but in doing so, they were "proceeding entirely at their own risk." The result was the "chaos in the air" that Hoover had predicted. It was worse than before the 1912 Act because so many more transmitters existed and they were so much more powerful. Stations popped up, jumped all over the frequency spectrum in search of open air, and turned up their transmission power to the maximum to drown out competing signals. Radio became virtually useless, especially in cities. Congress finally was forced to act.

## The Spectrum Nationalized

The premises of the Radio Act of 1927 are still in force. The spectrum has been treated as a scarce national resource ever since, managed by the government.

The purpose of the Act was *to maintain the control of the United States over all the channels of ... radio transmission; and to provide for the use of such channels, but not the ownership thereof, by individuals, firms, or corporations, for limited periods of time, under licenses granted by Federal authority....* The public could use the spectrum, under conditions stipulated by the government, but could not own it. A new authority, the Federal Radio Commission (FRC), made licensing decisions. The public had a qualified expectation that license requests would be granted: *The licensing authority, if public convenience, interest, or necessity will be served thereby, ... shall grant to any applicant therefor a station license....* The Act recognized that demand for licenses could exceed the supply of spectrum. In case of competition among applicants, *the licensing authority shall make such a distribution of licenses, bands of frequency..., periods of time for operation, and of power among the different States and communities as to give fair, efficient, and equitable radio service to each....*

*The premises of the Radio Act of 1927 are still in force. The spectrum has been treated as a scarce national resource ever since, managed by the government.*

> ### THE "RADIO COMMISSION" GROWS
>
> In 1934, the FRC's name was changed to the Federal Communications Commission—the FCC—when telephone and telegraph regulation came under the Commission's oversight. When a separate chunk of radio spectrum was allocated for television, the FCC assumed authority over video broadcasts as well.

The language about "public convenience, interest, or necessity" echoes Hoover's 1922 speech about a "national asset" and the "public interest." It is also no accident that this law was drafted as the Teapot Dome Scandal was cresting. Oil reserves on federal land in Wyoming had been leased to Sinclair Oil in 1923 with the assistance of bribes paid to the Secretary of the Interior. It took several years for Congressional investigations and federal court cases to expose the wrongdoing; the Secretary was eventually imprisoned. By early 1927, the fair use of national resources in the public interest was a major concern in the United States.

With the passage of the Act of 1927, the radio spectrum became federal land. International treaties followed, to limit interference near national borders. But within the U.S., just as Hoover had asked five years earlier, the federal government took control over who would be allowed to broadcast, which radio waves they could use—and even what they could say.

## Goat Glands and the First Amendment

The Radio Act of 1927 stipulated that the FRC could not abridge free speech over the radio. *Nothing in this Act shall be understood or construed to give the licensing authority the power of censorship..., and no regulation or condition ... shall interfere with the right of free speech by means of radio communications.* Inevitably, a case would arise exposing the implicit conflict: On the one hand, the Commission had to use a public interest standard when granting and renewing licenses. On the other, it had to avoid censorship. The pivotal case was over the license for KFKB radio, the station of the Kansas goat-gland doctor, John Romulus Brinkley (see Figure 8.2). The wrath brought down on CBS in 2004 for showing a flash of Janet Jackson's breast—and which the networks feared if they broadcast *Saving Private Ryan* on

*New York Evening Journal,* September 11, 1926. Microfilm courtesy of the Library of Congress.

FIGURE 8.2    A planted newspaper article about "Dr." Brinkley's goat-gland clinic. The doctor himself is shown at the left, holding the first baby—named "Billy," of course—conceived after a goat-gland transplant.

Veterans' Day or President Bush muttering to Tony Blair—descends from the FCC's action against this classic American charlatan.

Brinkley, born in 1885, became a "doctor" licensed to practice in Kansas by buying a degree from the Eclectic Medical University in Kansas City. He worked briefly as a medic for Swift & Co., the meatpackers. In 1917, he set up his medical practice in Milford, a tiny town about 70 miles west of Topeka. One day, a man came for advice about his failing virility, describing himself as a "flat tire." Drawing on his memory of goat behavior from his days at the slaughterhouse, Brinkley said, "You wouldn't have any trouble if you had a pair of those buck glands in you." "Well, why don't you put 'em in?" the patient asked. Brinkley did the transplant in a back room, and a business was born. Soon he was performing 50 transplants a month, at $750 per surgery. In time, he discovered that promising sexual performance was even more lucrative than promising fertility.

As a young man, Brinkley had worked at a telegraph office, so he knew the promise of communication technology. In 1923, he opened Kansas's first radio station, KFKB—"Kansas First, Kansas Best" radio, or sometimes "Kansas Folks Know Best." The station broadcast a mixture of country music, fundamentalist preaching, and medical advice from Dr. Brinkley himself. Listeners sent in their complaints, and the advice was almost always to buy some of Dr. Brinkley's mail-order patent medicines. "Here's one from Tillie," went a typical segment. "She says she had an operation, had some trouble 10 years ago. I think the operation was unnecessary, and it isn't very good sense to have an ovary removed with the expectation of motherhood resulting therefrom. My advice to you is to use Women's Tonic No. 50, 67, and 61. This combination will do for you what you desire if any combination will, after three months persistent use."

KFKB had a massively powerful transmitter, heard halfway across the Atlantic. In a national poll, it was the most popular station in America—with four times as many votes as the runner-up. Brinkley was receiving 3,000 letters a day and was a sensation throughout the plains states. On a good day, 500 people might show up in Milford. But the American Medical Association—prompted by a competing local radio station—objected to his quackery. The FRC concluded that "public interest, convenience, or necessity" would not be served by renewing the license. Brinkley objected that the cancellation was nothing less than censorship.

An appeals court sided with the FRC in a landmark decision. Censorship, the court explained, was prior restraint, which was not at issue in Brinkley's case. The FRC had "merely exercised its undoubted right to take note of appellant's past conduct." An arguable point—as Albert Gallatin said more than 200 years ago about prior restraint of the press, it was "preposterous to say, that to punish a certain act was not an abridgment of the liberty of doing that act."

The court used the public land metaphor in justifying the FRC's action. "[B]ecause the number of available broadcasting frequencies is limited," wrote the court, "the commission is necessarily called upon to consider the character and quality of the service to be rendered.... Obviously, there is no room in the broadcast band for every business or school of thought."

"Necessarily" and "obviously." It is always wise to scrutinize arguments that proclaim loudly how self-evident they are. Judge Felix Frankfurter, in an opinion on a different case in 1943, restated the principle in a form that has often been quoted. "The plight into which radio fell prior to 1927 was attributable to certain basic facts about radio as a means of communication—its facilities are limited; they are not available to all who may wish to use them; the radio spectrum simply is not large enough to accommodate everybody. There is a fixed natural limitation upon the number of stations that can operate without interfering with one another."

These were facts of the technology of the time. They were true, but they were contingent truths of engineering. They were never universal laws of physics, and are no longer limitations of technology. Because of engineering innovations over the past 20 years, there is no practically significant "natural limitation" on the number of broadcast stations. Arguments from inevitable scarcity can no longer justify U.S. government denials of the use of the airwaves.

The vast regulatory infrastructure, built to rationalize use of the spectrum by much more limited radio technology, has adjusted slowly—as it almost inevitably must: Bureaucracies don't move as quickly as technological innovators. The FCC tries to anticipate resource needs centrally and far in advance. But technology can cause abrupt changes in supply, and market forces can cause abrupt changes in demand. Central planning works no better for the FCC than it did for the Soviet Union.

Moreover, plenty of stakeholders in old technology are happy to see the rules remain unchanged. Like tenants enjoying leases on public land, incumbent radio license holders have no reason to encourage competing uses of the assets they control. The more money that is at stake, the greater the leverage of the profitable ventures. Radio licenses had value almost from the beginning, and as scarcity increased, so did price. By 1925, a Chicago license was sold for $50,000. As advertising expanded and stations bonded into networks, transactions reached seven figures. After the 1927 Act, disputes between stations had to be settled by litigation, trips to Washington, and pressure by friendly Congressional representatives—all more feasible for stations with deep pockets. At first, there were many university stations, but the FRC squeezed them as the value of the airwaves went up. As non-profits, these stations could not hold their ground. Eventually, most educational stations sold out to commercial broadcasters. *De facto*, as one historian put it, "while talking in terms of the public interest, ... the commission actually chose to further the ends of the commercial broadcasters."

# The Path to Spectrum Deregulation

When you push a button on your key fob and unlock your car doors, you are a radio broadcaster. The signal from the key fob uses a bit of the spectrum. The key fob signal obeys the same basic physical laws as WBZ's radio broadcasts in Boston, which have been going on continuously since WBZ became the first Eastern commercial station in 1921. But the new radio broadcasts are different in two critical respects. There are hundreds of millions of them going on every day. And while WBZ's broadcast power is 50,000 watts, a key fob's is less than .0002 of a watt.

If the government still had to license every radio transmitter—as Congress authorized in the aftermath of the radio chaos of the 1920s—neither radio key fobs nor any of hundreds of other innovative uses of low-power radio could have come about. The law and the bureaucracy it created would have snuffed this part of the digital explosion.

Another development also lay behind the wireless explosion. Technology had to change so that the available spectrum could be used more efficiently. Digitalization and miniaturization changed the communications world. The story of cell phones and wireless Internet and many conveniences as yet unimagined is a knot of politics, technology, and law. You can't understand the knot without understanding the strands, but in the future, the strands need not remain tied up in the same way as they are today.

## *From a Few Bullhorns to Millions of Whispers*

Thirty years ago, there were no cell phones. A handful of business executives had mobile phones, but the devices were bulky and costly. Miniaturization helped change the mobile phone from the perk of a few corporate bigwigs into the birthright of every American teenager. But the main advance was in *spectrum allocation*—in rethinking the way the radio spectrum was used.

In the era of big, clunky mobile phones, the radio phone company had a big antenna and secured from the FCC the right to use a few frequencies in an urban area. The executive's phone was a little radio station, which broadcast its call. The mobile phone had to be powerful enough to reach the company's antenna, wherever in the city the phone might be located. The number of simultaneous calls was limited to the number of frequencies allocated to the company. The technology was the same as broadcast radio stations used, except that the mobile phone radios were two-way. The scarcity of spectrum, still cited today in limiting the number of broadcast channels, then limited the number of mobile phones. Hoover understood this way back in 1922. "Obviously," he said, "if 10,000,000 telephone subscribers are crying through the air for their mates ... the ether will be filled with frantic chaos, with no communication of any kind possible."

Cellular technology exploits Moore's Law. Phones have become faster, cheaper, and smaller. Because cell phone towers are only a mile or so apart, cell phones need only be powerful enough to send their signals less than a mile. Once received by an antenna, the signal is sent on to the cell phone company by "wireline"—i.e., by copper or fiber optic cables on poles or under-ground. There need be only enough radio spectrum to handle the calls within the "cell" surrounding a tower, since the same frequencies can be used simul-taneously to handle calls in other cells. A lot of fancy dancing has to be done to prevent a call from being dropped as an active phone is carried from cell to cell, but computers, including the little computers inside cell phones, are smart and fast enough to keep up with such rearrangements.

Cell phone technology illustrates an important change in the use of radio spectrum. Most radio communications are now over short distances. They are transmissions between cell phone towers and cell phones. Between wireless routers at Starbucks and the computers of coffee drinkers. Between cordless telephone handsets and their bases. Between highway toll booths and the transponders mounted on commuters' windshields. Between key fobs with buttons and the cars they unlock. Between Wii remotes and Wii game machines. Between iPod transmitters plugged into cars' cigarette lighters and the cars' FM radios.

Even "satellite radio" transmissions often go from a nearby antenna to a customer's receiver, not directly from a satellite orbiting in outer space. In urban areas, so many buildings lie between the receiver and the satellite that the radio companies have installed "repeaters"—antennas connected to each other by wireline. When you listen to XM or Sirius in your car driving around a city, the signal is probably coming to you from an antenna a few blocks away.

*The radio spectrum is no longer mainly for long-range signaling.*

The radio spectrum is no longer mainly for long-range signaling. Spectrum policies were set when the major use of radio was for ship-to-shore transmissions, SOS sig-naling from great distances, and broadcast-ing over huge geographic areas. As the nation has become wired, most radio signals travel only a few feet or a few hundred feet. Under these changed conditions, the old rules for spectrum management don't make sense.

## Can We Just Divide the Property Differently?

Some innovations make better use of the spectrum without changing the fundamental allocation picture shown in Figure 8.1. For example, HD radio squeezes an unrelated low-power digital transmission alongside the analog AM and FM radio channels. ("HD" is a trademark. It doesn't stand for "high definition.") On AM HD radio, the HD transmission uses the guard bands on either side of an AM station for entirely different broadcast content (see Figure 8.3). Most AM radios filter out any signal in the channels adjacent to the one to which it is tuned, so the HD transmission is inaudible on an ordinary radio, even as noise. The HD radio broadcast can be heard only on a special radio designed to pick up and decode the digital transmission.

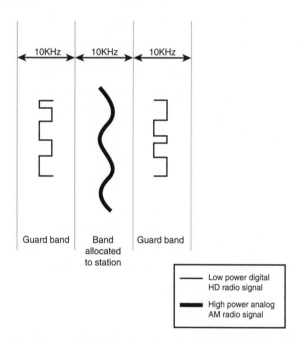

FIGURE 8.3   HD radio uses guard bands to broadcast digital signals at low power. In the AM spectrum, the 10kHz bands on either side of the band allocated to an ordinary analog broadcast station may be used for an entirely independent digital broadcast, limited to low power so that it does not interfere with reception of the analog broadcast.

HD radio is a clever invention, and by opening the spectrum to HD broadcasts, the FCC has been able to squeeze in more broadcast stations—at least for those willing to buy special radios. But it doesn't challenge the fundamental model that has been with us since the 1920s: Split up the spectrum and give a piece to each licensee.

Even parts of the spectrum that are "allocated" to licensees may be drastically underused in practice. A 2002 Federal Communications Committee Report puts it this way: "... the shortage of spectrum is often a *spectrum access problem*. That is, the spectrum resource is available, but its use is compartmented by traditional policies based on traditional technologies." The committee came to this conclusion in part by listening to the air waves in various frequency blocks to test how often nothing at all was being transmitted. Most of the time, even in the dense urban settings of San Diego, Atlanta, and Chicago, important spectrum bands were nearly 100% idle. The public would be better served if others could use the otherwise idle spectrum.

For about ten years, the FCC has experimented with "secondary spectrum marketing." Someone wanting some spectrum for temporary use may be able to lease it from a party who has a right to use it, but is willing to give it up in exchange for a payment. A university radio station, for example, may need the capacity to broadcast at high power only on a few Saturday afternoons to cover major football games. Perhaps such a station could make a deal with a business station that doesn't have a lot of use for its piece of the spectrum when the stock markets are closed. As another example, instead of reserving a band exclusively for emergency broadcasts, it could be made available to others, with the understanding—enforced by codes wired into the transmitters—that the frequency would be yielded on demand for public safety broadcasts.

As the example of eBay has shown, computerized auctions can result in very efficient distribution of goods. The use of particular pieces of the spectrum—at particular times, and in particular geographic areas—can create efficiencies if licensees of under-utilized spectrum bands had an incentive to sell some of their time to other parties.

But secondary markets don't change the basic model—a frequency band belongs to one party at a time. Such auction ideas change the allocation scheme. Rather than having a government agency license spectrum statically to a single party with exclusive rights, several parties can divide it up and make trades. But these schemes retain the fundamental notion that spectrum is like land to be split up among those who want to use it.

## Sharing the Spectrum

In his 1943 opinion, Justice Frankfurter used an analogy that unintentionally pointed toward another way of thinking. Spectrum was inevitably scarce, he opined. "Regulation of radio was therefore as vital to its development as traffic control was to the development of the automobile."

Just as the spectrum is said to be, the roadways are a national asset. They are controlled by federal, state, and local governments, which set rules for their use. You can't drive too fast. Your vehicle can't exceed height and weight limits, which may depend on the road.

But everyone shares the roads. There aren't any special highways reserved for government vehicles. Trucking companies can't get licenses to use particular roads and keep out their competitors. Everybody shares the capacity of the roads to carry traffic.

The roads are what is known in law as a "commons" (a notion introduced in Chapter 6). The ocean is also a commons, a shared resource subject to international fishing agreements. In theory at least, the ocean need not be a commons. Fishing boats could have exclusive fishing rights in separate sectors of the ocean's surface. If the regions were large enough, fishermen might be able to earn a good living under these conditions. But such an allocation of the resources of the ocean would be dreadfully inefficient for society as a whole. The oceans better satisfy human needs if they are treated as a commons and fishing boats move with the fish—under agreed limits about the intensity of fishing.

> Yochai Benkler's site, www.benkler.org, has several important and readable papers for free download, including the classic "Overcoming Agoraphobia." His book, *The Wealth of Networks* (Yale University Press, 2007), details these and other concepts.

The spectrum can be shared rather than split up into pieces. There is a precedent in electronic communications. The Internet is a digital commons. Everyone's packets get mixed with everyone else's on the fiber optics and satellite links of the Internet backbone. The packets are coded. Which packet belongs to whom is sorted out at the ends. Anything confidential can be encrypted.

Something similar can be done with broadcasts—provided there is a basic rethinking of spectrum management. Two ideas are key: first, that using lots of bandwidth need not cause interference and can greatly increase transmission capacity; and second, that putting computers into radio receivers can greatly improve the utilization of the spectrum.

## The Most Beautiful Inventor in the World

Spread spectrum was discovered and forgotten several times and in several countries. Corporations (ITT, Sylvania, and Magnavox), universities (especially MIT), and government laboratories doing classified research all shared in giving birth to this key component of modern telecommunications—and were often unaware of each other's activities.

By far the most remarkable precedent for spread spectrum was a patented invention by Hollywood actress Hedy Lamarr—"the most beautiful woman in the world," in the words of movie mogul Louis Mayer—and George Antheil, an avant-garde composer known as "the bad boy of music."

Lamarr made a scandalous name for herself in Europe by appearing nude in 1933, at the age of 19, in a Czech movie, *Ecstasy*. She became the trophy wife of Fritz Mandl, an Austrian munitions maker whose clients included both Hitler and Mussolini. In 1937, she disguised herself as a maid and escaped Mandl's house, fleeing first to Paris and then to London. There she met Mayer, who brought her to Hollywood. She became a star—and the iconic beauty of her screen generation (see Figure 8.4).

In 1940, Lamarr arranged to meet Antheil. Her upper torso could use some enhancement, she thought, and she hoped Antheil could give her some advice. Antheil was a self-styled expert on female endocrinology, and had written a series of articles for *Esquire* magazine with titles such as "The Glandbook for the Questing Male." Antheil suggested glandular extracts. Their conversation then turned to other matters—specifically, to torpedo warfare.

A torpedo—just a bomb with a propeller—could sink a massive ship. Radio-controlled torpedoes had been developed by the end of World War I, but were far from foolproof. An effective countermeasure was to jam the signal controlling the torpedo by broadcasting loud radio noise at the frequency of the control signal. The torpedo would go haywire and likely miss its target. From observing Mandl's business, Lamarr had learned about torpedoes and why it was hard to control them.

Lamarr had become fiercely pro-American and wished to help the Allied war effort. She conceived the idea of transmitting the torpedo control signal in short bursts at different frequencies. The code for the sequence of frequencies would be held identically within the torpedo and the controlling ship. Because the sequence would be unknown to the enemy, the transmission could not be jammed by flooding the airwaves with noise in any limited frequency band. Too much power would be required to jam all possible frequencies simultaneously.

© Bettmann/CORBIS

FIGURE 8.4   Hedy Lamarr, at about the age when she and George Antheil made their spread spectrum discovery.

Antheil's contribution was to control the frequency-hopping sequence by means of a player piano mechanism—with which he was familiar because he had scored his masterpiece, *Ballet Mécanique*, for synchronized player pianos. As he and Lamarr conceived the device (it was never built), the signal would therefore hop among 88 frequencies, like the 88 keys on a piano keyboard. The ship and the torpedo would have identical piano rolls—in effect, encrypting the broadcast signal.

In 1941, Lamarr and Antheil assigned their patent (see Figure 8.5) to the Navy. A small item on the "Amusements" page of the *New York Times* quoted an army engineer as describing their invention as so "red hot" that he could not say what it did, except that it was "related to the remote control of apparatus employed in warfare." Nonetheless, the Navy seems to have done

> The story of Antheil and Lamarr, and the place of their invention in the history of spread spectrum, is told in *Spread Spectrum* by Rob Walters (Booksurge LLC, 2005).

nothing with the invention at the time. Instead, Lamarr went to work selling war bonds. Calling herself "just a plain gold-digger for Uncle Sam," she sold kisses, and once raised $4.5 million at a single lunch. The patent was ignored for more than a decade. Romuald Ireneus 'Scibor-Marchocki, who was an engineer for a Naval contractor in the mid-1950s, recalls being given a copy when he was put to work on a device for locating enemy submarines. He didn't recognize the patentee because she had not used her stage name.

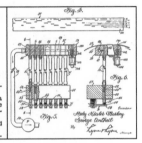

## UNITED STATES PATENT OFFICE

2,292,387

SECRET COMMUNICATION SYSTEM

Hedy Kiesler Markey, Los Angeles, and George Antheil, Manhattan Beach, Calif.

Application June 10, 1941, Serial No. 397,412

6 Claims.   (Cl. 250—2)

This invention relates broadly to secret communication systems involving the use of carrier waves of different frequencies, and is especially useful in the remote control of dirigible craft, such as torpedoes.

An object of the invention is to provide a method of secret communication which is relatively simple and reliable in operation, but at the same time is difficult to discover or decipher.

Fig. 2 is a schematic diagram of the apparatus at a receiving station;

Fig. 3 is a schematic diagram illustrating a starting circuit for starting the motors at the transmitting and receiving stations simultaneously;

Fig. 4 is a plan view of a section of a record strip that may be employed;

Fig. 5 is a detail cross section through a rec-

U.S. Patent Office.

FIGURE 8.5   Original spread spectrum patent by Hedy Lamarr (*née* Kiesler—Gene Markey was her second husband, of six) and George Antheil. On the left, the beginning of the patent itself. On the right, a diagram of the player-piano mechanism included as an illustration in the patent.

And that, in a nutshell, is the strange story of serendipity, teamwork, vanity, and patriotism that led to the Lamarr-Antheil discovery of spread spectrum. The connection of these two to the discovery of spread spectrum was made only in the 1990s. By that time, the influence of their work had become entangled with various lines of classified military research. Whether Hedy Lamarr was more a Leif Erikson than a Christopher Columbus of this new conceptual territory, she was surely the most unlikely of its discoverers. In 1997, the Electronic Frontier Foundation honored her for her discovery; she welcomed the award by saying, "It's about time." When asked about her dual achievements, she commented, "Films have a certain place in a certain time period. Technology is forever."

## Channel Capacity

Lamarr and Antheil had stumbled on a particular way of exploiting a broad frequency range—"spreading" signals across the spectrum. The theoretical foundation for spread spectrum was one of the remarkable mathematical results of Claude Shannon in the late 1940s. Although no digital telephones or radios existed at the time, Shannon derived many of the basic laws by which they would have to operate. The Shannon-Hartley Theorem predicted spread spectrum in the same way that Maxwell's equations predicted radio waves.

Shannon's result (building on work by Ralph Hartley two decades earlier) implies that "interference" is not the right concept for thinking about how much information can be carried in the radio spectrum. Signals can overlap in frequency and yet be pulled apart perfectly by sufficiently sophisticated radio receivers.

Early engineers assumed that communication errors were inevitable. Send bits down a wire, or through space using radio waves, and some of them would probably arrive incorrectly, because of noise. You could make the channel more reliable by slowing the transmission, they supposed, in the same way that people talk more slowly when they want to be sure that others understand them—but you could never guarantee that a communication was errorless.

Shannon showed that communication channels actually behave quite differently. Any communication channel has a certain *channel capacity*—a number of bits per second that it can handle. If your Internet connection is advertised as having a bit rate of 3Mbit/sec (3 million bits per second), that number is the channel capacity of the particular connection between you and your Internet Service Provider (or should be—not all advertisements tell the truth). If the connection is over telephone wiring and you switch to a service that runs over fiber optic cables, the channel capacity should increase.

However large it is, the channel capacity has a remarkable property, which Shannon proved: Bits can be transmitted through the channel, from the source to the destination, *with negligible probability of error* as long as the transmission rate does not exceed the channel capacity. Any attempt to push bits down the channel at a rate higher than the channel capacity will inevitably result in data loss. With sufficient cleverness about the way data from the source is encoded before it is put in the channel, the error rate can be essentially zero, as long as the channel capacity is not exceeded. Only if the data rate exceeds the channel capacity do transmission errors become inevitable.

### ERRORS AND DELAYS

Although transmission errors can be made unlikely, they are never impossible. However, errors can be made far less probable than, for example, the death of the intended recipient in an earthquake that just happens to occur while the bits are on their way (see the Appendix). Guaranteeing correctness requires adding redundant bits to the message—in the same way that fragile postal shipments are protected by adding styrofoam packing material. Attaining data rates close to the "Shannon limit" involves pre-processing the bits. That may increase *latency*—the time delay between the start of the "packing" process and the insertion of bits into the channel. Latency can be a problem in applications such as voice communication, where delays annoy the communicants. Happily, phone calls don't require error-free transmission—we are all used to putting up with a little bit of static.

## Power, Signal, Noise, and Bandwidth

The capacity of a radio channel depends on the frequencies at which messages are transmitted and the amount of power used to transmit them. It's helpful to think about these two factors separately.

### BANDWIDTH

Because channel capacity depends on frequency bandwidth, the term "bandwidth" is used informally to mean "amount of information communicated per second." But technically, bandwidth is a term about electromagnetic communication, and even then is only one of the factors affecting the capacity to carry bits.

A radio broadcast is never "at" a single frequency. It always uses a range or *band* of frequencies to convey the actual sounds. The only sound that could be carried at a single, pure frequency would be an unvarying tone. The *bandwidth* of a broadcast is the size of the frequency band—that is, the difference between the top frequency and the bottom frequency of the band. Hoover, to use this language, allotted 10kHz of bandwidth for each AM station.

If you can transmit so many bits per second with a certain amount of bandwidth, you can transmit twice that many bits per second if you have twice as much bandwidth. The two transmissions could simply go on side by side, not interacting with each other in any way. So, *channel capacity is proportional to bandwidth.*

The relation to signal power is more surprising. To use simple numbers for clarity, suppose you can transmit one bit, either 0 or 1, in one second. If you could use *more power* but *no more time or bandwidth*, how many bits could you transmit?

One way a radio transmission might distinguish between 0 and 1 is for the signals representing these two values to have different signal powers. To continue to oversimplify, assume that zero power represents 0, and a little more power, say 1 watt, represents 1. Then to distinguish a 1 from a 0, the radio receiver has to be sensitive enough to tell the difference between 1 watt and 0 watts. The uncontrollable noise—radio waves arriving from sunspots, for example—also must be weak enough that it does not distort a signal representing 0 so that it is mistaken for a signal representing 1.

Under these conditions, four times as much power would enable transmission of two bits at once, still in one second. Power level 0 could represent 00; 1 watt, 01; 2 watts, 10; and 3 watts could represent 11. Successive power levels have to be separated by at least a watt to be sure that one signal is not confused with another. If the power levels were closer together, the unchanged noise might make them impossible to distinguish reliably. To transmit three bits at a time, you'd need eight times as much power, using levels 0 through 7 watts—that is, the amount of power needed increases exponentially with the number of bits to be transmitted at once (see Figure 8.6).

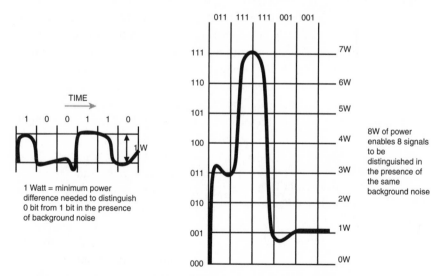

FIGURE 8.6  Shannon-Hartley. Signal levels must be far enough apart to be distinguishable in spite of the distortion caused by noise. Tripling the bit rate requires eight times as much power.

So the Shannon-Hartley result says that *channel capacity depends on both bandwidth and signal power,* but *more bandwidth is exponentially more valuable than more signal power.* You'd have to get more than *a thousand times* more signal power to get the same increase in channel capacity as you could get from having just ten times more bandwidth (because 1024 = $2^{10}$). Bandwidth is precious indeed.

## One Man's Signal Is Another Man's Noise

The consequences of the Shannon-Hartley result about the value of bandwidth are quite astonishing. If WBZ were transmitting digitally with its 50,000 watt transmitter, it could transmit the same amount of information (over shorter distances) using less power than a household light bulb—if it could get 100kHz of bandwidth rather than the 10kHz the FCC has allowed it.

Of course, no station could get exclusive use of 100kHz. Even giving each station 10kHz uses up the spectrum too quickly. The spectrum-spreading idea works only if the spectrum is regarded as a commons. And to see the consequences of many signals broadcasting in the same spectrum, one more crucial insight is needed.

The power level that affects the capacity of a radio channel is not actually the signal power, but the ratio of the signal power to the noise power—the so-called *signal-to-noise ratio.* In other words, you could transmit at the same bit rate with one watt of power as with ten—*if* you could also reduce the noise by a factor of ten. And *"noise" includes other people's signals.* It really doesn't matter whether the interference is coming from other human broadcasts or from distant stars. All the interfering broadcasts can share the same spectrum band, to the extent they could coexist with the equivalent amount of noise.

A readable account of spread spectrum radio appeared in 1998: "Spread-Spectrum Radio" by David R. Hughes and DeWayne Hendricks (*Scientific American*, April 1998, 94–96).

A surprising consequence of Shannon-Hartley is that *there is some channel capacity even if the noise (including other people's signals) is stronger than the signal.* Think of a noisy party: You can pick out a conversation from the background noise if you focus on a single voice, even if it is fainter than the rest of the noise. But the Shannon-Hartley result predicts even more: *The channel can transmit bits flawlessly, if slowly, even if the noise is many times more powerful than the signal. And if you could get a lot of bandwidth, you could drastically reduce the signal power without lowering the bit rate at all* (see Figure 8.7). What would seem to be just noise to anyone listening casually on a particular frequency would actually have a useful signal embedded within it.

The Shannon-Hartley Theorem is a mathematician's delight—a tease that limits what is possible in theory and gives no advice about how to achieve it in practice. It is like Einstein's $E = mc^2$—which at once says nothing, and everything, about nuclear reactors and atomic bombs. Hedy Lamarr's frequency hopping was one of the spread spectrum techniques that would eventually be practical, but other ingenious inventions, named by odd acronyms, would emerge in the late twentieth century.

Two major obstacles stood between the Shannon-Hartley result and usable spread spectrum devices. The first was engineering: computers had to become fast, powerful, and cheap enough to process bits for transmission of high-quality audio and video to consumers. That wouldn't happen until the 1980s. The other problem was regulatory. Here the problem was not mathematical or scientific. Bureaucracies change more slowly than the technologies they regulate.

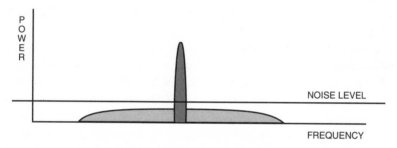

**FIGURE 8.7**   The spread spectrum principle. The same bit rate can be achieved at much lower power by using more bandwidth, and the signal power can even be less than the noise.

## Spectrum Deregulated

Today, every Starbucks has WiFi—that is, wireless Internet access. Hotel rooms, college dormitories, and a great many households also have "wireless." This happened because a tiny piece of the spectrum, a slice less than a millimeter wide in Figure 8.1, was deregulated and released for experimental use by creative engineers. It is an example of how deregulation can stimulate industrial innovations, and about how existing spectrum owners prefer a regulatory climate that maintains their privileged position. It is a story that could be repeated elsewhere in the spectrum, if the government makes wise decisions.

Michael Marcus is an improbable revolutionary. An MIT-trained electrical engineer, he spent three years as an Air Force officer during the Vietnam war, designing communications systems for underground nuclear test detection at a time when the ARPANET–the original, military-sponsored version of the Internet–was first in use. After finishing active duty, he went to work at a Pentagon think tank, exploring potential military uses of emerging communications technologies.

In the summer of 1979, Marcus attended an Army electronic warfare workshop. As was typical at Army events, attendees were seated alphabetically. Marcus's neighbor was Steve Lukasik, the FCC's chief scientist. Lukasik had been Director of ARPA during the development of the ARPANET and then an ARPANET visionary at Xerox. He came to the FCC, not generally considered a technologically adventurous agency, because Carter administration officials were toying with the idea that existing federal regulations might be stifling innovation. Lukasik asked Marcus what he thought could stimulate growth in radio communications. Marcus answered, among other things, "spread spectrum." His engineering was sound, but not his politics. People would not like this idea.

The military's uses of spread spectrum were little known to civilians, since the Army likes to keep its affairs secret. The FCC prohibited all civil use of spread spectrum, since it would require, in the model the Commission had used for decades, trespassing on spectrum bands of which incumbents had been guaranteed exclusive use. Using lots of bandwidth, even at low power levels, was simply not possible within FCC regulations. Lukasik invited Marcus to join the FCC, to champion the development of spread spectrum and other innovative technologies. That required changing the way the FCC had worked for years.

Shortly after the birth of the Federal Radio Commission, the U.S. plummeted into the worst depression it had ever experienced. In the 1970s, the FCC was still living with the culture of the 1930s, when national economic policies benevolently reined in free-market capitalism. As a general rule, innovators hate regulation, and incumbent stakeholders love it–when it protects their established interests. In the radio world, where spectrum is a limited, indispensable, government-controlled raw material, this dynamic can be powerfully stifling.

Incumbents, such as existing radio and TV stations and cell phone companies, have spectrum rights granted by the FCC in the past, perhaps decades ago, and renewed almost automatically. Incumbents have no incentive to allow use of "their" spectrum for innovations that may threaten their business. Innovators can't get started without a guarantee from regulators that they will be granted use of spectrum, since investors won't fund businesses reliant on resources the government controls and may decide not to provide.

Regulators test proposals to relax their rules by inviting public comment, and the parties they hear from most are the incumbents—who have the resources to send teams to lobby against change. Their complaints predict disaster if the rules are relaxed. In fact, their doomsday scenarios are often exaggerated in the hope the regulators will exclude competition. Eventually, the regulators lose sight of their ultimate responsibility, which is to the public good and not to the good of the incumbents. It is just easier to leave things alone. They can legitimately claim to be responding to what they are being told, however biased by the huge costs of travel and lobbying. Regulatory powers meant to prevent electromagnetic interference wind up preventing competition instead.

And then there is the revolving door. Most communications jobs are in the private sector. FCC employees know that their future lies in the commercial use of the spectrum. Hundreds of FCC staff and officials, including all eight past FCC chairmen, have gone to work for or represented the businesses they regulated. These movements from government to private employment violate no government ethics rules. But FCC officials can be faced with a choice between angering a large incumbent that is a potential employer, and disappointing a marginal start-up or a public interest non-profit. It is not surprising that they remember that they will have to earn a living after leaving the FCC.

In 1981, Marcus and his colleagues invited comment on a proposal to allow low-power transmission in broad frequency bands. The incumbents who were using those bands almost universally howled. The FCC beat a retreat and attempted, in order to break the regulatory logjam, to find frequency bands where there could be few complaints about possible interference with other uses. They hit on the idea of deregulating three "garbage bands," so called because they were used only for "industrial, scientific, and medical" (ISM) purposes. Microwave ovens, for example, cook food by pummeling it with 2.450GHz electromagnetic radiation. There should have been no complaints—microwave ovens were unaffected by "interference" from radio signals, and the telecommunications industry did not use these bands.

RCA and GE complained anyway about possible low-power interference, but their objections were determined to be exaggerated. This spectrum band was opened to experimentation in 1985, on the proviso that frequency hopping or a similar technique be used to limit interference.

Marcus did not know what might develop, but engineers were waiting to take advantage of the opportunity. Irwin Jacobs founded QUALCOMM a few months later, and by 1990, the company's cell phone technology was in wide-spread use, using a spread spectrum technique called CDMA. A few years later, Apple Computer and other manufacturers agreed with the FCC on standards to use spread spectrum for radio local area networks—"wireless routers," for which Apple's trademarked device is called the Airport. In 1997, when the FCC approved the 802.11 standard and the spectrum bands were finally available for use, the press barely noticed. Within three years, wireless networking was everywhere, and virtually all personal computers now come ready for WiFi.

Michael Marcus's web site, www.marcus-spectrum.com, has interesting materials, and opinions, about spectrum deregulation and spread spectrum history.

For his efforts, Marcus was sent into internal exile within the FCC for seven years but emerged in the Clinton era and returned to spectrum policy work. He is now retired and working as a consultant in the private sector.

The success of WiFi has opened the door to discussion of more radical spectrum-spreading proposals. The most extreme is UWB—"ultra wide band" radio. UWB returns, in a sense, to Hertz's sparks, splattering radiation all across the frequencies of the radio spectrum. There are two important differences, however. First, UWB uses extremely low power—feasible because of the very large bandwidth. Power usage is so low that UWB will not interfere with any conventional radio receiver. And second, UWB pulses are extremely short and precisely timed, so that the time between pulses can symbolically encode a transmitted digital message. Even at extremely low power, which would limit the range of UWB transmissions to a few feet, UWB has the potential to carry vast amounts of information in short periods of time. Imagine connecting your high definition TV, cable box, and DVD player without cables. Imagine downloading your library of digital music from your living room audio system to your car while it is parked in your garage. Imagine wireless video phones that work better than wired audio phones. The possibilities are endless, if the process of regulatory relaxation continues.

# What Does the Future Hold for Radio?

In the world of radio communications, as everywhere in the digital explosion, time has not stopped. In fact, digital communications have advanced less far than computer movie-making or voice recognition or weather prediction, because only in radio does the weight of federal regulation retard the explosive increase in computational power. The deregulation that is possible has only begun to happen.

## What If Radios Were Smart?

Spread spectrum is a way of making better use of the spectrum. Another dramatic possibility comes with the recognition that ordinary radios are extremely stupid by comparison with what is computationally possible today. If taken back in time, today's radios could receive the broadcasts of 80 years ago, and the AM radios of 80 years ago would work as receivers of today's broadcasts. To achieve such total "backward compatibility," a great deal of efficiency must be sacrificed. The reason for such backward compatibility is not that many 80-year-old radios are still in service. It's that *at any moment in time*, the incumbents have a strong interest in retaining their market share, and therefore, in lobbying against efforts to make radios "smarter" so more stations can be accommodated.

*If radios were intelligent and active, rather than dumb and passive, vastly more information could be made available through the airwaves.*

If radios were intelligent and active, rather than dumb and passive, vastly more information could be made available through the airwaves. Rather than broadcasting at high power so that signals could travel great distances to reach passive receivers, low-power radios could pass signals on to each other. A request for a particular piece of information could be transmitted from radio to radio, and the information could be passed back. The radios could cooperate with each other to increase the information flux received by all of them. Or multiple weak transmitters could occasionally synchronize to produce a single powerful beam for long-range communication.

### What Does "Smart" Mean?

"Intelligent" or "smart" radio goes by various technical names. The two most commonly used terms are "software-defined radio" (SDR) and "cognitive radio." Software-defined radio refers to radios capable of being reprogrammed to change characteristics usually implemented in hardware today (such as whether they recognize AM, FM, or some other form of modulation). Cognitive radio refers to radios that use artificial intelligence to increase the efficiency of their spectrum utilization.

Such "cooperation gains" are already being exploited in *wireless sensor networking*. Small, low-power, radio-equipped computers are equipped with sensors for temperature or seismic activity, for example. These devices can be scattered in remote areas with hostile environments, such as the rim of a smoldering volcano, or the Antarctic nesting grounds of endangered penguins. At far lower cost and greater safety than human observers could achieve, the devices can exchange information with their neighbors and eventually pass on a summary to a single high-power transmitter.

There are vast opportunities to use "smart" radios to increase the number of broadcast information options—if the regulatory stranglehold on the industry can be loosened and the incentives for innovation increased.

Radios can become "smarter" in another respect. Even under the "narrowband" model for spectrum allocation, where one signal occupies only a small range of frequencies, cheap computation can make a difference. The very notion that it is the government's job to prevent "interference," enshrined in legislation since the 1912 Radio Act, is now anachronistic.

Radio waves don't really "interfere," the way people in a crowd interfere with each other's movements. The waves don't bounce off each other; they pass right through each other. If two different waves pass through the antenna of a dumb old radio, neither signal can be heard clearly.

To see what might be possible in the future, ask a man and a woman to stand behind you, reading from different books at about the same voice level. If you don't focus, you will hear an incoherent jumble. But if you concentrate on one of the voices, you can understand it and block out the other. If you shift your focus to the other voice, you can pick that one out. This is possible because your brain performs sophisticated signal processing. It knows something about male and female voices. It knows the English language and tries to match the sounds it is hearing to a lexicon of word-sounds it expects English speakers to say. Radios could do the same thing—if not today, then soon, when computers become a bit more powerful.

But there is a chicken-and-egg cycle. No one will buy a "smart" radio unless there is something to listen to. No one can undertake a new form of broadcasting without raising some capital. No investor will put up money for a project that is dependent on uncertain deregulation decisions by the FCC. Dumb radios and inefficient spectrum use protect the incumbents from competition, so the incumbents lobby against deregulation.

Moreover, the incumbent telecommunications and entertainment industries are among the leading contributors to congressional election campaigns. Members of Congress often pressure the FCC to go against the public interest and in favor of the interests of the existing stakeholders. This problem was apparent even in the 1930s, when an early history of radio regulation stated, "no quasi-judicial body was ever subject to so much congressional pressure as the Federal Radio Commission." The pattern has not changed.

In other technologies, such as the personal computer industry, there is no such cycle. Anyone who wants to innovate needs to raise money. Investors are inhibited by the quality of the technology and the market's expected reaction to it—but not by the reactions of federal regulators. Overextended copyright protections have chilled creativity, as was discussed in Chapter 6, but lawmakers are to blame for that problem, not unelected commissioners.

From cell phones to wireless routers to keychain auto locks, wireless innovations are devoured by the public, when they can be brought to market at all. To foster innovation, the regulatory stranglehold needs to be broken throughout the wireless arena, including broadcast technologies. The regulations are now the source of the scarcity that is used to justify the regulations!

> **TV, ENTERTAINMENT, AND CONGRESS**
>
> In the 2006 election campaigns, the TV, movie, and music industries contributed more than $12 million to the re-election campaigns of incumbents, more than the oil and gas industry. The three biggest contributors were Comcast Corp., Time Warner, and the National Cable and Telecommunications Association.

*The regulations are now the source of the scarcity that is used to justify the regulations!*

## But Do We Want the Digital Explosion?

Technologies converge. In 1971, Anthony Oettinger foresaw the line blurring between computing and communications. He called the emerging single technology "compunication." Today's computer users don't even think about the fact that their data is stored thousands of miles away—until their Internet connection fails. Telephones were first connected using copper wires, and television stations first broadcast using electromagnetic waves, but today most telephone calls go through the air and most television signals go through wires.

Laws, regulations, and bureaucracies change much more slowly than the technologies they govern. The FCC still has separate "Wireless" and "Wireline" bureaus. Special speech codes apply to "broadcast" radio and television, although "broadcasting" is an engineering anachronism.

The silo organization of the legal structures inhibits innovation in today's layered technologies. Regulation of the content layer should not be driven by an outdated understanding of the engineering limits of the physical layer. Investments made in developing the physical layer should not enable the same companies to control the content layer. The public interest is in innovation and efficiency; it is not in the preservation of old technologies and revolving doors between regulators and the incumbents of the regulated industry.

But if the spectrum is freed up—used vastly more efficiently than it now is, and made available for innovative wireless inventions and far more "broadcast" channels—will we like the result?

There are general economic and social benefits from innovations in wireless technology. Garage door openers, Wiis, and toll booth transponders do not save lives, but wireless fire detectors and global positioning systems do. The story of WiFi illustrates how rapidly an unforeseen technology can become an essential piece of both business and personal infrastructure.

But what about television and radio? Would we really be better off with a million channels than we were in the 1950s with 13, or are today with a few hundred on satellite and cable? Won't this profusion of sources cause a general lowering of content quality, and a societal splintering as *de facto* authoritative information channels wither? And won't it become impossible to keep out the smut, which most people don't want to see, whatever the rights of a few?

As a society, we simply have to confront the reality that our mindset about radio and television is wrong. It has been shaped by decades of the scarcity argument. That argument is now brain-dead, kept breathing on artificial life support by institutions that gain from the speech control it rationalizes. Without the scarcity argument, TV and radio stations become less like private leases on public land, or even shipping lanes, and more like ... books.

There will be a period of social readjustment as television becomes more like a library. But the staggering—even frightening—diversity of published literature is not a reason not to have libraries. To be sure, there should be determined efforts to minimize the social cost of getting the huge national investment in old TV sets retired in favor of million-channel TV sets. But we know how to do that sort of thing. There is always a chicken-and-egg problem when a new technology comes along, such as FM radios or personal computers.

When market forces govern what gets aired, we may *not* be happy with the results, however plentiful. But if what people want is assurance about what they *won't* see, then the market will develop channels without dirty words and technologies to lock out the others. The present system stays in place because of the enormous financial and political influence of the incumbents—and because the government likes speech control.

## How Much Government Regulation Is Needed?

Certainly, where words end and actions begin, people need government protection. Dr. Brinkley lost his medical license, which was right then, and would be right today.

In the new wireless world, government needs to enforce the rules for spectrum sharing—technologies that can work only if everyone respects power and bandwidth restraints. The government has to ensure that manufactured devices obey the rules, and that rogues don't violate them. The government also has to help develop and endorse standards for "smart" radios.

It also has the ultimate responsibility for deciding if the dire warnings of incumbents about the risks imposed by new technologies are scientifically valid, and if valid, of sufficiently great social importance to block the advancement of engineering. A typical caution was the one issued in the fall of 2007 by the National Association of Broadcasters as it rolled out a national advertising campaign to block a new technology to locate unused parts of the TV spectrum for Internet service: "While our friends at Intel, Google, and Microsoft may find system errors, computer glitches, and dropped calls tolerable, broadcasters do not." Scientific questions about interference should be settled by science, not by advertisements or Congressional meddling. We will always need an independent body, like the FCC, to make these judgments rationally and in the public interest.

If all that happens, the scarcity problem will disappear. At that point, government authority over content should—and constitutionally *must*—drop back to the level it is at for other non-scarce media, such as newspapers and books. Obscenity and libel laws would remain in place for wireless communication as for other media. So would any other lawful restrictions Congress might adopt, perhaps for reasons of national security.

Other regulation of broadcast words and images should end. Its legal foundation survives no longer in the newly engineered world of information. There are too many ways for the information to reach us. We need to take responsibility for what we see, and what our children are allowed to see. And they must be educated to live in a world of information plenty.

There is no reason to re-establish a "Fairness Doctrine," like that which until 1987 required stations to present multiple points of view. If there were more channels, the government would not have any need, or authority, to second-guess the editorial judgment of broadcasters. Artificial spectrum scarcity has, in the words of Justice William O. Douglas, enabled "administration after administration to toy with TV or radio in order to serve its sordid or its benevolent ends." Justice Frankfurter's claim that "there is no room in the broadcast band for every business or school of thought" is now false.

※

Bits are bits, whether they represent movies, payrolls, expletives, or poems. Bits are bits, whether they are moved as electrons in copper wire, light pulses in glass fiber, or modulations in radio waves. Bits are bits, whether they are stored in gigantic data warehouses, on DVDs sent through the mail, or on flash drives on keychains. The regulation of free speech on broadcast radio and television is but one example of the lingering social effects of historical accidents of technology. There are many others—in telephony, for example. Laws and policies regulating information developed around the technologies in which that information was embodied.

The digital explosion has reduced all information to its lowest common denominator, sequences of 0s and 1s. There are now adapters at all the junctions in the world-wide networks of information. A telephone call, a personal letter, and a television show all reach you through the same mixture of media. The bits are shunted between radio antennas, fiber-optic switching stations, and telephone wiring many times before they reach you.

*Bits are bits, whether they represent movies, payrolls, expletives, or poems.*

The universality of bits gives mankind a rare opportunity. We are in a position to decide on an overarching view of information. We can be bound in the future by first principles, not historical contingencies. In the U.S., the digital explosion has blown away much of the technological wrapping obscuring the First Amendment. Knowing that information is just bits, all societies will be faced with stark questions about where information should be open, where it should be controlled, and where it should be banned.

# Conclusion

## *After the Explosion*

---

## Bits Lighting Up the World

In Greek mythology, Prometheus stole Zeus's fire and brought it from Olympus to Earth, along with the useful arts of civilization. Zeus retaliated for Prometheus's trickery by visiting upon humanity the ills and evils that beset us. We have been trying to make the best of things ever since.

The Prometheus myth is about technology. Technology, like fire, is neither good nor bad—its value depends on how we use it. And once we start using a technology, society itself changes. It is never the same again.

Information technologies spark a special kind of fire. Bits are the atomic particles of the information flames. With our information tools, we can do things, both good and bad, that we could not have done unassisted. For better or worse, these technologies enable us to think, reason, create, express, debate, compromise, learn, and teach in ways never before possible. They connect people across physical space, both in pairs and in groups. They extend the reach of our voices and the range of our hearing. They also amplify our capacity to frighten, harass, and hate other people, and to misrepresent ourselves to others. They enable us to earn and to spend money without going anywhere, and also to steal money from the comfort of our homes.

So central was Prometheus, the fire-bringer, to the Greek conception of humanity that in later retellings of the myth, he is credited with creating the human species itself. What changes to society will information technologies yield, in a decade or two, when the ongoing digital explosion has unimaginable power?

We don't know, of course. But if things go on changing as they are changing today, there are likely to be dramatic changes to three distinctive aspects of human culture: our sense of personal identity and privacy, our capacity for free speech, and the creativity that drives human progress.

## Privacy and Personhood

As the digital explosion was beginning, the struggle over privacy seemed to be a war. Individuals wanted to protect themselves from invasive forces. Institutions, both corporations and government, wanted the benefit of information that individuals would rather not reveal.

In actual practice, things have turned out to be much more complicated.

Technologies improved so that data gathering became easier and less annoying. Modest incentives induced individuals to sacrifice their personal privacy—often before they understood what they were giving up. Relatively few people today worry about stores keeping track of their purchases. Even without loyalty cards, a credit card swipe, together with bar code scans at the cash register, link a customer's name to his preferences in candy and condoms. You have to give up many conveniences to protect your privacy, and most people are not willing to do it.

The next generation may not even see the loss of privacy as a sacrifice. Socrates said that the unexamined life was not worth living, but people who have grown up with Gmail and MySpace may find life fully exposed to public view simply normal. As Sun Microsystem CEO Scott McNealy quipped: "You have zero privacy anyway. Get over it."

Yet getting over it is not so simple when social interactions happen through the computer screen. When most personal interactions were face-to-face or over the telephone, we mistrusted people claiming to represent our bank and trusted people we felt we had gotten to know. In the electronic world, we do the opposite—we trust our bank's web site with large sums of our money, but we have to be reminded that close electronic friends may be impostors. Where is the border for children between the personal and the public? Will we need laws about fraudulent friendships?

As electronic privacy becomes lost in the cloud of bits and caution gives way to social networking, what societal structures will break down? What will evolve to replace them? Society as we know it functions because of a web of trusting relationships between parties who are independently responsible for their own actions. What will replace that if the concept of personal identity becomes meaningless? Will the very notions of privacy and identity be destroyed in the explosion?

## What Can We Say, and Who Will Be Listening?

The digital explosion revolutionizes human communication. Earlier technologies for disseminating text, spoken words, and images also changed the world—but all included choke points. A million eyes might read your book, but only if you could get it published. You might discover a scandal that would bring down a government, but only if you could get a newspaper to expose it to public view. A million ears might hear your speeches, but only if you could control a radio station.

No longer are speakers bound by the whims of those who control the loudspeakers and printing presses. In the U.S., anyone can say anything, without permission from church or state, and be audible to millions. No one has to listen, but it is easy to put the message where millions can hear it.

> ### An Earlier Information Revolution
>
> *It is the mother of revolution. It is the mode of expression of humanity which is totally renewed; it is human thought stripping off one form and donning another; it is the complete and definitive change of skin of that symbolical serpent which since the days of Adam has represented intelligence.* —Victor Hugo, of printing (from *The Hunchback of Notre Dame*).

And yet there is a cost. Not a financial cost—web sites are cheap, and email is even cheaper. The cost is that the speaker relies on many intermediaries to handle the messages, and so there are many opportunities for eavesdropping, filtering, and censoring. The choke points have multiplied and become more diffuse, but they have not disappeared. The very technological miracles that have created the communication revolution have also created a big-brother revolution. With speech recognition and language understanding improving every year, we have to expect that, before long, every email, telephone call, blog, and television show may be monitored by the technological equivalent of a human listener. Machines will be waiting attentively for someone to say the "wrong" thing—whatever that is deemed to be.

Governments eavesdrop to protect national security, political opposition, and public morality. Communication companies want to listen to what their networks are being used for, so that they can tailor their service to the content in the most profitable way—a soft form of corporate censorship, in which unwanted communications are slowed down or made costly. Service providers want to listen in so they can add advertising to the content they deliver.

In spite of the unimaginable expansion of communications over the past quarter-century, the jury is still out on whether speech will be freer or less free in the future than it was in the past, even in the U.S. with its uncompromising First Amendment. And like the tree falling in the forest, of what use will free speech be if no one is listening? The dramatic pluralism of our information sources threatens to create a society where no one learns anything from people with whom they disagree. It is simply too easy for people to decide whom they want to hear and to ignore everyone else. Will the digital explosion in fact make information more limited?

> *In spite of the unimaginable expansion of communications over the past quarter-century, the jury is still out on whether speech will be freer or less free in the future than it was in the past.*

## A Creative Explosion, or a Legal Explosion?

In the same letter quoted in Chapter 1 Thomas Jefferson wrote, *He who receives an idea from me, receives instruction himself without lessening mine; as he who lights his taper at mine, receives light without darkening me.* Will the digital explosion be used to enlighten the world, or to create illusions and to blind us to the truth?

The digital explosion has started a legal revolution. In the past, teenagers were not routinely threatened with federal criminal charges. Today, such warnings about downloading music and movies are commonplace. In the past, if a political advertisement included a few seconds of video of a candidate debating his opponents, he did not fear the wrath of the television network that broadcast the debate. But Fox News Channel went after John McCain in the fall of 2007 for doing exactly that. If you want to silence your critics under the new legal regime, you may threaten to sue them simply for showing that you said something. That's what Uri Geller, the "paranormalist," did when prominent skeptic James Randi debunked Geller's powers in a YouTube clip that included eight seconds of Geller's activities. Even universities misuse copyright law to stanch the flow of information. A widely reported public statement by Harvard's president (Figure 4.3) could not be shown in this book because the university denied the publisher's request to print it.

Patent and copyright laws in the U.S. were designed to promote individual creativity in the interest of the progress of society. The law struck a balance between providing financial incentive to the creator and high social benefit to the population at large. The term for which artists and inventors maintained exclusive control over their creations was designed to be long enough to provide a financial return and short enough to provide an incentive for continued creativity. And  there was a high threshold on what could be protected at all, so that the system did not encourage lawyerly inventiveness rather than artistic and engineering creativity.

As mechanical tools have been supplanted by information-processing tools, and all manner of writing, music, and art have gone digital, the rules of the game have changed. The parties who receive the strongest protections are now major corporations, rather than the original creators or the ultimate consumers. At a time where information technology promises disintermediation— getting rid of the middle-man—those middle-men are becoming more powerful, not less.

The legal power of the powerful intermediaries, protecting their economic interests, has increased at the same time as new technologies have empowered the creators to reach their consumers directly.

Similar tensions are visible in the world of invention. The antitrust actions against Microsoft by the European Union stem from a fear that a software monopoly will stifle the creativity that might be shown by other software creators, were they able to survive. The power of the incumbent radio and television broadcast industries to exclude newcomers from the airwaves restrains both speech and invention, limiting radio communications and keeping useful devices off the market.

Will the United States move toward being an information democracy or an information oligarchy? Whose hands will be on the controls that regulate the way we produce and use bits in the future?

# A Few Bits in Conclusion

The worldwide bits explosion is lighting up the world (see Figure C.1). Most of the illumination today is in Europe and North America, but it is growing brighter almost everywhere. There is no physical reason it can't continue to grow. Bits are not like oil or coal. They take almost no raw materials to produce, and only tiny amounts of electricity. They flow through glass fibers in astonishing numbers, and they radiate through space, over short distances and long. With our cameras and computers, we produce them at will, in unintelligibly larger numbers every year. Existing dark spots—North Korea, for example—may remain black for a time, but eventually even these regions may glow brighter. And all that data and thought-stuff, all those atoms of light, can be captured and stored on disk for eternity.

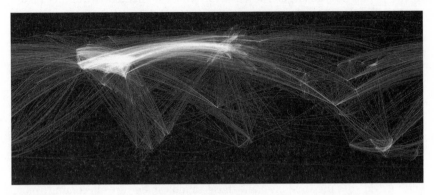

Chris Harrison, Human-Computer Interaction Institute, Carnegie Mellon University.
www.chrisharrison.net/projects/InternetMap/high/worldBlack.png.

FIGURE C.1   A map of the world, showing the number of Internet connections between routers. At present, the U.S. and Europe are heavily interconnected. If the volume of data transmissions were depicted instead (giving more prominence, for example, to areas with heavily used Internet cafés), Africa, Asia, and South America might show more prominently.

The explosion happened through technological inventions supported by political and economic freedoms. Gutenberg laid the foundation when he invented the printing press, and Morse's telegraph, Bell's telephone, and Edison's phonograph were all precursors. Claude Shannon was the bits Prometheus. After the Second World War, his mathematical insights lit the flame of communication and computing technologies, which have now illuminated the earth with bits.

The bits explosion is not over. We are in the middle of it. But we don't know whether it will be destructive or enlightening. The time for deciding who will control the explosion may soon be past. Bits are still a new phenomenon—a new natural resource whose regulatory structures and corporate ownership are still up for grabs. The legal and economic decisions being made today, not just about bits but about everything that depends on bits, will determine how our descendants will lead their lives. The way the bits illuminate or distort the world will shape the future of humanity.

# The Internet as System and Spirit

This Appendix explains how the Internet works and summarizes some larger lessons of its remarkable success.

## The Internet as a Communication System

The Internet is not email and web pages and digital photographs, any more than the postal service is magazines and packages and letters from your Aunt Mary. And the Internet is not a bunch of wires and cables, any more than the postal service is a bunch of trucks and airplanes. The Internet is a system, a delivery service for bits, whatever the bits represent and however they get from one place to another. It's important to know how it works, in order to understand why it works so well and why it can be used for so many different purposes.

### Packet Switching

Suppose you send an email to Sam, and it goes through a computer in Kalamazoo—an Internet *router*, as the machines connecting the Internet together are known. Your computer and Sam's know it's an email, but the router in Kalamazoo just knows that it's handling bits.

Your message almost certainly goes through some copper wires, but probably also travels as light pulses through fiber optic cables, which carry lots of bits at very high speeds. It may also go through the air by radio—for example, if it is destined for your cell phone. The physical infrastructure for the Internet is owned by many different parties—including telecommunications firms in the

U.S. and governments in some countries. The Internet works not because anyone is in charge of the whole thing, but because these parties agree on what
to expect as messages are passed from one to another. As the name suggests,
the Internet is really a set of standards for **inter**connecting **networks**. The individual networks can behave as they wish, as long as they follow established
conventions when they send bits out or bring bits in.

In the 1970s, the designers of the Internet faced momentous choices. One
critical decision had to do with message sizes. The postal service imposes size
and weight limits on what it will handle. You can't send your Aunt Mary a
two-ton package by taking it to the Post Office. Would there also be a limit
on the size of the messages that could be sent through the Internet? The
designers anticipated that very large messages might be important some day,
and found a way to avoid any size limits.

A second critical decision was about the very nature of the network. The
obvious idea, which was rejected, was to create a "circuit-switched" network.
Early telephone systems were completely circuit-switched. Each customer was
connected by a pair of wires to a central switch. To complete a call from you
to your Aunt Mary, the switch would be set to connect the wires from you to
the wires from Aunt Mary, establishing a complete electrical loop between you
and Mary for as long as the switch was set that way. The size of the switch
limited the number of calls such a system could handle. Handling more simultaneous calls required building bigger switches. A circuit-switched network
provides reliable, uninterruptible connections—at a high cost per connection.
Most of the switching hardware is doing very little most of the time.

So the early Internet engineers needed to allow messages of unlimited size.
They also needed to ensure that the capacity of the network would be limited
only by the amount of data traffic, rather than by the number of interconnected computers. To meet both objectives, they designed a *packet-switched
network*. The unit of information traveling over the Internet is a packet of
about 1500 bytes or less—roughly the amount of text you might be able to
put on a postcard. Any communications longer than that are broken up into
multiple packets, with serial numbers so that the packets can be reassembled
upon arrival to put the original message back together.

The packets that constitute a message need not travel through the Internet
following the same route, nor arrive in the same order in which they were
sent. It is very much as though the postal service would deliver only postcards with a maximum of 1500 characters as a message. You could send *War
and Peace*, using thousands of postcards. You could even send a complete
description of a photograph on postcards, by splitting the image into thousands of rows and columns and listing on each postcard a row number, a column number, and the color of the little square at that position. The recipient

could, in principle, reconstruct the picture after receiving all the postcards. What makes the Internet work in practice is the incredible speed at which the data packets are transmitted, and the processing power of the sending and receiving computers, which can disassemble and reassemble the messages so quickly and flawlessly that users don't even notice.

## Core and Edge

We can think of the ordinary postal system as having a *core* and an *edge*—the edge is what we see directly, the mailboxes and letter carriers, and the core is everything behind the edge that makes the system work. The Internet also has a core and an edge. The edge is made up of the machines that interface directly with the end users—for example, your computer and mine. The core of the Internet is all the connectivity that makes the Internet a network. It includes the computers owned by the telecommunications companies that pass the messages along.

An *Internet Service Provider* or *ISP* is any computer that provides access to the Internet, or provides the functions that enable different parts of the Internet to connect to each other. Sometimes the organizations that run those computers are also called ISPs. Your ISP at home is likely your telephone or cable company, though if you live in a rural area, it might be a company providing Internet services by satellite. Universities and big companies are their own ISPs. The "service" may be to convey messages between computers deep within the core of the Internet, passing messages until they reach their destination. In the United States alone, there are thousands of ISPs, and the system works as a whole because they cooperate with each other.

Fundamentally, the Internet consists of computers sending bit packets that request services, and other computers sending packets back in response. Other metaphors can be helpful, but the service metaphor is close to the truth. For example, you don't really "visit" the web page of a store, like a voyeuristic tourist peeking through the store window. Your computer makes a very specific request of the store's web server, and the store's web server responds to it—and may well keep a record of exactly what you asked for, adding the new information about your interests to the record it already has from your other "visits." Your "visits" leave fingerprints!

## IP Addresses

Packets can be directed to their destination because they are labeled with an *IP address*, which is a sequence of four numbers, each between 0 and 255. (The numbers from 0 to 255 correspond to the various sequences of 8 bits, from 00000000 to 11111111, so IP addresses are really 32 bits long. "IP" is an abbreviation for "Internet Protocol," explained next.) A typical IP address is 66.82.9.88. Blocks of IP addresses are assigned to ISPs, which in turn assign them to their customers.

There are 256 × 256 × 256 × 256 possible IP addresses, or about 4 billion. In the pre-miniaturization days when the Internet was designed, that seemed an absurdly large number—enough so every computer could have its own IP address, even if every person on the planet had his or her own computer. Figure A.1 shows the 13 computers that made up the entire network in 1970. As a result of miniaturization and the inclusion of cell phones and other small devices, the number of Internet devices is already in the hundreds of millions (see Figure A.2), and it seems likely that there will not be enough IP addresses for the long run. A project is underway to deploy a new version of IP in which the size of IP addresses increases from 32 bits to 128—and then the number of IP addresses will be a 3 followed by 38 zeroes! That's about ten million for every bacterium on earth.

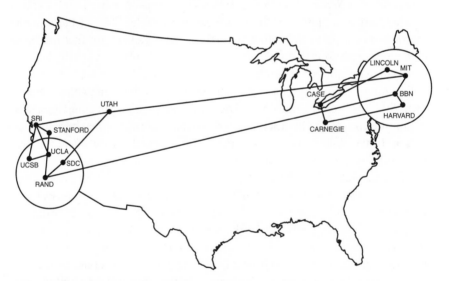

Source: Heart, F., McKenzie, A., McQuillian, J., and Walden, D., ARPANET Completion Report, Bolt, Beranek and Newman, Burlington, MA, January 4, 1978.

FIGURE A.1    The 13 interconnected computers of the December, 1970 ARPANET (as the Internet was first known). The interconnected machines were located at the University of California campuses at Santa Barbara and at Los Angeles, the Stanford Research Institute, Stanford University, Systems Development Corporation, the RAND Corporation, the University of Utah, Case Western Reserve University, Carnegie Mellon University, Lincoln Labs, MIT, Harvard, and Bolt, Beranek, and Newman, Inc.

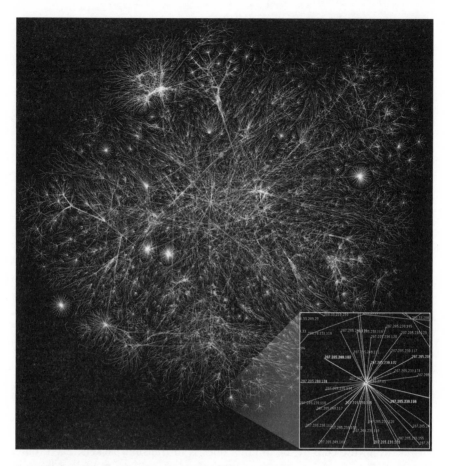

Source: Wikipedia, http://en.wikipedia.org/wiki/Image: Internet_map_1024.jpg. This work is licensed under the Creative Commons Attribution 2.5 License.

FIGURE A.2   Traffic flows within a small part of the Internet as it exists today. Each line is drawn between two IP addresses of the network. The length of a line indicates the time delay for messages between those two nodes. Thousands of cross-connections are omitted.

An important piece of the Internet infrastructure are the *Domain Name Servers*, which are computers loaded with information about which IP addresses correspond to which "domain names" such as harvard.edu, verizon.com, gmail.com, yahoo.fr (the suffix in this case is the country code for France), and mass.gov. So when your computer sends an email or requests a web page, the translation of domain names into IP addresses takes place before the message enters the core of the Internet. The routers don't know about domain names; they need only pass the packets along toward their destination IP address numbers.

## IP ADDRESSES AND CRIMES

The recording industry identifies unlawful music downloads by the IP addresses to which the bits are sent. But an IP address is rarely the exclusive property of an individual, so it is hard to be sure who is doing the downloading. A provider of residential Internet service allocates an address to a home only temporarily. When the connection becomes inactive, the address is reclaimed so someone else can use it. If NAT is in use or if many people use the same wireless router, it can be impossible to establish reliably who exactly used an IP address. If you don't activate the security on your home wireless router, neighbors who poach your home network signal may get you in serious trouble by their illegal downloads!

An enterprise that manages its own network can connect to the Internet through a single gateway computer, using only a single IP address. Packets are tagged with a few more bits, called a "port" number, so that the gateway can route responses back to the same computer within the private network. This process, called *Network Address Translation* or *NAT*, conserves IP addresses. NAT also makes it impossible for "outside" computers to know which computer actually made the request—only the gateway knows which port corresponds to which computer.

## The Key to It All: Passing Packets

At heart, all the core of the Internet does is to transmit packets. Each router has several links connecting it to other routers or to the "edge" of the network. When a packet comes in on a link, the router very quickly looks at the destination IP address, decides which outgoing link to use based on a limited Internet "map" it holds, and sends the packet on its way. The router has some memory, called a *buffer*, which it uses to store packets temporarily if they are arriving faster than they can be processed and dispatched. If the buffer fills up, the router just discards incoming packets that it can't hold, leaving other parts of the system to cope with the data loss if they choose to.

Packets also include some redundant bits to aid error detection. To give a simple analogy, suppose Alice wants to guard against a character being smudged or altered on a post card while it is in transit. Alice could add to the text on the card a sequence of 26 bits—indicating whether the text she has put on the card has an even or odd number of As, Bs, ..., and Zs. Bob can check whether the card seems to be valid by comparing his own reckoning with the 26-bit "fingerprint" already on the card. In the Internet, all the routers do a similar integrity check on data packets. Routers discard packets found to have been damaged in transit.

The format for data packets—which bits represent the IP address and other information about the packet, and which bits are the message itself—is part of the *Internet Protocol*, or IP. Everything that flows through the Internet— web pages, emails, movies, VoIP telephone calls—is broken down into data packets. Ordinarily, all packets are handled in exactly the same way by the routers and other devices built around IP. IP is a "best effort" packet delivery protocol. A router implementing IP tries to pass packets along, but makes no guarantees. Yet guaranteed delivery is possible within the network as a whole—because other protocols are layered on top of IP.

## *Protocols*

A "protocol" is a standard for communicating messages between networked computers. The term derives from its meaning in diplomacy. A diplomatic protocol is an agreement aiding in communications between mutually mistrustful parties—parties who do not report to any common authority who can control their behavior. Networked computers are in something of the same situation of both cooperation and mistrust. There is no one controlling the Internet as a whole. Any computer can join the global exchange of information, simply by interconnecting physically and then following the network protocols about how bits are inserted into and extracted from the communication links.

The fact that packets can get discarded, or "dropped" as the phrase goes, might lead you to think that an email put into the network might never arrive. Indeed emails can get lost, but when it happens, it is almost always because of a problem with an ISP or a personal computer, not because of a network failure. The computers at the edge of the network use a higher-level protocol to deliver messages reliably, even though the delivery of individual packets within the network may be unreliable. That higher-level protocol is called "Transport Control Protocol," or TCP, and one often hears about it in conjunction with IP as "TCP/IP."

To get a general idea of how TCP works, imagine that Alice wants to send Bob the entire text of *War and Peace* on postcards, which are serial numbered so Bob can reassemble them in the right order even if they arrive out of order. Postcards sometimes go missing, so Alice keeps a copy of every postcard she puts in the mail. She doesn't discard her copy of a postcard until she has received word back from Bob declaring that he has received Alice's postcard. Bob sends that word back on a postcard of his own, including the serial number of Alice's card so Alice knows which card is being confirmed. Of course,

Bob's confirming postcards may get lost too, so Alice keeps track of when she sent her postcards. If she doesn't hear anything back from Bob within a certain amount of time, she sends a duplicate postcard. At this point, it starts getting complicated: Bob has to know enough to ignore duplicates, in case it was his acknowledgment rather than Alice's original message that got lost. But it all can be made to work!

TCP works the same way on the Internet, except that the speed at which packets are zipping through the network is extremely fast. The net result is that email software using TCP is failsafe: If the bits arrive at all, they will be a perfect duplicate of those that were sent.

TCP is not the only high-level protocol that relies on IP for packet delivery. For "live" applications such as streaming video and VoIP telephone calls, there is no point in waiting for retransmissions of dropped packets. So for these applications, the packets are just put in the Internet and sent on their way, with no provision made for data loss. That higher-level protocol is called UDP, and there are others as well, all relying on IP to do the dirty work of routing packets to their destination.

The postal service provides a rough analogy of the difference between higher-level and lower-level protocols. The same trucks and airplanes are used for carrying first-class mail, priority mail, junk mail, and express mail. The loading and unloading of mail bags onto the transport vehicles follow a low-level protocol. The handling between receipt at the post office and loading onto the transport vehicles, and between unloading and delivery, follows a variety of higher-level protocols, according to the kind of service that has been purchased.

In addition to the way it can be used to support a variety of higher-level protocols, IP is general in another way. It is not bound to any particular physical medium. IP can run over copper wire, radio signals, and fiber optic cables—in principle, even carrier pigeons. All that is required is the ability to deliver bit packets, including both the payload and the addressing and other "packaging," to switches that can carry out the essential routing operation.

There is a separate set of "lower-level protocols" that stipulate how bits are to be represented—for example, as radio waves, or light pulses in optic fibers. IP is doubly general, in

### IP OVER CARRIER PIGEON

You can look up RFC 1149 and RFC 2549 on the Web, "Standard for the Transmission of IP Datagrams on Avian Carriers" and "IP over Avian Carriers with Quality of Service." They faithfully follow the form of true Internet standards, though the authors wrote them with tongue firmly planted in cheek, demurely stating, "This is an experimental, not recommended standard."

that it can take its bit packets from many different physical substrates, and deliver those packets for use by many different higher-level services.

## The Reliability of the Internet

The Internet is remarkably reliable. There are no "single points of failure." If a cable breaks or a computer catches on fire, the protocols automatically reroute the packets around the inoperative links. So when Hurricane Katrina submerged New Orleans in 2005, Internet routers had packets bypass the city. Of course, no messages destined for New Orleans itself could be delivered there.

In spite of the redundancy of interconnections, if enough links are broken, parts of the Internet may become inaccessible to other parts. On December 26, 2006, the Henchung earthquake severed several major communication cables that ran across the floor of the South China Sea. The Asian financial markets were severely affected for a few days, as traffic into and out of Taiwan, China, and Hong Kong was cut off or severely reduced. There were reports that the volume of spam reaching the U.S. also dropped for a few days, until the cables were repaired!

Although the Internet *core* is reliable, the computers on the edge typically have only a single connection to the core, creating single points of failure. For example, you will lose your home Internet service if your phone company provides the service and a passing truck pulls down the wire connecting your house to the telephone pole. Some big companies connect their internal network to the Internet through two different service providers—a costly form of redundancy, but a wise investment if the business could not survive a service disruption.

# The Internet Spirit

The extraordinary growth of the Internet, and its passage from a military and academic technology to a massive replacement for both paper mail and telephones, has inspired reverence for some of its fundamental design virtues. Internet principles have gained status as important truths about communication, free expression, and all manner of engineering design.

## The Hourglass

The standard electric outlet is a universal interface between power plants and electric appliances. There is no need for people to know whether their power is coming from a waterfall, a solar cell, or a nuclear plant, if all they want to do is to plug in their appliances and run their household. And the same electric outlet can be used for toasters, radios, and vacuum cleaners. Moreover, it will instantly become usable for the next great appliance that gets invented, as long as that device comes with a standard household electric plug. The electric company doesn't even care if you are using its electricity to do bad things, as long as you pay its bills.

The outlet design is at the neck of a conceptual hourglass through which electricity flows, connecting multiple possible power sources on one side of the neck to multiple possible electricity-using devices on the other. New inventions need only accommodate what the neck expects—power plants need to supply 115V AC current to the outlet, and new appliances need plugs so they can use the current coming from the outlet. Imagine how inefficient it would be if your house had to be rewired in order to accommodate new appliances, or if different kinds of power plants required different household wiring. Anyone who has tried to transport an electric appliance between the U.S. and the U.K. knows that electric appliances are less universal than Internet packets.

The Internet architecture is also conceptually organized like an hourglass (see Figure A.3), with the ubiquitous Internet Protocol at the neck, defining the form of the bit packets carried through the network. A variety of higher-level protocols use bit packets to achieve different purposes. In the words of the report that proposed the hourglass metaphor, "the minimal required elements [IP] appear at the narrowest point, and an ever-increasing set of choices fills the wider top and bottom, underscoring how little the Internet itself demands of its service providers and users."

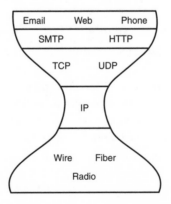

FIGURE A.3   The Internet protocol hourglass (simplified). Each protocol interfaces only to those in the layers immediately above and below it, and all data is turned into IP bit packets in order to pass from an application to one of the physical media that make up the network.

For example, TCP guarantees reliable though possibly delayed message delivery, and UDP provides timely but unreliable message delivery. All the higher-level protocols rely on IP to deliver packets. Once the packets get into the neck of the hourglass, they are handled identically, regardless of the higher-level protocol that produced them. TCP and UDP are in turn utilized by even higher-level protocols, such as HTTP ("HyperText Transport Protocol"), which is used for sending and receiving web pages, and SMTP ("Simple Mail Transport Protocol"), which is used for sending email. Application software, such as web browsers, email clients, and VoIP software, sit at a yet higher level, utilizing the protocols at the layer below and unconcerned with how those protocols do their job.

Below the IP layer are various physical protocol layers. Because IP is a universal protocol at the neck, applications (above the neck) can accommodate various possible physical implementations (below the neck). For example, when the first wireless IP devices became available, long after the general structure of the Internet hourglass was firmly in place, nothing above the neck had to change. Email, which had previously been delivered over copper wires and glass fibers, was immediately delivered over radio waves such as those sent and received by the newly developed household wireless routers.

Governments, media firms, and communication companies sometimes wish that IP worked differently, so they could more easily filter out certain kinds of content and give others priority service. But the universality of IP, and the many unexpected uses to which it has given birth, argue against such proposals to re-engineer the Internet. As information technology consultant Scott Bradner wrote, "We have the Internet that we have today because the Internet of yesterday did not focus on the today of yesterday. Instead, Internet technology developers and ISPs focused on flexibility, thus enabling whatever future was coming."

Indeed, the entire social structure in which Internet protocols evolved prevented special interests from gaining too much power or building their pet features into the Internet infrastructure. Protocols were adopted by a working group called the Internet

> ### THE FUTURE OF THE INTERNET— AND HOW TO STOP IT
>
> This excellent book by Jonathan Zittrain (Yale University Press and Penguin UK, 2008) sees the vulnerabilities of the Internet—rapidly spreading viruses, and crippling attacks on major servers—as consequences of its essential openness, its capacity to support new inventions—what Zittrain calls its "generativity." The book reflects on whether society will be driven to use a network of less-flexible "appliances" in the future to avoid the downsides of the Internet's wonderfully creative malleability.

Engineering Task Force (IETF), which made its decisions by rough consensus, not by voting. The members met face to face and hummed to signify their approval, so the aggregate sense of the group would be public and individual opinions could be reasonably private—but no change, enhancement, or feature could be adopted by a narrow majority.

The larger lesson is the importance of minimalist, well-selected, open standards in the design of any system that is to be widely disseminated and is to stimulate creativity and unforeseen uses. Standards, although they are merely conventions, give rise to vast innovation, if they are well chosen, spare, and widely adopted.

## Layers, Not Silos

Internet functionality could, in theory, have been provided in many other ways. Suppose, for example, that a company had set out just to deliver electronic mail to homes and offices. It could have brought in special wiring, both economical and perfect for the data rates needed to deliver email. It could have engineered special switches, perfect for routing email. And it could have built the ideal email software, optimized to work perfectly with the special switches and wires.

Another group might have set out to deliver movies. Movies require higher data rates, which might better be served by the use of different, specialized switches. An entirely separate network might have been developed for that. Another group might have conceived something like the Web, and have tried to convince ordinary people to install yet a third set of cables in their homes.

The magic of the hourglass structure is not just the flexibility provided by the neck of the bottle. It's the logical isolation of the upper layers from the lower. Inventive people working in the upper layers can rely on the guarantees provided by the clever people working at the lower layers, without knowing much about *how* those lower layers work. Instead of multiple, parallel vertical structures—self-contained silos—the right way to engineer information is in layers.

And yet we live in an information economy still trapped, legally and politically, in historical silos. There are special rules for telephones, cable services, and radio. The medium determines the rules. Look at the names of the main divisions of the Federal Communications Commission: Wireless, wireline, and so on. Yet the technologies have converged. Telephone calls go over the Internet, with all its variety of physical infrastructure. The bits that make up telephone calls are no different from the bits that make up movies.

Laws and regulations should respect layers, not the increasingly meaning-less silos—a principle at the heart of the argument about broadcast regulation presented in Chapter 8.

## End to End

"End to End," in the Internet, means that the switches making up the core of the network should be dumb—optimized to carry out their single limited func-tion of passing packets. Any functionality requiring more "thinking" than that should be the responsibility of the more powerful computers at the edge of the network. For example, Internet protocols could have been designed so that routers would try much harder to ensure that packets do not get dropped on any link. There could have been special codes for packets that got special, high-priority handling, like "Priority Mail" in the U.S. Postal Service. There could have been spe-cial codes for encrypting and decrypting packets at certain stages to provide secrecy, say when packets crossed national borders. There are a lot of things that routers might have done. But it was better, from an engineering standpoint, to have the core of the network do the minimum that would enable those more com-plex functions to be carried out at the edge. One main reason is that this makes it more likely that new applications can be added without having to change the core—any operations that are application-specific will be handled at the edges.

> ### STUPID NETWORKS
> Another way to understand the Internet's end-to-end philosophy is to realize that if the computers are powerful at the edge of the net-work, the network itself can be "stupid," just delivering packets where the packets themselves say they want to go. Contrast this with the old telephone network, in which the devices at the edge of the network were stupid tele-phones, so to provide good service, the switching equipment in the telephone office had to be intelli-gent, routing telephone signals to where the network said they should go.

This approach has been staggeringly successful, as illustrated by today's amazing array of Internet applications that the original network designers never anticipated.

## Separate Content and Carrier

The closest thing to the Internet that existed in the nineteenth century was the telegraph. It was an important technology for only a few decades. It put

> **THE VICTORIAN INTERNET**
>
> That is the title of an excellent short book by Tom Standage (Berkley Books, 1999), making the argument that many of the social consequences of the Internet were seen during the growth of the telegraph. The content-carrier conflict is only one. On a less-serious level, the author notes that the telegraph, like the Internet, was used for playing games at a distance almost from the day it came into being.

the Pony Express out of business, and was all but put out of business itself by the telephone. And it didn't get off to a fast start; at first, a service to deliver messages quickly didn't seem all that valuable.

One of the first big users of the telegraph was the Associated Press—one of the original "wire services." News is, of course, more valuable if it arrives quickly, so the telegraph was a valuable tool for the AP. Recognizing that, the AP realized that its competitive position, relative to other press services, would be enhanced to the extent it could keep the telegraph to itself. So it signed an exclusive contract with Western Union, the telegraph monopoly. The contract gave the AP favorable pricing on the use of the wires. Other press services were priced out of the use of the "carrier." And as a result, the AP got a lock on news distribution so strong that it threatened the functioning of the American democracy. It passed the news about politicians it liked and omitted mention of those it did not. Freedom of the press existed in theory, but not in practice, because the content industry controlled the carrier.

> **MORE ON INFORMATION FREEDOM**
>
> The SaveTheInternet.com Coalition is a pluralistic group dedicated to net neutrality and Internet freedom more generally. Its member organizations run the gamut from the Gun Owners of America, to MoveOn.org, to the Christian Coalition, to the Feminist Majority. Its web site includes a blog and a great many links. The blog of law professor Susan Crawford, `scrawford.net/blog`, comments on many aspects of digital information freedom, and also has a long list of links to other blogs.

Today's version of this morality play is the debate over "net neutrality." Providers of Internet backbone services would benefit from providing different pricing and different service guarantees to preferred customers. After all, they might argue, even the Postal Service recognizes the advantages of providing better service to customers who are willing to pay more. But what if a movie studio buys an ISP, and then gets creative with its pricing and service structure? You might discover that your movie downloads are far cheaper to watch, or arrive at your home looking and sounding much better, if they happen to be the product of the parent content company.

Or what if a service provider decides it just doesn't like a particular customer, as Verizon decided about Naral? Or what if an ISP finds that its customer is taking advantage of its service deal in ways that the provider did not anticipate? Are there any protections for the customer?

In the Internet world, consider the clever but deceptive scheme implemented by Comcast in 2007. This ISP promised customers unlimited bandwidth, but then altered the packets it was handling to slow down certain data transmissions. It peeked at the packets and altered those that had been generated by certain higher-level protocols commonly (but not exclusively) used for downloading and uploading movies. The end-user computer receiving these altered packets did not realize they had been altered in transit, and obeyed the instruction they contained, inserted in transit by Comcast, to restart the transmission from scratch. The result was to make certain data services run very slowly, without informing the customers. In a net neutrality world, this could not happen; Comcast would be a packet delivery service, and not entitled to choose which packets it would deliver promptly or to alter the packets while handing them on.

In early 2008, AT&T announced that it was considering a more direct violation of net neutrality: examining packets flowing through its networks to filter out illegal movie and music downloads. It was as though the electric utility announced it might cut off the power to your DVD player if it sensed that you were playing a bootleg movie. A content provider suggested that AT&T intended to make its content business more profitable by using its carrier service to enforce copyright restrictions. In other words, the idea was perhaps that people would be more likely to buy movies from AT&T the content company if AT&T the carrier refused to deliver illegally obtained movies. Of course, any technology designed to detect bits illegally flowing into private residences could be adapted, by either governments or the carriers, for many other purposes. Once the carriers inspect the bits you are receiving into your home, these private businesses could use that power in other ways: to conduct surveillance, enforce laws, and impose their morality on their customers. Just imagine Federal Express opening your mail in transit and deciding for itself which letters and parcels you should receive!

## Clean Interfaces

The electric plug is the interface between an electric device and the power grid. Such standardized interfaces promote invention and efficiency. In the

Internet world, the interfaces are the connections between the protocol layers—for example, what TCP expects of IP when it passes packets into the core, and what IP promises to do for TCP.

In designing information systems, there is always a temptation to make the interface a little more complicated in order to achieve some special functionality—typically, a faster data rate for certain purposes. Experience has shown repeatedly, however, that computer programming is hard, and the gains in speed from more complex interfaces are not worth the cost in longer development and debugging time. And Moore's Law is always on the side of simplicity anyway: Just wait, and a cruder design will become as fast as the more complicated one might have been.

Even more important is that the interfaces be widely accepted standards. Internet standards are adopted through a remarkable process of consensus-building, nonhierarchical in the extreme. The standards themselves are referred to as RFCs, "Requests for Comment." Someone posts a proposal, and a cycle of comment and revision, of buy-in and objection, eventually converges on something useful, if not universally regarded as perfect. All the players know they have more to gain by accepting the standard and engineering their products and services to meet it than by trying to act alone. The Internet is an object lesson in creative compromise producing competitive energy.

> **RFCs AND STANDARDS**
>
> The archive of RFCs creates a history of the Internet. It is open for all to see—just use your favorite search engine. All the Internet standards are RFCs, although not all RFCs are standards. Indeed, in a whimsically reflexive explanation, "Not all RFCs are standards" is RFC 1796.

# Endnotes

---

## Chapter 1

1  *"On September 19, 2007, while..."* Jennifer Sullivan, "Last phone call steered search," *Seattle Times*, October 2, 2007; William Yardley, "Missing woman found alive in wrecked car after 8 days," *New York Times*, September 29, 2007.

2  *"The March 2008 resignation ..."* How an information system helped nail Eliot Spitzer and a prostitution ring, `blogs.zdnet.com/BTL/?p=8211&tag=nl.e540`.

3  *"A company will give you..."* Pudding Media, `puddingmedia.com`.

3  *"So much disk storage is..."* Adapted from Latanya Sweeney, Information Explosion. *Confidentiality, Disclosure, and Data Access: Theory and Practical Applications for Statistical Agencies*, L. Zayatz, P. Doyle, J. Theeuwes, and J. Lane (eds), Urban Institute, Washington, DC, 2001.

5  *"Consider the story of Naral..."* Adam Liptak, "Verizon reverses itself on abortion messages," *New York Times*, September 28, 2007.

6  *"Its peculiar character, too, is..."* Letter from Thomas Jefferson to Isaac McPherson, August 13, 1813. Jefferson, *Writings 13:333–35.* `press-pubs.uchicago.edu/founders/documents/a1_8_8s12.html`.

8  *"If it can't be found..."* This maxim emerged in the late 1990s. See Scott Bradner, "How big is the world?," *Network World*, October 18, 1999. `http://www.networkworld.com/archive/1999b/1018bradner.html`.

8  *"Moore's Law"* Gordon Moore, "Cramming more components onto integrated circuits," *Electronics*, Vol. 38, No. 8, April 19, 1965. `ftp://download.intel.com/research/silicon/moorespaper.pdf`. Moore's original paper is worth a look—it was written for a popular electronics publication. Later articulations of the "Law" state that the doubling period is 18 months rather than two years. A very extensive (but not wholly persuasive) "debunking" appears in `arstechnica.com/articles/paedia/cpu/moore.ars`.

10 *"In 1983, Christmas shoppers could..."* Carol Ranalli, "Digital camera lets computers see," *Infoworld*, November 21, 1983.

10 *"Even 14 years later, film..."* "Kodak, GE, Digital report strong quarterly results," *Atlanta Constitution*, January 17, 1997.

10 *"The move would cost the..."* Claudia H. Deutsch, "Shrinking pains at Kodak," *New York Times*, February 9, 2007.

10 *"That is the number of..."* The expanding digital universe, IDC white paper sponsored by EMC, March 2007. `www.emc.com/about/destination/digital_universe/pdf/Expanding_Digital_Universe_IDC_WhitePaper_022507.pdf` and The Diverse and Expanding Digital Universe, March 2008, `www.emc.com/collateral/analyst-reports/diverse-exploding-digital-universe.pdf`.

12 *"Along with processing power and..."* Data from Internet Systems Consortium, ISC Domain Survey: Number of Internet Hosts. `www.isc.org/index.pl?/ops/ds/host-count-history.php`.

13 *"The story dropped off the..."* Seth Mydans, "Monks are silenced, and for now, Internet is, too," *New York Times*, October 4, 2007; OpenNet initative, "Pulling the Plug: A Technical Review of the Internet Shutdown in Burma." `http://opennet.net/research/bulletins/013`.

13 *"It may prove simpler to..."* Rachel Donadio, "Libel without borders," *New York Times*, October 7, 2007.

15 *"Recent federal laws, such..."* Uniting and Strengthening America by Providing Appropriate Tools Required to Intercept and Obstruct Terrorism Act of 2001 (Public Law 107–56), signed into law by President George Bush on October 26, 2001. This law expanded the legal authority of law enforcement agencies to search electronic communications and records in order to combat domestic terrorism.

15 *"Now when any newcomer comes..."* L. Jon Wertheim, "Jump the Shark," *New York Times*, November 24, 2007.

16 *"That woman's lawyer later blamed..."* Steve Pokin, "A real person, a real death," *St. Charles (Missouri) Journal*, November 10, 2007; Christopher Maag, "A hoax turned fatal draws anger but no charges," *New York Times*, November 28, 2007; Rebecca Cathcart, "MySpace is said to draw subpoena in hoax case," *New York Times*, January 10, 2008.

# Chapter 2

19 *"The attack on the transit..."* Of the many descriptions of the event, one of the most complete is available from Wikipedia at `en.wikipedia.org/wiki/7_July_2005_London_bombings`.

19 *"Hundreds of thousands of surveillance..."* Sarah Lyall, "London Bombers Visited Earlier, Apparently on Practice Run," *New York Times*, September 21, 2005.

19 *"BIG BROTHER IS WATCHING YOU..."* George Orwell, *1984,* Signet Classics, 2003, p. 2.

20 *"According to a 2007 Pew/Internet......"* Digital Footprints, "Online identity management and search in the age of transparency," Pew Internet and American Life Project, 2007. www.pewinternet.org.

20 *"Many of us publish and..."* Digital Footprints.

20 *"A third of the teens with..."* Teens and Social Media, Pew Internet & American Life Project report, December 19, 2007, p. 13. www.pewinternet.org/pdfs/PIP_Teens_Social_Media_Final.pdf.

21 *"More than half of all..."* Ibid.

23 *"'The fact that this girl...'"* O'Ryan Johnson, "Green Line Groper Arrested," *Boston Herald,* December 8, 2007.

23 *"Mr. Berman claims he is innocent..."* "Newton man arraigned in groping case," *Boston Globe,* December 11, 2007.

23 *"In June 2005, a woman..."* Sarah Boxer, "Internet's Best Friend (Let Me Count the Ways)," *New York Times,* July 30, 2005.

23 *"It is unlikely that the..."* Jonathan Krim, "Subway Fracas Escalates Into Test of the Internet's Power to Shame," *Washington Post,* July 7, 2005.

24 *"One fan got a pre-release..."* Jonathan Richards, "Digital DNA could finger Harry Potter leaker," *The Times of London,* July 19, 2007.

24 *"They knew where he was, ..."* Christopher Elliot, "Some Rental Cars Are Keeping Tabs on the Drivers," *New York Times,* January 13, 2004.

26 *"They can be almost undetectable."* http://www.rfid-asia.info/2007/02/digestible-rfid-tag-alternative-for.htm. See U.S. Patent Application 20070008113, filed by the Eastman Kodak Company, titled "System to monitor the ingestion of medicines." It describes "a digestible radio frequency identification (RFID) tag."

27 *"The technology is there to..."* Rhea Wessel, Metro Groups Galeria Kaufhof Launches UHF Item-Level Pilot, *RFID Journal,* September 20, 2007, www.rdifjournal.com/article/articleview/3624/1/1/.

27 *"When questioned, Trooper Rasinski said..."* Alex Taylor III, "Corzine crash spotlights SUV Safety," *Fortune,* April 19, 2007.

27 *"We know his exact speed..."* Tom Hester, Jr. (Associated Press), "Trooper speeding revealed in Corzine crash," *USA Today,* April 18, 2007.

27 *"Your insurance company is probably..."* Jeff Gamage, "Car's 'black box' and what it tells," *Philadephia Inquirer,* November 24, 2007. Bob Holliday, "Little black box: Friend or foe?," *The Pantagraph* (Bloomington, Illinois), March 4, 2007.

28 *"EDRs capture information about speed, ..."* Bill Howard, "The Black Box: Big Brother's Still Watching," *TechnoRide,* April 19, 2007. www.technoride.com/2007/04/the_black_box_big_brothers_sti.php.

28  *"CSX Railroad was exonerated..."* Leo King, "CSX wins wrongful death suit," *National Corridors Newsletter*, Vol. 3, No. 45, November 4, 2002. www.nationalcorridors.org/df/df11042002.shtml.

28  *"Taking bits from the car was..."* *The People of the State of New York v. Robert Christmann*, Justice Court of New York, Village of Newark, 3 Misc. 3d 309; 776 N.Y.S.2d 437, decided January 16, 2004.

29  *"Researchers at Purdue have developed..."* John Mello, "Codes Make Printers Stool Pigeons," *TechNewsWorld*, October 18, 2005. The web site for the Purdue research group is cobweb.ecn.purdue.edu/~prints/index.shtml.

30  *"Because his ticket did not..."* Matt Daniel, "Starts and Stops," *Boston Globe*, March 25, 2007.

31  *"On October 18, 2007, a..."* Eric Pfanner, "Britain tries to explain data leak affecting 25 million," *New York Times*, November 22, 2007.

32  *"When a federal court released..."* Jeffrey Heer, "Exploring Enron." jheer.org/enron/v1/.

34  *"To use the official lingo, ..."* An excellent overview of de-identification and related topics can be found at the web site of the Carnegie Mellon University Laboratory for International Data Privacy. It can be found at privacy.cs.cmu.edu.

34  *"According to the Cambridge voter..."* Latanya Sweeney, Recommendations to Identify and Combat Privacy Problems in the Commonwealth, Testimony before the Pennsylvania House Select Committee on Information Security (House Resolution 351), Pittsburgh, PA, October 5, 2005; available at privacy.cs.cmu.edu/dataprivacy/talks/Flick-05-10.html.

34  *"Nationally, gender, zip code, and..."* Latanya Sweeney, Comment of the Department of Health and Human Services on "Standards of Privacy of Individually Identifiable Health Information;" available at privacy.cs.cmu.edu/dataprivacy/HIPAA/HIPAAcomments.html.

35  *"'There is no patient confidentiality,'..."* Michael Lasalandra, "Panel told releases of med records hurt privacy," *Boston Herald*, March 20, 1997.

36  *"In 2003, Scott Levine, owner..."* Jalkumar Vijayan, "Appeals Court: Stiff prison sentence in Acxiom data theft case stands," *ComputerWorld*, Febraruy 23, 2007.

36  *"Millions of Americans are victimized..."* Javelin Strategy & Research, 2007 Identity Fraud Survey Report, February, 2007. A summary appears at www.privacyrights.org/ar/idtheftsurveys.htm.

37  *"These records can be subpoenaed, ..."* Daniel B. Wood, "Radio ID tags proliferate, stirring privacy debate," *Christian Science Monitor*, December 15, 2004; Debbie Howlett, "Motorists can keep on rolling soon," *USA Today*, May 26, 2004; "High-Tech Evidence, A lawyer's friend or foe?," *National Law Journal*, August 24, 2004.

40  *"In 1988, when a videotape..."* 18 USC Sect. 2710, 1988.

41  *"A university president had to..."* "Salisbury U. president removes Facebook profile after questions," *Associated Press*, October 17, 2007.

41   *"You can read the 'About Me'..."* Her web site is at www.smokeandashes.net.

41   *"Or consider that there is..."* Andrew Levy, "The ladettes who glorify their shameful drunken antics on Facebook," *Daily Mail,* November 5, 2007.

43   *"Absolutely not, says the Brown..."* Rachel Arndt, "Admissions officers poke around Facebook," *The Brown Daily Herald,* September 10, 2007.

44   *"For a little money, you..."* www.americablog.com/2006/01/americablog-just-bought-general-wesley.html.

44   *"It was a great service..."* Frank Main, "Everyone can buy cell phone records," *Chicago Sun-Times,* January 5, 2006.

45   *"Beverly O'Brien suspected her..."* O'Brien v. O'Brien, No. 5D03-3484, 2005 WL 322367 (Fla. Dist. Ct. App. February 11, 2005); available at www.5dca.org/Opinions/Opin2005/020705/5D03-3484.pdf.

47   *"Anyone could figure out where..."* John S. Brownstein, Christopher A. Cassa, and Kenneth D. Mandl, "No place to hide—reverse identification of patients from published maps," *New England Journal of Medicine,* 355:16, October 19, 2007, 1741–1742.

48   *"Yet they were able to..."* The data sources the MIT students used are readily available. The Illinois crime data can be found at www.icpsr.umich.edu/NACJD/help/faq6399.html. You can search the Social Security Death Index at ssdi.rootsweb.com/.

49   *"According to a report in..."* Keith Bradsher, "China Enacting a High-Tech Plan to Track People," *New York Times,* August 12, 2007.

49   *"Many cell phones can be..."* See, for example, Department of Energy web page on cell phone vulnerabilities, www.ntc.doe.gov/cita/CI_Awareness_Guide/V2comint/Cellular.htm.

49   *"A federal court ruled that..."* United States of America v. John Tomero, et al., S2 06 Crim. 0008 (LAK), United States District Court for the Southern District of New York, 462 F. Supp. 2d 565, Opinion of Judge Lewis A. Kaplan, November 27, 2006.

49   *"Tomero could have prevented it..."* Declan McCullagh and Anne Broache, "FBI taps cell phone mic as eavesdropping tool," *CNET News.com,* December 1, 2006. www.news.com/2100-1029_3-6140191.html.

49   *"OnStar warns, 'OnStar will cooperate...'"* OnStar "Helpful Info" web page. www.onstar.com/us_english/jsp/explore/onstar_basics/helpful_info.jsp?info-view=serv_plan.

49   *"The FBI has used this method..."* Declan McCullagh, "Court to FBI: No spying on in-car computers," *CNET News.com,* November 19, 2003. www.news.com/2100-1029_3-5109435.html.

50   *"You have chosen to say, ..."* Ellen Nakashima, "FBI Prepares Vast Database Of Biometrics; $1 Billion Project to Include Images of Irises and Faces," *Washington Post,* December 22, 2007.

52   *"In what is generally agreed..."* "Creating a new Who's Who," *Time Magazine,* July 9, 1973.

52  *"Specifically, it states, 'No agency...'"* 5 USC sect. 552(b).

53  *"In January 2002, just a..."* There is a good exposition of the Total Information Awareness Office on the site of EPIC, http://epic.org/privacy/profiling/tia/.

53  *"In a May 2002 email..."* Email dated May 21, 2002, released on January 23, 2004 to David L. Sobel of the Electronic Privacy Information Center under a Freedom of Information Act request.

54  *"The* New York Times *broke..."* John Markoff, "Pentagon plans a computer system that would peek at personal data of Americans," *New York Times,* November 9, 2002.

54  *"In his June 2007 report..."* Michael J. Sniffen, "Homeland Security drops data-mining tool," *Washington Post,* September 6, 2007.

55  *"That project sought to compile..."* Walter Pincus, "Pentagon Will Review Database on U.S. Citizens Protests Among Acts Labeled 'Suspicious,'" *Washington Post,* Thursday, December 15, 2005.

56  *"After testifying in an antitrust..."* 1995 email from Bill Gates, quoted by Steve Lohr in Antitrust case is highlighting role of email, *New York Times,* November 2, 1998.

57  *"Electronic files, e-mail, data files, ..."* Harvard University Personnel Manual for Administrative/Professional Staff and Non-Bargaining Unit Support Staff, Section 2.6.C (December, 2007).

59  *"That is actually not a..."* Danny Sullivan, "Nielsen NetRatings Search Engine Ratings," *Search Engine Watch,* August 22, 2006.

60  *"In this particular case, we..."* thesarc.blogspot.com/2006/08/aol-user-says-just-kidding-about.html.

61  *"Instantaneous photographs and newspaper enterprise..."* Samuel Warren and Louis Brandeis, "The Right to Privacy," *Harvard Law Review,* IV, 5 (December 15, 1890).

62  *"Yet the Warren-Brandeis definition..."* R. M. Fano, "Review of Alan Westin's *Privacy and Freedom,*" *Scientific American,* May 1968, 148–152.

63  *"The result was a landmark study..."* Alan F. Westin, *Privacy and Freedom,* Atheneum, 1967.

63  *"The following are suggested as..."* *Privacy and Freedom,* p. 370.

64  *"In 1973, the Department of Health, ..."* U.S. Dep't. of Health, Education, and Welfare, Secretary's Advisory Committee on Automated Personal Data Systems, Records, computers, and the Rights of Citizens viii (1973). Text courtesy of EPIC at www.epic.org/privacy/consumer/code_fair_info.html.

65  *"Although the U.S. sectorial approach..."* www.export.gov/safeharbor/.

66  *"Only 0.3% of Yahoo! users..."* Saul Hansell, "Compressed data: The big Yahoo privacy storm that wasn't," *New York Times,* May 13, 2002.

66  *"Now many phone calls travel..."* Eric Lichtblau, James Risen, and Scott Shane, "Wider spying fuels aid plan for Telecom industry," *New York Times,* December 16, 2007.

67  *"So your computer might send..."* Ben Edelman, "The Sears 'Community' Installation of ComScore." `www.benedelman.org/news/010108-1.html`.

67  *"Dr. Roberta Ness, president of..."* "Privacy Rule slows scientific discovery and adds cost to research, scientists say," *Science Daily,* November 14, 2007, `www.sciencedaily.com/releases/2007/11/071113165648.htm`.

68  *"Sociologist Amitai Etzioni repeatedly asks..."* Amitai Etzioni, quoted by Fred H. Cate, "The failure of Fair Information Practice Principles," in Jane K. Winn, ed., *Consumer Protection in the Age of the "Information Economy,"* Ashgate, 2006.

68  *"Those laws have become unmoored..."* Cate, "The failure of Fair Information Practice Principles."

69  *"His data trail indicated that..."* Chris Cuomo, Eric Avram, and Lara Setrakian, "Key Evidence Supports Alibi in Potential Rape Defense for One Indicted Duke Player," ABC News at `abcnews.go.com/GMA/LegalCenter/story?id=1858806&page=1`.

70  *"Although the individual might have..."* D. Weitzner, "Beyond Secrecy: New Privacy Protection Strategies for Open Information Spaces," *IEEE Internet Computing,* September/October 2007. `dig.csail.mit.edu/2007/09/ieee-ic-beyond-secrecy-weitzner.html`.

70  *"We all have a right to..."* David Brin, *The Transparent Society,* Perseus Books, 1998, p. 334.

70  *"Some ongoing research is..."* Daniel J. Weitzner, Harold Abelson, Tim Berners-Lee, Joan Feigenbaum, James Hendler, and Gerald Jay Sussman, *Information Accountability,* MIT CSAIL Technical Report, MIT-CSAIL-TR-2007-034, June 13, 2007.

71  *"We are alone."* *1984,* Chapter 2, Section 8.

# Chapter 3

73  *"The U.S. produced a 42-page..."* The report, in its redacted and unredacted form, is available on the Web—for example, on Wikipedia at `en.wikisource.org/wiki/Calipari Report`.

73  *"The redacted report was posted..."* "Operation Iraqi Freedom, the official web site of the Multi-National Force," at `www.mnf-iraq.com`. The report was removed as soon as the error was discovered, but by that time, copies had already been made.

74  *"The revelations were both dangerous..."* Gordon Housworth, "Insurgents harvest secret NORORN materials from botched redaction of Nicola Calipari-Giuliana Sgrena incident report," Intellectual Capital Group. `spaces.icgpartners.com/apps/discuss.asp?guid=25930D60E7294C459DB22915B37F3F46`.

75  *"The article was posted on..."* `www.nytimes.com/library/world/mideast/041600iran-cia-index.html`.

75 *"A controversy ensued about the..."* cryptome.org/cia-iran.htm.

76 *"As posted on the* Post*'s..."* Serge F. Kovaleski and Sari Horwitz, "In letter, killer makes demands and threats," *Washington Post*, October 26, 2002, A14.

76 *"The paper fixed the problem..."* "Washington Post's scanned-to-PDF sniper letter more revealing than intended," PlanetPDF web site, October 26, 2002, www.planetpdf.com/mainpage.asp?webpageid=2434. Figures from presentation slides by Steven J. Murdoch and Maximillian Dornseif, "Hidden data in Internet published documents," University of Cambridge, December 27, 2004, www.ccc.de/congress/2004/fahrplan/files/316-hidden-data-slides.pdf.

77 *"The report was not final..."* James Bone and Nicholas Blanford, "UN office doctored report on murder of Hariri," *Times* of London, October 22, 2005; Michael Young, Assad's dilemma, *International Herald Tribune*, October 28, 2005. The report is available on the *Washington Post* web site: www.washingtonpost.com/wp-srv/world/syria/mehlis.report.doc.

78 *"In particular, when the change..."* Stephen Shankland and Scott Ard, "Hidden text shows SCO prepped lawsuit against BofA," *ZDNet*, March 4, 2004. news.zdnet.com/2100-3513_22-5170073.html.

79 *"According to the Evening Standard..."* Joe Murphy, "Campbell aide and team behind the dodgy dossier," *Evening Standard (London)*, June 25, 2003.

80 *"But it turns out that..."* Tuomas Aura, Thomas A. Kuhn, and Michael Roe, "Scanning electronic documents for personally identifiable information," *WPES '06*, October 30, 2006, 41–49.

83 *"One of the earliest triumphs..."* Thomas Stockham, "Restoration of Old Acoustic Recordings by means of Digital Signal Processing," *Audio Engineering Society*, 1971.

83 *"A special camera..."* The Canon EOS-1 SLR offers this option. See "Original Image Verification System," www.canon.com/technology/canon_tech/category/35mm.html.

84 *"Congress outlawed such virtual kiddie..."* Child Pornography Protection Act of 1996 (CPPA), 18 U.S.C. 2256(8)(B).

84 *"If a digital camera has..."* David Pogue, "Breaking the myth of megapixels," *New York Times*, February 8, 2007.

93 *"Some documents created with Word 2007..."* See, for example, Shan Wang, "New 'Word' frustrates users," *Harvard Crimson*, November 26, 2007.

93 *"The world is about open standards..."* Massachusetts Verdict: MS Office Formats Out, eWeek.com, www.eweek.com/article2/0,1895,1863060,00.asp.

94 *"Microsoft says they disagree and..."* Robert Weisman, "Microsoft fights bid to drop Office software," *Boston Globe*, September 14, 2005.

94 *"Quinn suspected 'Microsoft money and..."* www.groklaw.net/article.php?story=20060123132416703.

94 *"Nonetheless, other software companies would..."* Commonwealth of Massachusetts, Information Technology Division web site, page on "OpenDocument File Format."

97 *"During World War I, the German..."* D. Kahn, *The Codebreakers*, Scribner, 1996.

97    *"The first letters of the..."* Adam McLean, ed., *The Steganographia of Johannes Trithemius*, Magnum Opus Hermetic Sourceworks, Edinburgh, 1982.

99    *"Who uses steganography today..."* Jack Kelley, "Terror groups hide behind web encryption," *USA Today*, February 5, 2001. See also Farhad Manjoo, "The case of the missing code," Salon.com, July 17, 2002.

99    *"But most of the drives..."* Simson Garfinkel and Abhi Shelat, "Remembrance of Data Passed: A Study of Disk Sanitization Procedures," *IEEE Security and Privacy*, January/February 2003, 17–27.

102    *"The Federal Trade Commission now..."* Federal Trade Commission, 16 CFR Part 682, Disposal of Consumer Report Information and Records.

102    *"2007 Massachusetts Law about security breaches."* Commonwealth of Massachusetts, Chapter 82 of the Acts of 2007, "An act relative to security freezes and notification of data breaches," Chapter 93I.

103    *"A researcher bought ten cell..."* Larry Magid, "Betrayed by a cell phone," *CBS News*, August 30, 2006.
www.cbsnews.com/stories/2006/08/30/tech/main1949206.shtml.

105    *"Mocking the project's grand ambitions..."* Robin McKie and Vanessa Thorpe, *Guardian Unlimited*, March 3, 2002; The BBC Domesday Project web site at www.atsf.co.uk/dottext/domesday.html.

106    *"The data was recovered, though..."* Jeffrey Darlington, Andy Finney, and Adrian Pearce, "Domesday redux: The rescue of the BBC Domesday Project videodiscs," *Ariadne*, No. 36, www.ariadne.ac.uk/issue36/tna/; see also www.domesday1986.com.

106    *"The recovered modern Domesday Book..."* www.atsf.co.uk/dottext/domesday.html.

106    *"Even the data files of..."* www.domesdaybook.co.uk/index.html.

# Chapter 4

109    *"'It's something magic.'"* Eva Wolchover, "Web reconnects cousins cut off by Iron Curtain," *Boston Herald*, December 18, 2007; "Web post reunites cousins after 70 years," *Associated Press Online*, December 19, 2007; Email from Sasha Berkovich.

112    *"It was amusing to know..."* www.google.com/intl/en/press/zeitgeist2007/mind.html.

115    *"The reporter then published an..."* Alex Berenson, "Lilly said to play down risk of top pill," *New York Times*, December 17, 2006; Alex Berenson, "Drug files show maker promoted unapproved use," *New York Times*, December 18, 2006.

117    *"'Limiting the fora available to...'"* U.S. District Court, Eastern District of New York, Zyprexa Litigation, 07-CV-0504, In re Injunction, I, IV.F, February 13, 2007.

119  *"It appeared in the* Atlantic Monthly..." Vannevar Bush, "As we may think," *Atlantic Monthly,* July 1945.

120  *"There is no practical obstacle..."* H.G. Wells, "The idea of a permanent world encylopaedia," in *World Brain,* Methuen, 1938, 60–61. Available online at sherlock.sims.berkeley.edu/wells/world_brain.html.

122  *"Speaking to the Association of..."* Eric Schmidt, "Technology is Making Marketing Accountable," speech before the Association of National Advertisers, October 8, 2005; available at www.google.com/press/podium/ana.html.

122  *"That's just a bit more..."* www.ericdigests.org/2002-2/hidden.htm.

124  *"For example, after 9/11, a..."* "Information that was once available," BBC News Online, Intelligence data pulled from web sites, October 5, 2001.

125  *"Because the pages had been..."* Chris Sherman, "Deleted "Sensitive" Information Still Available via Google," Search Engine Watch, October 9, 2001.

131  *"'The Anatomy of a Large-Scale...'"* infolab.stanford.edu/~backrub/google.html.

131  *"'Modern Information Retrieval: A Brief Overview'"* IEEE Data Engineering Bulletin, 24(4), pp. 35–43, 2001.

131  *"'The Most Influential Paper Gerald...'"* "Library Trends," Spring 2004. findarticles.com/p/articles/mi_m1387/is_4_52/ai_n7074022.

136  *"On March 19, 2005, ..."* According to Kinderstart's Complaint for Injunctive and Declaratory Relief and Damages, U.S. District Court, Northern District of California, San Jose Division, Case No. C 06-2057 RS, March 17, 2006; available at blog.ericgoldman.org/archives/kinderstartgooglecomplaint.pdf.

136  *"Google's public description of its..."* Google's webmaster help center, "Little or no original content." www.google.com/support/webmasters/bin/answer.py?answer=66361.

136  *"Plaintiff KinderStart contends that..."* "Google's motion to dismiss Kinderstart lawsuit," quoted by Eric Goldman. blog.ericgoldman.org/archives/2006/05/kinderstart_v_g.htm.

136  *"'PageRank,' claimed KinderStart..." Kinderstart.com LLC, on behalf of itself and all others similarly situated, v. Google,* U.S. District Court for the Northern District of California, Case C 06-2057 JF (RS), opinion of Judge Jeremy Fogel, July 13, 2006.

137  *"The page Google indexed was..."* Matt Cutts blog, "Gadgets, Google, and SEO, Ramping up on international webspam," February 4, 2006. www.mattcutts.com/blog/ramping-up-on-international-webspam/.

137  *"But a coding trick caused..."* "BMW given Google 'death penalty,'" *BBC News,* February 6, 2006. news.bbc.co.uk/1/hi/technology/4685750.stm.

137  *"Don't deceive your users or..."* Google Webmaster Guidelines. www.google.com/support/webmasters/bin/answer.py?hl=en&answer=35769.

138  *"More than 90% of online..." Digital Footprints,* "Online identity management and search in the age of transparency," Pew Internet and American Life Project, 2007, www.pewinternet.org, p. 5.

139  *"He published a paper about..."* Brian Pinkerton, "Finding What People Want,"
*Second International WWW Conference.* thinkpink.com/bp/WebCrawler/
WWW94.html.

139  *"The 1997 academic research paper..."* Sergey Brin and Lawrence Page, "The
Anatomy of a Large-Scale Hypertextual Web Search Engine," Stanford
University Computer Science Department, 1997.
infolab.stanford.edu/~backrub/google.html.

139  *"To this day, Stanford University..."* U.S. Patent #6285999, "Method for node
ranking in a linked database," Filed January 9, 1998 and issued September 4,
2001. Inventor: Lawrence Page; Assignee: The Board of Trustees of the Leland
Stanford Junior University.

141  *"Sounding every bit like a..."* Danny Sullivan, "GoTo Going Strong, Search
Engine Watch," July 1, 1998. http://searchenginewatch.com/showPage.
html?page=2166331.

142  *"Microsoft's MSN offered a creative..."* Verne Kopytoff, "Searching for profits:
Amid tech slump, more portals sell search engine results to highest bidder," *San
Francisco Chronicle,* June 18, 2001.

142  *"'We can't afford to have...'"* Kopytoff, "Searching for profits."

142  *"If they are going to stuff..."* Commercial Alert Files Complaint Against Search
Engines for Deceptive Ads, *Commercial Alert* web site, July 16, 2001.
www.commercialalert.org/news/news-releases/2001/07/commercial-
alert-files-complaint-against-search-engines-for-deceptive-ads.

144  *"Google's technology was brilliant, ..."* A good history of the development of the
search business is John Battelle, *The Search,* Portfolio, 2005.

145  *"Among the items and services..."* AdWords Advertising Policies, Content Policy.

145  *"But bias can be coded..."* Eric Goldman, "Search Engine Bias and the Demise of
Search Engine Utopianism," *Yale Journal of Law & Technology,* 2005–2006.
Available at SSRN: http://ssrn.com/abstract=893892.

146  *"In so doing, the company..."* Laurie J. Flynn, "Amazon says technology, not
ideology, skewed results," *New York Times,* March 20, 2006.

146  *"Only 12% of the first..."* "Different Engines, Different Results," A Research
Study by Dogpile.com in collaboration with researchers from Queensland
University of Technology and the Pennsylvania State University, 2007. (Dogpile
offers a Metasearch engine, so the results of the study make a case for the
usefulness of its product. Although the study could be questioned on that
ground, the report fully details its methodology, so an independent researcher
could attempt to test or duplicate the results.)

146  *"An industry research study found..."* iProspect Search Engine User Behavior
Study, April 2006; available at www.iprospect.com/premiumPDFs/WhitePaper_
2006_SearchEngineUserBehavior.pdf.

147  *"A study of queries to..."* B.J. Jansen, A. Spink, and T. Saracevic, 2000. "Real life,
real users, and real needs: A study and analysis of user queries on the web,"
*Information Processing & Management, 36*(2), 207–227.

147  *"Google's experience is even more..."* Private correspondence to Hal Abelson.

147  *"36% of users thought seeing..."* iProspect study, page 4.

149  *"Google proclaims of its Page..."* http://www.google.com/intl/en/corporate/
tenthings.html.

150  *"In his book,* Ambient Findability..." Peter Morville, *Ambient Findability,*
O'Reilly Media, 2005.

150  *"Marek is now facing three..."* blogoscoped.com/archive/2007-09-11-n78.
html.

151  *"Montcrief's innocent site fell to..."* *The Search,* Chapter 7.

152  *"Google in particular was unavailable..."* "China blocking Google," BBC News,
September 2, 2002, news.bbc.co.uk/2/hi/technology/2231101.stm; "Google fights
Chinese ban," *BBC News,* September 3, 2002, news.bbc.co.uk/1/hi/
technology/2233229.stm.

152  *"The company reluctantly decided not..."* "China, Google News and source
inclusion," *The Official Google Blog,* September 27, 2004. googleblog.
blogspot.com/2004/09/china-google-news-and-source-inclusion.html.

153  *"How would it balance its..."* www.google.com/corporate/.

153  *"'It is unfair and smacks...'"* Peter Pollack, "Congress grills tech firms over China
dealings," *Arstechnica,* February 15, 2006. arstechnica.com/news.ars/
post/20060215-6192.html.

153  *"'While removing search results is...'"* Kevin J. Delaney, "Google launches
service in China," *Wall Street Journal,* January 25, 2006.

153  *"A disappointed libertarian commentator countered..."* Pamela Geller Oshry,
quoted by Hiawatha Bray, "Google China censorship fuels calls for U.S. boycott,"
*Boston Globe,* January 28, 2006.

154  *"'I cannot understand how your...'"* Verne Kopytoff, "Lawmakers bash top high-
tech firms for yielding to China," *San Francisco Chronicle,* February 16, 2006.

154  *"One researcher tested the Chinese..."* blogoscoped.com/archive/
2006-06-18-n85.html.

156  *"You're here as a volunteer; ..."* Quoted in *The Search,* p. 228.

156  *"Public image-matching services include..."* Ray Blitstein, "Image analysis
changing way we search, shop, share photos," *San Jose Mercury News,*
April 30, 2007.

156  *"Chinese dissidents were imprisoned when..."* Ariana Eunjung Cha and Sam
Diaz, "Advocates sue Yahoo in Chinese torture case," *Washington Post,* April 19,
2007.

159  *"And competition there is..."* "Summary of Antitrust Analysis: Google's Proposed
Acquisition of DoubleClick," Microsoft memorandum available at Google Watch,
December 24, 2007. googlewatch.eweek.com/content/google_vs_microsoft/
meet_google_search_giant_monopolist_extraordinaire.html.

159 *"For that, we will launch..."* Kevin J. O'Brien, "Europeans weigh plan on Google challenge," *International Herald Tribune*, January 18, 2006. "Attack of the Eurogoogle," *Economist.com*, March 9, 2006.

159 *"A year later, Germany dropped..."* The Theseus image and video search project, Pandia Search Engine News, November 28, 2007. `http://www.pandia.com/sew/570-theseus.html`.

# Chapter 5

161 *"'It used to be,' the..."* Congressional Record, September 13, 2001, p. S9357.

161 *"'The technology has outstripped...'"* Quoted by John Schwartz, "Disputes on electronic messages: Encryption takes on new urgency," *New York Times*, September 25, 2001.

161 *"'I just assumed,' he said..."* Schwartz, "Disputes," *NYT*.

162 *"If you don't try, you're..."* Schwartz, "Disputes," *NYT*.

162 *"'We are not working on...'"* Declan McCullagh, "Senator backs off backdoors," *Wired News*, October 17, 2001.

162 *"Senator Gregg's proposal was a..."* "Whoever, after January 31, 2000, sells in interstate or foreign commerce any encryption product that does not include features or functions permitting duly authorized persons immediate access to plaintext or immediate decryption capabilities shall be imprisoned for not more than 5 years, fined under this title, or both." 105th Congress, H.R. 695. House Report 104–108, part 4 "Security and Freedom Through Encryption (SAFE) Act of 1997," Section 2803.

163 *"The report concluded that on..."* National Research Council, *Cryptography's Role in Securing the Information Society*, Kenneth W. Dam and Herbert S. Lin, Editors, National Academy Press, 1996.

163 *"FBI Director Louis Freeh testified..."* Testimony of FBI Director Louis Freeh, before the Senate Judiciary Committee Hearing on Encryption, United States Senate, Washington, D. C., July 9, 1997.

164 *"'The question,' posed MIT's Ron Rivest, ..."* Statement by Ron Rivest at MIT Press Forum on Encryption, MIT, April 7, 1998.

165 *"If anyone wishes to decipher..."* Suetonius, *The Lives of the Caesars: The Life of Julius Caesar*, Chapter 56, from the Loeb Classical Library, 1913.

166 *"The Caesar cipher is really..."* Actually, the Romans didn't use J, U, or W, so Caesar had only 22 shifts available.

166 *"Parts of this manual, which..."* Folio 30 *verso* of Peterhouse MS. 75.I. For the dispute on the authorship, see Derek J. Price, *The Equatorie of the Planetis*, Cambridge University Press, 1955, and Kari Anne Rand Schmidt, *The Authorship of The Equatorie of the Planetis*, Chaucer Studies XIX, D.S. Brewer, 1993.

171 *"Babbage never published his technique, ..."* Babbage's contribution remained unknown until 1970.

172 *"There is a deep relation..."* Claude Shannon, "Communication Theory of Secrecy Systems," *Bell System Technical Journal*, Vol. 28-4 (1949), pp. 656–715.

173 *"The Soviet KGB fell victim..."* www.nsa.gov/publications/publi00039.cfm.

174 *"The messages included correspondence between..."* Rossella Lorenzi, *Discovery News*, 2007.

174 *"Although Babbage and Kasiski had..."* "A new cipher code," *Scientific American Supplement*, v.58 (January 27, 1917), p. 61. From the Proceedings of the Engineers Club of Philadelphia. [Baker Business Library, Historical Collection, By appointment only]. Available online at www.nku.edu/~christensen/Sciamericansuppl17January1917.pdf.

175 *"In the absence of a..."* As coined by Charlie Kaufman, Radia Perlman, and Mike Speciner in *Network Security: Private Communication in a Public World*, Prentice-Hall, 1995, p. 40.

176 *"In 2001, however, WEP was..."* Nikita Borisov, Ian Goldberg, and David Wagner, *Intercepting Mobile Communications: The Insecurity of 802.11*, Proceedings of the Seventh Annual International Conference on Mobile Computing and Networking, July 16–21, 2001.

176 *"A spokesman for Texas Instruments, ..."* "RFID crack raises spector [sic] of weak encryption: Steal a car—and the gas needed to get away," *Computerworld*, March 17, 2005; available at www.computerworld.com/mobiletopics/mobile/technology/story/0,10801,100459,00.html.

177 *"The Flemish linguist Auguste Kerckhoffs..."* Auguste Kerckhoffs, "La cryptographie militaire," *Journal des sciences militaires*, Vol. IX, pp. 5–38, January 1883, pp. 161–191, February 1883. Available on the Web at www.petitcolas.net/fabien/kerckhoffs/crypto_militaire_1.pdf.

177 *"Claude Shannon restated Kerckhoffs's Principle..."* This adage has come to be known as Shannon's maxim. Shannon, "Communication Theory of Secrecy Systems," 662ff.

177 *"The method was kept secret..."* Jeffrey A. Bloom, Ingemar J. Cox, Ton Kalker, Jean-Paul M.G. Linnartz, Matthew L. Miller, and C. Brendan Traw, "Copy Protection for DVD Video," Proceedings of the IEEE, Vol. 87, No. 7, July 1999, pp. 1267–1276.

178 *"A newer standard, Advanced Encryption..."* Federal Information Processing Standards Publication 197, Advanced Encryption Standard. csrc.nist.gov/publications/fips/fips197/fips-197.pdf.

179 *"This is what the paper..."* Whitfield Diffie and Martin Hellman, "New directions in cryptography," IEEE Transactions on Information Theory, November 1976. An important piece of the puzzle was contributed by Berkeley graduate student Ralph Merkle, and today Diffie, Hellman, and Merkle are typically given joint credit for the innovation.

179 *"It was revealed in 1997..."* James Ellis, "The History of Non-secret Encryption;" available at www.cesg.gov.uk/site/publications/media/ellis.pdf.

181 *"The key agreement protocol starts..."* The particular one-way computation of Diffie and Hellman is the remainder of $x^y$ when divided by $p$, where $p$ is an industry-standard, fixed prime number.

185 *"One can multiply numbers in..."* To be precise, multiplication of $n$-bit numbers can be done in slightly super-linear time, while fastest factoring algorithms take time exponential in the cube root of $n$.

186 *"Anyone who wants to use..."* This idea, and the use of the word "certificate," were introduced by Loren Kohnfelder in his 1978 MIT bachelor's thesis. Loren M. Kohnfelder, "Towards a Practical Public-key Cryptosystem," MIT S.B. Thesis, May 1978 (unpublished).

187 *"At first, public-key encryption..."* As quoted in "The Science of Secrecy: The birth of the RSA cipher." www.channel4.com/science/microsites/S/secrecy/page5b.html.

187 *"They simply did not appreciate..."* Conversation between Bobby Ray Inman and Hal Abelson, February 1995. Shortly after RSA appeared, the NSA asked MIT not to publish the paper, but MIT refused, citing academic freedom.

189 *"This is analogous to driftnet..."* Testimony of Philip Zimmermann to Subcommittee for Economic Policy, Trade, and the Environment, U.S. House of Representatives, October 12, 1993.

190 *"In Zimmermann's own words..."* Zimmermann, Congressional testimony, October 12, 1993.

191 *"For example, the Chinese government..."* Regulation of Commercial Encryption Codes, China State Council Directive No. 273.

191 *"In 2007, the United Kingdom enacted..."* Part 3, Section 49 of the Regulation of Investigatory Powers Act.

191 *"But it is up-to-date..."* Patrick Radden Keefe, *Chatter: Dispatches from the Secret World of Global Eavesdropping*, Random House, 2005.

192 *"A series of executive orders..."* The Protect America Act of 2007, §1927 of the Foreign Intelligence Surveillance Act

192 *"Such developments may stimulate encryption..."* Patricia J. Williams, "The protect Alberto Gonzales Act of 2007," *The Nation*, August 27, 2007.

193 *"On the one hand, encryption technology..."* www.strategypage.com/dls/articles/2004850.asp.

# Chapter 6

195 *"But, he warned, once the..."* Andersen's story is described in Ashbel S. Green, "Music Goliath unloads on wrong David," *The Oregonian*, July 1, 2007, at www.oregonlive.com. Further details can be found in the lawsuit *Andersen v. Atlantic Recording Corporation et al.*, case number 3:2007cv00934, U.S. District Court of Oregon at Portland, filed June 22, 2007, at www.ilrweb.com.

196 *"When they could not produce..."* Janet Newton, "RIAA named in first class action," *p2planet*, August 16, 2007, at www.p2pnet.net/story/13077. The actual complaint can be found at www.ilrweb.com, Amended Complaint 070816.

196 *"The RIAA has filed more..."* Cited in Joshua Freed (Associated Press), "RIAA: Expect More Music Download Suits," *lexisone*, October 4, 2007, at www.lexisone.com/news/ap/ap100407e.html.

196 *"There's even a web site, ..."* Ray Beckerman, "How the RIAA Litigation Process Works," info.riaalawsuits.us/howriaa_printable.htm. Also see the declaration of Carlos Linares, RIAA VP for Anti-Piracy Legal Affairs, U.S. District Court, MA, filed as part of many John Doe lawsuits—for example, U.S. District Court of Massachusetts, Case 1:07-cv-10834-NG, filed May 2, 2007; available at www.ilrweb.com, 070502LineresDeclaration. The RIAA's p2plawsuits.com web site was visited August 3, 2007.

197 *"But we also realize that..."* Quoted in Dennis Roddy, "The Song Remains the Same," *Pittsburgh Post-Gazette*, September 14, 2003, at www.post-gazette.com.

197 *"Besides Andersen, other snared 'dolphin'..."* Lowell Vickers, "Family sued by recording industry," *Rockmart Journal*, Rockmart Georgia, April 24, 2006, news.mywebpal.com. Also *Walter v. Paladuk*, U.S. District Court of Eastern Michigan described in "RIAA Sues Stroke Victim in Michigan," recordingindustryvspeople.blogspot.com. Also Eric Bangemann, "I Sue Dead People," *Ars Technica*, February 4, 2005, arstechnica.com/news.ars/post/20050204-4587.html.

197 *"For defendants who can prove..."* The fines (as of 2007) are stipulated in 17 USC 504 (2007).

198 *"Said the RIAA's lawyer after..."* David Kravets, "RIAA Juror: 'We Wanted to Send a Message'," *Wired Blog Network*, October 9, 2007, at blog.wired.com/27bstroke6/2007/10/riaa-juror-we-w.html.

199 *"Without a commercial motive, there..."* For a detailed discussion of the increasing penalties up through 1999, see Lydia Pallas Loren, "Digitization, Commodification, Criminalization: The Evolution of Criminal Copyright Infringement and the Importance of the Willfulness Requirement," *Washington University Law Quarterly*, 77:835, 1999.

200 *"The Boston U.S. Attorney issued..."* Quoted in Josh Hartmann, "Student Indicted on Piracy Charges," *The Tech*, April 8, 1994, at the-tech.mit.edu/V114/N19/piracy.19n.html.

200 *"He cited Congressional testimony from..."* United States District Court District of Massachusetts, 871 F. Supp. 535, December 28, 1994.

201 *"Its supporters argued that NET..."* See the statement before the Senate by Senator Leahy of Vermont, Congressional Record: July 12, 1999 (Senate) page S8252-S8254; available at cyber.law.harvard.edu/openlaw/DVD/dmca/cr12jy99s.txt.

203 *"A year later, after an..."* The full story has a lot of legal twists and turns. Even after declaring bankruptcy and having its assets bought, Napster survives today as a pay-per-track music service. For a complete timeline, see Stephanie

Hornung, "Napster: The Life and Death of a P2P Innovator," *Berkeley Intellectual Property Weblog*, January 15, 2003, at journalism.berkeley.edu/projects/ biplog/archive/000428.html.

204 *"Systems incorporating peer-to-peer communication..."* Steve Crocker, "Host Software," *Network Working Group Request for Comment: Number 1*, April 7, 1969, at www.apps.ietf.org/rfc/rfc1.html.

204 *"As one 2001 review gushed, ..."* Clay Shirky, Kelly Truelov, Rael Dornfest, and Lucas Gonze, *2001 P2P Networking Overview*, O'Reilly, 2001. The $500 million investment estimate is quoted at www.oreilly.com/catalog/p2presearch/ summary/index.html.

205 *"But the success of decentralized..."* See, for example, Hari Balakrishnan, M. Frans Kaashoek, David Karger, Robert Morris, and Ion Stoic, "Looking Up Data in P2P Systems," *Communications of the ACM*, February 2003/Vol. 46, No. 2; also Stephanos Androutsellis-Theotokis and Diomidis Spinellis, "A Survey of Peer-to-Peer Content Distribution Technologies," *ACM Computing Surveys*, Vol. 36, No. 4, December 2004, pp. 335–371.

206 *"In October 2001, the RIAA..."* The complaint is *MGM etc. al. v. Grokster et al.*, at www.eff.org/IP/P2P/MGM_v_Grokster/20011002_mgm_v_grokster_ complaint.pdf.

206 *"'I say to you that the...'"* Testimony of MPAA President Jack Valenti in Hearings on the Home Recording of Copyrighted Works before the Subcommittee on Courts, Civil Liberties, and the Administration of Justice of the Committee on the Judiciary, House of Representatives, April, 12, 1982, at cryptome.org/ hrcw-hear.htm.

206 *"In a narrow 5 to 4..."* *Sony Corp. of America v. Universal City Studios, Inc.*, 464 U.S. 417 (1984).

207 *"In April 2003, the Central California..."* U.S. District Court Judge Stephen V. Wilson, at www.eff.org/IP/P2P/MGM_v_Grokster/030425_order_on_ motions.pdf.

207 *"In reaction, the RIAA immediately..."* RIAA News Release, June 25, 2003, "Recording Industry to Begin Collecting Evidence and Preparing Lawsuits Against File [sic]," at riaa.com.

207 *"In short, from the evidence..."* www.eff.org/IP/P2P/MGM_v_Grokster/ 20040819_mgm_v_grokster_decision.pdf.

207 *"In June 2005, the Court..."* *MGM Studios v. Grokster, Ltd.*, 545 U.S. 913 (2005).

208 *"Many people certainly thought so, ..."* From testimony by Chairman and CEO of the Walt Disney Company, President Michael Eisner, in hearings on Protecting Content in a Digital Age, U.S. Senate Committee on Commerce, Science, and Transportation, February 28, 2002, 37.

208 *"That's more than a trillion..."* Revenues were $33.6 billion in 2006, per news.bbc.co.uk/2/hi/entertainment/4639066.stm.

208 *"The company that bought Replay's..."* See Fred von Lohmann and Wendy Seltzer, "Death by DMCA," *IEEE Spectrum Online*, June 2006, at www.spectrum. ieee.org/jun06/3673.

209 *"Non-coincidentally, in 2002, the..."* Turner Broadcasting System CEO Jamie Kellner, interviewed in *Cableworld*, April 29, 2002, at www.2600.com/news/050102-files/jamie-kellner.txt.

209 *"In 1993, a U.S. Federal Circuit..."* MAI *Systems Corp. v. Peak Computer, Inc.*, 991 F.2d 511 (9th Cir. 1993). The 9th Circuit's rigid interpretation of copying here has been widely criticized by legal scholars, but it has also been the basis for subsequent court rulings. For a discussion, see Joseph P. Liu, "Owning Digital Copies: Copyright Law and the Incidents of Copy Ownership," *42 Wm. & Mary L. Rev.* 1245, 1255–78 (2001). The copyright statute was modified in 1998 to also permit copying the code into memory for the purpose of maintenance or repair (17 USC 117).

209 *"A 1995 report from the Department..."* Bruce A. Lehman, *Intellectual Property and the National Information Infrastructure: The Report of the Working Group on Intellectual Property Rights*, 1995, pp. 64–66, at www.uspto.gov/web/offices/com/doc/ipnii/.

210 *"Similarly, if Fortress prepares music files..."* See *Adobe LiveCycle Enterprise Suite*, at www.adobe.com/products/livecycle/. Also *Windows Media Rights Manager 10.1.2 SDK*, at msdn2.microsoft.com/en-us/library/bb649422.aspx.

210 *"DRM systems are widely used..."* One such system is *XrML* (eXtensible rights Markup Language), based on work originally done at Xerox Palo Alto Research Center and licensed by Microsoft. See www.xrml.org.

211 *"Encrypting the files helps, but..."* For an example, see "Microsoft Windows Media copy protection broken," *informity*, September 12, 2006, at informitv.com/articles/2006/09/12/microsoftwindowsmedia/. As the article quotes a Microsoft representative, "Microsoft has long stated that no DRM system is impervious to circumvention—a position our content partners are aware of as well." PDF decrypters are readily found on the Web. We'd provide links in this note, but our publisher is wary of possible DMCA violations.

211 *"This basic technique was worked..."* Some of this early work is S. T. Kent, "Protecting externally supplied software in small computers," Ph.D. dissertation, Massachusetts Institute of Technology. Dept. of Electrical Engineering and Computer Science, 1981. Also S. R. White and L. Comerford, "ABYSS: An Architecture for Software Protection," *IEEE Trans. Softw. Eng.* 16, 6 (June 1990), 619–629. Also Ryoichi Mori and Masaji Kawahara, "Superdistribution: The Concept and the Architecture," *Transactions of the IEICE*, Vol. E 73, No. 7, July 1990, pp. 1133–1146.

211 *"The required chip, called a Trusted..."* See the organization's web site at https://www.trustedcomputinggroup.org. The original name of this organization was the Trusted Computing Platform Alliance, and the original members were Intel, Microsoft, HP, Compaq, and IBM.

211 *"One industry estimate shows that..."* Shane Rau, "IDC Executive Brief: The Trusted Computing Platform Emerges and Industry's First Comprehensive Approach to IT Security," February 2006, at https://www.trustedcomputinggroup.org/news/Industry_Data/IDC_448_Web.pdf.

212 *"As one security researcher warned: ..."* Talk by Lucky Green, at the Berkeley Conference on the State of Digital Rights Management, February 28, 2003, reported in transcript at www.law.berkeley.edu/institutes/bclt/drm/ trans/drm-2-28-p2.htm.

213 *"A world of trusted systems..."* Jonathan Zittrain, in *The Future of the Internet and How to Stop It*, argues that the viability of the Internet as a "generative platform" is being threatened by the lock-in motivated by concerns for security.

213 *"Windows Vista implements this in..."* See Dave Marsh, *Output Content Protection and Windows Vista*, April 27, 2005, at www.microsoft.com/ whdc/device/stream/output_protect.mspx.

213 *"In the words of one..."* Bruce Schneier, "The Futility of Digital Copy Prevention," *CRYPTO-GRAM*, May 15, 2001, at www.schneier.com/crypto-gram-0105.html.

214 *"A New York U.S. District..."* *Universal City Studios, Inc. v. Corley*, 273 F.3d 429 (2d Cir. 2001) decision available at www.eff.org/IP/Video/MPAA_DVD_cases/ 20011128_ny_appeal_decision.html.

214 *"Alternative proposals that would have..."* Defeated alternative versions were the "Digital Copyright Clarification and Technology Act of 1997," S. 1146 (Ashcroft), 105th Cong. (1997) in the Senate, and the "Digital Era Copyright Enhancement Act," H.R. 3048, 105th Cong. (1997) (Boucher).

215 *"That is, allowing anti-circumvention devices..."* Letter from U.S. Rep. Barney Frank to Hal Abelson, July 6, 1998.

215 *"There are many published explanations..."* For example, Matt Blaze, "Cryptology and physical security: Rights amplification in master-keyed mechanical locks," *IEEE Security and Privacy*, March/April 2003, at www.crypto.com/papers/mk.pdf.

215 *"Indeed, AT&T threatened legal action..."* David Kravitz, "Unlocking Your iPhone is Legal; Distributing the Hack, Maybe Not," *Wired Blog Network*, August 27, 2007, at blog.wired.com/27bstroke6/2007/08/to-unlock-the-i.html. The Librarian of Congress's ruling is "Exemption to Prohibition on Circumvention of Copyright Protection Systems for Access Control Technologies," November 27, 2006, *Federal Register*, Vol. 71, No. 227. Rules and regulations, pp. 68472–68480. www.copyright.gov/fedreg/2006/71fr68472.html.

216 *"It took two years for the case..."* *Chamberlain v. Skylink*, 381 F.3d 1178 (Fed. Cir. 2004). Initial December 2002, DMCA complaint available at www.eff.org/ legal/cases/Chamberlain_v_Skylink/MotionSummJudgment.pdf.

216 *"The ruling was overturned on..."* *Lexmark International v. Static Control Components*, 387 F.3d 522 (6th Cir. 2004), at www.eff.org/legal/cases/ Lexmark_v_Static_Control/20041026_Ruling.pdf.

216 *"Had the appeals court not..."* *Storage Technology Corp. v. Custom Hardware Engineering & Consulting*, 2005 U.S. App. LEXIS 18131 (Fed. Cir. 2005), at fedcir.gov/opinions/04-1462.pdf.

217 *"Any company marketing a product..."* See www.dvdcca.org/.

217 *"Another start-up working on a..."* Rick Merritt, "Judge rules against DVD consortium," *EE Times*, March 29, 2007, at www.eetimes.com/news/latest/showArticle.jhtml?articleID=198701186.

218 *"In 2002, Congress considered a..."* This was the "Consumer Broadband and Digital Television Promotion Act," introduced by Senator Fritz Hollings (D-SC) in March 2002.

218 *"By outlawing technology for circumventing..."* Timothy B. Lee, "Circumventing Competition: The Perverse Consequences of the Digital Millennium Copyright Act," CATO Institute, Policy Analysis no. 564, March 21, 2006, at www.cato.org/pub_display.php?pub id=6025.

219 *"The relentless message is that..."* See www.koyaanasqatsi.org. Ironically, the film, which some people have praised as the greatest film ever made, was unavailable during most of the 1990s due to a copyright dispute.

219 *"The period of copyright was..."* The image from the *Centinel* is from microfilm in the Harvard University Library. The current law is available from the U.S. Copyright Office at www.copyright.gov/title17/circ92.pdf.

220 *"For digital satellite radio, you..."* See 17 USC §110(6), §121(a)(2), and §114.

221 *"In contrast, in an October..."* Pariser's testimony is quoted in: Eric Bangeman, "Sony BMG's chief anti-piracy lawyer: 'Copying' music you own is 'stealing'," *Ars technica*, October 2, 2007, at http://arstechnica.com/news.ars. When subsequently questioned about this, RIAA President Cary Sherman claimed that Pariser had "mis-spoken" and had misheard the question. (*NPR Talk of the Nation*, January 3, 2008.) The RIAA's legal advice on CD copying is at http://www.riaa.com/physicalpiracy.php. The *LA Times* survey is described in Charles Duhigg, "Is Copying a Crime? Well...," August 9, 2006, at www.latimes.com.

222 *"That resentment can easily grow..."* John Gilmore, "What's Wrong with Copy Protection," February 16, 2001, at www.toad.com/gnu/whatswrong.html.

222 *"As the president of the MPAA..."* Estimate from MPAA news release, June 21, 2007, "Lights ... camera ... busted!," available at www.mpaa.org/PressReleases.asp. The quotation is from MPAA President Dan Glickman, commenting in response to the 9th Circuit Court's ruling in *Grokster* (subsequently overturned), January 25, 2005, at www.riaa.com/newsitem.php/news_room.php.

223 *"In Jobs's view, a world..."* Steve Jobs, "Thoughts on Music," February 6, 2007, at http://www.apple.com/hotnews/thoughtsonmusic/.

223 *"Musicload asserted that DRM makes..."* "Die Nutzung von Musik für der Verbraucher erschweren und verhindern, dass sich der legale Download zum Massenmarkt entwickelt." Quoted in *Heise Online*, March 17, 2007, at www.heise.de/newsticker/meldung/86944.

223 *"Its director general claimed that..."* Bayley, quoted in Andrew Edgecliffe-Johnson, "Anti-piracy moves 'hurt sales'," *Financial Times*, November 20, 2007, at www.ft.com.

223 *"By the summer of 2007, ..."* "Apple Launches iTunes Plus: Higher Quality DRM-Free Tracks Now Available on the iTunes Store Worldwide," May 30, 2007, at

www.apple.com/pr/library/2007/05/30itunesplus.html. Also Ken Fisher, "Universal to track DRM-free music online via watermarking," August 15, 2007, at arstechnica.com/news.ars/post/20070815-universal-to-track-drm-free-music-online-via-watermarking.html.

223 *"The same perspective can apply..."* See D. Weitzner, H. Abelson, T. Berners-Lee, J. Feigenbaum, J. Hendler, and G. Sussman, "Information Accountability," MIT Comp. Sci. and Artificial Intelligence Lab Technical Report, No. 2007-34, June 13, 2007. Available at hdl.handle.net/1721.1/37600.

223 *"A few months later, even..."* Eliot Van Buskirk, "Some of Amazon's MP3 Tracks Contain Watermarks," *Wired Blog Network*, Sept. 25, 2007, at blog.wired.com/music/2007/09/some-of-amazons.html.

223 *"When Jobs made his February..."* Gregg Keizer, "Warner Chief Calls Jobs' DRM Fight 'Without Logic'," *Computerworld*, February 10, 2007.

224 *"Before the end of the..."* Jessica Mintz, "Warner offers DRM-free music on Amazon," *Associated Press*, December 28, 2007.

224 *"One plan links the service..."* "Universal Music Takes on iTunes," *Business Week News*, October 22, 2007, at www.businessweek.com/magazine/content/07_43/b4055048.htm?chan=rss_topStories_ssi_5.

224 *"New companies are emerging that..."* One example is Ruckus Network, which offers content from its catalog of music and videos to students on participating campuses, where the content is delivered as streaming media. See www.ruckusnetwork.com. One weakness of the model is its use of DRM—the music can be downloaded but not burned to CDs—but that might change with the increasing move toward DRM-free distribution.

224 *"People can make unlimited use..."* One such effort, a start-up with participants from Harvard Law School called Noank Media, is planning pilots with several Chinese universities.

224 *"Stimulating open sharing on the..."* For a thorough discussion of commons, and especially their relation to the digital environment, see Yochai Benkler, *The Wealth of Networks: How Social Production Transforms Markets and Freedom*, Yale University Press, 2006.

225 *"Success could pave the way..."* One example: Bruce Lehman, Undersecretary of Commerce during the Clinton administration and author of the copyright report mentioned in endnote 29, was a major architect of the DMCA. In a panel discussion held at McGill University on March 25, 2007, he admitted that "our Clinton administration policies didn't work out very well" and "our attempts at ... copyright control have not been successful," and he criticized the recording industry for their failure to adapt to the online marketplace. Video available at video.google.com/videoplay?docid=4162208056624446466.

226 *"At issue is the fact..."* The Google books library project is described at books.google.com/googlebooks/library.html. The lawsuits are described at Elinor Mills, *CNET News.com*, "Authors Guild Sues Google over library project," September 20, 2005, news.com.com/2100-1030 3-5875384.html; Alorie Gilbert, *CNET News.com*, "Publishers sue Google over book search project," October 19,

2005, news.com.com/Publishers+sue+Google+over+book+search+project/
2100-1030_3-5902115.html. The comment by Authors' Guild president Nick
Tayor appears in a debate over the issue held at the New York Public Library on
November 17, 2005. The transcript can be found at www.nypl.org/research/
calendar/imagesprog/google111705.pdf.

227 *"These were major controversial issues..."* In the U.S., details of these rights,
called *riparian rights*, differ from state to state. A seminal case in the West here
is *Strickler v. Colorado Springs*, 16 Colo. 61, 70, 26 P. 313, 316 (1891). We're
grateful to Danny Weitzner for pointing out the connection between information
and water.

227 *"From ancient times, property rights..."* For a discussion from the perspective of
the 1920s, see Hiram L. Jome, "Property in the Air as Affected by the Airplane
and the Radio," *The Journal of Land & Public Utility Economics*, Vol. 4, No. 3.
(August 1928), pp. 257–272. "The Latin common law maxim, formulated in the
early part of the sixteenth century, [was] *Cuius est solum, eius est usque ad
caelum* (He who owns the soil, owns it up to the sky)." Jome discusses the
example of the owner of the "Cackle Corner Poultry Farm," who complained to
the U.S. Postmaster General about low-flying mail planes frightening his hens
and lowering egg production. The U.S. Air Commerce Act of 1926 nationalized
the navigable airspace (see 49 USC §40103). It's intriguing to compare this
"creation of a new national resource" with the almost simultaneous
nationalization of the spectrum by the Radio Act of 1927, as described in
Chapter 8, "Bits in the Air."

227 *"Congress forestalled the growth of..."* The parallel between air rights and
information rights is drawn by Larry Lessig in *Free Culture: How Big Media Uses
Technology and the Law to Lock Down Culture and Control Creativity* (Penguin,
2004), and before that by Keith Aoki in "(Intellectual) Property and Sovereignty:
Notes toward a Cultural Geography of Authorship," *Stanford Law Review*, Vol.
48, No. 5 (May 1996), pp. 1293–1355. Technology-stimulated controversies over
ancient doctrines of land ownership have also extended into modern times. In
1976, Ecuador, Colombia, Brazil, Congo, Zaire, Uganda, Kenya, and Indonesia
adopted the Bogota Declaration, which claimed the right of national sovereignty
for equatorial countries over portions of geostationary orbits over their territory.

# Chapter 7

229 *"She found his profile on..."* Erin Alberty, "A love that clicked," *Saginaw News*,
December 10, 2006.

229 *"Lester tricked her mother into..."* David N. Goodman, "Michigan girl heading
home from Jordan after attempted rendezvous with man she met on
MySpace.com," *Minneapolis Star-Tribune*, June 9, 2006.

230 *"Do you know where your..."* Julian Sher, "The not-so-long arm of the law,"
*USA Today*, May 1, 2007.

231  *"But on September 12, 2007, ..."* abclocal.go.com/wjrt/story?section=local&id=5653762.

231  *"The affair finally ended a..."* "MySpace Teen breaks up on 'Dr. Phil,'" WNEM.com, November 27, 2007. www.wnem.com/news/14702796/detail.html.

232  *"What are the rules of..."* John Perry Barlow, "The economy of ideas," May 1994. www.wired.com/wired/archive/2.03/economy.ideas_pr.html.

232  *"For example, when Pete Solis..."* Alison Hoover, "Keeping MySpace safe," *The Washington Times*, June 28, 2006.

233  *"If a government seeks to..."* This analysis, and Figure 7.1, are based on Jonathan Zittrain, Internet Points of Control, 43 B. C. L. Rev. 653 (2003).

235  *"The case of Cubby v. ..."* *Cubby v. CompuServe*, No. 90 Civ. 6571 (PKL), U.S. District Court for the Southern District of New York, October 29, 1991.

235  *"Sometimes, though, it takes away..."* Eugene Volokh, "Chilled Prodigy," *Reason*, August/September 1995.

236  *"The whole company was a..."* *Stratton Oakmont, Inc., and Daniel Porush, v. Prodigy Services Co.*, Index No. 31063/94, Supreme Court of New York, Nassau County, May 24, 1995.

237  *"To determine whether material is..."* U.S. Supreme Court, *Miller v. California*, 413 U.S. 15 (1973).

238  *"Bob and Carleen were not indicted..."* David Loundy, "Whose Standards? Whose Community?," *Chicago Daily Law Bulletin*, August 1, 1994, 5. www.loundy.com/CDLB/AABBS.html.

238  *"Shipping the bits was just..."* 1996 FED App. 0032P (6th Cir.), United States Court of Appeals, Sixth Circuit, *U.S. v. Robert Alan Thomas and Carleen Thomas*, decided and filed January 29, 1996. www.epic.org/free_speech/censorship/us_v_thomas.html.

239  *"On those Usenet newsgroups where..."* Philip Elmer-DeWitt, "On a screen near you," *Time Magazine*, July 3, 1995.

240  *"[Y]ou are trying to ward..."* John Perry Barlow, "A declaration of the independence of Cyberspace," February 8, 1996. homes.eff.org/~barlow/Declaration-Final.html.

241  *"As the most participatory form..."* *ACLU v. Reno*, Civil action no. 96-963, U.S. District Court for the Eastern District of Pennsylvania, June 12, 1996.

242  *"For example, he told adult..."* Tristan Louis, "Dirty business at CMU," *Internet World*, October 1995. www.tnl.net/who/bibliography/rimm/.

242  *"He published a book called..."* Casino Forum, March 1995.

243  *"'No provider or user of an...'"* CDA, §230(c)(1,2).

243  *"'We doubt,' wrote the appeals..."* Fair Housing Council of San Fernando Valley, et al., v. Roommates.com, 04-56916 and 04-57173, U.S. Court of Appeals for the Ninth Circuit, May 15, 2007.

244  *"One man who made it..."* www.cnn.com/US/OKC/daily/9512/12-30/index.html.

245 *"But the Good Samaritan provision..."* Kenneth M. Zeran v. America Online, *Inc.*, No. 97-1523, U.S. Court of Appeals for the Fourth Circuit, 129 F. 3d 327, November 12, 1997. legal.web.aol.com/decisions/dldefam/zeranapo.html.

245 *"Much as he may have..."* Zeran v. Diamond Broadcasting, Inc., U.S. Court of Appeals, Tenth Circuit, Nos. 98-6092 and 98-6094, filed January 28, 2000. legal.web.aol.com/decisions/dldefam/zerandia.html.

246 *"The court sided with AOL..."* Sidney Blumenthal and Jacqueline Jordan Blumenthal v. Matt Drudge and America Online, Inc., Civil action No. 97-1968, U.S. District Court for the District of Columbia, April 22, 1998. www.techlawjournal.com/courts/drudge/80423opin.htm.

247 *"The sequence of decisions 'thrusts...'"* Jane and John Doe v. America Online, Supreme Court of Florida, March 8, 2001, No. SC94355, dissent of J. Lewis. www.eff.org/legal/ISP_liability/CDA230/doe_v_aol.pdf.

249 *"Much as he was sympathetic..."* U.S. District Court for the Eastern District of Pennsylvania, *ACLU v. Gonzalez*, Civil Action 98-5591, Final Adjudication, March 22, 2007. www.paed.uscourts.gov/documents/opinions/07D0346P.pdf.

250 *"When she sent them away..."* "After 5 years on the Internet, Pathfinder reaches its final destination," *Cleveland Plain Dealer*, May 3, 1999.

250 *"In fact, the 'woman' sending..."* "Computer stalking case a first for California," *New York Times*, January 25, 1999; Valerie Alvord, "Cyberstalkers must beware of the e-law," *USA Today*, November 8, 1999.

250 *"Only when a message is..."* Brandenburg v. Ohio, 395 U.S. 444 (1969).

250 *"No danger flowing from speech..."* Whitney v. California, 274 U.S. 357, 375–76 (1927). Justice Holmes joined this opinion.

251 *"Reasonable jurists could, and did..."* Rene Sanchez, "Abortion foes' Internet site on trial; Doctors' fear of violence collides with radical opponents' rights to free speech," *Washington Post*, January 15, 1999; *Planned Parenthood of the Columbia/Willamette Inc., et al., v. American Coalition of Life Activists, et al.*, U.S. Court of Appeals for the Ninth Circuit, No. 04-35214, 422 F.3d 949. Decision dated September 6, 2005.

251 *"The '2005 Violence Against Women...'"* H.R. 3402, §113(a).

252 *"The Telecommunications Act of 1934..."* §223(a)(1)(B). www.dinf.ne.jp/doc/english/Us_Eu/ada_e/telcom_act/47/223.htm.

252 *"The law was challenged by..."* The Suggestion Box, Inc. v. Gonzales. Quotes from www.theanonymousemail.com/.

252 *"So the law is in force..."* TheAnonymousEmail.com successfully obtains clarification of Federal "Annoyance Law" in its suit against Attorney General Gonzalez and the Federal Government. www.hotstocked.com/news/suggestion-box-inc-SGTB-4182764.html.

253 *"The congressional sponsors have succumbed..."* RH 5319, 109th Congress, 2nd session, July 27, 2006.

253 *"But in the words of one..."* Alexander Meiklejohn, "Testimony on the Meaning of the First Amendment to the Senate Judiciary Subcommittee on Constitutional Rights," 1955.

254 *"In Thailand,* www.stayinvisible.com *is blocked..."* Examples from the OpenNet Initiative.

254 *"Google has even hired a..."* Christopher S. Rugaber, "Google ask feds to fight Internet censorship abroad," *Houston Chronicle,* June 22, 2007.

255 *"On October 30, 2000, the..."* Bill Alpert, Unholy gains, *Barron's,* October 30, 2000.

255 *"The Australian court agreed with Gutnick..."* High Court of Australia, *Dow Jones and Co. v. Gutnick* [2002] HCA 56 (December 10, 2002). www.austlii. edu.au/au/cases/cth/high_ct/2002/56.html#fn204.

255 *"Gutnick ultimately won an apology..."* "Gutnick settles suit," *The Advertiser,* November 12, 2004.

255 *"Is it possible that a rogue..."* Felicity Barringer, "Internet makes Dow Jones open to suit in Australia," *New York Times,* December 11, 2002.

255 *"By imposing death sentences..."* Warren Richey, "Once it's on the Web, whose law applies?," *Christian Science Monitor,* December 19, 2002.

256 *"'We should not allow a...'"* Court of Appeals for the Ninth Circuit, *Yahoo! Inc. v. La Ligue Contree Le Racisme et al.,* No. 01-17424, D. C. No. CV-00-21275,-JF, p. 505.

257 *"But as one British commentator..."* John Naughton, "The Germans get their Flickrs in a twist over 'censorship,'" *The Observer,* June 17, 2000.

# Chapter 8

259 *"The cable network CNN carried..."* www.cnn.com/2006/POLITICS/07/17/bush. tape/index.html.

259 *"Most broadcast stations bleeped out the expletive."* Jeff Jarvis, "America gives a shit," *Reason Magazine,* October 2006. www.reason.com/news/show/36821.html.

259 *"The FCC ruled that this..."* This seems a curiously self-referential standard, since the broadcast community gets to see and hear only what the FCC rulings permit.

259 *"It promised to fine and even..."* www.fcc.gov/eb/Orders/2004/FCC-04-43A1.html.

260 *"Have you ever tried to..."* www.fcc.gov/omnibus_remand/FCC-06-166.pdf.

260 *"A federal court reversed the..."* Fox Television Stations et al. v. Federal Communications Commission, U.S. Court of Appeals for the Second Circuit, Docket Nos. 06-1760-ag (L), 06-2750-ag (CON), 06-5358-ag (CON), June 4, 2007

260 *"Congress quickly introduced legislation to..."* The Protecting Children from Indecent Programming Act introduced by Senator John Rockefeller (D-WV) would effectively overturn the court decision on the *Fox Television Stations v. FCC,* pressesc.com/01184929170_senate_indecency_bill, Linda Greenhouse "Justices take up on-air vulgarity again," *New Your Times,* March 18, 2008.

260  *"Congress may have thought that..."* Notices of Apparent Liability and Memorandum Opinion and Order, March 15, 2006, FCC 06-17, 1.

260  *"The Supreme Court struck down..."* U.S. Supreme Court, *Miami Herald Publishing Company v. Tornillo*, 418 U.S. 241 (1974).

260  *"In spite of the spike..."* www.televisionwatch.org/junepollresults.pdf.

260  *"Because the broadcast media have..."* Opinion of Justice Stevens in *Federal Communications Commission v. Pacifica Foundation et al.*, 438 U.S. 726, 748.

261  *"Indeed, federal legislation has been..."* The Family and Consumer Choice Act of 2007 is cosponsored by Rep. Daniel Lipinski (D-IL) and Rep. Jeff Fortenberry (R-NE).

262  *"Lower Manhattan communicated for several..."* Peter Meyers, "In crisis zone, a wireless patch," *New York Times*, October 4, 2001.

263  *"The main job of the ship's..."* www.titanic-titanic.com/warnings.shtml.

263 *"Who would pay to send..."* The term "radio" became standard only after World War II.

264  *"A completely different ship reported..."* Karl Baarslag, *S O S to the Rescue*, Oxford University Press, 1935, 72.

265  *"Some people could 'catch the...'"* "Wireless melody jarred," *New York Times*, January 14, 1910, 2.

265  *"'When the world weeps together...'"* www.titanicinquiry.org/USInq/USReport/AmInqRepSmith01.php.

265  *"The Radio Act of 1912..."* An act to regulate radio communication, August 13, 1912, 1.

267  *"Sports broadcasting was born with..."* Erik Barnouw, *A Tower in Babel*, Oxford University Press, 1966, 69, 85.

267  *"The first five radio stations..."* Barnouw, 91, 104.

267  *"The number of radio receivers..."* "Asks radio experts to chart the ether," *New York Times*, February 28, 1922, 16.

267  *"Intercity sued Hoover to have..."* *Hoover v. Intercity Radio, Inc.*, No. 3766, Court of Appeals of District of Columbia, 52 App. D.C. 339, February 5, 1923.

267  *"The spectrum was 'a great...'"* Herbert Hoover, Speech to the first National Radio Conference (February 27, 1922), *Memoirs of Herbert Hoover, v. 2: The Cabinet and Presidency*, MacMillan, 1952, 140.

267  *"'[T]he large mass of subscribers...'"* *NYT*, February 28, 1922.

268  *"After all, their money would..."* The reminiscences of Herbert Clark Hoover, Oral History Research Project, Radio Unit, Columbia University, January 1951, 12.

268  *"But as the slicing got..."* End Cincinnati radio row, *New York Times*, February 15, 1925.

268  *"Hoover fined Zenith; Zenith challenged..."* *UNITED STATES v. ZENITH RADIO CORPORATION et al.*, District Court, N.D. Illinois, E.D., 12 F.2d 614; April 16, 1926.

268 *"Anyone could start a station..."* Hoover asks help to avoid air chaos, *New York Times*, July 10, 1926.

268 *"Congress finally was forced to act."* Daniel Klein argues in "Rinkonomics" that regulation may be unnecessary where there is enough coincidence of interest. www.econlib.org/library/Columns/y2006/Kleinorder.html.

269 *"In case of competition among..."* The Radio Act of 1927, Public Law No. 632, February 23, 1927, 1, 9.

270 *"Nothing in this Act shall..."* Radio Act of 1927, 29.

271 *"In time, he discovered that..."* Barnouw, 169ff; Gerald Carson, *The Roguish World of Dr. Brinkley*, Rinehart and Co., 1960, 33ff. A new biography of Brinkley has appeared: Pope Brock, *Charlatan*, Crown, 2008.

271 *"This combination will do for..."* KFKB Broadcasting Assn, Inc., v. Federal Radio Commission, 60 App. D.C. 79, 47 F.2d 670, February 2, 1931.

271 *"In a national poll, it..."* Carson, 143.

271 *"An arguable point—as Albert..."* Quoted by Anthony Lewis in *Make No Law*, Vintage, 1991, 60. Lewis cites Levy, *Emergence of a Free Press*, 302–303.

272 *"There is a fixed natural..."* NATIONAL BROADCASTING CO., INC. ET AL. v. UNITED STATES ET AL., No. 554, SUPREME COURT OF THE UNITED STATES, 319 U.S. 190; 63 S. Ct. 997; 87 L. Ed. 1344; 1943 U.S. LEXIS 1119; 1 Media L. Rep. 1965; February 10 and 11, 1943, Argued; May 10, 1943, Decided. This passage cites two radio engineering textbooks, one published in 1933, and the other in 1937.

272 *"Central planning works no better..."* This analogy is due to Michael Marcus.

273 *"De facto, as one historian..."* E. Pendleton Herring, "Politics and radio regulation," *Harvard Business Review*, January 1935.

274 *"Hoover understood this way back..."* NYT, February 28, 1922.

274 *"When you listen to XM..."* Mark Lloyd, "The strange case of satellite radio," *Center for American Progress*, February 8, 2006.

276 *"That is, the spectrum resource..."* Federal Communications Commission, Spectrum Policy Task Force, Report of the Spectrum Efficiency Working Group, November 15, 2002, 9.

276 *"Perhaps such a station could..."* Mark M. Bykowsky and Michael J. Marcus, "Facilitating spectrum management reform via callable/interruptible spectrum," *FCC*, September 13, 2002.

277 *"Everybody shares the capacity of..."* Credit for this analogy to Eli M. Noam, "Taking the next step beyond spectrum auctions: Open spectrum access." www.columbia.edu/dlc/wp/citi/citinoam21.html.

277 *"Something similar can be done..."* See, for example, Lawrence Lessig, "Code and the Commons," Keynote address at a conference on *Media Convergence*, February 9, 1999; Yochai Benkler, "The commons as a neglected factor of information policy," 26th Annual Telecommunications Conference, October 3–5, 1998; Benkler, "Overcoming Agoraphobia," Harvard J. L. & Tech., 287 (Winter

1997–98); Benkler, "Property, commons, and the First Amendment," white paper for the First Amendment Program, Brennan Center for Justice at NY School of Law; Jon M. Peha, "Emerging technology and spectrum policy reform," International Telecommunications Union (ITU) Workshop on Market Mechanisms for Spectrum Management, Geneva, January 2007.

277   *"Two ideas are key: first, ..."* For other examples, see Kevin Werbach, "Open spectrum: the new wireless paradigm," *New American Foundation*, Spectrum series working paper 6, October 2002.

278   *"Spread spectrum was discovered and..."* Robert A. Scholtz, The origins of spread-spectrum communications, *IEEE Trans. Communications*, COM-30, No. 5, May 1982, 822–853; Notes on spread-spectrum history, COM-31, no. 1, January 1983, 82–84; Robert Price, "Further notes and anecdotes on spread-spectrum origins," ibid., 85–97; Rob Walters, *Spread Spectrum*, Booksurge LLC, 2005.

278   *"Antheil was a self-styled expert..."* George Antheil, "Glands on a hobby horse," *Esquire*, April 1936, 47; "Glandbook for the questing male," May 1936, 40; "The glandbook in practical use," June 1936, 36.

278   *"Antheil suggested glandular extracts."* George Antheil, *Bad Boy of Music*, Doubleday, Doran & Co., 1945, 327–332.

279   *"A small item on the 'Amusements'..."* Hedy Lamarr Inventor, *New York Times*, October 1, 1941, 24.

280   *"Calling herself 'just a plain...'"* "$4,547,000 Bonds," *New York Times*, September 2, 1942; "Hollywood puts on a show," *Time Magazine*, October 12, 1942.

280   *"He didn't recognize the patentee..."* www.rism.com/.

284   *"All the interfering broadcasts can..."* For this reason, modern treatments of information theory use the letter $I$, for "interference," instead of $N$ for "noise." One man's signal is another man's noise. Physically, it's all just interference with the signal of interest.

285   *"It is a story that could..."* Web page on "Early civil spread spectrum history" at www.marcus-spectrum.com/SSHistory.htm.

286   *"In the radio world, where..."* See Debora L. Spar, *Ruling the Waves*, Harvest, 2003; also a presentation by Marcus, collegerama.tudelft.nl/mediasite/ Catalog/?cid=73e977a6-0283-4ee6-9813-a61df0dd1778.

286   *"Incumbents, such as existing radio..."* Ironically, the regulatory structures can hold in place entitlements that were secured in the pre-regulatory period. The very corporations that profited from the early absence of government control now depend on government regulation to protect them.

287   *"Hundreds of FCC staff and..."* Center for Public Integrity, "Networks of Influence," February 28, 2004.

287   *"In 1981, Marcus and his..."* Notice of inquiry, Authorization of spread spectrum and other wideband emissions not presently provided for in the FCC rules and regulations, Gen Docket No. 81-413, September 15, 1981, www.marcus-spectrum.com/documents/SpreadSpectrumNOI.pdf. This inquiry was informed

by a report prepared for the FCC by the MITRE Corporation, "Potential use of spread spectrum techniques in non-government applications," Walter C. Scales, December 1980, www.mitre.org/work/tech_papers/tech_papers_07/ MTR80W335/MTR80W335.pdf.

287 *"There should have been no..."* "A brief history of Wi-Fi," *Economist*, June 10, 2004.

287 *"RCA and GE complained anyway..."* FCC 84-169, Further notice of inquiry and notice of proposed rulemaking, in the matter of authorization of spread spectrum and other wideband emissions not presently provided for in the FCC rules and regulations, Gen Docket No. 81-413, May 21, 1984; Authorization, June 18, 1985. www.marcus-spectrum.com/documents/SpreadSpectrumFNOINPRM.pdf, www.marcus-spectrum.com/documents/81413RO.txt.

288 *"In 1997, when the FCC..."* One of the very few newspaper articles that mentioned the beginning of WiFi was "FCC OK's short-range wireless communications," *Chicago Sun-Times*, January 10, 1997, 50 (in the "Financial" section). By contrast, an auction of spectrum for cell phone use was covered in almost every business page on January 14 or 15.

290 *"There are vast opportunities to..."* See David Reed, "The sky's no longer the limit," *Context Magazine*, Winter 2002–2003, and testimony of David P. Reed before the FCC Spectrum Policy Task Force, July 8, 2002, www.newamerica. net/publications/resources/2002/david_reed_comments_to_fcc_ spectrum_policy_task_force.

290 *"This problem was apparent even..."* Laurence F. Schmeckebier, *The Federal Radio Commission*, The Brookings Institute, Institute for Government Research, Service Monographs of the United States Government, No. 65, 55.

291 *"The three biggest contributors were..."* opensecrets.org/industries/ mems.asp.

291 *"In 1971, Anthony Oettinger foresaw..."* "Compunications in the National Decision Making Process," in *Computers, Communications and the Public Interest*, Martin Greenberger (ed.), Johns Hopkins University Press, Baltimore, Maryland, 1971 (with discussion by Ithiel Pool, Alain Enthoven, and David Packard).

293 *"A typical caution was the..."* Alan Frank, quoted in Broadcasters launch ads against device, Yahoo! Finance (biz.yahoo.com), September 10, 2007.

293 *"At that point, government authority..."* Lawrence Lessig and Yochai Benkler, "Net Gains: Will Technology Make CBS Unconstitutional?", The New Republic, December 14, 1998, 14.

293 *"Artificial spectrum scarcity has, in..."* *Columbia Broadcasting System v. Democratic National Committee*, 412 U.S. 94, 154, May 29, 1973.

# Conclusion

296  *"As Sun Microsystems CEO Scott McNealy..."* Polly Sprenger, "Sun on Privacy: 'Get over it,'" *Wired*, January 26, 1999. www.wired.com/politics/law/news/1999/01/17538.

297  *"It is the mother of revolution."* Chapter 24. www.online-literature.com/victor_hugo/hunchback_notre_dame/24/.

298  *"In the same letter quoted..."* Jefferson to Isaac McPherson, August 13, 1813, Writings, 13:333–35.

298  *"But Fox News Channel went..."* www.publicknowledge.org/node/1247.

298  *"That's what Uri Geller, the..."* Rob Beschizza, "Creationist vs. atheist YouTube war marks new breed of copyright claim," *Wired*, September 25, 2007.

# Appendix

310  *"A variety of higher-level..."* The Internet Hourglass was first laid out in Section 2 of *Realizing the Information Future*, a 1994 report by the National Academy of Sciences (www.nap.edu/readingroom/books/rtif/). A later important report that also appeals to the hourglass model is *The Internet's Coming of Age*, the report of the Committee on the Internet in the Evolving Information Infrastructure, Computer Science and Telecommunications Board, Commission on Physical Sciences, Mathematics, and Applications, National Research Council (The National Academies Press, 2001), p. 36.

311  *"Instead, Internet technology developers and..."* "The fallacy of short-term thinking about the Internet," *Network World*, October 17, 2007.

313  *"'End to End,' in the..."* J.H. Saltzer, D.P. Reed, and D.D. Clark, "End-to-end arguments in system design," *ACM Transactions on Computer Systems*, 2(4), 277–288 (1984).

313  *"Stupid Networks"* For a very clear explanation of the advantages of what are called "stupid networks," see David S. Isenberg, "The dawn of the stupid network," *ACM Networker 2.1*, February/March 1998, 24–31. Available online at isen.com/papers/Dawnstupid.html.

315  *"In the Internet world, consider..."* Peter Svensson, "Comcast blocks some subscriber Internet traffic, AP testing shows," *Associated Press*, October 20, 2007.

315  *"In other words, the idea..."* "Should AT&T police the Internet?," *CNET News.com*, January 17, 2008. http://www.news.com/Should-ATT-police-the-Internet/2100-1034-6226523.html?part=dht&tag=nl.e703.

# Index

## M

## S